The Florida Heritage Series
Edited by Jim Miller

Florida's Colonial Architectural Heritage

Elsbeth Gordon

Foreword by
Janet Snyder Matthews

University Press of Florida
Gainesville · Tallahassee · Tampa · Boca Raton
Pensacola · Orlando · Miami · Jacksonville · Ft. Myers

Copyright 2002 by Florida Department of State, Division of Historical Resources
Printed in the United States of America on acid-free paper
All rights reserved
A Florida Heritage Publication

07 06 05 04 03 02   6 5 4 3 2 1

Library of Congress Cataloging-in-Publication Data
Gordon, Elsbeth K.
Florida's colonial architectural heritage / Elsbeth Gordon.
p. cm. — (The Florida heritage series)
Includes bibliographical references and index.
ISBN 0-8130-2463-3 (cloth : alk. paper)
1. Architecture, Colonial—Florida. I. Title. II. Series.
NA730.F6 G67 2002
720'.09759—dc21   2002016580

The University Press of Florida is the scholarly publishing agency for the State
University System of Florida, comprising Florida A&M University, Florida Atlantic
University, Florida Gulf Coast University, Florida International University, Florida
State University, University of Central Florida, University of Florida, University of
North Florida, University of South Florida, and University of West Florida.

University Press of Florida
15 Northwest 15th Street
Gainesville, FL 32611-2079
http://www.upf.com

To Roy Hunt and Blair Reeves,

and to Mike, Huntly, and Beth.

Each makes architecture directly perceptible to the heart.

CONTENTS

ILLUSTRATIONS

COLOR PLATES, FOLLOWING PAGE 132

Foreword

Professor Roy Hunt, special advisor for international affairs, Historic Preservation and Cultural Resources, Florida Department of State, writes, "Elsbeth Gordon's *Florida's Colonial Architectural Heritage* aids substantially in our search for cultural identity, a necessary prelude to the cultural stability so desperately needed in today's society. Her groundbreaking research tells us much about who we are and where we came from."

The publication of Gordon's study of the colonial era (1513 to 1821) is part of a cooperative agreement between the Florida Department of State, Division of Historical Resources, and the University Press of Florida to publish material in the Florida Heritage Series in the areas of Florida history, archaeology, folklife, museums, historic preservation, and heritage tourism. This project is also made possible through a matching Community Education Grant from the Florida Department of State, Division of Historical Resources' Historic Grants-in-Aid Program.

Elsbeth Gordon ("Buff" to her friends) is a humanist whose degrees in American history and fine arts include a master's thesis on architecture of the Yucatan. Her oils on canvas focus on the indigenous peoples of Latin America. Her Martin Luther King statue stands in bronze in the city center of Gainesville. In this colonial study, she was inspired by a decade as head of a company that restored buildings in Florida. The result is her compilation of a new contextual history of colonial architecture in Florida—evidence that the understanding of this important period in Florida is constantly changing by virtue of documentary research and new physical discoveries.

Gordon illumines her subject through painstaking research on both sides of the Atlantic. Exhaustive searches of original customs records, correspondence, and building surveys by Spain and England support a reconsideration of previously known accounts in light of voluminous new details found within those originals. Thus Ms. Gordon contributes a fresh view of Florida that provides context for an understanding of colonial sites accessible to the public today. For the visitor and the researcher, she patinates the period, characterizing lifestyle by implication. Governmental property inventories paint a persona on the designers and build-ers of doors and windows, trim colors, linens and wines, place settings, and imported furnishings. She underlines the sequential frailty of the built environment in the face of fire and hurricane, insects and moisture, war and pestilence. She identifies the contributions of both free and slave laborers, of ship chandlers, merchant traders, public officials, clergy, mili-tary personnel, and the diverse residents themselves.

Florida's colonial years defined a particular political unit, a colony, and named the land whose vibrant places and pathways belonged by tra-dition to Native Americans holding regional areas of authority. The name La Florida originated with Ponce de León's arrival in 1513. Divided by the English in 1763 into East and West Florida, the land passed through two English colonial decades (1763–83) and a second Spanish period before establishment in 1821 of today's political boundaries as a U.S. territory.

Florida has the longest coastline of the contiguous forty-eight states with shallow, sandy shores punctuated by a few deep-water ports. Mari-time access defined Florida's early history, nowhere more so than at the colonial capitals of St. Augustine and Pensacola. Climate also played a pivotal role. The shallow coastal shelf wraps a landmass whose elevation rises from sea level and an annual temperature of 77.8° in the tropical Florida keys to 220 feet and 67.2° in the red clay hill country of today's state capital in Tallahassee. Elevations, water systems, temperatures, hu-midity, and soil types define the building materials peculiar to Florida's regions. From vernacular materials men and women built dwellings, in-dustrial structures, vessels, places of worship, and governmental monu-ments. In this, colonials followed precedent. They often occupied Native American dwellings within the established village centers.

Both the Spanish and the English erected familiar forms on this dis-tant colony. For today's Castillo de San Marcos, builders first erected in wood, then replaced aging structures with coquina shellstone quarried on Anastasia Island for an intimidating, lasting fortress similar in shape to those towering above European shores. The Castillo was sited strategi-cally to protect Spain's homeward-bound annual treasure fleet propelled just offshore in the northerly flow of the Atlantic current. That govern-mental monument proclaimed the might of empire, the psychological and aesthetic divide between the governing and the governed. Block by block, the Castillo rose up to underline the critical fiscal importance of captured New World treasure in gold and silver, mined and smelted by forced labor of indigenous peoples.

Pensacola, the regional center Native Americans referred to as Panzacola, was the object of a colonial undertaking in 1559. Fifteen hundred settlers and sailors embarked from Mexico, led by Tristán de Luna y Arellano. Eleven ships arrived in Pensacola Bay just before a September hurricane. The detailed story of the stranded colonists is the focus of modern study through underwater archaeology. A second Spanish effort succeeded in 1698, as did one in 1719 by the French, and another in 1763 by the British. Fortifications and the town grew during colonial rule, and Gordon details the architectural information provided in government documents to add to the existing record.

At Mission San Luis de Apalachee in Tallahassee, the imposing church built by Native Americans of wood and thatch represents the exalted role of the Spanish crown's religious authority in a chain of seventeenth-century missions stretching from the coastal Carolinas to Cape Canaveral, and from St. Augustine to Tallahassee. From a summit in that region no longer ruled by the Apalachee people, the church dominated the surrounding village. The sanctuary sheltered images and relics, providing an indoor burying ground in the European tradition for Spanish rulers and their Apalachee converts.

A handful of colonial Florida sites are National Historic Landmarks. This designation, established in 1960 and initiated within the National Park Service, today comprises only 2,300 nationwide designations, possessing the legal requisite stated on today's NPS Web site: "exceptional value or quality in illustrating or interpreting the heritage of the United States."

Of some 35 National Historic Landmarks in Florida, fewer than a dozen emanate from the colonial period. The designations reflect both an evolving consciousness of cultural inclusivity and the necessity of ongoing documentation. Fort San Marcos de Apalachee on the St. Marks River in Wakulla County was designated in 1966. Listed in 1994, the site of Gracia Real de Santa Teresa de Mose on the Atlantic coast dates at least from 1687. The NHL Web page describes the significance of Fort Mose as "the first legally sanctioned free Black community within the present boundaries of the United States . . . mainly runaway Black slaves from the British colonies of South Carolina and Georgia, who escaped to freedom in Spanish Florida." The St. Augustine town plan is a National Historic Landmark; laid out by 1598 around a central plaza, it includes streets in use today. Pensacola landmarks designated in 1960 are Fort San Carlos de Barrancas on the bay and Plaza Ferdinand VII, the town site where military governor Andrew Jackson proclaimed the end of the colonial period with Florida's transfer from Spain to the United States. On the same day in St. Augustine, exchange also took place under Jackson's aide and legal ward, Robert Butler.

The significance of some archaeological sites, such as the Safety Harbor site in Pinellas County, relies on the documented history of European contact at a Native American center. San Luis de Apalachee in Tallahassee became a National Historic Landmark in 1960. The seventeenth-century Apalachee council house, Spanish mission church, convent, and houses were reconstructed from documentary and archaeological evidence around a central plaza on today's state-owned 60-acre site, acquired through Conservation and Recreational Lands Trust (CARL) funds.

The National Historic Preservation Act of 1966 created a National Register of Historic Places. This pivotal legislation provided congressional funds to each state, specifically providing for comprehensive historic surveys and plans and expanding criteria to include the state or local level. Of more than 74,000 listings throughout the nation, 1,364 in Florida include approximately 52 whose significance relates to the colonial period. Such sites include a British sugar mill ruin at Smyrna and the DeSoto archaeological site at the mouth of the Manatee River, studied by the Smithsonian Institution in 1939, as authorized by Congress. National Register listings include colonial shipwrecks. Hurricanes sank entire Spanish fleets in 1559, 1622, 1715, and 1733. Discovered in 1992, a galleon of the Tristán de Luna fleet at Pensacola remains the earliest of those in Florida's waters. Off Fort Pierce, the site of *Urca de Lima*, a cargo ship of 1715, is also listed. Off the Florida Keys lie the wrecksites of three vessels of the 1733 fleet disaster—*San José* off Key Largo, and *San Felipe* and *San Pedro* off Islamorada. Such sites are touchstones with the colonial past, providing future information. Through the legislative intent of the National Historic Preservation Act, underwater wrecksites and those on land become modern planning tools.

William Murtagh, first Keeper of the National Register and founder of preservation programs at Columbia and elsewhere, underlines the essential intent of the Act and the effect of the Register in his 1997 book, *Keeping Time: The History and Theory of Preservation in America*. According to Murtagh, "The historical and cultural foundations of the Nation . . . give a sense of orientation to the American people . . . in the face of ever increasing extensions of urban centers, highways and . . . insure future generations a genuine opportunity to appreciate and enjoy the rich heritage of our nation."[1]

Historian Daniel J. Boorstin, former Librarian of Congress and former director of the National Museum of Science and Technology at the Smithsonian, like Murtagh, decries a national loss of a sense of place. Boorstin emphasizes the value of historical study and preservation planning: "Neither our classroom lessons nor our sermons nor our books nor the things we live with nor the houses we live in are any longer strong ties to our past.... We have lost our sense of history. Without the materials of historical comparison, we are left with nothing but abstractions."[2] Elsbeth Gordon's *Florida's Colonial Architectural Heritage* works to fill that vast void, giving detailed definition to the architecture of a period transitional from Native American, adding significantly to a sense of Florida history, a sense of Florida places.

Richard Moe is president of the National Trust for Historic Preservation, an organization chartered by Congress in 1949 through legislation introduced by Representative J. Hardin Peterson of Florida. Following attacks in September 2001 on national monuments—the Pentagon and New York City's World Trade Center, Moe wrote to the Trust advisors, "People look for reassurance to the continuity provided by both national and community landmarks that represent our collective heritage, and we are of course in the business of preserving those landmarks." In a troubled and confusing time, historic landmarks more than ever serve as important points of reference, reminding us of the continuity of life and community and of our collective heritage. *Florida's Colonial Architectural Heritage* reexamines those landmarks, substantially redefining the importance of diverse influences in our collective heritage.

Janet Snyder Matthews
State Historic Preservation Officer and Director
Division of Historical Resources
Florida Department of State

FOREWORD   XXI

PREFACE

Four hundred and thirty-six years have passed since the Spanish settlers of St. Augustine first brought European building practices to Florida. Yet the story of the making of architecture in Florida is little known. It is a story so rich in human endeavor, one book alone cannot tell the whole story.

Florida's Colonial Architectural Heritage is the first book of a planned series about Florida architecture. It is the story of Florida governed by Spain and England, when people from many regions of the world came together and constructed the first European buildings across northern Florida. Future books will explore the making of Florida architecture after the colonial period ended in 1821 and new builders arrived with different hopes and viewpoints, extending the frontiers and expanding architectural ideals. The purpose of this book, and of those yet to come in the series, is to relate the story of Florida's buildings by resurrecting their designs, their materials, and their building practices from documents, archaeological evidence, and extant historic structures; and to reconstruct the lives and personal stories of their owners, designers, and craftsmen.

This illustrated history is for readers who are intrigued by vernacular and classical building practices and how local materials, environment, history, culture, and personal tastes shaped "architecture" on new frontiers. It is a book for the curious who, with Florida's historians, would solve puzzles in ancient documents; for the armchair archaeologist who would climb into the trenches with Florida's archaeologists; for the architect, builder, mason, and carpenter who would know the minds and hearts of Florida's earliest designers and builders. For the preservationists, this book will make connections with what buildings to save, and why.

The Florida peninsula was a vast frontier encompassing a diversity of building sites for a very long time that attracted many exceptional people with extraordinary design and construction talents. *Colonial Florida* seeks to tell the exciting stories of these people. Making architecture on

Florida's frontier during the colonial period was a far greater and richer experience than previously thought.

ACKNOWLEDGMENTS

There are many people to thank. They all made this book better.

Roy Hunt, distinguished service professor emeritus of law, University of Florida, and special advisor for historic preservation and cultural resources, Florida Department of State, who opened many doors, and who, with F. Blair Reeves, F.A.I.A., professor emeritus of architecture, University of Florida, urged me to write this book and continued to have faith in its author;

George Bedell, Walda Metcalf, and Meredith Morris-Babb at the University Press of Florida, who launched this project, kept it afloat, and brought it to completion, with generous amounts of their time, a few lunches, loaned books, patience and encouragement even though the project took much longer than they expected; and

Charles Tingley, manager, St. Augustine Historical Society Research Library, for reading the manuscript as it evolved, making many suggestions, discreetly correcting and educating the author, and sharing his personal library and prodigious knowledge of St. Augustine's history.

I cannot thank enough my readers of the manuscript as it developed from the first very rough drafts and helped me improve it through all the versions that followed: Jerald T. Milanich, curator in archaeology, Florida Museum of Natural History, and Jean Parker Waterbury, St. Augustine author and editor of *El Escribano,* who read portions of the earliest manuscript; Herschel E. Shepard, F.A.I.A. emeritus and professor emeritus of architecture, University of Florida, for reading a manuscript-in-progress, sharing his discoveries and ideas about historic building technologies, and helping me eliminate speculations that drifted too far away from reality; Samuel Proctor, distinguished service professor emeritus of history, University of Florida, for reminding me that adjectives can sometimes get in the way of history; Donald Curl, author and architectural historian, for reading the nearly finished manuscript and his very valuable suggestions for improvement; Michael Gannon, distinguished service professor emeritus of history, University of Florida, and director of the Institute for Early Contact Period Studies, for his encouragement and thoughtful insights, and for eloquently letting Americans know that our history and first Thanksgiving did not begin with the pilgrims in New England.

Much gratitude is owed to the many men and women—architects, historians, and preservationists—whose detailed research, publications, and community activism over many years have enabled me to present this overview, only some of whom could be cited in the notes and bibliography. I particularly want to thank archaeologists Bonnie G. McEwan and Kathleen Deagan for interviews and tours of their very impressive work at their archaeological sites in Tallahassee and St. Augustine, respectively; Eugene Lyon, for sharing some of his profound knowledge of early Florida and for his invaluable published translations of old documents in Spanish and Cuban archives, for which all of us are far "richer than we thought"; Susan Parker, St. Augustine historian, for her ideas about colonial St. Augustine architecture; Isabel Rigol Savio, Directura del Centro Nacional de Conservación, Restauración y Museología de Cuba, and her fellow architects and historians in Havana, Camagüey, Santiago de Cuba, and Trinidad, for their hospitality and tour of architecture in Cuba, and for sharing their love of Cuba's Spanish colonial architectural heritage.

Many librarians and curators helped with research and supplied the illustrations, and all of them made the creation of this book a joy. I greatly appreciate the help of Bruce Chappell, at the P. K. Yonge Library of Florida History, University of Florida; Taryn Rodriguez-Boette, director of the St. Augustine Historical Society; Hugh Alexander, Image Library assistant manager, Public Record Office, Kew, England; Joan Morris, archives supervisor; Leslie Lawhon, archivist, Florida Photographic Collection, Florida State Archives; Michael Zimny, assistant editor, *Florida History and the Arts* magazine; Bruce Graetz, curator, the Museum of Florida History; Dean DeBolt, university librarian, Special Collections, University of West Florida Library; Elise LeCompte, Jeff Gage, and Merald Clark, Florida Museum of Natural History, University of Florida; Dr. Miguel A. Bretos, Smithsonian Center for Latin Initiatives; Betty Rogers, records manager, Jackson County Archives, Mississippi; and the staffs of the P. K. Yonge Library of Florida History, St. Augustine Historical Society Library, the British Library, and the Public Record Office, England. Ken Barrett, Jr., photographer, made miracles in the darkroom and in the sunshine. His precision and attention to detail were greatly needed. Peg Richardson's watercolor painting added an artist's touch to a monastery that no longer exists.

To Janet Snyder Matthews, my thanks for being the guiding light as the director of the Florida Division of Historical Resources, Department of State, Florida. Without her tireless efforts, we would pull up our historical roots and drift into architectural obscurity.

To Gillian Hillis, my project editor, and to each of the talented persons at the University Press of Florida who have created and produced this book, thank you for transforming words and sentences into a work of art.

To my many friends, thank you for remaining my friends, and to Roger and Linda Blackburn, thank you for loving Wuffy, my dog, in my many absences researching this book.

To my son, Huntly, and daughter, Beth, who still do not believe I have finished this project, now I can say, I have. Finally, I thank Michael Gordon, my husband, best friend, and partner, for assisting me with the photography and arranging trips to England, Spain, and Cuba, but mainly for his love and support during the entire period of creation.

This publication has been financed in part with historical preservation grant assistance provided by the National Park Service, U.S. Department of the Interior, administered through the Bureau of Historic Preservation, Division of Historical Resources, Florida Department of State, assisted by the Historic Preservation Advisory Council. However, the contents and opinions do not necessarily reflect the views and opinions of the Department of Interior of the Florida Department of State, nor does the mention of trade names or commercial products constitute endorsement or recommendation by the Department of Interior of the Florida Department of State. This program receives Federal financial assistance for identification and protection of historic properties. Under Title VI of the Civil Rights Act of 1964, Section 504 of the Rehabilitation Act of 1973, and the Age Discrimination Act of 1975, as amended, the U.S. Department of the Interior prohibits discrimination on the basis of race, color, national origin, disability, or age in its federally assisted programs. If you believe you have been discriminated against in any program, activity, or facility as described above, or if you desire further information, please write to: Office of Equal Opportunity, National Park Service, 1849 C Street, NW, Washington, D.C., 20240.

ABBREVIATIONS

AGI: Archivo General de Indias at Seville, Spain, on microfilm at SAHS, and in the P. K. Yonge Library of Florida History at the University of Florida.

F.A.I.A.: Fellow American Institute of Architects.

FHQ: *The Florida Historical Quarterly.*

HABS: Historic American Buildings Survey

PRO: Public Record Office, the National Archives, Kew, Richmond, Surrey, England.

SAAA: St. Augustine Archaeological Association.

SAHS: St. Augustine Historical Society.

Introduction

Either a building is part of a place or it is not.
Once that kinship is there, time will make it stronger.

Willa Cather

This book is intended to change the way Florida thinks of itself, and of its built environment.

At first, I set out to prove a point in response to an incident that occurred in St. Augustine five years ago. I gave an architectural tour of the historical city to an eminent educator from New England. We began at Henry Flagler's beautiful, Spanish-inspired, Hotel Ponce de Leon (1887), now Flagler College, and then walked through the streets that had been laid out in 1572 and arrived at the plaza and Government House of 1598. I finished the tour with my favorite line from Michael Gannon's *Florida, A Short History:* "by the time the Pilgrims came ashore at Plymouth, St. Augustine was up for urban renewal." In fact, the town was up for its *second* urban renewal! The first had taken place in 1587, after the town was ransacked and burned by Francis Drake in 1586. My New England guest, however, said that this early architectural history did not count, because it was Spanish!

Thus I set out to prove that Spanish Florida did indeed launch not just Florida's post-Columbian architectural history, but our nation's European architectural heritage as well. By the time the ink was drying on the Declaration of Independence, the capital city of the first permanent colony in what is now the United States was already two hundred years old. By 1821, when Florida was acquired through territorial expansion, an enormous amount of construction had been realized over two and one-half centuries; thousands of buildings had been erected, razed and rebuilt, or converted on the peninsula by European residents and governments. Why is it that Florida's colonial period has been excluded from architectural histories for so long?

The story of Florida's Spanish architecture begins on September 8, 1565, when some eight hundred colonists arrived in sailing vessels off the northeast coast of Florida and peered toward shore, no doubt with fear, anxiety, and even regrets. They were from various regions of Spain, following a Spanish entrepreneur named Pedro Menéndez de Avilés. The site chosen for their landing was at an inlet, where a river curled around an island to meet the Atlantic Ocean, and where the small harbor in the lee of the island was inviting and felt safe. They chose well, and survived. They settled near an Indian village and converted at least one large Indian structure to serve their colony. The settlement grew into a town peopled by Europeans, Africans, and Native Americans who called their new home San Agustín de La Florida. They never gave up, and never abandoned their colony. Their success was not matched anywhere else in the United States, by any other European peoples, until a half century later at Plymouth in 1620.

When Florida became a U.S. territory in 1821, its architectural landscape was layered with 256 years of French, Spanish, English, African, and Native American building practices. There were temporary buildings at first—expedient dwellings, churches, and forts—before more permanent structures were erected. We may never know the true picture of the wood buildings that were the result of their best efforts because these perished in the Florida climate or were destroyed in the flames of European competition for ownership of Florida. During the eighteenth century, however, the Spanish colonists turned to the local coquina stone. Some of their achievements still stand. Some are national monuments. But even where buildings have perished there is still history.

And so the search for Florida's colonial buildings began, but as the research progressed, it became more and more important to draw a larger picture about them, their builders, and the society and environment that produced them. Many were described and drawn by the colonists themselves in what are now old and fragile documents. Others can be resurrected based on archaeological findings, but the majority are presented here, either as they stand today, or as their planners intended them, conserved in the archives in engineers' plans, craftsmen's invoices, owners' letters and claims, and governments' descriptive accounts. This book is about seeing Florida's past carefully, and presenting a plausible historical picture sensitive to the era. By the book's end, the search should have proved beyond any doubt or bias that colonial Florida's exceptionally long architectural heritage is rich, and a national treasure.

The picture of Florida's colonial architecture is, however, far from complete, awaiting the archaeologists' trowels and the discovery of more documents in Spain, Cuba, Mexico, and Great Britain. The complexity of the historical puzzle is exemplified in St. Augustine, where city blocks, streets, and houses laid out since 1572 are today part of a busy city of the twenty-first century where residents live, work, and worship on colonial sites and in buildings stratified by four hundred years of continuous human presence. The architectural beginnings and truths are buried in the labyrinth of the overlays and historical myths. Examples include the coquina and tabby house walls that line the old narrow streets and enclose eighteenth-century rooms that sit on top of sixteenth- and seventeenth-century house foundations and floors. The massive late seventeenth-cen-

1. *St. Augus. de Floride*, 1683, published by cartographer/engineer Alain Manesson Mallet (1630–1706) in his *Description de l'Univers*. Myths about Florida's architecture were fed by the imaginations of artists who never set foot on the region's shores. They exaggerated descriptions of the first settlements to sell to Europeans hungry for views of the New World. (Collection of E. Gordon; photocopy by Ken Barrett, Jr.)

tury stone fort overlooks the river harbor on the site where once stood a series of sixteenth- and early seventeenth-century wooden forts, the number and shapes of which might never be known due to development and erosion. The river that is the town's most important physical landmark has always flowed twice a day to and from the ocean inlet, its currents, floods, and storm surges continuously changing the contours of the harbor and rewriting architectural history along its banks.

"Architecture," however, did not begin in Florida with the Europeans in St. Augustine. In this book, discovery of the state's building heritage will start with the structures of the "first builders," the Indians of Florida before they were discovered and subjugated by Europeans. The buildings of the Calusa, Apalachee, and Timucua will be seen through the eyes of the explorers who saw them in 1528 and 1539 during the expeditions of Pánfilo de Narváez and Hernando de Soto as they searched the region between Tampa Bay and Tallahassee. The discovery then leapfrogs to Indian structures on the east coast where Pedro Menéndez made his historic campsite in 1565 in a preexisting Timucua village, and where a Timucua building became his headquarters.

The conversion of an Indian building marked the beginning of more than a century of collaboration in construction, during which Indian labor and building practices were largely responsible for the successes of the Spanish Franciscan missions that stretched across Florida's wilderness. The archaeology and reconstruction of the enormous Apalachee Indian buildings at Mission San Luis in present-day Tallahassee challenge past histories and demonstrate how little we know about the complexities of Indian knowledge and abilities. According to Bonnie McEwan, director of archaeology at the mission, the Apalachee Council House of 1656 was erected without European tools or hardware and was large enough to hold up to three thousand people. Even earlier, prior to European contact, enormous earthen platform mounds were formed as raised foundations on which to exalt Indian structures. William H. Marquardt, curator in archaeology, Florida Museum of Natural History, has revealed that one such elevated structure built by the Calusa was described in 1566 as being large enough for two thousand to stand inside without being very crowded. These were no rude huts, but two of the largest buildings erected in the colonial southeast. Chapter 1 and the story of the first builders is thus the prelude to the European-derived architecture that began in Florida in earnest after 1564.

Spain governed Florida for the first 198 years of the colonial period, before ceding the peninsula to England in 1763. For Spain, ownership of La Florida was important to protect the *flota plata,* the annual convoy of

HABITS ET MAISONS
DES FLORIDIENS.

2. *Habits et Maisons des Floridiens,* 1757, by Jacques Nicolas Bellin (1702–1772). European publishers were still whetting the public imagination with imaginary views of Florida well into the eighteenth century. Bellin was the most influential chart publisher in eighteenth-century France, commissioned to map all known coasts of the world. (Collection of E. Gordon)

ships carrying millions of dollars worth of silver and gold from Mexico and South America to Cuba, thence through the Straits of Florida and along the coast before crossing the Atlantic to Spain. Much of this treasure went to pay for Spanish hegemony in Europe. Since there were no profitable commodities to be extracted in Florida that offered adequate returns for huge investments, the large territory remained dependent, and largely underdeveloped, settled by too few with too little resources. It fell to the Franciscan missions to secure La Florida for Spain. Together, friar and Indian constructed more than 140 missions across the Florida wilderness. Chapter 2 exposes what archaeology has discovered to date about the construction of the religious buildings, the churches and monasteries, and the secular buildings of the Indian villages they served.

Wood and palm thatch were plentiful, but impermanent. No wooden buildings erected by the first Spanish settlers survive. However, St. Augustine's fifteenth- and sixteenth-century town plans and the organizational layout of houses and lots still exist. Many early wooden architectural elements influenced later construction when the native shellstone replaced wood and gave the town a sense of permanency. Chapter 3 is therefore the first discussion about architecture as a product of history and culture, adapted to climate and available local materials, a theme that will weave through each of the remaining chapters.

Chapter 4 is the most detailed and is devoted to the eighteenth-century stone architecture in St. Augustine. It dispels an often quoted assumption that St. Augustine was impoverished and a backwoods Spanish military colony bereft of significant architecture. Professional engineer-architects and civilian master masons drew plans and supervised the construction of many buildings that were in fashion with current ideas in Europe and Spanish America. Their scaled plans, found in the archives, speak for themselves.

Chapter 4 also reveals that when Great Britain governed Florida (1763–83 by treaty, but evacuation was drawn out until 1785), the English did not tear down Spanish St. Augustine as is often alleged. They did not remake it into an "English" town, but instead moved into existing Spanish buildings, converted them to new uses, and nurtured their Caribbean-style elements. The English governors, for example, spent large sums of money to maintain the Spanish-built governor's house, used the Spanish hospital (formerly the residence of Don Francisco Menéndez Marqués) for their courthouse, and converted the *palacio episcopal* (bishop's house) into their statehouse. In actuality, the Spanish themselves tore down their oldest churches and the former *palacio episcopal* (remade into English statehouse) during the second Spanish period (1783–1821) in order to recycle the stones and save money for their new parish church, the Cathedral.

The Spanish and English alike had great respect for architecture that was responsive to environment. Chapter 5 traces how the local coquina stone and the climate brought Spanish, English, and Caribbean architectural traditions together to create a cohesive St. Augustine style of architecture, a regional style with great strengths for Florida.

Chapter 6 is about English architecture in Pensacola, in dreams as well as in reality. The Spanish had only six short years (1757–63) at the site they called San Miguel de Panzacola before it became part of British West Florida, which stretched to the Mississippi River. The British laid out a new town and, with the exception of the Spanish commandant-governor's house of bousillage construction, rebuilt most of the buildings. Their designs reveal cultural and environmental determinants, French and Caribbean colonial practices, English symmetry, multiple verandas, single-depth rooms, and cross-ventilating doors and windows. The story is told in their plans, many drawn by Captain Elias Durnford, chief engineer of Pensacola. Plans for buildings that were never built or completed are included in the story, because they reveal the cultural aspirations and tell us much about a town and the people who wanted to make it happen.

By 1783, Spanish and English residents of urban St. Augustine and Pensacola, the capitals of East and West Florida, had seen buildings embellished with stone carvings, stepped and curved belfries, arcaded loggias, and classical Ionic and Doric orders. Their cityscape soared with crenellated battlements and domed towers, tall cupolas, brick chimneys, and three-story buildings. An eighty-foot-tall church spire designed in the style of one of England's finest neo-Palladian architects, James Gibbs, pierced the skyline of St. Augustine. Residents knew central hall plans, symmetry, and proportional geometry. Spanish and English governors, as well as Chief Justice James Hume and Lieutenant Governor John Moultrie, created acres of grandiose pleasure gardens enclosed in fencing

3. Charlotte Street, St. Augustine, 1880s. The narrow street plan has not changed much since it was laid out in 1572 and is today a National Historic Landmark. (Photocopy courtesy of Florida State Archives)

with formal walkways, vistas, orchards, ponds with freshwater fish, and even a bowling green.

Floor plans, sections, and elevations drawn by English engineers reveal earlier Spanish-built buildings in St. Augustine and Pensacola; conversely, the drawings of Spanish engineers after the Spanish returned in 1784 depict how the buildings had been adapted by the English.

England ruled Florida for twenty-one years, a short period by comparison with the total years of Spanish governance, but English contribution to Florida's colonial architecture was significant, the result of a substantial plantation economy and affluent citizenry. Britain encouraged economic independence, granted large tracts of land in East and West Florida, and proffered the civil establishment an annual allowance to stimulate the production of silk, vines, cotton, rice, and indigo. Large capital investments were made by wealthy entrepreneurs on tracts of twenty thousand acres. Plantation architecture in chapter 7 is described in plans, inventories, and descriptions found in the National Archives in England (Public Record Office). One West Florida plantation twelve miles from Pensacola, for example, was inventoried with an extensive library of more than ninety volumes ranging from Cicero to Shakespeare, Homer to Don Quixote. The main house, bulging with musical instruments, china, mahogany tables and chairs, carpets, silverware, silver tea services, gilt mirror, and extra rolls of wallpaper, hints of a lifestyle lived with dignity.

Chapter 8 continues the story of plantation architecture with the history of Kingsley Plantation on Fort George Island, north of present-day Jacksonville. Architecturally, it is a story of modular geometry and symmetry, and of local materials and how they were manufactured into building materials. However, the more important story is the human story, that of the owners and, most of all, that of the slaves, the craftsmen and -women who worked the indigenous materials into homes for themselves and their owners. Enslaved people from Africa erected the buildings and cultivated the cash crops and domestic gardens that maintained the plantation and made some of the owners wealthy. Their skills as carpenters and masons are nowhere more evident than at Kingsley Plantation, Florida's only intact colonial plantation. The remains of their tabby houses are poignant reminders that people were wrongfully enslaved.

Chapter 9 ends the book with a brief overview of the forts and other defensive military constructions that enabled Spain, then England, and Spain again, to establish footholds and protect settlements. Defense always seemed to be the most pressing issue of the day. Relics of colonial defense are few, but once again the engineers' plans in the archives help to tell the story. Most defenses required enormous expenditures, and exacted a high cost in lives. One cannot imagine today the effort of Indians and slaves and European artisans who dug and cut moats and stone by hand, who crushed and burned enough oyster shells to construct the behemoth Castillo de San Marcos to guard the harbor at St. Augustine. This huge artifact is the oldest stone fort in North America, and a National Monument. It is hoped that the weight of the story highlights the hardships involved in defending homes in new frontiers.

Many ingredients went into the making of Florida's colonial architecture: available local materials and skills, prevalent building technologies and fashions, climate, personal histories, tastes, and wealth. Sudden cataclysmic events, town fires, hurricanes, and wars also influenced the way buildings were made. The fortunes of the mother countries, and their bureaucracies that controlled financial support, determined building sizes, materials, and decoration. The Spanish crown's annual subsidy from Mexico, for example, was continually in arrears. The English in Florida were similarly exasperated by their "contingency fund" system and how it had to be manipulated in order to construct, maintain, and embellish public buildings, but only with the approval of the king's agent in America, who did not always have an accounting of such funds. Governor Grant was driven to set up a slush fund with Henry Laurens in Charleston to pay vouchers in a timely manner.

It is not provident to compare or measure Florida's colonial architecture with structures built in the northern English colonies. Buildings on Florida's frontiers were molded by the state's *own* unique heritage and speak with a voice of their own. For example, the decision by the Spanish to replace their latest wood fort with a stone fort in 1672 came after two incidents: First, the pirate Robert Searles sailed into St. Augustine's harbor in 1668, past a useless rotting wooden fort, and, second, the English had established a foothold at Charleston in 1670 from where they could initiate attacks on Spanish St. Augustine. This prompted the design of the defensive Castillo de San Marcos and launched a stone industry with professional engineer-architects, masons, cutters, and lime-makers. After the English attacked and burned the town's wooden buildings in 1702, the destruction was an additional catalyst that turned builders away from wood and toward the "fireproof" material; stone improved the economy and architectural expectations.

To understand Florida's colonial builders, the reader needs to put aside twenty-first-century perspectives and perceptions about building construction. If a limewash or mortar was needed, homeowners constructed wheelbarrows and kilns, fetched oyster shells and firewood, and

4. View of the fort and city of St. Augustine, Florida, anonymous, drawn from a ship at anchor in the Matanzas Bay harbor about 1835. (Courtesy of SAHS)

burned the shells to make quicklime, which was thrown into a pit in the backyard and mixed with water and sand. If wood was part of their building plans, trees had to be felled, hand-hewn into heavy timbers (scantling), rived (hand-split) or pit-sawn into boards and shingles, and air-dried up to several years for warp-free doors, floors, and windows. Not until the 1760s, during the British Period, did water-driven sawmills start producing quantities of commercial lumber. If bricks had to be made, they were molded, air-dried, stacked, and fired in a tedious, unpredictable method in a "clamp" that was a stack of green bricks covered with clay. It was stoked with wood fires up to five days and cooled down for several weeks, after which only half the bricks were hard enough to use. Other materials and tools took ages to arrive, if they arrived at all, from centers of commerce distanced from Florida by a treacherous ocean or gulf crossed only under sail. Appended at the back of this book are construction costs and builders' vocabulary.

Descriptions in historical documents are rife with biases and gamesmanship. To wrest more pesos or pounds sterling from crown coffers, poor conditions and small sizes of buildings were exaggerated by colonial officials. "Dilapidated," "ready to fall down," "too small," "bad," and "leaking like a sieve" were frequently used misrepresentations employed in correspondence to justify the need for more money for buildings. A Spanish priest, for example, describes his congregation standing in the street suffering in the rain to hear mass because the church was too small, but an engineer's scaled drawing reveals it had considerable square foot-

FLORIDA'S COLONIAL ARCHITECTURAL HERITAGE

age. Officials learned that to be clever about fund-raising, one had to be evasive and lean with praises. When a politically naive Spanish report described one of the aging wood forts in "fair" condition, new money was immediately canceled.

Buildings are cultural history books. Florida's colonial landscape was initially shaped by building practices brought to Florida from other regions of the world, but compromises and accommodation took place as people learned they had to make changes to meet the conditions and needs imposed by the site and Florida's climate. For example, the Spanish-style flat roofs were not a good idea in the wet climate, but traditions from Spain died hard; it was not until the British arrived that flat roofs ceased to be built. Similarly, the British military made a very costly mistake when they ignored the benefits learned by the Spanish, that the local coquina stone and southern pine lasted longer than imported northern woods.

Africans have been a part of Florida's colonial history since the beginning. They came with the Spanish and worked on Spanish buildings, including the stone Castillo. They cleared the land and built the British plantations. They also built Gracia Real de Santa Teresa de Mose, the first legally sanctioned free black town in the United States, two miles north of St. Augustine. I have recently heard two African American professors at the University of Florida say plantation buildings and historic courthouses should be torn down because they are symbols of racism. This argument will not be taken up in this book, which is about architectural history and the way in which buildings were designed and constructed. The tabby slave houses at Kingsley Plantation and the ruins of the Bulow sugar mill, as examples, by being preserved, burn into the collective memory of both black and white the heritage of this state, the value of individuals long gone, and the evils of slavery and Indian removal.

Historic buildings have a poignant presence in our daily lives, connecting generations, reminding us of origins, passages, and transitions, that countless people have come before, and that others will follow in endless generations. Building designs now, as well as then, seek solutions that respond to climate, hurricanes, materials, and real needs for safety, durability, comfort, and neighborhood. Some of today's designs are reinterpreting the colonial period's best solutions. They include balconies, galleries, loggias, courtyards, side entrances, and lot arrangements where houses are closer to the streets, conserving the rear for family activities and the garages and guest houses that are today's outbuildings. There is an old adage, "we are what we build." To know more about earlier buildings is to know who we are, what we build and why.

Fortunately, during the last two decades, the discovery, preservation, and maintenance of historic architecture and archaeological sites have been nurtured by a vigorous program of grants by the state of Florida.

Marjory Stoneman Douglas, the uncompromising protagonist for the Everglades and author of the classic *River of Grass,* comes to mind when considering what "old" buildings to save and why. She had a humble house built for her in 1926 in Coconut Grove when Miami was a frontier. It never had air-conditioning. She approached her one hundredth birthday with an autobiography, *Voice of the River,* in which she discussed the meaning of her life. "The house was a great influence on my life, and so important that I often think of it more than the other things I was doing in those years." For those of us who can never personally know Marjory, or Miami before air-conditioning, it will be important to preserve her house as part of the story of how Florida grew and developed.

1 | THE FIRST BUILDERS

*Architecture and Construction must be . . . practiced simulta-
neously; Construction is the means, Architecture is the result.*

EUGENE EMMANUEL VOILLET-LE-DUC

The history of Florida's architecture begins somewhere in the mists of
time. The written story starts on a spring day in April 1528 with the landing of Spanish conquistadors near Tampa Bay. The leader was Pánfilo de
Narváez, a cruel commander who had played a role in the Spanish conquest of Mexico. His expedition of four hundred men trekked northward
toward today's Tallahassee. All but four men eventually died. One of the
survivors, Álvar Núñez Cabeza de Vaca, took note of native structures.
His descriptions of mound platforms and buildings of timber, thatch, and
matting are the earliest eyewitness accounts known to date that record
construction practices in Florida.

The Indian dwellings that glowed in the sunsets over Tampa Bay in
1528 or backed up to cornfields along the Spaniards' northern route were
numerous. They were still numerous in 1539, when members of the expedition led by Hernando de Soto also noted many Indian towns between
Tampa Bay and Tallahassee. Every day of the march they reached a town
that was prosperous enough to feed the army's six to seven hundred
men.[1]

Thus the practice of architecture in Florida began with indigenous
peoples living among the scrub oaks, pines, and palmettos, and along
sand dunes, swamps, and savannas long before they were discovered by
Europeans. They were Florida's first builders, artisans who had learned
how best to exploit locally available materials and adapt construction
methods to the hot, humid, and hurricane-prone climate. Many centuries
before Frank Lloyd Wright's architecture was described as "organic," the
Indians in Florida erected structures that had a close relationship with

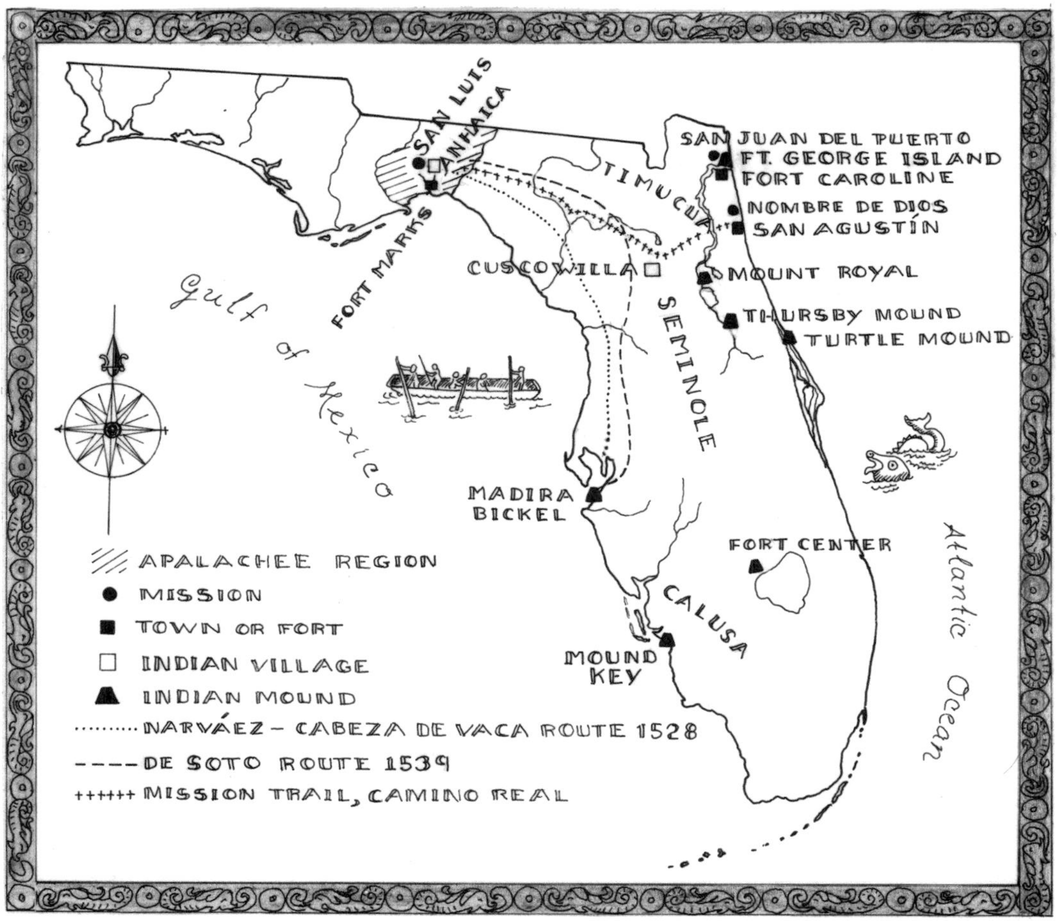
SAN LUIS
ANHAICA
FORT MARKS
SAN JUAN DEL PUERTO
FT. GEORGE ISLAND
FORT CAROLINE
TIMUCUA
NOMBRE DE DIOS
SAN AGUSTÍN
CUSCOWILLA
MOUNT ROYAL
SEMINOLE
THURSBY MOUND
TURTLE MOUND
Gulf of Mexico
MADIRA BICKEL
FORT CENTER
Atlantic Ocean
CALUSA
MOUND KEY
APALACHEE REGION
MISSION
TOWN OR FORT
INDIAN VILLAGE
INDIAN MOUND
NARVÁEZ – CABEZA DE VACA ROUTE 1528
DE SOTO ROUTE 1539
MISSION TRAIL, CAMINO REAL

1. Indian mounds and building sites. (Map drawn by E. Gordon)

the land, that blended comfortably into their setting, and that were the products of careful use of the natural materials.

After the European conquest, Indians constructed the string of Spanish Franciscan missions that stretched across Florida. They also helped to construct crown projects in the capital, St. Augustine, including the governor's house, wood forts, and the stone Castillo de San Marcos. They erected the fort at Pueblo San Luis, hereinafter called Mission San Luis, now Tallahassee. But in building a future for the Spanish in Florida, the Indians quickened their own demise. Their dwellings and villages were destroyed in the flames of the European contest for Florida, and they themselves went down with European diseases. The first builders of Florida did not survive the Spanish colonial period, but a few of their building practices are retrieved and described below.

EARTH MOVERS

Earth mounds began to rise along Florida's coasts and rivers about 3000 B.C. Defying the flat terrain of the peninsula, Florida's aboriginal first builders constructed massive truncated pyramidal earth and shell mounds in which to bury their dead and to elevate their most important buildings, the charnel houses and large houses of the chiefs. It was a staggering feat when the tools were human hands, baskets, and axes made from stone, animal bones, and flint.

Mounds of various shapes rose in many places during the next three millennia. Beginning about 500 B.C., a large complex with several mounds, drainage ditches, canals, ceremonial ponds, and "highways" rose in the vast savannah around Lake Okeechobee (Mayaimi to the Indians), and its construction continued for two thousand years; the site is known today to archaeologists as Fort Center. From Tampa Bay to Crystal River, more than one hundred mounds have been discovered, excavated, or documented. The Madira Bickel Mound, on Terra Ceia Island, is a twenty-foot-tall flat-topped mound, rising out of an impressive base 100 feet by 170 feet. From the long side of the platform mound, a ten-foot-wide earth ramp descended to a plaza. Another large mound in the Tampa Bay area measured 148 by 62 feet, stood 11 feet tall, and also had an earth ramp to the village plaza. South of Fort Myers, in Estero Bay, a truncated cone of earth rose 31 feet high on Mound Key with a 75-foot diameter at the top. It was constructed by the Calusa Indians, whose ten thousand members lived in an estimated seventy villages that sprawled from Charlotte Harbor to the Florida Keys. Mound Key might have been Calos, their capital (pl. 1).[2]

Mound platforms were equally impressive in North Florida. William Bartram, the intrepid explorer-botanist from Philadelphia, was awe-struck in 1774 by the massive size of the mound still evident at Mount Royal (today's Fruitland), just north of Lake George, the work of Indians of the St. Johns River region. He described it as a "magnificent Indian mount" which once "possessed an almost inexpressible air of grandeur, . . . But what greatly contributed toward the magnificence of the scene, was a noble Indian highway, which led from the great mount, on a straight line, three-quarters of a mile, . . . this grand highway was about fifty yards wide, sunk a little below the common level, and the earth thrown up on each side, making a bank of about two feet high."[3]

Almost ten years earlier (1765), William's father, John Bartram, also a botanist, had described the same "Indian tumulus." He measured it at 300 feet in diameter and 20 feet high, nearly round and so old that large live oak trees grew upon it. The highway, he noted, was as level as a floor from bank to bank for three-quarters of a mile. Excavations have confirmed what the Bartrams had seen. The mound had been capped with a red-ochre sand stratum, and the causeway that led to a small lake was 820 yards long. It had been scraped from the earth, the scrapings piled in ridges about 3 feet high and 12 feet wide sometime between A.D. 1050 and 1500.[4]

The Bartrams also visited an Indian mound and highway south of New Smyrna Beach, known as Turtle Mound, or the mound of Surruque, built during A.D. 800–1400. Its huge mass of oyster shells once stood 75 feet high and covered more than two acres. It was one of the largest shell mounds in North America. Today, the artifact is a landmark in the Canaveral National Seashore, located on a barrier island. Erosion has reduced its height to about 50 feet.[5]

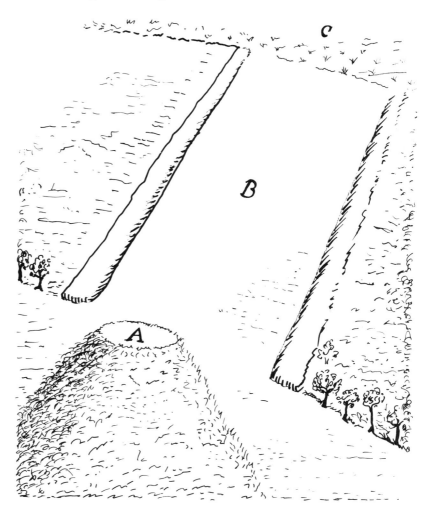

1.1. Mount Royal, A.D. 1050–1500, sketched by William Bartram, 1765?. William and his father, John, visited the site in 1765 and 1774 and were greatly impressed by the size of the "magnificent Indian mount" (A), and its "noble Indian highway" (B), "about fifty yards wide, sunk a little below the common level." The causeway was 820 yards long and led to a small lake (C). (Redrawn by E. Gordon after Edwin H. Davis, National Anthropological Archives, Smithsonian Institution)

Turtle Mound was but one of many Indian shell mounds that made the Florida coastline look as if it had hills or even mountains to sailors offshore, depicted in early published views of Florida. The mounds were high enough to serve as landmarks, lookouts, and navigational aids for European sailors and soldiers during the sixteenth to eighteenth centuries. Many of these mounds were mined during the colonial period to make lime mortar and tabby for the construction of east coast plantations and the buildings in St. Augustine. Even as late as the twentieth century, the shell mounds continued to be a source of construction material. The mounds at Matanzas Inlet, for example, supplied the road bed for the A1A highway and the mattress of oyster shells for the 1924 stabilization and restoration of Fort Matanzas.[6] An Indian mound in St. Petersburg, however, became a tourist site with a stairway to the top.

Mound building ceased when the Spanish arrived, and the mound builders and their descendants were entirely gone by the time the Spanish left Florida in 1763.[7] Fortunately, and despite the tidal wave of population and bulldozers in the twentieth century, many Indian mound sites in Florida are being protected by the state of Florida and listed in the National Register of Historic Places.

1.2. Indian shell mound, A.D. 800–1400, New Smyrna Beach. Photographed for a postcard about 1910, the sender attributed the mound to the "appetites of the aborigines and the early Spanish adventurers" and described it as "one of the immense piles of shells 20 feet high which are now mined to form the beautiful shell roads so prevalent throughout Florida." No wonder the early explorers on ships saw "mountains" on the Florida landscape! (Photocopy courtesy of Florida State Archives)

Right, 1.3. Indian shell mound, Fort George Island. When photographed more than a century ago, the prehistoric mound of shells had long been mined. During the colonial period, its oyster shells were used for roads and building construction. (Stereoscopic photograph by George Barker, 1886; photocopy courtesy of Florida State Archives)

Below, 1.4. Indian shell mound, St. Petersburg. The prehistoric mound became a tourist attraction, with stairs and a platform, and was featured on a vintage tinted picture postcard, ca. 1910, for telling the folks back home about the climb. The mound in the postcard has disappeared; today a hospital stands on the site. (Collection of E. Gordon)

Wizards of Thatch and Matting

The conquest of Florida by Europeans and the cessation of mound building did not, however, end all traditional Indian building practices. Community and residential structures similar to those described by early explorers continued to be erected well into the Spanish colonial period. In 1528, in the Tampa Bay area, Cabeza de Vaca had been so impressed with the size of a native house that he described it as holding more than three hundred people![8] What he saw was probably the chief's house or the principal *bohío* (council house), the most important public building. Council houses might have served multicommunities for administrative meetings, feasts, and dances, as well as for overnight lodging. They were constructed with a timber framework covered with palm thatch, and were the largest of the traditional native structures. The size of the southwest coast Calusa king's "house" prompted Solís de Merás to note that it was large enough for two thousand people to stand in (pl. 1). During the mission period, Fray Alonso de Jesús in 1630 noted one he thought would hold up to four thousand people, and the visiting bishop of Santiago de Cuba, Gabriel Díaz Vara Calderón, wrote in 1675 that a council house in one of the missions he visited in the northern mission field could accommodate some two to three thousand people! The enormous council house at Mission San Luis in Tallahassee has recently been reconstructed based on archaeological findings, and the exuberant descriptions are confirmed. It had been erected ca. 1656 without European tools or hardware and forces one to look again at Indian construction (pls. 2, 3, 4; figs. 2.6, 2.13).[9]

The Narváez expedition passed many thriving towns on its route to the region of the Apalachee, a Muskhogean group living between the Aucilla and Ochlockonee Rivers. Cabeza de Vaca recorded "small and low houses, reared in sheltered places, out of fear of the great storms that continuously occur in the country."[10]

A decade later, Hernando de Soto and his men bivouacked in the town of Ucita, north of Little Manatee River on Tampa Bay. With them was an anonymous Portuguese gentleman from Elvas, who wrote, "The town was of seven or eight houses built of timber covered with palm leaves. The Chief's house stood near [next to or on] the beach, upon a very high mount made by hand for defense; at the other end of the town was a temple, on the top of which perched a wooden fowl with gilded eyes." De Soto's private secretary, Rodrigo Ranjel, thought one of the large cabins in the town was similar to structures he had "seen in the Indies." De Soto lodged himself in the largest house, belonging to the chief, and the army stayed six weeks.[11]

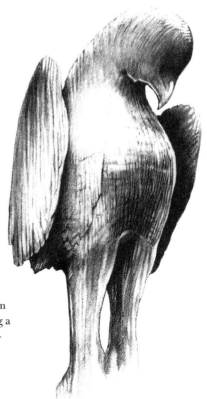

1.5. Carved wood eagle, A.D. 300–400, Fort Center, near Lake
Okeechobee. Larger than life (63 inches tall) and acutely observed from
nature, the eagle was one of many carved birds and animals supporting a
burial platform in a pond. The site was a large Indian ceremonial complex formed between 500 B.C. and A.D 1700. (Drawing by Patricia
Altman, courtesy of the Anthropology Division, Florida Museum of
Natural History)

The "temple" with the carved wooden fowl was probably a charnel
house, used to clean, prepare, and store bodies and bones for burials.
The "mount" on which it stood was an earth mound 6 feet high and 60
feet in diameter that served both as a building platform and a burial
mound. Archaeologists found it contained 112 burials that had been dug
down from the top.[12]

Drawings of charnel houses in Florida were not made by the first
Spanish explorers. However, an Englishman, John White, made hundreds of field drawings and studies in 1585 in what is now North Carolina, including one of an Indian charnel house raised on pilings. The
drawing today is in the collection of the British Library. It was engraved
and published in Frankfurt in 1590 by Theodor de Bry, of Liège, Flan-
ders, as Part I of the series *America,* with the notation that its timber
frame was 9 to 10 feet high and covered with matting.[13] Another charnel
house was sketched by Le Page du Pratz, a French engineer-architect
who spent time observing Indian construction in Louisiana. He published a woodcut in his *Histoire de la Louisiane* (Paris, 1758) that shows a
mortuary temple with carved wooden birds on top.[14]

Animal and bird effigies have been found in Florida at mortuary sites.
Their gifted carvers keenly observed the animals and birds that had special meaning to their people. At the Fort Center site in the Lake

Okeechobee basin, about A.D. 300–400, they had carved the tops of vertical support timbers of a burial platform to look like life-size bobcats, bears, and a beautiful, larger-than-life eagle. Smaller carved animals and birds, with tenon bases, were mortised on the tops of poles along the edges of the platform. At the Thursby Mound ceremonial complex (in today's Volusia County), archaeologists found a six-foot great horned owl effigy, a pelican, and an otter holding a fish. Each had been carved about A.D. 1200 from a single pine log with a shark tooth tool and stone knife.[15]

When de Soto's army moved northward from Tampa Bay during the fall of 1539, various men in the expedition noted they passed "many towns," "more towns," "a large town," and "a village of pleasant aspect and abundant food." The de Soto chroniclers left the impression that the western half of the Florida peninsula had been "developed" with numer-

Left, 1.6. Burial platform, A.D. 300–400, Fort Center, near Lake Okeechobee, conceptual drawing. The burial platform was constructed in an artificial pond dug about 120 feet across by 5 feet deep. The vertical posts supporting the platform, on which 150 bundles of skeletal remains had been placed, were carved with life-size animals and larger-than-life birds. (Photocopy by Merald Clark, copyright Florida Museum of Natural History)

Right, 1.7. Carved wood horned owl, ca. A.D. 1200, Thursby Mound, Volusia County. The six-foot owl is believed to have once been part of an Indian charnel house, where the dead were prepared for burial. (Photocopy courtesy of Florida State Archives)

ous "towns" (community centers) and "suburbs" (dispersed habitations), to use the terminology of today. The diary of de Soto's private secretary, Rodrigo Ranjel, noted that at the center of Uriutina, "there was in it a very large cabin with a large open court in the middle."[16] De Soto and his men spent the five winter months of 1539–40 in Anhaica (also Inihaica), the largest community center of the Apalachee province. Once again de Soto lodged himself in the houses belonging to the chief, which were the largest and located on one side of the town. He quartered his entire army nearby, in "two-hundred and fifty large and substantial houses."[17]

The site of Anhaica and de Soto's winter camp was excavated in 1987–88, on the grounds of the home of former Governor John W. Martin in Tallahassee. Archaeologists found traces of circular pole-frame Apalachee dwellings. Wood posts made from small trees had been set directly in the ground as vertical supports and were lashed with smaller horizontal poles and cordage, forming the framework. The floors were packed clay. Most likely, walls were covered with palm thatch, similar to the chief's house at today's reconstructed Mission San Luis, the mission village that rose later and slightly to the west of Anhaica.[18]

The sixteenth-century Spanish explorers, including Adelantado Pedro Menéndez, founder of St. Augustine (1565), "had no appreciation of comparative religions" nor "any objective interest in native cultures as such."[19] They made no drawings, wrote no objective studies, and took no measurements of native cultural artifacts. The more ethnographically minded French, however, made drawings and wrote descriptions of Timucuan architecture near the East Coast in 1564, which were published in Europe. Thus the story of Timucua Indian architecture can move forward with somewhat more visibility and form as it awaits verification by archaeologists.

Village of Seloy

The Timucuan people inhabited most of northeast Florida. Chief Saturiba (a.k.a. Saturiwa, Satouriona) ruled over a region of many villages located along the St. Johns River and today's Jacksonville. In June of 1564, French men, women and children of the Protestant Huguenot religion established a colony on the south side of the river they named May River (F. Maij), today's St. Johns River, because they had discovered the river on May 1. Within three to four miles of Saturiba's own village, they built a triangular wooden fort that they named Fort Caroline (fig. 9.1).[20]

The leader of the French colony was René de Laudonnière, a French nobleman who wrote an intriguing little book about Florida, *L'Histoire notable de la Florida*. It was published in Paris in 1586 posthumously, twenty years after he fled from Fort Caroline during an attack by the Spanish, who had recently arrived and founded St. Augustine.[21] Laudonnière had brought to Florida the artist-cartographer Jacques le Moyne de Morgues, who made drawings not only of Fort Caroline, but of a Timucua village as well (fig. 1.8). Years later he re-created paintings from memory in Europe, because he too was forced into a hasty lifesaving swim to a French ship during the Spanish raid. Engravings of these paintings, cut in copper, were published in Frankfurt in 1591 by Theodor de Bry in *Brevis narrato eorum quae in Florida Ameridae*, Part II of his fourteen-volume series *America*. All but one of le Moyne's paintings, however, have disappeared, leaving de Bry's engravings as the earliest known images of a European fort and Indian architecture in Florida.[22]

A year and several months after the French had built Fort Caroline, the Spanish founded St. Augustine (September 8, 1565). Pedro Menéndez de Avilés and some eight hundred colonists began their settlement in association with the Timucuan village of Chief Seloy, about forty miles south of Fort Caroline. Excavations at the village have uncovered layers of human occupation spanning thousands of years. The parameters of the large Indian village are still undefined, but the work of archaeologist Kathleen Deagan over the past fifteen years reveals that it included today's Fountain of Youth park and surrounding neighborhoods. The Spanish associated with the village of Seloy for almost a year.[23]

The Spanish colony's first construction of any consequence was the conversion of the chief's house into the Spanish fortified government house, described as a "very large house . . . on the river bank." The Spanish "ordered a ditch and a moat made around the house, with a rampart of earth and fagots [bundle of sticks]." Thus fortified, the Spanish headquarters was divided into rooms that served as the residence and office of Menéndez (as *adelantado*, he represented the King as governor and captain-general of the colony) and his lieutenants. It also served as storehouse for the records of the colony, and probably as the treasury and armory.[24]

Archaeologist Kathleen Deagan, excavating the Menéndez campsite, has called it the "Spanish Plymouth Rock." On April 19, 1566, it burned. Dr. Deagan thinks the building sequestered gunpowder and subsequently exploded. The Spanish relationship with the Timucua had badly dete-

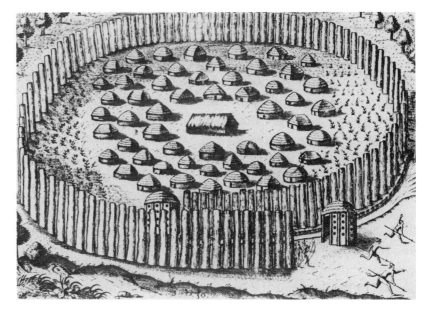

1.8. A typical Indian village of 1564, near present-day Jacksonville, engraving number 30 by Theodore de Bry, published 1591. The Timucua village enclosed in a palisade was sketched by Jacques le Moyne, the artist-cartographer with the French settlement at Fort Caroline (1564–65) on the St. Johns River. (Photocopy from engraving in *Brevis narrato eorum quae in Florida Ameridae,* courtesy of Florida State Archives)

riorated; thus it may never be known if the fire was purposely set by Indians, or was the unclaimed accident of a carelessly lighted Spanish candle.[25]

Albert Manucy, a well-known historian of St. Augustine, depicted Seloy's house in a conceptual view as round and thatched.[26] Nicholas le Challeux, a French carpenter who had escaped with Laudonnière and le Moyne from Fort Caroline, wrote in his own diary that Timucuan "houses are round, similar to dove cotes, with palm leaves on the roofs, and with foundations and structures of large trees."[27]

Round, conical thatched structures were also characteristic of the Apalachee region and widespread across the American southeast,[28] from where the style migrated across the Mississippi River with Indians moving west and was recorded in the age of photography at an Omaha village.[29] Hernando de Mestas's sketch, *Pueblo de yndios nombre de Dios,* of a council house about 1593 is probably closer to the truth. Pueblo Nombre de Dios was an Indian village associated with a Franciscan mission by about 1587, located near where Menéndez had landed. Mestas depicted the council house as the largest building—round, palm-thatched, and windowless, but with a large opening in the center of the roof to vent the hearth (figs. 2.1, 2.2). The excavation and research by Dr. Deagan will no doubt reveal its structural plan, its configuration, and how the Spanish applied their exterior defense scheme. The details are important because it is the foremost building associated with the founding of Florida.

Some Timucuan buildings may have been very large multifamily dwellings. Laudonnière described a house near Fort Caroline "from which about fifty Indians emerged;"[30] Gonzolo Solís de Merás, brother-in-law of Pedro Menéndez, described Saturiba's village as "a pueblo of 25 large houses, where in each one live eight or nine Indians with their wives and children."[31]

Le Moyne himself is thought to have written the caption that accompanies de Bry's engraving of his sketch of a typical Indian [Timucuan] village:

> The Indians usually built their village in the following way. Having chosen a suitable site near some fast flowing river they made it level as best they could. Then they built a ditch round it and planted thick round wooden posts, twice the height of a man, side by side in the ground in a circle. At the entrance to the town the circle of posts continued further round, like a snail's shell, but so closely that not more than two people abreast could enter. Then they diverted the channel of the river to this place. At the entrance they built a small round house at each end. These two houses had lots of holes and vertical openings and were built in the beautiful tradition of that country. In these houses they put guards ... The chief's house was situated in the middle and slightly sunk below ground level to protect it against the heat of the sun. Around it were built the houses of his noblemen covered thinly with palm leaves for they used these houses for only nine months of the year. Spending the other three in the woods. When they returned from the woods they inhabited their houses again but if they were burnt down they simply rebuilt them.[32]

One wonders if moving with the seasons was a system of natural sanitation, and whether houses were purposely burned to eliminate fleas and roaches in the palm thatch. Laudonnière wrote in his *L'Histoire* that when the Timucua chief or priest died, his house was set on fire with all his goods "in such a way that nothing is ever seen of it again."[33]

The two circular guardhouses depicted in the village engraving are wattle-and-daub construction. Upright earthfast poles were interwoven with twigs or cane withes to form a wattle (lath) framework on which clay was daubed (plastered) which hardened in the sun like adobe. Perhaps the roof was put on first to protect the "green" clay daub from the weather until it hardened.

Le Moyne's more interesting architectural observations include the ditch and palisade, the diverted river, and the chief's house built slightly below grade to protect it against the heat of the sun. Florida architect

1.9. Florida Museum of Natural History (formerly Florida State Museum), Dickinson Hall, south facade, University of Florida, Gainesville. The design (1969) was inspired by Indian mounds and platforms. The colder north facade was banked with earth, while the warmer south facade was stepped and terraced. The concept was a climate-responsive building naturally insulated and cooled. (Architect: William N. Morgan, F.A.I.A.; drawing courtesy of the Florida Museum of Natural History)

William N. Morgan, F.A.I.A., made a study of Indian earthworks[34] and adapted a similar earth-insulated concept for modern living when he designed the Florida Museum of Natural History in 1968–71 (fig. 1.9) and Forest House, a private residence in north Florida, in 1975. By depressing the buildings and banking their exterior walls with earth, he proved that earth does insulate and reduces the need for air-conditioning.

When René Laudonnière had a barn built to protect his military supplies at Fort Caroline, he asked the Timucua chief to command his Indian subjects to make a roof of palm leaves "for they use nothing else to cover their houses." The chief "commanded all the Indians of his company, starting the next morning, to prepare such a great number of palm leaves that the barn was covered within two days . . . During those two days, the Indians did nothing but labour—some in bringing palm leaves, others in weaving them together."[35]

Palm-thatched roofs properly constructed will last from twelve to twenty years. The steeper the pitch, the faster it sheds the rain, and the longer it lasts. Palm thatch was typically used for roofing by pre-Columbian Indians in Florida, the West Indies, and Mexico. Post-conquest accounts throughout these regions reveal that thatched roof forms varied, from cone to gable to hip, with smoke vents either at the top of the cone or below the gable ridge. Friar Diego de Landa, in 1540 in the Yucatan, for example, was one of the earliest Europeans to advocate the excellent qualities of the "leaves of palm" adapted to roofs, "the roof being very steep to prevent its raining through."[36] Long after the Indians were gone from Florida, palm fronds covered entire buildings of American pioneers who pushed the wilderness frontiers southward (fig. 3.10). In Cuba and Mexico, palm fronds are still commonly used in rural village construction, and "palapa" roofs are now popular on very expensive houses designed by prominent architects in Mexico.[37]

John White made a painting in 1585 of "The Towne of Pomeiock," an Indian village in North Carolina. De Bry published it as "The Towne of Pomeiooc," with the note: "the townes of this countrie are in a manner like unto those which are in Florida."[38] Two original drawings by White depict Pomeiock with a palisade and entrance that are very similar to le Moyne's "typical Timucua town" in Florida engraved by de Bry.[39] White's drawings were serious studies, keenly observed, and accurate where modern archaeology has checked. The original drawings of black lead pencil and watercolor are preserved in the British Library and reveal that de Bry's engravings were faithful. However, since White is known to have exchanged ideas with le Moyne, the similarity between the villages (or between the drawings) begs to be questioned.[40]

White's note on his painting is revealing: "The Towne of Pomeiock and true forme of their howses, covered and enclosed some wth matts, and some wth barcks of trees." De Bry's engraving of his drawing explained, "Their dwellings are builded with certaine potes [posts] fastened together and covered with matts which they turne op [up] as high as they thinke good . . ." probably for receiving light and air because there were no windows. "Some are also covered with boughs of trees."[41] They are depicted as rectangular or square at the base, framed with bent and tied poles that form rounded or semicylindrical roofs. The matting is expertly fashioned in long strips and covers the arched framework. An additional long section of matting runs the length of the ridge of the roof. Some of the houses are said to have been as large as 72 by 36 feet. All are shown with benches lining the walls and covered with mats for sleeping, similar to those of the Apalachee council houses in Florida described by explorers and Franciscan friars, and confirmed by archaeological data at Mission San Luis (pls. 3, 4).

White described houses covered with "barcks of trees." The British in 1764 found slabs of "bark of trees" covering roofs and walls of Spanish houses in Pensacola built with Indian help,[42] and when the Spanish repossessed Pensacola twenty years later, "bark" roofs again were a solution. "Bark" was also the material of French builders on the Gulf Coast, presumably influenced by earlier Indian practices.[43]

Construction methods for Indian dwellings, round and square, in

French Louisiana were recorded by Le Page du Pratz, an architect living in Natchez and New Orleans in 1718–34, and his observations below are as informative as John White's depictions:

> The natives go back into the woods to seek poles . . . four inches in diameter by eighteen to twenty feet long. They plant the thickest ones in the four corners to form its width and the dome . . . they prepare the scaffold . . . composed of four poles attached together at the top, and the bottom ends are secured to the four corners. On these four poles others are attached across at a foot apart. This whole makes a four faced ladder or four ladders joined together.
>
> That done, the other poles are planted in the ground in a straight line between the corner ones . . . strongly tied to a pole which crosses them inside each face. For this purpose they use thick cane wicker for tying them at the height of five or six feet according to the size of the cabin. This is what forms the walls. These standing poles are distant from each other only around fifteen inches. A young man afterwards mounts to the end of one of the corner poles with a cord in his teeth. He attaches the cord to the pole and as he climbs on the inside, the pole bends because those who are at the bottom draw the cord in order to make the pole bend as much as is necessary.[44]

In the du Pratz narrative, the poles at the opposite angles were similarly bent and strongly attached to each other, and were joined to the point, "which all together makes the figure of a garden bower, such as we have in France."[45]

The wattle work of canes was then attached across the vertical poles at around eight inches apart and up to about 5 or 6 feet, the height of the walls. This wattle or lath framework was then packed with "clay mortar" made of "earth in which sufficient Spanish moss is put." The only opening in the Indian structure was a door about 2 by 4 feet or smaller. The roof was covered with bundles of grass reeds 4 or 5 feet long attached with heavy canes and wicker, also of cane, and covered with mats of cane. "[H]however great the wind might come, it can do nothing against the cabin. Then these roofs endure twenty years without doing anything to them."[46]

In Florida's climate the preservation of food required specific architecture. Le Moyne observed Timucua Indians gathering and filling their canoes with fruits to be transported to storehouses that he described as: "low, built of stones and earth with roofs of thickly laid palm leaves and soft soil. These kinds of huts were usually built near the river at the foot of a hill or rock where the sun's rays did not penetrate to stop the fruit from

1.10. "The Indians take their harvest to a store-house," 1564, engraving number 22 by Theodore de Bry, published 1591. Jacques le Moyne is said to have written the text accompanying this sketch, describing the Timucua storehouses as "built of stones and earth with roofs of thickly laid palm leaves and soft soil." (Photocopy from engraving in *Brevis narrato eorum quae in Florida Ameridae,* courtesy of Florida State Archives)

going rotten." Smoked meat and fish were also stored in similar storehouses.[47]

The storage of corn was not described by le Moyne or Laudonnnière, but it was essential to protect it from mice and animals. The Timucua might have used corncribs similar to those noted in the Apalachee region by the anonymous Portuguese gentleman with de Soto in 1539 that were made of cane and called "barbacoas," houses raised aloft on wood posts. Two possible granaries in Mestas's drawing of ca. 1593, *Pueblo de yndios nombre de Dios,* are depicted as thatch buildings raised on pilings and blessed with a cross (figs. 2.1, 2.2). Since Pueblo Nombre de Dios was a Spanish period village, this might account for the crosses, still a common practice on granaries in Galicia, Asturias, and Cantabria, Spain. Later, during the mission period, Bishop Gabriel Díaz Vara Calderón described Indian granaries in a letter in 1675 to Queen Mariana of Spain following his ten-month tour of the missions: "On one side [of the native house] is a granary supported by twelve beams, which they call a garita, where they store the wheat, corn and other things they harvest."[48] One hundred years later, in 1774, William Bartram described similar granaries at the Seminole (Creek) town of Cuscowilla, south of present-day Gainesville.[49] Granaries and corncribs built with cane or wattle-and-daub were common in Indian villages throughout Spanish America.[50] In Mexico, the form is still constructed today (fig 2.12).

Timucua and Apalachee Indians had access to diverse materials.

There was an abundance of large and small timbers, palm logs and palm fronds, reeds, clayey mud, moss, animal and plant cordage. In René de Loudonnière's account of construction at Fort Caroline in 1564, he sent men daily to an arm of the St. Johns River "to get clay to make bricks and mortar for our houses." During the colonial period, there was enough clay on the St. Johns River at Ortega to support a commercial brick-making operation.[51] There was also plenty of clay in the Apalachee region and layer of clayey river mud along North Florida's creeks and rivers. John Bartram observed grass reeds or canes growing four or five feet tall in the marsh between St. Augustine and Woodcutters Creek (Moultrie Creek).[52] Pieces of coquina shellstone were probably strewn along the beaches of Anastasia Island just as they are today.

Florida's first builders knew their indigenous construction materials well. Even after European colonization, they had no need for iron fastenings. At the missions they engineered enormous pole frames into circles, and notched and lashed them securely with fibers and animal gut. They drew upon seven thousand years of tradition in matting and twining fiber cordage from Sabal palms, saw palmettos, grass, and other plants. Remnants of such perishable materials have been found in the Windover Pond site (circa 5,000 B.C.) in Brevard County, preserved in peat beside the skulls, brains and genetic material of the people themselves.[53]

Florida's first builders were intelligent builders. They knew that cypress poles lasted longer than pine in wetlands (cypress contains cypresene, a natural preservative). Their thatch roofs were waterproof and easily repaired. They designed pits in which to burn corncobs slowly in low-oxygen fires to produce smoke that repelled mosquitoes. Experience taught Florida's first builders that round buildings fared better in tropical storms, that earth insulated, and that air ventilated.

The "conquest" signaled the end. The Calusa, Apalachee, and Timucua builders died by the thousands during the colonial period because they had no immunity against the epidemics of European measles, smallpox, and yellow fever. They had numbered about 350,000 on the eve of the arrival of Spanish ships. By 1763, when Great Britain acquired Florida, the first builders and their buildings were gone.[54] Two hundred years after the Spanish bedded down in his house and his village, Chief Seloy could never have imagined a loss so total so soon.

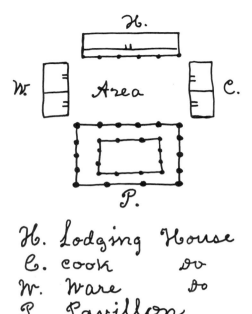

H. Lodging House
C. cook ᵈᵒ
W. Ware ᵈᵒ
P. Pavillon

1.11. Creek Indian house plan, 1770s, sketched by William Bartram. Creek Indians moved into Florida early in the 1700s, where they became known as Seminoles. (Redrawn by E. Gordon after Edwin H. Davis, National Anthropological Archives, Smithsonian Institution)

CUSCOWILLA

Indians of the Chattahoochee River Basin north of Florida began to migrate southward into the peninsula in the early 1700s. They came from different towns and they spoke different languages. They spoke Oconee, Muskogee, Yuchi, Apalachicola, and Hitchiti, but were called Creek and, later, Seminole and Miccosukee. Seminole came from the word *simanoli,* a Muskogee corruption of the Spanish word *cimarrón,* meaning wild ones, or outsiders, running from creeping white civilization. The English called them *Semenolas* and by the late colonial period, all Florida's Indians were called Seminoles.[55]

The Creek (Seminoles) spread across Florida and grew in numbers during the colonial period. Additional refugees from the northern Creek confederacy arrived and were joined by escaping African slaves who took up living under the protection of Seminole chiefs. When the Creek transplanted themselves to Florida, they transplanted their architecture and building methods. By 1774, nine substantial Seminole towns had been built in Florida. They were characterized by the traditional Creek pairs of dwellings, square yards slightly below grade, airy pavilions for banqueting, and council houses.[56]

In 1774 William Bartram visited Cuscowilla, a Seminole town south of today's Gainesville in Alachua County. He was royally entertained by Ahaye, chief of the Hitchiti-speaking Oconee Seminoles (Bartram called

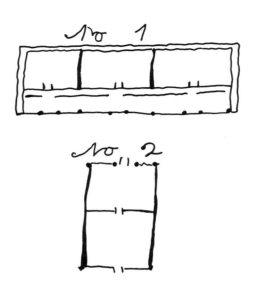

1.12. Seminole house plan, 1770s, Cuscowilla, south of Gainesville near Micanopy, sketched by William Bartram. Cuscowilla dwellings consisted of a pair of frame houses with notched log sides, each 30 feet by 12 feet, with cypress roofs. (Redrawn by E. Gordon after Edwin H. Davis, National Anthropological Archives, Smithsonian Institution)

them Lower Creek).[57] Ahaye was also known as Cowkeeper, because of his extensive herd of cattle. He hated the Spanish and was a shrewd leader in his negotiations with the British at the Congress held at Picolata in 1765.[58] Bartram was greatly impressed by the Cuscowilla council house, public square, private dwellings and granaries, as well as its orange groves, innumerable droves of cattle, and large publicly owned plantation and granary.

He counted thirty habitations, each consisting of two houses 30 by 12 feet. One house was divided into apartments for the "cook room," common hall, and lodging. The second house was two stories tall and divided into two apartments with one end open on three sides, forming a roofed porch. It was accessed by a ladder, and was pleasantly cool. This was where the head of the family rested or received guests. The other end was an enclosed food warehouse, the lower floor for potatoes and the upper for corn and produce from their gardens. The frame construction had large strong corner pillars and posts in between set in the ground, cross bracing, and a roof of cypress bark. The sides were notched logs. Cowkeeper's house was the same but larger. The airy loft where he met with Bartram was 12 feet high.[59]

At Cuscowilla and at another Creek settlement in present-day St. Marks, Wakulla County, Bartram was feted in a banqueting house that was an "apartment of the public square, constructed and appointed for feasting." The pavilions in which Bartram was received were "delightful and airy." Woven cane mats dyed different colors covered platforms around the sides. The benches were built to different heights for people of rank, for white people, and for Indians of other towns.[60]

Joseph Purcell, an English surveyor, drew a map in 1778 of the road from Pensacola to St. Augustine as ordered by the superintendent of Indian affairs of the Southern District, Colonel John Stuart. On the map is noted that he visited six "Semenola" towns. One of these was "Tallahassa," beside the ruins of the "St. Louis fort and town." In this town were thirty-six houses, a square, sixteen families, and thirty gunmen, with a headman called Tonaby. Another town visited was "Micasucky," with sixty houses and a square.[61]

Black Seminoles increased in number in the last half of the colonial period. They were slaves who had escaped from plantations in Georgia and Carolina, living as Seminoles in separate villages near the Seminole Indians and paying tribute in exchange for protection.[62] Until archaeology proves otherwise, it is suggested they constructed log or wood frame dwellings, some raised and some open, with bark or palm thatch roofs similar to those described by Bartram at Cuscowilla.

When Spain departed Florida for the second time in 1821, and Florida became an American territory, the number of white settlers increased. The competition for Florida's rich farming fields and timber stands led to tremendous tension between Americans and Seminoles. The land claims pitted white settler against Indian and African, and all were determined to protect their homesteads at any cost. The American thirst for

1.13. Seminole dwelling (chickee), 1884. To avoid deportation to the West, a few Seminoles fled into the Everglades and Big Cypress Swamp, where they adapted their house construction to the environment. (Drawing by Clay MacCauley, courtesy of Florida State Archives)

1.14. Seminole Chickee, 1950s construction. The Seminoles who fled to the Everglades used local materials to construct their houses. The chickee could be erected by one man, and was raised off the ground and left open to provide maximum ventilation. (Photocopy courtesy of Florida State Archives)

land, however, was unquenchable. Treaties were signed and broken, and politicians, generals, and settlers alike called for "extermination" of the Seminoles and their removal to reservations in the West. Seminoles who resisted removal had bounties placed on their heads.

A few Seminoles fled deep into hiding in the Everglades and Big Cypress Swamp, where they adapted their building practices to the hot, wet environment. Their dwellings, called *chickees*, had simple frames of upright logs and pitched roofs of small poles covered with palmetto thatch. They averaged 8 by 15 feet, smaller than their ancestral homes, but they could be built by one man. The floors of split logs or boards were raised off the ground about 18 inches, and the sides and ends were left open to provide maximum ventilation. The cooking houses were separate. By 1858, the Seminole population had been reduced from five thousand to two hundred,[63] and their villages, granaries, and dwellings, like those of the first builders, the Calusa, Apalachee, and Timucua, had been removed from the face of the land.

2 | THE SPANISH MISSIONS

*They deprive us of every vestige of happiness which our
ancestors obtained for us, in exchange for which they hold
out the hope of joys of Heaven.*

JUANILLO, HEIR APPARENT, TOLOMATO CHIEFDOM

Juanillo, quoted above, was beheaded in 1601. The dwellings and community buildings of the Tolomato have long been erased from Florida's landscape, but vestiges of the Tolomato peoples live on in place names like Tolomato River and Tolomato Cemetery in St. Augustine.[1] However, during the collision of European and Indian cultures symbolized by Juanillo's fate, scores of Franciscan friars and thousands of Florida's natives managed to salvage some sense of humanity and a little something of grace, if not an architectural miracle. Together, they constructed more than 140 missions up and down Florida's east coast and westward into the red hills of Tallahassee.[2] The missions too are gone, but their buildings and commitment reappear in the descriptions to follow.

INSTRUMENTS OF FAITH, CHURCH, AND CROWN

Jesuits arrived first, in 1566, to begin the evangelization of Florida's Indians. The territory was formidable, stretching endlessly through thick woods and wetlands, from the realms of the Guale, Timucua, and Ais in the north and east, to the Apalachee in the northwest, to the Calusa in the southwest, to the Tequesta on Biscayne Bay. The first Jesuit to set foot on land to look for Indians was said to have been strangled underwater and then clubbed. Somewhat daunted, the Jesuits built their first churches behind the protection of garrisons and fort palisades. The association with soldiers, however, who cruelly mistreated the Indians, proved disas-

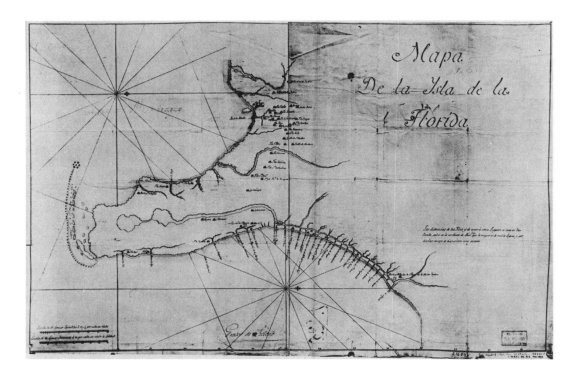

2. Mission map, 1683, showing some of the estimated 140 missions (*pueblos*) established along the *camino real* and coasts of Florida between 1587 and 1702. (Anonymous, Spanish, Ministry of War, Madrid; photocopy, Library of Congress, courtesy of Florida State Archives)

trous at fort-missions on Biscayne Bay and the Gulf Coast. The Jesuits scurried back to Spain in 1572.[3]

The Franciscans arrived in the 1580s, wearing the brown or blue monastic habit of colonial Franciscans on foreign missions. Felipe II was King of Spain; Elizabeth was Queen of England. The Renaissance had been flowering for a hundred years in Italy, but North America was a vast uncharted wilderness. One hundred and eighty years more would have to pass before Father Junipero Serra would found the first mission in California.

During the rest of the sixteenth and for all of the seventeenth century, Franciscan friars trekked from St. Augustine, the mission headquarters, north to the coastal islands of the Carolinas (then part of Spanish Florida), south to Cape Canaveral, and west to present-day Tallahassee. More than three hundred friars are estimated to have served in Florida, but the turnover rate was very high because many perished or fell ill in the crushing isolation.[4] Somehow, these undaunted bearers of Catholic faith and their Indian converts accommodated their cultural differences and constructed the hundred-plus missions. The missions were held together by something more than Spanish handwrought nails and Indian cordage.[5] In *Death Comes for the Archbishop,* a novel about the experiences of a priest among Indians in New Mexico, Willa Cather expresses plainly that no man can know what triumph of faith happened there, where white man and Indian met torture and death—or what visions and revelations God may have granted to soften the brutal end.[6]

The Franciscan friars in Florida were men who were members of the Roman Catholic mendicant religious order founded by St. Francis of Assisi in 1207. They combined monastic life with work in the outside world. The order that took charge of the missions in Florida was directed by the commissary general of the Indies from a convent in Madrid. They were a custody of the Franciscan province of Santo Evangelico de Nueva España (Mexico) until 1609, when they were fused with the Franciscan monastery in Cuba. After 1612, their headquarters in Florida was the monastery in St. Augustine then known as the Convento de la Concepción Inmaculada, south of the Plaza, today called by archaeologists Convento de San Francisco. Here they convened every two to four years to elect their administrators, subject to the supervision and subsidies of the viceroy of New Spain. Some friars might have received training at the Franciscan college of San Fernando in Mexico City before heading into Florida's wilderness, like the many who fanned out into New Mexico and eventually California.[7]

Friars in Florida were far distanced from their church centers in Europe, Cuba, or Mexico, but they brought with them a centuries-old attitude toward church architecture. Their accomplishments would spring from their ability not only to engage Indians in a new system of beliefs, but to convince them to build traditional European religious buildings. Their churches and monasteries would have to be constructed according to European practices with European tools, but with indigenous materials and native labor, in the simplest way, restrained by the unfamiliar and with no pretense of monumentality.

The most substantial mission buildings erected in the late 1500s in present-day Florida were at Pueblo Nombre de Dios (north of St. Augustine), Pueblo San Juan del Puerto (on Ft. George Island), and the Convento de la Concepción Inmaculada. Before long, their friars would be boasting of ornate churches, belfries, statues of saints, organs, and a large library at the mission headquarters. Mestas's drawing, ca. 1593, labeled *Pueblo de yndios nombre de Dios,* is the earliest depiction of a Florida mission (fig. 2.1).

Pueblo Nombre de Dios is thought to have been the first mission village, initiated shortly after the Spanish landed in 1565. The Mestas drawing may be revealing three architectural complexes: the complex of European-style buildings (Franciscan religious complex of church, friary, and kitchen) erected beginning in 1587; the complex of Indian buildings, possibly preexisting the Franciscan mission (council house with huge roof-

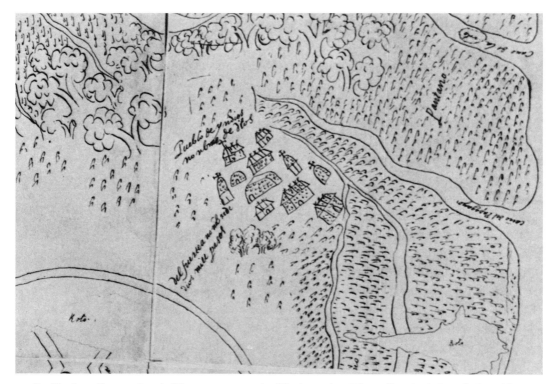

2.1. Pueblo de yndios nombre de Dios, ca. 1593, north of St. Augustine. The earliest depiction of a Spanish Franciscan mission village in Florida is attributed to Hernando de Mestas. All the buildings, European and Timucuan, had pole frames set directly in the ground and covered with palm thatch, but their forms differed greatly. The European-style church and friary were rectangular and gabled, built with hewn timbers and iron hardware. The chief's house and the Timucua council house were round, built with round poles and cordage from plants and animals. (Photocopy courtesy of Florida State Archives)

top vent, chief's house, and granaries raised on poles, marked later with crosses in the Spanish custom); and the complex of the residential area, with either Spanish or multifamily Timucua houses (fig. 2.2). More humble beginnings, however, might have been a cross driven into the ground and a bell hung in a tree before the first temporary thatch chapel was erected.

The mission at Pueblo San Juan del Puerto, founded in 1587, gave its name to the St. Johns River. It was the residence of Friar Pareja, a very dedicated and capable friar who wrote a grammar and a catechism in the Timucuan language, published in Mexico in 1614. Father Pareja died at his mission in 1628 after serving thirty-one years.[8] Jonathan Dickinson stopped at the mission in 1696 and described its location in the middle of the island as having a church, a friary, a corn house, and a large council house. He also noted many hogs and chickens. The mission was burned in 1702 but was revived during 1715–36. When John Bartram visited the site in 1765, he noted that the mission was once a "fine settlement" with its "cedar posts still standing on each side of their fine straight avenues."[9] By 1736, the mission had functioned for almost 136 years.

Despite terrible odds, the Franciscan vernacular architecture was successful. By 1635, Fray Francisco de Ocaña estimated that 170,000 Indians had been baptized in Spanish Florida.[10] But by 1704, Florida's mission field was in ruins, a victim of Spanish mismanagement and cruelty, epidemics of European diseases, and a deadly contest between Spain and England for control of Florida. A series of raids from 1702 to 1704 led by Colonel James Moore and Captain Robert Daniel, from the English colony of South Carolina, destroyed most of Florida's missions. Also among the raiders, however, were Florida Indians who were dissatisfied with Spanish government officials, abusive hacienda owners, and the friars themselves. The destruction was so complete the Apalachee region lost not only all the missions, but also the Spanish ranches and the Spanish fort and town of San Luis (fig. 9.13), and its entire native population.[11] The English had stopped the missions from supplying sustenance to the Spanish capital.

The missions along the coasts and in the wilderness beside the Apalachee Trail (*camino real,* royal road) were never rebuilt to grow and cap-

Mission Nombre de Dios in 1593

2.2. Mission Nombre de Dios, north of St. Augustine, redrawn from Hernando de Mestas's drawing of ca. 1593 with suggested spheres of building organization and uses: *A.* European religious buildings; *B.* Traditional Indian buildings; *C.* Residential, either Spanish or Indian. *A1.* church, *A2.* friary, *A3.* kitchen; *B4.* council house with large roof opening, *B5.* chief's house, *B6.* granary, raised on pilings, with cross in Spanish tradition; *C7.* residences, *C8.* first chapel, built before construction of larger church. (Drawing by E. Gordon)

2.3. Apalachee Indians of Louisiana, descendants of Florida's Apalachee Indians who left the region after the destruction of the missions in 1704. The young girl in the left-hand corner, Francis Vallery (born 1908), is the mother of the current chief, Gilmer Bennett. (Photograph courtesy of Florida Division of Historical Resources)

ture the imagination of future generations, as happened in the American Southwest and California. The bells were silenced at missions that once had sonorous names like Santa Catalina de Guale, Santa Fé de Toloca, San Luis de Talimali, San Pedro y San Pablo de Patale, and San Martín de Timucua, to name only a very few. Their sites and structural remnants were covered over with grassland and forests, or slipped into meandering inlets and rivers. They were forgotten for about two hundred and fifty years, until unearthed late in the twentieth century.[12]

Missions closer to the capital, St. Augustine, however, were rebuilt. Nuestra Señora de la Leche, the church at Mission Nombre de Dios, was rebuilt with stone closer to town in the eighteenth century (fig. 4.22). Nuestra Señora de Guadalupe at the Tolomato mission was also reconstructed, as were the friary and church at La Concepción, the Franciscan headquarters (pl. 12).[13] La Leche and La Concepción each had 175 years of history by 1763, when Spain ceded Florida to Great British.

The state of Florida is presently reconstructing and furnishing the major structures that once existed from 1656 to 1704 at Mission San Luis in Tallahassee, based on the data retrieved from archaeological excavations. The church, council house, chief's house, *convento* (monastery), and its *cocina* (kitchen) are completed, and work on the fort will begin soon. The magnitude of the accomplishments of the friars and Indian builders is astonishing, grasped only by actually standing inside their church (fig. 2.8; pls. 5, 6), the largest built in Florida, and the immense council house, the largest colonial period Indian structure in the American southeast (pl. 4).

Mission villages were small centers of commerce and education that strengthened Spain's foothold in Florida. The missions engaged in trade with the Indians, and they supplied St. Augustine, the capital, with foodstuffs. They also sent Indian laborers, required under the *repartimiento* system, to work on public construction projects. The string of missions came at a bargain price when compared to the cost of maintaining an army and string of forts to protect Spain's claim to the peninsula and ships bearing gold and silver in the shipping lanes close by the coastline. The sharp Friar Pareja put it bluntly in 1613 on behalf of the Franciscans: "We are the ones who are bearing the burden and the heat and we are the ones who are conquering and subduing the land."[14]

The Mission Village, Church, and Convento

The friars generally did not choose the mission sites, but supervised their establishment at the behest of Indian villages that already existed. However, they moved missions to new sites along the westward *camino real* from St. Augustine to the Apalachee region, following reorganization orders of the Spanish governors when mission villages were destroyed in rebellion or decimated by diseases.[15] The missions were spaced a day's walk from each other, providing safety and overnight hospitality. The Indians along the way were converted Christians and posed little threat. All the missions, however, had to be located in places suited to agriculture.

Archaeologists are not yet in agreement on an architectural mission village model, or whether one even existed.[16] The Franciscan church, monastery, *atrio,* kitchen, and granary must have had certain requirements, but each mission's architecture would have been subject to concessions and accommodation, influenced by whether the village was preexisting, the village size, site topography, local materials, the prior building experiences and skills of each friar-designer and his Indian artisans. The mission churches, however, might have had a model plan based on whole or sacred numbers in simple ratios.

Mission San Luis was the largest and most important mission in the Apalachee region. To date, it is the most thoroughly investigated, and the only one to be reconstructed. Although it was unique in having a sizable European population, some of its architectural characteristics might be indicative of what existed at some of the other missions. For example, Mission San Luis had an immense circular plaza (410 feet in diameter) that was the central element of the mission village. In prominent positions close to the plaza stood the European church and convento, and the Indian council house and chief's house, each a symbol of authority. Spanish dwellings were clustered to one side; Indian dwellings and granaries were dispersed.[17]

This plaza, however, was atypical of the square or rectangular plaza mandated by the Laws of the Indies for New World Spanish towns.[18] However, it accommodated the differences between the two cultures, facilitating their union by serving as a main stage for communication, uniting as well as separating their economic, social, and ceremonial activities, from ball games to religious processions. Plazas had been known to both cultures long before they were laid out at Florida's Spanish missions. In Europe, plazas had spread across the continent into Spain with the Romans. In the New World, Indian plazas had been centers of activities and markets for almost two thousand years before the arrival of the Spanish. In Florida, the Portuguese gentleman from Elvas, who chronicled the de Soto expedition in 1539, noted in an Indian village the existence of "the public yard of the town."[19]

Fray Alonso de Jesús wrote in 1630 of Indian skills, "for the construction of our temples and houses, we no longer have need of nails and iron tools," and "the temples are of timbers, built with as much perfection as those of the Spaniards." The archaeological data at Mission San Luis,

2.4. Apalachee chief's house (foreground) ca. 1656, Mission San Luis, Tallahassee, reconstructed 1999. It was a very large dwelling, round (65 feet diameter), and conical with a roof vent for light and hearth smoke. (Photograph by Merald Clark, copyright 2001 Florida Museum of Natural History)

FLORIDA'S COLONIAL ARCHITECTURAL HERITAGE

2.5. Apalachee chief's house, ca. 1656, framework of roof opening, Mission San Luis, Tallahassee, reconstructed in 1999 and looking like a giant spider web before the Zulu guest workers covered it with palm fronds. The identical timber frame was erected 350 years ago by Florida's Apalachee Indians without European tools or hardware. (Photograph courtesy of Florida Division of Historical Resources)

however, revealed that European tools and wrought iron spikes and nails had been used to construct the framework of the "European buildings," the church and friary. Until archaeologists find more evidence, one might conclude that churches and monasteries were designed by the friars on the spot, based on European models, Franciscan traditions, and specifications that met the liturgical requirements of the Catholic Church, but that they were constructed by Indian laborers using some of their own ingenuity and knowledge of the local materials, particularly as regards the palm roofs.[20]

The excavations at Mission San Luis also revealed that the Indian builder was reluctant to abandon his own customs when he built his traditional council house, his chief's house, and his own dwellings and granaries. The excavations did not find evidence that European hardware or tools were used, except perhaps the hatchet. A similar persistence in traditional building methods has been discovered at other mission sites in Florida.[21]

The methods for designing churches and for conveying the design particulars to the Indian builders are unknown. Friar and Indian might

2.6. Apalachee council house, ca. 1656, timber framework, Mission San Luis, Tallahassee, reconstructed 2000. Archaeology and reconstruction exposed the incredible size of the council house framing timbers. (Photograph by E. Gordon)

have worked out floor plans on the ground using cords and pegs in accordance with European practices, similar to the way in which the Castillo de San Marcos was staked out and cordoned off to size and shape.[22] Elevations could have been planned from a three-dimensional model like those used by the Jesuit Father Paul de Ru in Mississippi in 1700,[23] or from sketches roughed out in the soil or on a wood plank or clay slab. Friars might have been sent out with an assisting itinerant builder, or with instructions for developing church plans based on modules multiplied by sacred numbers or ratios. The church may have begun with the placement of the altar and sanctuary, the most sacred place, and walking off the nave east of the altar in simple multiples of its dimensions, reflecting the biblical proportions of Solomon's temple (60 by 30 by 20 cubits, in 1 Kings 6 and 2 Chronicles 3, 4) and Medieval practices. The direction of burials discovered in the twentieth century, and drawings of parish churches rendered by Boazio (1586) and Mestas (1593) indicate that altars in Spanish Florida were generally in the westerly quadrant.[24]

At Mission San Luis, the framing for the church and convento consisted of pine and cypress timbers set directly in the ground. Earthfast posts in the ground construction had been practiced by New World Indians and Europeans long before their cultures came together in America. Since the early 1500s, friars as well as Spanish settlers had been erecting earthfast buildings in Cuba and Mexico. In Cuba, poles were singed at the ends to produce a waterproof charcoal layer before they were set into the ground. In Florida, some post holes were lined or backfilled with oyster shells for stabilization and preservation; others were set down on clay pads or into clay-filled post holes.[25] The European buildings had squared beams that were joined by mortise and tenon, pegs, and wrought iron nails and spikes—techniques taught the Indians by the friars, or learned during apprenticeships under the *repartimiento* system of forced labor.[26] Indian buildings, however, did not have hewn timbers and were joined with animal or plant cordage.

The church and friary at Mission San Luis were roofed with palm thatch, perhaps with techniques more Indian than Spanish. The walling of the church was pitsawn vertical planks, a Spanish practice. The walling of the friary was clay packed on a wood frame (wattle-and-daub or *cuje y embarrado*), smoothed and covered with coats of whitewash, thought to waterproof, disinfect, and cool the building. This type of construction produced thick walls and had a very old history in both cultures. Sometimes moss or grass binders were mixed in the clay.

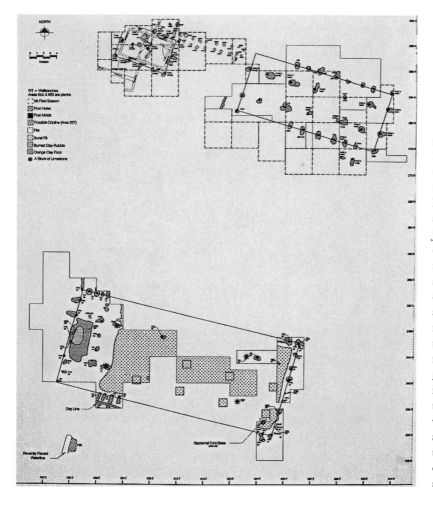

2.7. Archaeological Plan of the Religious Complex at Mission San Luis, ca. 1690, Tallahassee. *Top:* friary, about 70 feet by 30 feet, joined to kitchen by covered walkway, now reconstructed by the state of Florida to replicate the original wattle-and-daub structures roofed with palm thatch. *Bottom:* church, roughly 100–110 feet by 50 feet, reconstructed in 1999 according to the archaeological data, with wood plank walls and thatch roof. (Courtesy of Florida Division of Historical Resources)

One mission church in Spanish Florida was constructed with a combination of pine planking and wattlework. The front facade was entirely wattle-and-daub, anchored by four round poles set into shell-lined postholes. It was plastered white and perhaps was extended upward to form the traditional Spanish *espadaña,* an extension of the front wall above the gable roof.[27] Sometimes espadañas became belfries, pierced with openings in which bells were suspended, tied to a beam.

The skills and methods with which the Indians laid out the dimensions and worked the native materials affected the final appearance of each church and its friary. They manufactured everything at the site with minimal tools, handmade or brought from St. Augustine. Inventories of tools in late sixteenth-century St. Augustine included axes, adzes, spades, hoes, chisels, augers, drills, planes, saws, hammers, and nails.[28] Whatever they could not manufacture had to be carried to the sites in crates, sacks, or wooden barrels and olive jars (mainly for wine and olive "holy" oil) on "roads" that were Indian trails. The friar, therefore, would have depended on local Indian knowledge to maximize the advantages of the site and of local materials. The unknown construction details of the churches are still numerous, from the forms of belfries to the use of ridge poles, from the heights and shapes of roofs, windows, and chancel rails to the interior furnishings and church art.

A story associated with Fig Springs Mission in 1597 says much about the skills of the Indian mission builder: The Indians appealed to St. Augustine for a missionary, and they "were given two iron axes and a hoe" and told to build a church and a house for the priest who would follow upon its completion![29] Bishop Gabriel Díaz Vara Calderón, who visited the mission churches in 1674, wrote in a letter to Queen Mariana of Spain in 1675 that the natives were "great carpenters as is evidenced by the construction of their wooden churches which are large and painstakingly wrought."[30] Excavations show that the wood and thatch church constructed by the Apalachee at Mission San Luis was slightly larger in interior square footage than the thick-walled stone cathedral built in 1797 in St. Augustine.

The Spanish missions could not have survived as long as they did if the religious architecture had not met its evangelical, liturgical, and educational roles. Churches had to be impressive, mysterious, and tangible symbols or metaphors for the glory and power of God and Catholic doctrine. There is no reason to think that Franciscans in Florida did not follow the same rules applicable to building Catholic mission churches elsewhere, regardless of construction material—adobe, stone, wood or thatch. The rules were: the church must be consecrated, built to be a church and not used for other purposes; it must be a permanent structure, arranged with a sanctuary for the altar and celebrants, a nave for the congregation, a choir for singers, and a place to baptize. It was a sacrilege to break these rules.[31]

The dimensions of the San Luis church might not have been random but based on a proportional system similar to that used by Medieval and Renaissance church builders.[32] At the time of the formation and growth of the Franciscan movement in the thirteenth century, theologians and church architects conceived their church plans in geometric units (square sanctuaries and rectangular naves, for example), roughly calculated with imprecise methods using pegs and cords, multiplied or halved according to a system of numbers or Golden Ratios. The dimensions and proportions obtained on the ground were also employed for elevations and the interconnections between horizontal and vertical members, as well as heights of windows and roofs. The numbers and ratios bestowed cohesion on the aggregate of parts and became the very principle of church order and aesthetics.[33] In the fifteenth century, the ideal of strictly proportioned parts and harmony of the whole similarly captured the imagination of Renaissance church builders. Churches with harmonic dimensions were thought to reflect the fundamental laws of nature and of God.[34]

Much reduced and greatly simplified from its form in Europe, a Franciscan church model with proportional mathematics came to the missions in the West Indies and New Spain in the very early 1500s, and thence to Florida's wilderness. The church at Mission San Luis (1656–1704), thoroughly excavated and reconstructed, was long and narrow, some 100–110 feet long by 50 feet wide and 50 feet high. Herschel Shepard, architect and consultant to the San Luis project, believes the church's numerical modules might have diminished or increased in geometric proportions according to ratios of three, five, eight, and thirteen. A less complicated model might be found in its simple Solomonic multiples, in which its height was intended to equal its width, which was one-half its length. This single-nave, mendicant mission church, high on a hill on the edge of the frontier, *may* suggest that other Franciscan mission churches in Florida employed proportional number systems.[35]

For example, the Franciscan church at the mission headquarters in St. Augustine was described in 1759 by the parish priest Juan Joseph Solana as having a height equal to its width. He reported similar ratios between lengths, widths, and heights at the mission churches of Nuestra Señora de la Leche and Nuestra Señora de Guadalupe de Tolomato.[36] Moreover, measurements reported during a 1776 inventory of thirty Franciscan mis-

2.8 Church interior, ca. 1690, looking east to the entrance, Mission San Luis, Tallahassee, reconstructed 1999. Above the entrance was the choir loft. Music and music lessons were powerful Franciscan teaching aids. The Indians could participate in church ceremony by singing the mass. (Photograph by Frantisek Zvardon, courtesy of Diocese of Saint Augustine)

sion churches in New Mexico also reveal a formula of heights equal to widths.[37]

We can only imagine the effect of the long and dimly lit naves on the Indians. The nave propelled the eye to the heart of the structure, the mysterious sanctuary with its altar at the far end, the theater where the rituals of Catholic dogma would play, candle-lighted and pungent with smoke (pl. 6). The sanctuary at San Luis was raised and set apart from the nave by chancel rails. To each side were two small rooms, the sacristy and counter sacristy, built with wattle-and-daub and plastered, for the storage of the altar items: vestments, linens, candles, and the chalices and wines for holy communion. Transepts were absent, as they were in the mission churches of sixteenth-century Mexico and seventeenth-century New Mexico.[38]

Music was a powerful part of church ceremony, and one in which the Indians were participants. They sang the Virgin's mass on Saturdays.[39] Florida's Indians might have learned their music similarly to Indians in California, where Friar Narciso Durán painted the music lessons on walls, with different colored notes and shapes for the different parts of the choir. Choir lofts similar to those in extant contemporary Franciscan mission churches in Texas and New Mexico may have been constructed in Florida's mission churches above the entrances. The Franciscan headquarters church in St. Augustine had a wood "choir loft" in 1737, as well as in 1632 when the royal accountant, Nicolás Ponce de León, was reported to have slept in the loft in order to escape Sergeant Major Eugenio de Espinoas, who had threatened to cut off his head.[40]

A holy water font for the baptism was essential, as well as a holy water stoup for blessing oneself. In Catholic tradition, they would have been opposite the altar end, just inside the front entrance. The base of a limestone baptismal font was found on the Gospel side (left) in the church at Mission San Luis.[41] In Mexico, and later in the California missions, bap-

Above, 2.9. Baptismal font limestone base, ca. 1690, found in the church floor by archaeologists, Mission San Luis, Tallahassee. The baptismal font was just inside the front east entrance, on the Gospel side (left) of the nave. (Photograph courtesy of Florida Division of Historical Resources)

Right, 2.10. Conceptual rendering of baptism ceremony, ca. 1690, Mission San Luis, Tallahassee. More than 300 friars are thought to have served in Florida. One friar estimated that by 1635, some 170,000 Indians had been baptized in Spanish Florida. Beneath the church floor at San Luis there may be as many as 900 Christian Indian burials. Thousands were baptized, but thousands were lost with frightening speed to European epidemics. Spanish friar or Indian chief could never have imagined a loss so total, so swiftly. (Drawing courtesy of Florida Division of Historical Resources)

tismal fonts were made by copying drawings in books. If there were *atrios,* plazas or side patios, near the church entrance, they might have played a role in the ceremonial pomp and procession celebrating the baptism, a tradition throughout Spanish America.

Every mission church had a *campanario,* a belfry, with one to four bells that tolled and summoned, and organized the spiritual life of the mission. Bell towers traditionally soared to great heights and extravagance in both Europe and the colonial New World, but here in their initial stages in the Florida wilderness, where they were no less important, they were very much simplified. The Mestas drawing of the 1593 parish church in St. Augustine shows four bells hung from cross beams supported by four posts in the ground, and rung by rope pulls (figs. 3.5, 3.6). Eight church bells had come with Pedro Menéndez in 1565, and fourteen heavy bronze mission bells arrived in 1612. In 1613, Friar Pareja wrote that his "ornate" church at Mission San Juan del Puerto had a "bell tower." An inventory of Florida's missions in 1681 listed 92 bells to toll the mass, as well as 238 smaller bells to ring the sanctus. Fragments of brass and bronze bells have been found at various mission sites. Admiral Landeche's survey of 1705 at Mission San Luis noted on a map "the site where the bells were buried." Sixty years later, William Bartram noted "heavy church bells" among that same mission's ruins, as did Joseph Purcell and Colonel John Stuart in 1778. John Bartram in 1765 had described highly decorated stone bell towers at "ye indian or milk church" and at the monastery in St. Augustine.[42]

The palm thatch roof of the reconstructed church at Mission San Luis is steeply pitched, with a 50 percent slope to throw the rain off quickly. The framework has rafters made from poles with bark removed, their lower ends notched to fit the wall plate and the upper ends inclined toward the center. Sixteenth- and seventeenth-century gable roofs could have been joined at the peak with rafters either notched and lashed or sawn at an angle and joined with nails or pegs. A series of smaller poles (purlins) were lashed across the major rafters, parallel to the wall plate, to hold the palm fronds. These methods are similar to the *palapa* roofs still being constructed in Mexico and Cuba.[43]

St. Augustine's parish church, Nuestra Señora de los Remedios, was depicted by Baptista Boazio as it looked in 1586, before it was sacked and burned by Sir Francis Drake (fig. 3.4).[44] The church was rebuilt and depicted in Mestas's drawing about 1593 (figs. 3.5, 3.6).[45] Both of these pictures suggest that the mission churches were similarly long and narrow, with altars in the west. The 1593 church had vertical wood planks and a palm thatch roof. It burned in 1599, was rebuilt in 1605, and was described in 1697 as having a substantial portico.[46] These two churches imply that light penetrated naves from windows high in the east gable, that double doors marked the eastern main entrances, and that side doors might have led to choir lofts or baptismal fonts. They indicate churches had a cross on top of the east gable and a small side sacristy. In the mission wilderness, where sawn or rived planks, nails, and spikes were more expensive, the frontier builders might have resorted to palm thatching enclosing the gable ends and greater use of clay and lathwork where clay was available.

Church art was essential for teaching and conversion. Evidence of *santos* (holy images) and ritual materials have been found by archaeologists and historians. Inventories of sixteenth- and seventeenth-century mission church furnishings reveal hundreds of items in silver, brass, and linen, gilded crosses, gilded statues, worked leather, altar hangings, and a large *retablo* of Christ crucified. The seventeenth-century inventory also includes 444 pictures and canvases of figures, 69 engravings, 183 statues of the Virgin, the infant Jesus, and various saints, and three *reredos,* two of them gilded.[47] Since late in the sixteenth century there had been a statue of the Blessed Virgin nursing the Infant Jesus at the Mission Nombre de Dios (pl. 11).[48] In 1630, Friar Alonso de Jesús described the churches as "well decorated and adorned with ornaments."[49]

One mission wall, 48 feet long, was found by archaeologists to have once been decorated in places by figures sculpted in clay.[50] Other hints of interior decorations can be gleaned from documents. The vicar at Mission Nombre de Dios, Friar Barmejo, was pleased to report in 1602 that his church was adorned with statues of saints. In 1613, at Mission San Juan del Puerto on Fort George Island, Friar Francisco Pareja proudly noted that his impressive church was "ornate," constructed of heavy timbers, wattle-and-daub, and inside planking. It had a bell tower and beautifully crafted images of Christ and Mary, used in processions through the village. On May 20, 1702, the church at Mission Santa Fé was burned and the governor wrote that the attackers did not get "the images which with some risk were saved."[51]

The initial provisioning of statues and paintings came from Spain, Mexico, and Cuba, but eventually each mission might have produced its own wood panels, clay and wood *santos,* and paintings on whitewashed walls. The Timucua and Apalachee Indians were accomplished artists. They painted deerskins, dyed mats, painted the walls of their council houses, and tattooed their own skin with great exuberance (fig. 2.11).[52] They used vegetable dyes and mineral pigments like kaolin, hematite (iron oxide), and burned wood or bone. Water-soluble pigments might have been added to limewash and painted on walls. Laudonnière in 1564

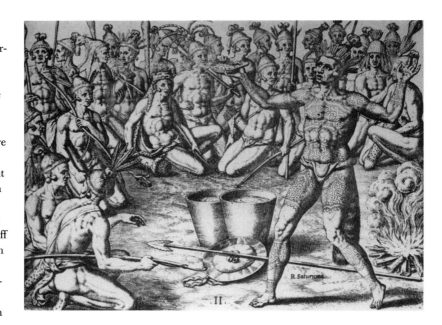

2.11. Timucua "body art," ca. 1564. The Florida missions had canvas paintings, *santos* (holy images), *retablos* (paintings on wood), *reredos* (altar screens), and statues. Some were brought from Spain, Mexico, and Cuba, but many might have been created by Indians at the missions. All were destroyed or carried off in 1702 and 1704, when the English and allied Indians had systematically burned the missions, or in 1763, when Spain ceded Florida. Theodor de Bry's engraving of 1591 depicting a Timucua chief's body painting hints of the Indians' artistic skills. (Photocopy courtesy of Florida State Archives)

described the paintings of the Timucua near today's Jacksonville: "The drawing was so natural and true to life, with all the rules of proportion exactly right, that there is no European painter skillful enough to duplicate it."[53]

Santos were symbols of holy personages and their invisible power to whom one addressed one's prayer. As long as they had the standard Christian iconography or attributes, they could be less than anatomically correct. They could have been copied from engravings in prayer books, simplified, and painted with the artist's choice of pigments. The destruction or dispersal of these images is a great loss.

Bishop Calderón's report to Queen Mariana of Spain in 1675 leaves no doubt that the buildings of the mission villages in Florida served their purpose well. He wrote that the natives attended mass "with regularity at 11 o'clock. . . . they observe the holy days of Christmas, . . . the Epiphany, the Purification of Our Lady, and the days of Saint Peter, Saint Paul, and All Saints Day. . . . on Sundays they attend the Rosario and the Salve in the afternoon. . . . they celebrate . . . the Birth of Our Lord, all attending the mass at midnight. . . . the children both male and female go to the church on work days to a religious school. . . . on Saturdays they attend when mass is sung."[54]

The clay floors of the mission churches kept their tragic secret for more than three centuries. The remains of hundreds of mission Indians have been found under nave floors, some stacked in layers three deep. At San Martín de Timucua (built ca. 1608) in today's Ichetucknee Springs State Park, four to five hundred Indians were buried under the church floor; at Santa Catalina de Guale, 430 have been counted. As many as nine hundred might have been buried under the church floor at Mission San Luis.[55] The thousands that were baptized were lost with frightening speed to epidemics of European diseases.

Missions generally had a *convento* (monastery, friary) close by the church, forming a religious complex with the church, kitchen, courtyard or patio, and kitchen garden (fig. 2.7). The convento was the domestic space for the friars. Friaries excavated in Florida reveal rectangular buildings of European design with plank and/or wattle-and-daub walling and palm thatch roofing. The Mission San Luis friary, built about 1690 and recently excavated and reconstructed, contained the friars' sleeping quarters, chapel, office, room for an assistant-interpreter, pantry for the storage of olive jars, and a loft for storage of food and supplies. The major beams are thought to have been mortised-and-tenoned and pegged, possibly assembled on the ground and raised.[56] The floor plan measured 30 by 70 feet; its thick and cool walls were made of clay. The wattle was lashed with leather thongs; the mud-clay was mixed with Spanish moss and dry, fibrous grasses and plastered on both sides, about six to eight inches thick, and lime-plastered or whitewashed. The roof might have gone on first, to protect the applications of clay from rain before it hardened and was plastered. At Mission Santa Catalina de Amelia (present-day Amelia Island) the walls of the friary were also wattle-and-daub. A doorway consisted of a hewn pine sill laid over a shell sleeper. The sill, posts, and large wrought nails are on display at the Amelia Island Museum of History, Fernandina Beach.[57]

Cooking at Mission San Luis took place in a separate building, the *cocina* (kitchen), removed from the friary probably because of the threat of fire, but attached by a covered walkway. The first kitchen had been planked but was rebuilt with the more fireproof clay. Its foundation imprints were still clearly visible in the clay floor after three centuries. The walkway was covered with a thatch roof supported on pillars, and led into the pantry at the west end of the convento, where oil and wine were stored in olive jars.[58] It is believed that the Franciscans had designated plots or fields for raising their garden subsistence as well as surplus crops that could be stored in granaries and sold for supplies and church furnishings.[59]

The largest convento in Florida was at La Concepción, the mission headquarters in St. Augustine. Construction began in 1588 with red cedar logs, planks, and thatch. It burned in 1599, and was rebuilt in wood with a shingle roof between 1603 and 1610. A large sum was spent on its furnishings, including an image of St. Francis of Assisi, perhaps receiving

2.12. Wattle-and-daub granary, Mexico. Granaries (called *garitas*) were built at mission villages, raised off the ground to protect the harvested corn, beans, pumpkins, berries, and nuts from rodents, birds, and other animals. They were described as having a dozen support beams. The example in the drawing is in Mexico, where granaries are still built today with colonial Hispano-Indian practices using wattle-and-daub and thatch roof. (Drawing by E. Gordon)

the stigmata. By mid-seventeenth century it had been enlarged with a library and laid out in a traditional mission quadrangle to accommodate thirty-five to forty missionaries and visiting dignitaries. It was destroyed by fire in 1702 during the James Moore raid. The monastery, cloister, and church rose again, however, during the first half of the eighteenth century, but this time the monks' rooms, refectory, library, arcaded cloister, and church were erected with large blocks of stone. Some stone cells and cloister voussoirs are still present today (pl. 12).[60]

COUNCIL HOUSE

After his ten-month tour of the Florida missions, Gabriel Díaz Vara Calderón, bishop of Santiago de Cuba, wrote that a principal *bohío* was large enough to accommodate two to three thousand people.[61] His astonishing description has proved to be true at Mission San Luis, where archaeologists discovered that the enormous circular council house had measured 120 feet in diameter when it was built about 1656 (pl. 2). The vast size and weights of its supporting timbers suggest complex seventeenth-century Indian building practices (pl. 4; fig. 2.6).

A ring of enormous earthfast tree-trunk poles, as well as eight massive major interior supports, formed the framework that required cranes and

56,000 palm fronds to cover during the recent reconstruction (fig. 2.13). In the center was a very large central hearth 14 feet in diameter, above which a huge roof opening 45 feet in diameter let in light and exhausted the smoke. The interior space had two concentric rows of benches covered with cane mats. The benches were more than a *vara* (32.9 inches) high, higher than a flea could jump. The chief's bench was raised above all the others. In the row furthest from the hearth, lining the perimeter, were "cabins" with back and side panels. Under each cabin was a clay-lined smudge-pit where corncobs were burned at low heat to repel mosquitoes (pl. 3).[62]

The Mission San Luis council house was an Indian building, from start to finish, unaffected by European presence and erected without European hardware. The massive, viscerally impressive building was secured with plant and animal cordage. Inside, the chiefs presided over annual feasts, regional meetings, ceremonies, and dances, and lodged their overnight guests.[63] Its reincarnation in 1999 is dramatic storytelling, leaving one to wonder how Florida's Indians accomplished what would be impossible today without precise measuring tools, chain saws, trucks, and cranes.

2.13. Council house, ca. 1656, schematic drawing showing major architectural features, Mission San Luis. The council house was the largest Indian building in the Southeast. Eight major interior pilings and a ring of outer wall posts supported the frame. (Drawing courtesy of Florida Division of Historical Resources)

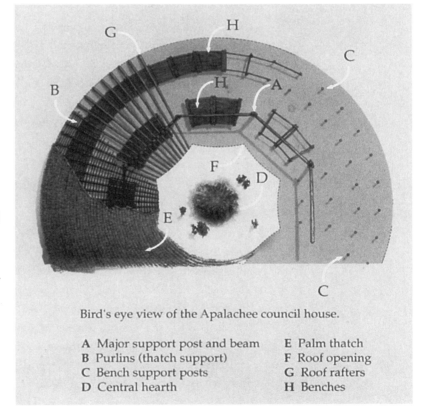

Bird's eye view of the Apalachee council house.

A Major support post and beam	E Palm thatch
B Purlins (thatch support)	F Roof opening
C Bench support posts	G Roof rafters
D Central hearth	H Benches

3 | THE DARKENED AGE OF WOOD

The Appalatchi and St. Pedro Old Fields bear the marks of once having been large and flourishing Spanish settlements, strongly proved by the Ruins of Fort, churches and other buildings; the cannon and church bells that are found lying about; the broad roads; and by the remains of causeways and bridges that are to be seen to this day.[1]

JOSEPH PURCELL, SURVEYOR AND MAPMAKER, 1778

Wood was colonial Florida's most plentiful building material, and its most transient. Wooden buildings rotted and perished in fires, hurricanes, and swarms of termites. They were replaced by tabby, stone, and brick when such materials became available and affordable. As the centuries turned over, the wood buildings of the sixteenth and seventeenth centuries slipped away. What is left of them today, in archives or in their archaeological footprints, is described below.

SAN AGUSTÍN DE LA FLORIDA, 1565–1702

San Agustín (St. Augustine) was founded in 1565 by Pedro Menéndez de Avilés and settlers from Spain. By unknown means, they requisitioned a large Indian building in which to live and make their important decisions. It is thought that the building was the chief's house in the Timucua village of Seloy. Divided into rooms and encircled with the traditional European defensive ditch and rampart of earth and fagots, the fortified Indian building became the settlement's most important first structure, serving as fort, government house, military headquarters, armory, storehouse, and residence for Menéndez and his officers. It is thought to have been a very large, circular, earthfast pole-frame building covered with palm thatch. The Spanish used it for almost one year.[2]

3.1. Pedro Menéndez de Avilés, 1519–1574, *adelantado*, governor and captain-general of La Florida. Menéndez and about 800 colonists from various regions in Spain landed on September 8, 1565, and founded San Agustín de la Florida, the first successful European colony in what is now the United States. (Photocopy courtesy of Florida State Archives)

The Spanish campsite is slowly revealing itself to archaeologist Kathleen Deagan, who has been working the site since the 1980s. To date, there is evidence the Spanish built seven to nine rectangular European structures with wood frames set on mud sleepers, probably planked or thatched. Construction details and the relationship of the campsite to the preexisting Timucua village and newly fortified chief's house are still being investigated. The Spanish, however, stayed too long, too close to Chief Seloy's village. Their headquarters was violently destroyed on April 19, 1566, in a fire. The excessive heat of the fire suggests that the Spanish had stored gunpowder inside.[3]

In May the colonists moved across the harbor to Anastasia Island to distance themselves from the Indians. The island's present name is a latter-day mystery; it has also been called *la Cantera,* the quarry, and *la Escolta,*[4] the escort, perhaps reflecting its barrier island position protecting the mainland. On the island they built their second and third forts and an adjacent town. This time, however, the buildings had to be constructed by the Spanish soldiers and residents themselves. The Timucua could not be counted on for labor, and the fifteen carpenters who had arrived with Menéndez had left with mutineers several months earlier. (Menéndez had also enlisted ten stone masons for his Florida expedition.) The first structures erected were small and flimsy, including the

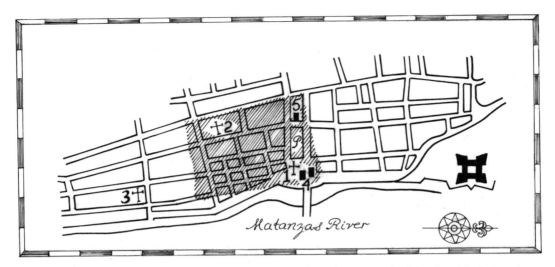

3. Sixteenth-century St. Augustine overlaid on today's street plan. The area south of the plaza (shaded area) was laid out ca. 1572, with town blocks and streets that exist today in nearly the same plan. 1. Parish church, Nuestra Señora de los Remedios, ca. 1572; 2. Hermitage, Nuestra Señora de la Soledad, ca. 1572 with hospital ca. 1597; 3. Franciscan monastery, Convento de la Concepción Inmaculada, ca. 1588; 4. Guardhouse and governor-general's house, ca. 1572; 5. Governor's house after 1598, when the present plaza (P) was laid out. (Drawn by E. Gordon based on excavations by archaeologists Kathleen Deagan and Carl Halbirt)

fort, barracks, palm-thatched storehouse, guardhouse, customs house, and town dwellings. They proved to be very inadequate.[5]

Seventeen relief ships with fifteen hundred troops arrived June 29 from Cuba. The ships' carpenters and soldiers were enlisted to build barracks, a bigger planked customs and storehouse, and to expand the fort and town to accommodate the population of about eighteen hundred. Historian Eugene Lyon has read documents in the Archivo General de Indias in Seville describing a two-story building, a forge, a church, and a jail inside the fort. The floors were lined with pine logs, wells were made from wood barrels, and roofs were thatched. Outside the fort were barracks and the Jesuits' friary and chapel. Taverns and brothels, while not in the official records, must also have existed. The town site is thought to have been at the north end of the island, near today's Salt Run. A new harbor entrance was dredged in the twentieth century, and the dredging and filling of Davis Shores in 1925–26 altered the island and its history.[6]

In 1566, the same year that the colonists moved to Anastasia Island, Pedro Menéndez established a new principal town and fort at Santa Elena (present-day Parris Island, in Port Royal Sound, once part of La Florida, but now in South Carolina). In 1571 he relocated his wife and his household furnishings, recently revealed to be quite luxurious, from San Agustín to Santa Elena, intending to govern the Spanish province of La

Florida from there. Santa Elena, however, was abandoned in 1586, and the Spanish headquarters was returned to San Agustín. In the meantime, the Anastasia Island fort and town had proved to be too exposed to erosion by the sea and too vulnerable to attacks by English ships; the town and its fort had been relocated back to the mainland early in 1572 (map 3).[7]

Thus began the urban enclave of the St. Augustine we know today. The sixteenth-century buildings were constructed in the area of the present plaza southward to Bridge Street. City archaeologist Carl Halbirt has excavated twelve wells in the plaza dating from the late 1500s. They are spaced across its east-west axis at forty-four-foot intervals, the width of the sixteenth-century Spanish house lots. The common settler built on one *peonía* (land given to a soldier); the gentlemen of means built on a *caballería,* equivalent to four lots. These urban lots and blocks laid out in a grid are depicted in the "battle plan" drawn by Baptista Boazio, the Italian artist and mapmaker living in London, who recorded the location and events of Sir Francis Drake's raid in 1586. The first edition of the engraving was published by Walter Bigges in Latin in 1588, bound and titled *Expeditio Francisci Draki*.[8]

The Boazio drawing is the earliest view of St. Augustine, and the *first* view of *any* town in the United States. There is no indication that Boazio

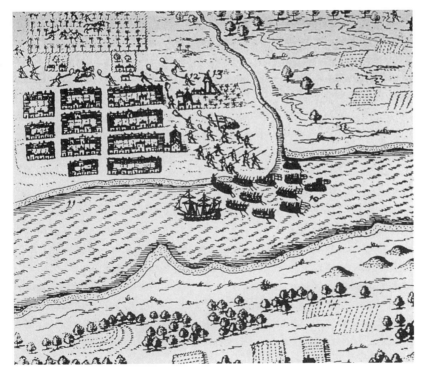

3.2. St. Augustine, 1586, detail from Sir Francis Drake's "battle plan" just before his raid on St. Augustine in 1586. The view of the town shows an orderly grid of eleven city blocks depicted south of the plaza, a street plan that remains today, unchanged by the intervening 400 years. The engraving was made from drawings by Baptista Boazio and first published in 1588 in *Expeditio Francisci Draki* by Walter Bigges. (Detail courtesy of SAHS)

3.3. Sir Francis Drake, 1540–1596. St. Augustine was celebrating its twenty-first year when Drake, a very bold privateer, sailed into the harbor in 1586, captured the wood fort *San Juan de Pinos*, and burned and pillaged the town. The portrait is similar to one of Drake engraved by Jodocus Hondius, the Flemish engraver, working in London ca. 1590. Drake was described by a contemporary as "Lowe of stature, of strong limbs, broade Breasted, round headed, browne hayre, full Bearded, his eyes round, Large and Cleare, well favoured, fayre and of a cheerefull countenance." Others called him a thief and a robber. (Photocopy courtesy of Florida State Archives)

was on the voyage, but he might have acquired sketches and descriptions from Drake himself, who is thought to have sketched his own plans and views during his circumnavigation voyage of 1577–80.[9] Boazio depicts an orderly town, laid out in a gridiron aligned with the cardinal points of the compass south and west of the parish church which stands prominently by the plaza and waterfront. Boazio's sixteenth-century street plan (fig. 3.2) is remarkably similar to the Elíxio de la Puente property map of 1764 and the plan of St. Augustine today (map 3). This town plan, and the plaza redefined in 1598, have been designated a National Historic Landmark.[10]

The Spanish, in transplanting themselves, transplanted their society and some architectural traditions of the regions they came from. They brought with them their social stratification, a hierarchy based on ancestry. Thus *castas* (mixed blood, nonwhite) were inferior, below *criollos* (creoles of Spanish descent born in the New World), who in turn were below *peninsulares* (born in Spain). This social hierarchy influenced where their dwellings would be located. The elites not only had larger lots, they had the choice lots closest to the plaza and centers of government and mercantile activities.[11] Their buildings were shaped by available materials, by the Indian labor, and eventually by some lessons learned from the climate. Post-molds found by archaeologists indicate some early buildings had earthfast frames, with pole supports set directly into the ground, and walls of thatch or perhaps palings, or *cuje y embarrado* (wattle-and-daub), or wood planks chinked with mud. The construction was essentially vernacular, Iberian building practices combined with Indian palm thatch roofing techniques, similar to methods acquired in Mexico and Cuba since the early 1500s.[12]

At Santa Elena, part of La Florida in 1580, Spanish houses had been constructed of "wood and mud, covered with lime inside and out [wattle-and-daub, plastered and whitewashed] and with flat roofs of lime." (Note this is not tabby.) In Andalucía today, flat roofs are still constructed in the same manner over simple box-type structures, using chestnut, eucalyptus, or poplar timbers covered with mats of canes woven together with grass, then a layer of brush (broom, thyme, oleander) and a final layer of a mud mortar to make it watertight. Some houses and roofs might have been similarly constructed in St. Augustine after the influx of residents who abandoned Santa Elena in 1586. The coastal capital had an abundance of oyster shells with which to make the lime mortar.[13]

The view of San Agustín drawn about 1593 by Hernando de Mestas depicts the town that had already undergone "urban renewal" after Drake's raid, the term used by historian Michael Gannon to point out the antiquity of St. Augustine versus Plymouth. For several days, Drake had

3.4. Parish church, Nuestra Señora de los Remedios, ca. 1572, St. Augustine, as depicted in 1586 on Boazio's "battle plan" of Francis Drake's raid of St. Augustine. The church was built with wood planks and palm thatch roof, and stood by the harbor waterfront, near the southeast corner of today's plaza. Drake ransacked and burned the church and carried everything of value to Portsmouth, England. (Drawing by E. Gordon after the Boazio battle plan, courtesy of SAHS)

looted and burned many buildings and carried off the hardware and tools (and a chest of six thousand ducats), which he planned to give the settlement at Roanoke. At Roanoke, a storm forced him to sail on to Portsmouth, England, with the St. Augustine loot. San Agustín, meanwhile, was quickly rebuilt and expanded to receive the residents from Santa Elena. The parish church, guardhouse, house of the commandant-governor, and town dwellings are shown in the Mestas sketch with vertical wood planks. The pitched thatch roofs might have been constructed by the Indians, whose own buildings had been covered with palm long be-

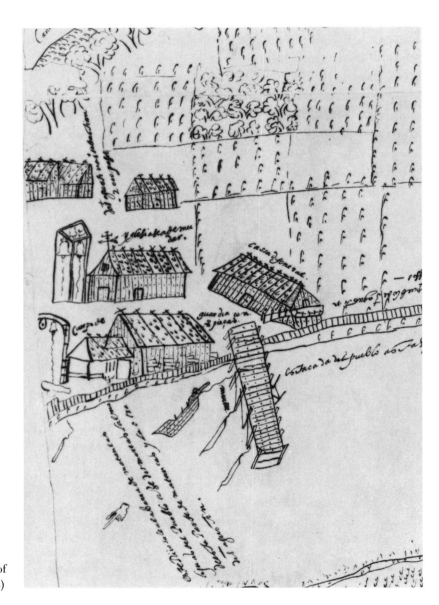

3.5. St. Augustine, ca. 1593. Detail from a drawing attributed to Hernando de Mestas about 1593 depicting the center of the town with the wharf, parish church, guardhouse, and governor's house (Government House). (Photocopy courtesy of Florida State Archives)

3.6. Parish church, Nuestra Señora de los Remedios, ca. 1572, St. Augustine, depicted in 1593, seven years after Drake's raid. The newly rebuilt church (1587?) was drawn with vertical planks and palm thatch roof. The interior was said to be richly appointed. The *campanario* (belfry) was a timber post-and-lintel construction with four bells that were tolled by pulling ropes, to ring the mass and to sound the alarm if another pirate came calling. A hurricane and fire destroyed the church in 1599. (Redrawn by E. Gordon after Mestas, ca. 1593)

3.7. Guardhouse, ca. 1593, St. Augustine. The guardhouse was sited close to the waterfront, behind a board fence running along the river's edge. Mestas depicted it with vertical siding, palm thatch roof, eight cannons, warning bell, hoist and pulley, and a large shady portico under which soldiers stood watch. (Redrawn by E. Gordon after Mestas, ca. 1593)

fore Europeans arrived. Indians had been brought to the city under a system of obligatory tribute of goods and labor initiated by Pedro Menéndez that became institutionalized during the mission period.[14]

When the sixteenth century came to a close, San Agustín had progressed toward the urban plan that exists today. In 1598, Governor Gonzalo Méndez de Canzo laid out the Plaza de Armas and moved his resi-

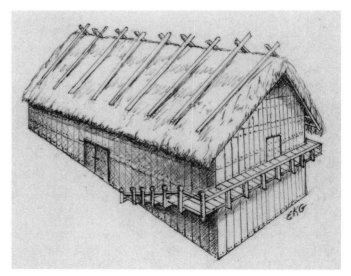

3.8. Governor's house (Government House), ca. 1593, St. Augustine. The large two-storied house of the captain-general and governor in 1593 was close to the harbor's edge and had an outside staircase. It was vertically planked and roofed with palm thatch. From the second-floor gallery, the governor could view the inlet, where ships bearing supplies and food—or pirates and English enemy—could mean the difference between life and death. (Redrawn by E. Gordon after Mestas, ca. 1593)

dence from the edge of the harbor to the site at the west end of the plaza where Government House stands today.[15] Plazas were part of the ideal city sketched out for the New World in regulations that were codified in 1573 in the *Leyes de las Indias.* If laid out accordingly, the plaza should have been treeless, rectangular, close to the harbor, and the nucleus of a grid of narrow streets.[16] The plaza was the heartbeat of the town and lively scene of social, religious, military, government, and market activities.[17]

The history of St. Augustine's architecture is filled with the inevitable disasters. A fire and hurricane swept the town in 1599. Storms blew in unexpectedly, and there were labor shortages due to epidemics. The Indians resisted the forced labor draft, and the pirate Robert Searles (alias John Davis) rode the tide into the harbor and sacked the town in 1668. Thirty-four years later, most of the wood buildings in town were set on fire during an English raid from Carolina.[18] The recitation of such events might lead one to the hasty conclusion that St. Augustine's residents had little incentive to build anything worthwhile, only buildings that were expedient, practical, cheap, and quickly replaceable. Buried in colonial reports, however, are proud descriptions; Governor Méndez Canzo reported, for example, that the new wood church of 1602 was the "neatest and best finished of its kind in the Indies."[19]

Repetitive disasters led to new solutions. A more permanent fort was built with blocks of coquina shellstone to replace the wood fort that was useless during the pirate attack by Searles and crew. This opened quarries and launched a cut-stone and lime-making industry; slabs of shellstone were quarried, cut, and shaped and oyster shells were calcined on a large scale. Masons, plasterers, stonecutters, and tabby concrete workers expanded the workforce.[20] Cataclysmic disasters gave the architecture of San Agustín a new imperative, and new direction. The masonry buildings, however, had roots in the wood architecture they replaced.

Pre-1702 wood buildings do not exist in St. Augustine. Clues as to how the seventeenth-century architecture was constructed must be conjectured from data culled from archives, archaeology, and Spanish ideals. The street plan had strong Roman and Islamic roots, in which traditional villages were geometrically laid out and had clear separation of public and private spaces. Narrow streets in hot climates from Mesopotamia to North Africa were shaded from the blazing sun by walls and facades.[21] Some streets in St. Augustine were even narrower than they are today.[22] Buildings were purposely placed up to the street edge—not only to shade

3.9. Treasury Street, St. Augustine, laid out during the Spanish colonial period. Many of the narrow colonial streets are present today. (Photocopy of original Albertype courtesy of Florida State Archives)

their interiors and pedestrians, but to maximize and protect backyards for domestic utilitarian activities that take place inside houses today. A dwelling consisted of a house for sleeping and eating and one for cooking. The yard was for kitchen gardens, bread ovens, storage, wells, trash pits, fruit trees, and animals. This lot organization was common for all households regardless of social status, income, or occupation, and persisted into the eighteenth century (fig 5.7).[23]

The population of the Spanish capital was culturally rich and ethnically diverse.[24] There were more than fifteen hundred residents at the end of the seventeenth century, and more than three thousand when the Spanish departed in 1763, greater than the permanent population of Williamsburg, Virginia, in 1775. When the first buildings were erected in the sixteenth century, San Agustín was a microcosm of Iberian Spain, peopled by recruits from Andalucía, Cataluña, Extremadura, and Castilla y León, each region known for its own distinctive architecture and construction methods. In addition, the colony was supported by a network of kinship and commercial ties with Asturias, Sevilla, Cádiz, Cuba, Puerto Rico, Santo Domingo, the Canary Islands, Cartagena de Indias, and Mexico.[25]

During the seventeenth century, more owner-builders were mestizos and Creoles, born in Florida, Cuba, and Mexico. Newcomers arrived from Spain, Portugal, France, Germany, Africa, and the Canary Islands. Many of the soldiers had come from Mexico.[26] Some residents had acquired enough wealth to own more than one building in town as well as a rural hacienda. Other residents engaged in external trade, both legal and

3.10. Palm thatch schoolhouse, 1890s. Palms were among the most important of local materials used by prehistoric Indians, the mission builders, and the early Spanish colonists of St. Augustine, San Luis, and Pensacola. Palm trunks and fronds were still the materials of choice late in the nineteenth century. A schoolhouse photographed in the 1890s had both walls and roof of palm thatch. A good palm thatch roof can last twenty years if built with a steep pitch to speed the runoff of rain water. (Photocopy courtesy of Florida State Archives)

FLORIDA'S COLONIAL ARCHITECTURAL HERITAGE

3.11. Palm trunks were widely used in construction by Florida's colonists well into the eighteenth century for redoubts, revetments, wharves, and palisades, if not buildings. The practice continued into the nineteenth and twentieth centuries, when palm trunks supported verandas and entrance porches, and walled entire houses. The owner of an early-1900s house built entirely of palm trunks in Volusia County says the vertical logs that compose the walls and porch of his house have become very hard and strong, impervious to rot and insects. (Photograph of "billiard house" porch behind Markland, St. Augustine, by M. Gordon)

illegal, and had far-reaching merchant networks and access to building products from Europe and the Spanish Caribbean, sending their ships directly to Spain, Havana, Veracruz, Campeche, the Canary Islands, and the British colonies.[27] After 1672, European-trained military engineer-architects, civilian *maestros de obras,* as well as skilled masons, stonecutters, and lime-makers had come to San Agustín to work on the stone Castillo de San Marcos. The engineers and *maestros* might have been commissioned to draw and execute designs for wood residences, warehouses, churches, and other buildings in town.

The widespread destruction of the town described by contemporaries in 1702 implies that the architecture of the seventeenth century had been predominantly wood. Tabby concrete made from lime, oyster shells, sand, and water does not appear to have been a primary load-bearing material until after 1702.[28] A study of tabby by Janet Bigbee Gritzner follows its development. Rammed earth construction called *tapia* or *pisé* was a folk building material in Andalucía by 1269. A thirteenth-century Moorish adaptation was stabilized with stone and lime (made from limestone), a mixture called *tabia* or *tabbi.* In Spain, this new development was called *tapia real.* During the sixteenth and early seventeenth centuries, *tapia real* was used as a building medium throughout the Spanish West Indies. Meanwhile, roof mortars were developed in La Florida about 1580 when quicklime was first produced from oyster shells. Roof mortar was a lime-sand or mud mixture similar to what was used in Spain, not the concrete known as tabby that developed later in Florida and used oyster or coquina shells for the aggregate. Tabby concrete came about only after lime from oyster shells was produced in great quantity as a precursor to the construction of the Castillo de San Marcos. Importing lime made in Cuba from limestone was too expensive. Once the local source was exploited, and oyster shells were substituted for stone aggregate, *tapia real* became tabby concrete.[29]

One can generalize that most newly arrived residents erected simple wood structures while they waited to move on to something better. Florida's plentiful native palms, cedar, and cypress trees made excellent expedient materials. River mud was used in *cuje y embarrado* construction, an example of which was noted by Engineer Mariano de la Rocque in 1788.[30]

Some seventeenth-century residents would have moved on to more permanent and satisfying architecture as quickly as their resources allowed, replacing earthfast pole frames with two-storied braced frames, constructed from heavy timbers, hewn logs, and split boards. Packed dirt floors were replaced with wide planks laid over log sleepers. Other improvements included tabby floors and larger kitchen houses that were detached from the main house to reduce the threat of fire. The house of Major Pedro Benedit de Horruytiner, nephew of governor Luis de Horruytiner (1633–38), was inventoried upon his death in 1684. It was wooden, near the waterfront, roofed with shingles, fenced with boards, and had a detached kitchen of the same material. Among his furnishings were four large canvas paintings, including ones of San José, San Antonio, and Nuestra Señora de la Soledad.[31]

Kitchens at first had been clay ovens in the back yards, probably similar to one noted by René Laudonnière in 1564 outside the walls of Fort Caroline: "I had an oven built at some distance . . . to avoid the risk of fire, since the houses were covered with palm leaves, which burn quickly once the fire takes hold of them so it is very difficult to put out."[32] De Bry's illustration of Laudonnière's oven at Fort Caroline is very similar to clay ovens built today in Mexico (fig. 9.1). In 1580, a house owner in San Agustín, Doña Mayor de Arango, ordered her manservant, Luis Rodríguez, to take a canoe and get a load of clay to build an oven.[33]

In *The Houses of St. Augustine,* Albert Manucy suggests the majority of houses were brace framed and planked by the end of the seventeenth century.[34] Spanish construction methods in West Florida, however, still used posts placed directly in the ground as late as 1758, when they constructed the governor's house with walls of bousillage.[35] Wall planks applied horizontally or vertically were rived or pit-sawn. (The earliest water-powered sawmills were built during the British period). They were

joined to the frame with wrought iron nails and spikes. Outside staircases led to second stories, the earliest example being illustrated by Mestas, ca. 1593 (fig. 3.8). Iberian architectural ideals persisted. Interior wood shutters in unglazed window openings kept out the cold and rain, and floor braziers added heat.

Wood shingles or boards replaced fire-prone palm thatch on gable roofs wherever possible. Shingles were hand-split from short logs, and nailed to horizontal poles and laths that allowed the roof to breathe and air out. They might have been preserved against the weather with a coating of pitch or tar oils as was practiced by the English in Pensacola in the 1760s.[36] Flat roofs with lime mortar, described earlier on late sixteenth-century houses, also existed in the seventeenth and eighteenth centuries, and were described by John Bartram in 1765.[37] Flat or nearly flat roofs, however, were a bad idea in wet tropical climates, but their presence in San Agustín was testament to colonial reluctance to some abandon traditional Spanish practices.[38] The Spanish built the same flat roofs of timbers, twigs, and earth mortar in the drier climates of New Mexico, and at the early Spanish missions in California. In 1675, a powder magazine built of stone at the Castillo de San Marcos was able to support a roof of barrel clay tile.[39]

Balconies had made their appearances by the seventeenth century. Their styles came with the artisans from Spain, Cuba, Mexico, and the

Canary Islands, where they were built on first-floor joists run out through the walls, suspending them over the streets.[40] The governor's house was described with a balcony in 1690 and 1713,[41] and the residence of Joseph Rodríguez Meléndez, which was noted as "the strongest, newest and highest," had a balcony that faced the fort in 1702.[42] Balconies became a leitmotif of St. Augustine's stone architecture in the eighteenth century (figs. 3, 5.9, 5.13).

Spanish windows in seventeenth-century San Agustín generally did not have glass. They were openings protected by exterior window lattice screens (*celosías*), grilles (*rejas*), and interior shutters (figs. 5.1, 5.17). Window screens ideally were made of intricate cedar latticework, and grilles were usually turned spindles or simple wood bars. A cloth or pigskin curtain, called a *guarda-polvo,* may have provided privacy and kept out dust and insects. The wood shutters may have had the traditional peep window (*postigo*). *Celosías* and *rejas* had originated in Islamic Spain[43] and came to Florida with carpenters from Spain, the Canary Islands, and Cuba. These same window schemes would prevail in the eighteenth century until the British arrived.

Seventeenth-century San Agustín was a waterfront town oriented to port activities. The houses and warehouses of the merchants engaged in coastal trade dominated the river's edge. One royal warehouse was described as holding 760 yards of sail canvas, including a ready-made mainsail, foresail, frigate's main topsail, a launch's mainsail, and twenty-five pounds of wax candles.[44] The customs house, guardhouse, and church were also close to the wharf, and one might assume so were the shops of the blacksmiths, coopers, ships' outfitters and carpenters, if not a brothel or two, and a few taverns. These wood buildings, however, were often flooded by storm surges before the stone seawall was built in 1700.[45] San Agustín's wooden buildings were always a work in progress.

San Luis 1656–1704

The second most important Spanish settlement in 17th century Florida was associated with Mission San Luis (Tallahassee). It was the western outpost of Spanish Florida from 1656 to 1704. Pueblo San Luis was a mission village with a large Franciscan church and monastery complex, the Apalachee chief's administrative headquarters, a fort, and a residential community of Spanish administrators, merchant-traders, and soldiers. In the "suburbs" were the dispersed dwellings of the fifteen hundred Christianized Apalachee Indians. They were descendants of the Indians who had built Anhaica, the former Apalachee capital that had been appropriated as a winter headquarters by Hernando de Soto in 1539. In 1656, the Apalachee chief promised to build a blockhouse (*casa fuerte*) for the Spanish, and consequently moved the council house and chief's dwelling westward of the former Anhaica, to the hill site that became San Luis.[46]

San Luis has been thoroughly excavated and reconstructed based on its archaeology. The Spanish community was not laid out with the central rectangular or square plaza and grid street plan as at San Agustín. The community appears instead to have "grown" in an informal manner with the growth of the mission and surrounding ranches and Indian trade. The center of activity, nevertheless, was a large circular plaza dominated by the Franciscan religious buildings and the immense Indian administrative buildings, the council house and chief's house.[47]

3.13. Interior, Spanish settler's residence, ca. 1690, Mission San Luis, Tallahassee, reconstructed 1999. Archaeological excavations revealed that the original walls of this settler's house had been thick and cool, constructed with wattle-and-daub and covered with lime plaster. (Photograph courtesy of Florida Division of Historical Resources)

The architecture of the first dwellings was probably like those of St. Augustine, expedient earthfast frames, covered with thatch or wood planks. They were improved, enlarged, and made more fireproof with *cuje y embarrado* construction (pl. 15). One substantial chunk of clay daub retrieved from the excavation of the settler's house shows the imprint of its wattle framework, a hefty three-inch limb. The thick clay walls were covered inside and out with a coat of lime plaster or whitewash to waterproof and repel insects; the skirting coat at the bottom might have received the most liberal coats, as they did in Spain. The region is rich with clay, mined from large borrow pits within the San Luis village boundaries. The Spanish house that has recently been reconstructed from architectural evidence has two ample rooms, one for sleeping and one for eating. The cooking house was a detached outbuilding.[48]

Surrounding San Luis in the 1670s were extensive cattle ranches and at least one known wheat hacienda, inventoried with four buildings of timber or clay and palm thatch, called Asile Farm by historians and archaeologists today. The haciendas or ranches were thriving enough for archaeologist Bonnie McEwan to describe their owners as a landed aristocracy. While San Luis had no harbor, the landing at the confluence of the St. Marks and Wakulla Rivers to the south served as a place from which to ship their products directly to Havana and San Agustín, and enabled the richest to import luxury goods.[49]

San Luis was abandoned in 1704 when the region was under assault by the English from South Carolina, led by James Moore and his followers—Apalachicola, Creek, and Apalachee Indians rebelling against abuses of the Spanish. As they withdrew from the region, the Spanish were ordered by the authorities in San Agustín to burn buildings and supplies. The village, the fort, and the ranches were destroyed, and the surviving Apalachee migrated from the region. A year after its abandonment and destruction, Admiral Antonio de Landeche made a reconnaissance with former soldier-residents and drew a map that depicts what had been San Luis (fig. 9.13).[50] Joseph Purcell, a British surveyor, noted on his map of the road between Pensacola and St. Augustine in 1778, "Ruins of St. Louis Fort and Town," beside a place he called "Tallahassa, or Taloosa, or Old Field Town . . . eighteen miles north of Ft. St. Marks."[51]

Panzacola Bay 1698–1763

The first attempt to settle what is now Pensacola occurred in August of 1559, led by Tristán de Luna y Arellano. Eleven ships from Mexico with one thousand settlers, five hundred sailors, and all their personal and household goods anchored in the bay known as Ochuse, renamed Bahía Filipina del Puerto de Santa María. The town site, layout, and buildings were chosen, but by September 19, the settlement was in big trouble. A hurricane sank their ships. Colonization was abandoned after two years of starvation and many deaths. The site of the planned town is still a mystery, but many artifacts retrieved from one of the sunken ships are beginning to reveal what supplies had been destined for the town.[52]

The second attempt, one hundred and thirty-nine years later, was successful. Panzacola began on the mainland, on bluffs at the harbor entrance, and like San Agustín in 1566, moved to an island, and relocated back to the mainland to a more protected site that is Pensacola today.

The story begins in 1698, when colonists again from Mexico entrenched themselves on the bluff (Barranca de Santo Tomé) overlooking the bay they called Bahía Santa María de Galve. They built a settlement that they named after the bay, now the site of Pensacola Naval Air Station. The area was home to native Indians, the Panzacola, a Choctaw word for "long haired." With time, the bay came to be called by the name associated with the Indians, hence Panzacola and, finally, Pensacola by the English after 1763. Captain Jaime Franck of Austria was the military engineer who designed the settlement fort. He named it San Carlos de Austria, in honor of the thirteen-year-old Charles who became Charles VI of the Holy Roman Empire. His materials were the nearby pine, cypress, clay, and moss.[53]

Wood buildings were erected inside and outside the fort, and included houses, a storehouse, hospital, church, and barracks. Their earthfast wood frames were walled with planks, bark slabs, and thatch. The next twenty-one years were not much of an architectural success for Santa María de Galve and its Fort San Carlos. Many of the soldier-builders were former prisoners from Mexico's jails, thieves who stole and deserted. "Massive violence and terrible diseases" killed an estimated twenty-five hundred people; mass graves have been discovered beneath the church inside the fort. Fires, hurricanes, and enemy sieges added to the woes and turned the architecture into a shabby village. The Gulf Coast and Panzacola Bay were embroiled in a constant tug-of-war between Spain, France, and Great Britain. Santa María de Galve surrendered to France in 1719, and was returned to Spain in 1722, but all buildings had been destroyed except a dilapidated cabin, a bake oven, and a lidless cistern.[54]

In 1723, the presidio was moved to the western tip of Santa Rosa Island at the harbor's entrance. Engineer Don José de Berbegal and his men constructed the usual buildings: church, warehouse, barracks, officers'

A view of the
Santa Rosa Island
settlement was drawn
by Dominic Serres
from a ship at anchor
in the harbor in 1743,
engraved and pub-
lished in 1763. Serres,
French born, became
captain of a Spanish
ship and ultimately an
artist of great renown
in England. (Photo-
copy courtesy of Flor-
ida State Archives)

quarters, hospital, civilian houses, bake oven, powder house, and dwelling for the commandant-governor. The lookout tower was said to be 60
feet high.[55]

Looking south at the island, a young French artist on a Spanish merchant ship in the bay made a drawing of Santa Rosa in 1743. It was engraved and published in London in 1763.[56] His drawing of the polygonal
church with a center belfry and the two-storied governor's house
crowned with *media naranja* domes would seem to be frontier fiction,
except for the later reputation of the artist (fig. 3.14). Dominic Serres
(1722–1793) was born in Gascony but ran away to Spain and became master of a vessel trading to Havana. He was captured by the British in 1752
and taken to London, where he became a founding member of the prestigious Royal Academy of Art in 1768. Well known for the accuracy of his
images, he was appointed maritime painter to King George III in 1780.
His paintings of the siege of Havana in 1762 hang at the Greenwich Maritime Museum. A decade later, he became the most successful English
painter of marine events during the American Revolution, his depictions
considered to be valuable historical documents, more accurate than
many written accounts.[57]

Santa Rosa's architecture was doomed by its location. The barrier island was at the mercy of violent storms that undermined and destroyed
the buildings. In November 1752, a hurricane delivered the mortal blow.
Only a storehouse, hospital, and blockhouse withstood the fury of wind,
water, and sand. Warehouses, a church, quarters, a stake palisade, and
new blockhouses were hastily rebuilt, but the precarious site could not
be permanent. In 1756, orders came from Mexico to relocate the presidio
to the mainland site where the Spanish had built a blockhouse in 1740

called Fort San Miguel. In 1757, a royal order named the third presidio San Miguel de Panzacola. It became today's Pensacola.[58]

Panzacola faced the bay, and was located between present-day Plaza Ferdinand VII and Seville Square. The commandant, who also acted as governor, was Don Miguel Román de Castilla y Lugo, and the royal engineer was Don Philipe Feringan Cortés. There were some seven hundred colonists, including approximately 184 women and children and 180 Christian Indians from nearby villages. Spain, however, was not committed to building a town of architectural substance. Once again, the construction workers were the military garrison, including undisciplined soldiers and criminals sentenced to hard labor. The practice of emptying Mexico's prisons to supply soldiers and construction labor for new Spanish settlements also occurred in California.[59]

Within the stockade, there was a house for the governor, a chapel, guardhouse, grocery warehouses, hospital, powder magazines, troop barracks, and some houses for officers and civilians (figs. 3.15, 3.16). Buildings were timber framed, the timber posts placed directly in the ground, walled with planks and bark slabs, and roofed with slabs of bark or palmetto. A new commandant-governor, Colonel Diego Ortiz Parrilla, an experienced Indian fighter, arrived in 1761. He was appalled at the condition of the buildings and rebuilt many during 1762. British plans of the presidio made shortly after Spain ceded Florida show many Spanish buildings with galleries and covered walks supported by round pillars.

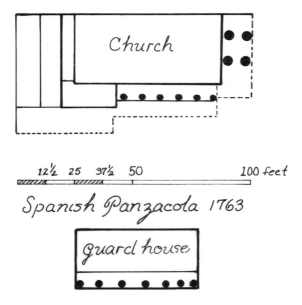

3.15. Spanish church and guardhouse, 1763, Pensacola. Plans drawn by English engineers shortly after Spain ceded Pensacola to the English depict the sizable church, with loggia and four-column belfry, and the major guardhouse with covered gallery across the length of the building. (Redrawn by E. Gordon after "Plans and Sections of the Fort at Pensacola," 1764, in *The Crown Collection of Photographs of American Maps*, courtesy of SAHS)

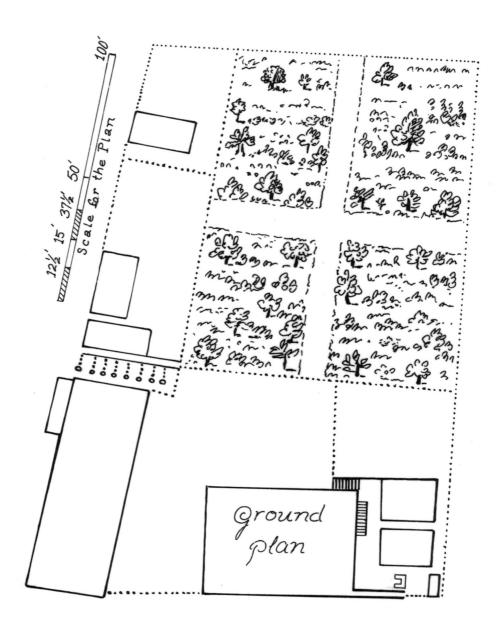

3.16. Spanish governor's house and gardens, 1763, Pensacola. Commandant-governors Don Miguel Román de Castilla and Col. Diego Ortiz Parrilla had an ample house, gardens, and stable inside the stockade. Walls were bousillage construction; the floors were planks covered with paving bricks. Slabs of cypress covered the roof. (Redrawn by E. Gordon, after "Plans and Sections of the Fort at Pensacola," 1764, in *The Crown Collection of Photographs of American Maps,* courtesy of SAHS)

The church, approximately 70 by 30 feet (nave 60 feet?), had a gallery and belfry.[60]

The governor's house was the best of the buildings, described by the Spanish as having a stone first floor that served as warehouse and two-room office of the paymaster. The second floor was the governor's residence, reached by an exterior staircase. The building was said to be 12 yards high; English measurements show the first floor dimensions to be about 60 by 43 feet. The exterior staircase and two attached outbuildings, one for kitchen and one for storage, are depicted on both Spanish and English presidio plans.[61]

A survey of the Spanish governor's house on September 28, 1770, by four British carpenters and chief Engineer Elias Durnford reads as follows: "The foundation consisted of posts in the ground filled up with stones about two feet above the surface, and above that with clay and moss, a coat of plaster on the outside."[62] This was typical of French bousillage construction known along the Gulf Coast since early 1700s. Walls of bousillage could be as thick as 2 feet, and were plastered inside and out. After decades, they hardened like cement.

The English report continued, "The posts are rotten with the surface of the ground, supported only by the brick chimney built by Governor Johnstone [English governor], and a few cedar posts as props which run through the center of the house underneath the large room, which are the entire support of a heavy floor consisting of heavy timbers and planks [puncheon floors], with two courses of Brick thereon." They noted the house had sunk some four inches in places and six inches in others. The kitchen was "built of posts in the ground with a new [English] shingled roof, the sides of which are only bark [slabs cut off the outside of timbers]." An outbuilding adjoining the kitchen was also built with posts in the ground and covered entirely with "bark."[63]

The Spanish had only six troubled years, 1757–63, at Panzacola before they had to abandon the settlement. During that time, a hurricane destroyed all the roofs of the buildings inside the stockade, and in 1760 the houses outside the fort belonging to civilians, officers, and soldiers were leveled to better defend the presidio during an impending Indian attack. In February 1763, "Panzacola" became British "Pensacola."[64] Notable architecture other than the governor's house could not be built under such conditions in so little time.

4 | The Power of Stone

*Lend me the stone strength of the past
and I will lend you the wings of the future.*

Daniel J. Boorstin

In San Agustín or St. Augustine, the colonial architectural environment ebbed and flowed like the tides that swept the harbor, bringing in and carrying out the Spanish, English, and American governments, new residents, and builders.

For the first two centuries, the town's architecture was wood and impermanent. During the eighteenth century, however, the waterfront capital of La Florida vibrated with hammers and chisels making a new stone architecture. Stone was more permanent. Stone gave the colonists new cultural expectations.

St. Augustine residents, like peoples around the world then and now, wanted to protect their buildings from fire, termites, rot, hurricanes, and enemy raids. They wanted habitations that met real needs in the hot and humid climate. They also wanted their buildings to bridge the lonely distances from the "mother countries," and so they constructed stone buildings that had the hallmarks of architecture in Spain, in Spanish America, in England, and in English West Indies. Stone dramatically changed the look of the town that had always renewed itself in thatch and wood planks.

St. Augustine's stone buildings have evolved from the wrenching changes in ownership of Florida. Building practices from the two mother countries had determined some initial directions of the town's architecture, but years of practical experience in the St. Augustine environment and the nature of the local shellstone ultimately shaped the architecture to the place. Long overshadowed by splendid baroque architecture south of Florida and Georgian-Palladian buildings to the north, St. Augustine's eighteenth-century and early-nineteenth-century masonry architecture has been overlooked and undervalued. This chapter and the next will present Florida's first regional style of architecture, its history and its strengths due to its own peculiar evolution.

EIGHTEENTH-CENTURY STONE FLORESCENCE

St. Augustine had been a town of wood and thatch from 1565 until the fateful English raid in 1702, with one very important exception, the masonry fort. After many wooden forts had rotted away, the final fort, the

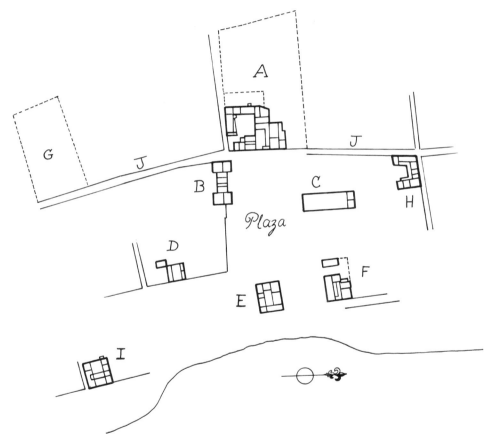

4. Eighteenth-century St. Augustine: *A,* Governor's House; *B,* British Statehouse (expansion of former *palacio episcopal,* Spanish bishop's house); *C,* Cathedral; *D,* British Courthouse (conversion of Spanish hospital, formerly the Menéndez Marquéz House); *E,* Guardhouse; *F,* Customs and Royal Treasury; *G,* site where Nuestra Señora de la Soledad and St. Peter's Church once stood; *H,* residence called "Spanish Treasurer's House" (home of Juan Estevan de Peña 1742–63 and home of Lieutenant Governor John Moultrie 1772–78; *I,* house of Elíxio de la Puente 1740s?–63 (Spanish treasury official) and William Drayton 1772–84, British chief justice; *J,* St. George Street. (Redrawn by E. Gordon from *Plano Particular de la Ciudad de Sn Agustín de la Florida . . . by Engineer Mariano de la Rocque,* 1788, and from *Plano General de la Ciudad de San Agustín de la Florida,* 1797 by Engineer Pedro Díaz Berrio, copies at SAHS)

Castillo de San Marcos, was begun in 1672 and was defensible by 1695 (pl. 7).[1] Its construction with blocks of coquina shellstone and tabby was designed and engineered by professionals. Inevitably, they created a stone industry and a stoneworking technology that awakened St. Augustine to new possibilities. Hewn stone (*cantería*) and roughly trimmed small stones for *mampostería* (rubble construction) began to find their way into other buildings: the church at Pueblo Nombre de Dios in 1678, the governor's house in 1690, and the hermitage of San Patricio on the outskirts of town in 1697.[2]

The Castillo stood fast and sound in 1702 when few other structures survived the fires of James Moore's raid.[3] The destruction of so many wood buildings became the catalyst that turned officials and weary residents in earnest to the fireproof building material of the fort. By about 1740, many buildings were being rebuilt with thick stone walls covered with white plaster and lime whitewash.

Coquina shellstone had been recognized as a building material at the end of the sixteenth century, when it was used to construct a powder magazine in one of the early forts.[4] However, the money and skills for

4.1. St. Augustine skyline, 1740, detail from a map drawn in ink and pencil illustrating the attack on the town by the English, led by General Oglethorpe. The style of the drawing is similar to a companion map signed by Lieutenant Todiman of the ship Phoenix. *A.* The town, with three belfries and large wall shielding the governor's house, its balustrade resembling windows; *B.* Fortified lookout tower on Anastasia Island; *C.* Quarries. Even though the churches were drawn with common English church map icons, and no attempt was made to be architecturally accurate, the skyline drawn from a distant ship suggests that the town's new stone architecture was taking shape by 1740. (Redrawn by E. Gordon from a drawing in the British Library, Maps K. Top. 122. 83a)

4.2. St. Augustine, 1740, detail from *A Drawing of Matanzas Inlet and Pengen Creek as taken by Lieutenant Todiman of the Phoenix who was sent with the Pilots of the Men of War on purpose to sound the same,* an ink and pencil preparatory drawing of the region showing General Oglethorpe's positions, with unfinished notes and key in pencil. This drawing shows four belfries, two at Indian mission villages north and south of the city outside the defenses, and two inside the walled town. The northern village is Nombre de Dios. (Photograph courtesy of the British Library, Maps. K. Top. 122. 83b)

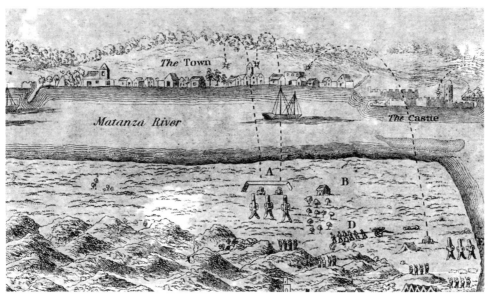

4.3. St. Augustine, 1740, from *A view of the Town and Castle of St. Augustine and the English Camp before it June 20, 1740,* engraved by Thomas Silver. The Silver engraving was made from the drawings of Lieutenant Todiman in figures 4.1 and 4.2. The engraving included two of Lieutenant Todiman's towers and the San Carlos Bastion sentry tower at the Castillo de San Marcos. The sentry tower was completed earlier in 1740. (Photocopy courtesy of Florida State Archives)

quarrying heavy blocks in great quantity and transporting and working them and smaller stones into civic, religious, and residential architecture on a large scale, were not present in St. Augustine until after the first phase of the construction of the fort in 1695. Early in the eighteenth century, professional engineers, stonecutters, and masons were brought to St. Augustine in increasing numbers from Spain, Mexico, and Cuba to work the coquina shellstone into neat building blocks, staircases, pilasters, and columns with classical capitals. By mid-century, they had erected pier arches, *media naranja* domes, stepped and curved gables, stone belfries, and portals with neoclassic arch orders. They embellished buildings with friezes, cornices, moldings, balusters, and keystones, and taught apprentice lime-makers and plasterers how to weatherproof the works with lime mortars. Large-scale limemaking prompted the development of oyster shell tabby concrete for load bearing walls as well as finer coquina tabby for floors.

The skills of St. Augustine's eighteenth-century masons were such that John Bartram described their work in 1765 as "a prodigious sight of carved stone," cut "as fine as if cut in ye fine marble." He was amazed that the stone of the "cemented shells" stood "ye chisel without flying to pieces or breaking farther then was designed."[5]

There is a myth, however, that St. Augustine was impoverished architecturally.[6] The myth was brewed by taking at face value disparaging adjectives in some historical documents describing colonial buildings as dilapidated and wretched, if not piles of ruins falling down. Most of these adjectives, however, were written by officials who exaggerated the state of buildings to procure more pesos and pounds from royal purses. Indeed, at one point, when the old wood fort was mentioned as being in "fair" condition, the money requested to build the stone fort was tabled.[7] English documents preserved in London are equally revealing of the hypocrisies of fund-raising gamesmanship in Florida.

A far different, unbiased picture of eighteenth-century colonial architecture emerges from the professional engineers' reports, maintenance records, and scaled drawings, together with contractors' vouchers, building inventories of departing and arriving governments and estates, and testimonials. Records of external trade—the cargo lists of the Spanish and English ships trading with Charleston, Savannah, Mexico, New England, the West Indies, Spain, and England—reveal enormous tonnage of many types of building materials and luxurious furnishings. The lists of imported exotic foods and spices, Madeiras and wines, china and mahogany furniture, silver and linens, cases of glass and tiles—to name only a few of the items arriving in large quantities in legal trade—denote an expectation of a certain standard of living. We will never know all that arrived in illegal trade that avoided customs, but it was substantial. The wealth represented in the holds of ships defies the image of an impoverished St. Augustine. Ultimately, however, archaeology must prove what actually existed.[8]

The individual building histories presented in this chapter are about materials, climate, and people. Coquina, oyster shells, sand, southern pine, and cypress were the materials. Heat, humidity, northeasters, and hurricanes were the climate extremes to plan for. Colonial officials, engineers, priests, itinerant craftsmen, slaves, and Indians were the builders and users; their cultural backgrounds, education, wealth, skills, handbooks, and own regional construction practices controlled the building plans and ornamentation.

The British have been accused of tearing down St. Augustine's Spanish architecture. This came from misinterpretations of a letter from John Bartram and a report by Spanish Governor Melchor Feliu of troops pulling down houses to get wood to burn during the winter.[9] The good masonry buildings standing in 1763 when the British arrived were still standing and recorded as carryovers in 1788 after the British had left. Wood buildings in poorest condition, or rotting beams in cracked tabby and thatch houses, became firewood, as they should have in any renewal undertaking. Bartram had qualified his remarks with, "the best houses stand."[10] General Gage and Governor Grant corresponded about the great shortage of housing for arriving British soldiers and officers,[11] and it is doubtful that decent wood or stone buildings were destroyed for firewood. British officials kept meticulous records of Spanish buildings they converted; the vouchers reveal that Spanish St. Augustine remained intact but with a "Caribbean Englishness" grafted onto Spanish beginnings. Underlying the amalgamation of Spanish and English building practices was a mutual respect for the local stone and architectural elements that responded to the climate.

The Spanish themselves after 1784 tore down the churches, La Leche, La Soledad (St. Peter's), and La Guadalupe, as well as the bishop's house (statehouse); with neglect, they lost others profiled in this chapter.

The eighteenth-century built environment is also about infrastructure. A great amount of energy and resources went into roads, lookouts, extensive fortifications, and cultural amenities. The colony required causeways and bridges, and miles of good road for carts and wagons. The Spanish built a stone seawall; the English extended wagon roads to Mosquito Inlet (today's Ponce de Leon Inlet) and north to the St. Mary's River, and eventually the "King's Road" ran from New Smyrna to

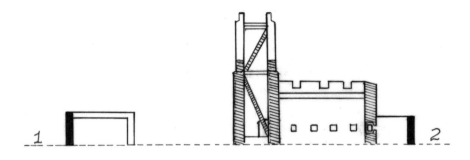

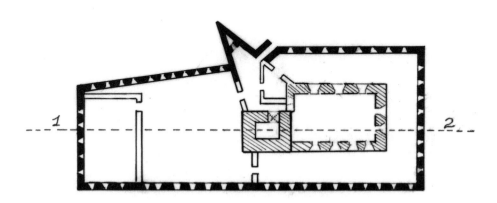

4.4. Lookout house, 1764, Anastasia Island, St. Augustine. (Redrawn by E. Gordon after William Brasier's "Plan and section of Look-out House, St. Augustine," Public Record Office, PRO: CO 700 Florida 29)

4.5. Lookout house, 1769, Anastasia Island, St. Augustine. (Drawing by Sam Roworth, deputy surveyor general, British Period; photocopy by Ken Barrett, Jr., courtesy of SAHS)

4.6. Lighthouse, 1823–80s, Anastasia Island, St. Augustine. The lantern was lighted April 5, 1824, with whale oil. In 1855, a rotating Fresnel lens brought it into the modern age. In the 1880s the historic lighthouse slipped into Saltwater Run, a victim of coastal erosion. (Photocopy courtesy of Florida State Archives)

Colerain, Georgia. Thomas Tustin was contracted to build a bathing house "for the use of the Inhabitants of St. Augustine," and Joseph Chetwood, clerk of the public market, was hired to oversee the construction of the public slaughtering pen at the barrier gate to the city. John Hewitt, master carpenter, built and painted a belfry on the market house and hung the market bell.[12]

The lookout tower on Anastasia Island was a stone structure that served both Spanish and English governments. Spanish construction began in 1673, with enlargements in 1739 for soldier's quarters and a chapel. The walls and tower had the battlemented parapets characteristic of Spanish architecture (figs. 4.1, 4.4). The British kept the "Moorish castle with ports and battlements," and added a wood tower on top of the stone tower in 1769, raising the height to 60 feet, surmounted with flags to announce ships arriving from north or south (fig. 4.5). In 1784, the Spanish added a new kitchen, storehouse, and powder magazine, and plastered and whitewashed the lookout. What a sight it must have made, a sparkling beacon to ships who set course for the harbor. Americans rebuilt the upper part of the tower, added a keeper's house, and turned it into the first lighthouse in Florida (fig. 4.6). Storms undermined its foundation during the 1870s, and in the summer of 1880 the lighthouse slipped under the sea and into oblivion.[13]

Many of St. Augustine's eighteenth-century stone buildings were designed and built by skilled professionals. Their plans were subject to approval by authorities in the mother countries and were held to current standards and tastes. The royal military engineers were direct envoys of the monarchies. The Spanish engineers who came from Havana were trained in Europe (Cuba did not have a professional school of engineering or design until mid-1800). Ignacio Daza, Juan de Císcara, Antonio de Arredondo, Pedro Ruiz de Olano, Pedro de Brozas y Garay, and Pablo Castelló were some of the capable professional engineer-architects (or *alarifes,* a term used by Father Solana) who masterminded St. Augustine's stone renewal.[14] They, and the English engineers who followed, were students of precision and accuracy. They studied mathematics and modular proportions, the classical orders and symmetry, and the fixed rules of dimensions. For inspiration and decorative classical language, they turned to architectural books written by the European architects of the Renaissance (pl. 8).

The highest-ranking Spanish builder was a well-trained artisan called *maestro de obras* (master of works). The *maestro de obras* was a civilian stonecutter or mason and professional contractor whose education included a formal system of apprenticeship training. He was capable of drawing and executing designs based on the accepted conventions of the day. He refined and oversaw the projects of the military engineers and commissioned the artisans to work on the forts, churches, and grand residences.[15] The *maestro de obras* at the Castillo in 1672 was Lorenzo Lajones, about fifty-six years old, a veteran master mason-stonecutter from France, Italy, and Havana. When he died, successive *maestros* came from Havana: Juan Márquez Molina, Cantillo, and Blas de Ortega, to mention a few. Africans, Indians, and even an Englishman worked their way up through the apprenticeship system to become masters of the quarries and lime-kilns, carpenters, and stone-cutters.[16]

Among the many drawings of these engineers are the beautifully rendered plans of the Castillo made by Engineer Pedro de Brozas y Garay. He had come from Ceuta (Spanish Morocco) to complete the fort started by Engineer Ignacio Daza in 1672.[17] His 1756 drawing shows the two-story-tall Doric pilasters across the courtyard wall that were translated nicely into the local coquina stone and oyster shell stucco, the materials closest at hand (pl. 9; fig. 9.7).

Scaled building plans by the English engineer James Moncrief (1744–1793) reveal valuable data about the Spanish buildings he renovated.

Moncrief graduated from the elite Royal Military Academy at Woolwich in 1759, and by 1776 had earned the rank of engineer extraordinary and captain-lieutenant. He arrived in St. Augustine in 1763, left in 1779 to fortify Savannah, and in 1780 became the chief engineer for the defense of Charleston. During his career, he acquired considerable wealth, including Airdrie in Scotland, purchased from Sir John Anstruther, and 7,560 acres in East Florida where he had two indigo plantations on Tomoka Creek and the Halifax River, each with dwelling houses, slave houses, and indigo works, valued at £2,570 and £2,787 respectively. While in Florida, he mapped St. Augustine and the East Florida territory from St. Mary's River to Ponce de Leon Inlet and worked on the conversions of the Spanish monastery, bishop's house, and hospital into barracks, the statehouse and courthouse (figs. 4.11, 4.14–4.21). His courthouse preparatory drawings expose the floor plan and elevation of what was once the Spanish hospital, which earlier had been the large home of the wealthy Menéndez Marquéz family. His 1765 drawing of temporary British barracks discloses the floor plan and loggia of the Spanish *palacio episcopal*.[18]

Governor Grant wrote in 1765 that Moncrief "is under the necessity of sending Copys to the Board of Ordinance of every Plan which I send to their Lordships [of the Board of Trade]" indicating that the designs of St. Augustine's buildings had to be approved before construction and payment, and had to meet the standards of the central Office of Works in London, which at the time was a stronghold of Palladianism.[19] The Florida National Guard Headquarters of today owes the concept of its design to Moncrief (figs. 4.15, 4.16, 4.39, 4.40).

John Hewitt was a master carpenter and the building contractor for many of the buildings of the British government, including St. Peter's Church. He arrived in 1768; by 1784 he owned seven parcels of land and several dwellings. On his thirteen-hundred-acre parcel on Pellicer Creek he built a two-storied water-powered sawmill, 51 feet long by 18.5 feet wide and 22 feet high (fig. 7.9). The mill is now an archaeological site, revealing its dam, spillway, millpond, planked floor, hewn timbers, oak blocks, and remnants of the rachet wheel, flutter water wheel, and pit wheel. Water sawmills of this type were capable of cutting five hundred to fifteen hundred feet of lumber a day.[20] Hewitt's accumulated properties reveal that contractors could acquire wealth in East Florida, an indication of a prosperous construction industry.

Mariano de la Rocque was the engineer responsible for buildings in St. Augustine during the first nine years of the second Spanish period. His plans and reports tell as much about British building conversions as

4.7. Government House, south entrance, 1937, St. Augustine. When Florida architects Mellen Clark Greely and Clyde Harris restored Government House to its colonial Spanish-period style in 1937, they included a neoclassic entrance that is similar to the 1785 design by Spanish engineer Mariano de la Rocque for the chapel entrance at the Castillo de San Marcos. (Photograph by F. Victor Rahner; photocopy courtesy of Ken Barrett, Jr.)

about the state of Spanish architecture after the British left in 1784. Rocque was born in Tarragona, Spain, in 1736, and came to Florida from assignments in Cuba. He died in Havana, Cuba, in 1795. His drawings reveal the British Statehouse and the British St. Francis Barracks, formerly the chapel of the Franciscan monastery (figs. 4.14, 4.15, 4.18). His lasting architectural achievements are his lot map of St. Augustine, documenting properties and buildings in 1788,[21] and his design for the Cathedral (fig. 4.33). One can also admire Rocque's work today at the fort, where he designed the neoclassical arch order entrance to the chapel (pl. 10). In homage to Rocque, a similar portal was added to the south wing of Government House in 1936 by Jacksonville architects Mellen Clark Greeley and Clyde Harris, but in marine fossil limestone quarried in south Florida instead of the local coquina stone.

"RICHER THAN WE THOUGHT"[22]

The building profiles below reveal an eighteenth-century reaching for higher architectural standards, continuous improvements, some grandiose if not ostentatious embellishments, and an identity with architecture in Europe tempered, however, with a practical sense of place.

GOVERNMENT HOUSE

The Spanish governors' residence and office (Government House) was one of the first large buildings to rise in stone after the English set the wooden town on fire in 1702. Its place in history is unique, because, more than any other building in Florida with the exception of the Castillo de San Marcos, it would cross many cultural and architectural boundaries during the next three centuries.

Government House history at the west end of the plaza begins in 1598, when Governor Gonzalo Méndez de Canzo redefined the town plaza and moved his own residence to its western end (map 3). His original house on the waterfront had been eroded by tides and storms. He moved into a wooden house owned by the widowed Doña María de Pomar. In 1604, the house was purchased by the Crown and became the official residence of the governors. By 1687, the wood structure was in disrepair and had to be rebuilt. The massive stone fort on the harbor was nearing completion and stone blocks were made available for the governor's house ground floor. Indians, crown-owned slaves, and soldiers were among the sawyers, carpenters, masons, and blacksmiths. The two-story house had a balcony and loggia. After the 1702 raid, its charred wood members were removed, and by 1713 the house had been rebuilt entirely of stone, coinciding with the date that Governor Francisco de Córcoles y Martínez first appeared on its balcony.[23]

Father Juan Joseph Solana, the parish priest, described the stone house with boarded roof in 1759. A more detailed description followed in the materials inventory prepared by Engineer Pablo Castelló in 1763 for the transition to an English government of Florida. After that date, records become more numerous, meticulously kept and sent to the Board of Trade in London with vouchers describing improvements, repairs, and costs. Between 1763 and the 1820s, many more descriptions flowed from the quills of Englishmen, as well as from returning Spanish, then from American tenants who depicted life in its tower and courtrooms. An anonymous English artist made a watercolor painting of its east plaza fa-

4.8. *View of the Publick Square in St. Augustine, Florida,* published 1835, *American Magazine of Useful Knowledge.* Government House is depicted at the far left, the cathedral at the far right. The drawing is significant because it confirms the longevity of Government House's Spanish tower, balcony, and side courtyard Doric entrance. The century-old tower, balcony, and portal were torn down in 1834 during renovations by Robert Mills, one of America's foremost architects and designer of the Washington Monument, who turned Government House into a federal building with an east facade in a current American style. He had not visited St. Augustine and did not conserve its Spanish heritage. (Photocopy courtesy of SAHS)

cade in November, 1764, depicting the balcony and Doric portal (pl. 13). In 1765, someone carved its silhouette on a powder horn (pl. 14).[24]

From all sources, the profile of a large and very handsome traditional Spanish house emerges. It was two-storied and had thick stone walls covered with plaster. At the northwest corner, there was a five-story stone observation tower, 14 by 20 feet at the base, 70 feet tall, with crenellated parapet, stairs, and railings, resembling battlemented towers built at the corners of domestic buildings in Castilla y León, Spain.[25]

By the 1780s the house complex included stone ovens with chimneys, a detached flat-roofed kitchen with a dining room and covered passageway, and another baking oven under a wood roof. Sixteen stone columns with capitals supported a second-story *corredor* (gallery) above the loggia bordering the main patio. This patio was south of the house, enclosed by a two-story wall on St. George's Street, and paved with small stones brought by ships as ballast, and later paved with tabby. A second patio and eight gates led to the formal gardens west of the house (map 4). In Spanish houses, the second and even a third patio were used for laundries and drying clothes. The governors' house had twelve wells lined with masonry,[26] a wood stable and carriage house, and roofed latrines during British occupancy.

The wood balcony that hung over "governor's street" (named St. George Street by the British) and looked toward the activities of the Plaza and harbor, was very elegant and finely embellished. It was corbelled on eight double beams running out through the wall, and supported with carved curving brackets. The 1764 watercolor painting at the British Library clearly shows triple cornices and eight white Doric columns with purposeful intercolumnation to define the central entrance to the balcony (pl. 13). Between the columns was a balustrade with twenty-two turned balusters; above was the cornice entablature, eggshell-blue-painted ceiling, and shingled roof. The resemblance to balconies of the Canary Islands and Andalucía is striking; it was Mudéjar-inspired and inherently decorative. The street door below the balcony had the typical Spanish *reja.*

One approached the governors' mansion through the south courtyard by way of the main portal, which was in the two-story wall along St. George Street. The massive wood door was flanked by paired Doric columns supporting a cornice entablature. On top of the wall was a balustrade. Columns, capitals, bases, pedestals, cornices, and balusters were formed gracefully and meaningfully in the local stone and white plaster.

4.9. James Grant, first governor of British East Florida, appointed in July 1763, arrived August 29, 1764. In July 1770, he inherited Ballindalloch Castle, and on May 9, 1771, he took a leave of absence from East Florida, intending to return in twelve to eighteen months. John Moultrie, lieutenant governor, became acting governor. During Grant's and Moultrie's administration, St. Francis Barracks, St. Peter's Church, the courthouse, and the statehouse were completed in St. Augustine, all housed in former Spanish buildings converted to new uses by English engineers. Grant did not return. Patrick Tonyn was appointed governor in 1774 and served until Florida was retroceded to Spain and the last of the English left in 1785. (Portrait attributed to Allan Ramsay, ca. 1760s. Photocopy courtesy of SAHS)

The high courtyard wall and balustrade might have been constructed in the 1730s in response to the growing English threat (fig. 4.1; pl. 14).

James Grant was appointed governor of East Florida in 1763. He is often misinterpreted for his view that Government House "was really a very bad Spanish House without a chimney, or even a Window except such as were made of boards."[27] Grant, who had been raised in Scotland, perceived comfort and fashion very differently than Spanish people from the warm climates of the Mediterranean, Mexico, and Cuba. In fact, Grant, and succeeding governors John Moultrie and Patrick Tonyn, spent generous amounts of money maintaining Government House and adding a few amenities that were "English." Some of the vouchers and receipts for work completed found to date in England's archives add up to £Stg.1,556.

Grant's use of the word "bad" did not mean dilapidated. Grant was expressing his taste and preference for the glazed windows, brick chimneys, and fireplace hearths of his native Scotland and London. Spanish windows, on the other hand, were products of warmer climates. They were large openings protected from rain and cold by interior wood shutters. Some had exterior *celosias* or *rejas*. For similar cultural reasons, the Spanish used charcoal braziers instead of wall fireplaces with chimneys.

Grant immediately hired John Volumns (New York mason sent by General Gage), Edward Shaw (mason), Andrew Allsopp and David McCluch (carpenters), and six "Negro workers" from Charleston to make glazed sashes. They worked 122 days making large sashes from cypress and pine to fit the large Spanish openings. The glazier, Joseph Thomas, glazed 144 panes of crown glass ten by twelve inches, and 54 panes eight by ten inches. The multipaned windows were counterbalanced with fourteen pulleys and lead weights. The sashes were painted white. All the materials were brought from Charleston.[28]

Window glass and hand-crafted sashes were very expensive. The best glass was called crown glass, blown in a circle called a "crown" or "table" with few irregularities.[29] The letters of Thomas Jefferson in 1774 concerning construction at Monticello indicate that it was cheaper to ship ready-made windows from Europe than to have them made in the colonies.[30] Governor Grant's new windows prompted William Stork in 1767 to write, "the apartments of which [at the governor's house] are spacious and suited to the climate, with high windows."[31]

In 1765, a new stable and coach house was built contiguous to the residence by George Brown, carpenter. The fifty-four-foot building had wood siding and floors, eight thousand wood shingles, and six glazed sash windows. No doubt it resembled plans in the then-current architectural handbooks published in London. The laundry with a room above was built by Solomon Griffiths, mason and bricklayer; the hardware was made by Robert Bonsall, blacksmith, and it was plastered and painted by Daniel Hounswith.[32] The wall was rebuilt that enclosed the formal garden and orchard planted by the Spanish with 114 orange trees and thirty-seven other fruit trees bearing lemons, peaches, pomegranates, figs, and grapefruit.[33]

Walls in Government House were plastered and "coloured" by Theophilus Armourer. Thomas Tustin, a carpenter-contractor from Pennsylvania, raised the observation tower and built two flights of stairs. The house roof was repaired, and a fireplace with chimney was built by Edward Marlin. John Hull built two new sentry boxes for the entrance, replacing the Spanish guardhouse that had a flat roof. In 1771, new locks and bolts were made, cupboards were built in (highly prized in colonial America), shelves were added to the study, and a closet was added under the staircase. A new staircase to the second-story gallery was built in the back yard. Fifteen interior doors, including two in the governor's study and one in the passage, and all the window shutters, were painted with an oil paint to imitate the color of stone. Handrails and banisters on the hall stairway were painted green. In 1773, masons Laidler and Patterson added 100 bricks to the kitchen chimney to cure the smoking, and used 150 bricks to build an oven. A large sum was paid in 1773–74 to John Hewitt, contractor, for "additional buildings to Government House," but the current governor, Patrick Tonyn was infamous for not sending itemized vouchers.[34]

It was a fine house, a mansion built for the climate, with library, office, dining parlor, drawing room, guest rooms, and probably a private chapel during the Spanish years. The resident Spanish and English governors hosted lavish dinners, lighted by sconces and candlelight, indulging themselves and their guests with gallons of imported wines and casks of Madeira, rum, and beer, barrels of spices, cheeses, herring, and olives, served on polychrome plates from the kilns of Spain and Hispanic America, or china and silver from England, accompanied by linens from France and the Netherlands, all listed on various ships' manifests.

When the Spanish returned to Florida in 1784, Engineer Rocque added new floors, enclosed and added windows in the north and south galleries, whitewashed the walls, and painted the trim in ochre. When the governors' house was damaged by a hurricane in October 1811,[35] it was not well repaired. An anonymous narrative in 1819 described it as "a very considerable house, the former residence of the governor of this settlement, but now in a state of dilapidation and decay, from age and inattention."[36] In 1821 and 1833, Americans repaired and renovated the "very considerable" historic house. It would have a new future as courthouse and post office.

FRANCISCAN MONASTERY AND CHURCH
(CONVENTO DE SAN FRANCISCO)

South of the city, in 1588, construction of the headquarters for Florida's mission system, consisting of a monastery and church, was begun. Costs of building were supported by annual subsidies from Mexico and Cuba. The Havana Franciscan monastery has been described as "very, very rich," with heavy tithes filling the coffers, where a novice entering the monastic orders was a son of the aristocracy and typically entered the convent accompanied by a slave. Several African slaves were present in the early years at the St. Augustine monastery.[37]

Brown- or blue-robed Franciscans in the sixteenth and seventeenth centuries knew the monastery as the Convento de la Concepción Inmaculada. Friars of the eighteenth century called it the Convento de San Francisco (pl. 12). The British converted the monastery into barracks, renaming it the Barracks at St. Francis Convent. Americans since the 1820s have used the term St. Francis Barracks. Today the site is the Florida National Guard Headquarters, south of the plaza at the corner of St. Francis and Marine Streets.

The earliest monastery buildings were wood planked and thatched. They were destroyed by fire in 1702 during James Moore's English raid. Reconstruction in stone began during 1717–18, when pesos were paid to superintendents and laborers for quarrying the stone. A boat was bought, and horses rented to transport stone, oyster shells, and firewood to the lime kilns. The walls went up slowly, the church being "built to half the height" in 1731. Lumber had yet to be bought for "entablatures, joists, roof shakes, doors, windows, and choir loft." The stone church was completed about 1737 with a single nave, sacristy, wood choir loft, cloister, and belfry at a cost estimated at five thousand pesos. The stone belfry dominated the southern end of town, symbolized in Lieutenant Todiman's ink and pencil drawings of 1740[38] and Thomas Silver's published version (figs. 4.1, 4.2, 4.3).

The friary, however, was not completed until about 1750, at an estimated cost of ten thousand pesos. It was said to have been built "the same size and measurements" as the friary destroyed in 1702, 56 varas long, 6 varas wide, and 6 varas high (or about 154 feet long, 16.4 feet wide, and 16.4 feet high, using 32.9 inches to the vara). These were the measure-

ments certified in 1724 by the Masters of Masonry, Ensign Bartholome Perez and Joseph de Espinosa, and Masters of Carpentry, Thomas de Balderama, Antonio González, Pedro Ruiz, and Diego Marquez Morales, who were to supervise rebuilding the friary in stone.[39]

Property maps drawn on location by Elíxio de la Puente (1764), engineer James Moncrief (1765), surveyor Joseph Purcell (1777), and engineer Mariano de la Rocque (1788) show the friary had two wings at right angles forming an L shape. A wall connected one end of the friary to the church, and thus the buildings and wall formed a quadrangle, wrapping around a courtyard (fig. 4.11). Since the Middle Ages, the cloister was traditionally the central element around which monastic buildings were organized.

John Bartram paced off the friary in 1765. Engineer James Moncrief made his survey the same year. Their measurements roughly match. Each segment of the L was about 126 to 135 feet long by 27 feet wide (Bartram: 45 paces long by 9 paces wide; Moncrief: 42 yards by 9 yards). The width included an arcaded walkway, which was 9 feet wide. Bartram counted ten arches for each segment, twenty arches in total. The friary's width without the arcade, therefore, would be roughly 18 feet, close to the 1724 Spanish measurements of the burned wood friary. Bartram estimated the friar's rooms to be 12 feet square, with walls 2 feet thick, again roughly totaling the Spanish measurements. He estimated that the wall connecting the church and monastery enclosed a church yard 90 feet square.

4.10. Convento de San Francisco, ca. 1750–63, conceptual view based on engineer James Moncrief's survey of 1765 and descriptions by Father Juan Joseph Solana (1759) and John Bartram (1765). Each wing of the friary had a 9-foot-wide arcaded loggia with ten arches. The church's front facade soared above the roof ridge of the nave to form the belfry (*espadaña*), about 40 feet high with five arches and four bells. (Drawing by E. Gordon)

4.11. Convento de San Francisco, lot plans before and after its conversion into English barracks. The church required extensive work during 1769–71. The conversion can be followed on the lot maps by: 1. Elíxio de la Puente (1764) and 2. Engineer James Moncrief (1765) both before conversion; 3. Surveyor Thomas Purcell (1777) and 4. Engineer Mariano de la Rocque (1788) after conversion. (Drawing by E. Gordon after the referenced lot maps)

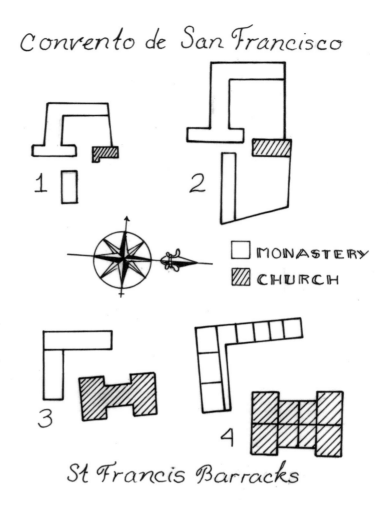

Convento de San Francisco

1   2

☐ MONASTERY
▨ CHURCH

3   4

St Francis Barracks

Moncrief's survey of the friary reveals it encompassed some 8,244 square feet (fig. 4.12).[40] Several of its stone walls, rooms, and remnants of its cloister arches can be seen today at the Florida National Guard Headquarters.

Father Solana described the monastery's church in 1759, and John Bartram described it in 1765. Their measurements are similar to the scaled drawing by Engineer Moncrief. The length (nave and presbytery) was roughly 75 feet, and width varied between 24 and 30 feet. (Solana: 27 varas by 10 varas and 10 varas high; Moncrief: 25 yards by 10 yards; and Bartram: 25 paces by 8 paces.)[41]

Father Solana noted that the front wall was the belfry. His description leads one to believe it was the typical Spanish *espadaña* belfry, with front facade raised higher than the roof ridge to add impressive height. The bells were hung in openings in the *espadaña*. Bartram estimated the belfy

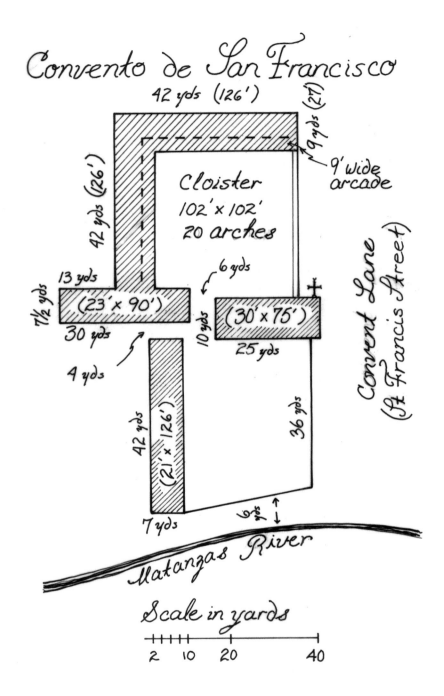

Convento de San Francisco

42 yds (126')

9 yds (27')

9' wide arcade

42 yds (126')

Cloister
102' x 102'
20 arches

6 yds

13 yds

7½ yds

(23' x 90')

(30' x 75')

30 yds

10 yds

25 yds

4 yds

36 yds

42 yds

(21' x 126')

Convent Lane
(St Francis Street)

7 yds

6 yds

Matanzas River

Scale in yards

2   10   20   40

4.12. Convento de San Francisco, plan by English engineer James Moncrief in 1765. The monastery had been the headquarters of the Spanish mission system in Florida since 1588. In 1702 its wood buildings were destroyed but the church was rebuilt with stone by 1737; the monastery was rebuilt by 1750 to the same dimensions as the destroyed monastery. (Redrawn by E. Gordon after Moncrief, 1765, Public Record Office, PRO: CO 700 Florida number 8)

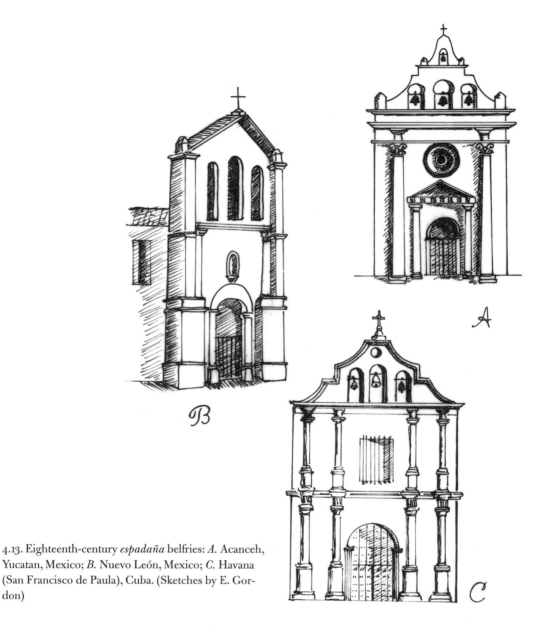

4.13. Eighteenth-century *espadaña* belfries: *A.* Acanceh, Yucatan, Mexico; *B.* Nuevo León, Mexico; *C.* Havana (San Francisco de Paula), Cuba. (Sketches by E. Gordon)

was 40 feet high, and wrote it had five arches, four of which had bells hung on cross bars. He added that the front was "curiously carved according to ye Spanish tast[e]."[42] The Franciscan belfry resembled the belfry at La Leche, the church of the mission at Pueblo Nombre de Dios, and Franciscan churches built during the same time in Mexico and San Antonio, Texas. Later, the St. Augustine Cathedral would be designed with the same style belfry.

Recent excavations reveal there had been stone columns along the west side of the church, suggesting that it too had a covered walkway open to the courtyard. It was about 3 feet wide and paved with crushed coquina. Another walled area east of the church (under Marine Street and a parking lot today) might have been the cemetery.[43]

St. Francis Barracks

In 1764 British Governor Grant set aside the Franciscan monastery to become officers' quarters, and its church to be converted into barracks for the soldiers. The thirty-two-year-old church underwent an extensive enlargement beginning in 1769 to its completion in 1771 (figs. 4.14, 4.15). Engineer Moncrief was "employed in the building of the Barracks of St. Francis." The width of the stone nave was doubled, and a second story and two pavilions north and south were added. The building formed the H plan popular in Palladian London. The square footage was roughly 15,800 square feet, eight large rooms for eight companies of soldiers.

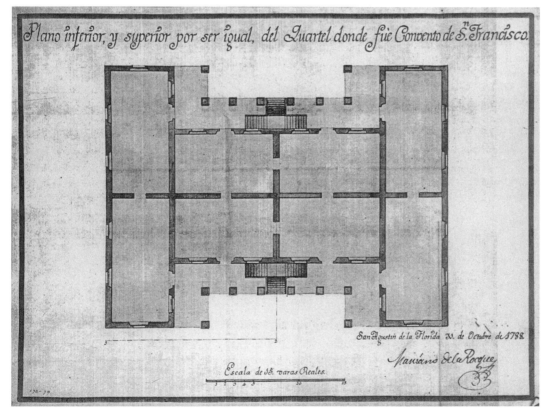

4.14. St. Francis Barracks, 1771, floor plan by Engineer Rocque, 1788, revealing how the British had converted the Spanish church of the Convento de San Francisco into troop barracks. (Photocopy by Ken Barrett, Jr., courtesy of SAHS)

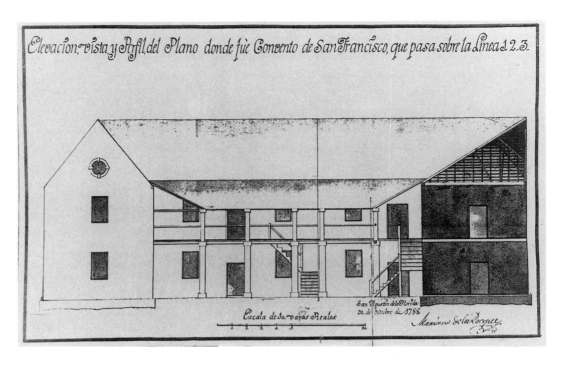

Elevacion, vista y Perfil, del Plano donde fue Convento de San Francisco, que pasa sobre la Linea 1, 2, 3.

Escala de 30. varas Reales

San Agustin de la Florida 31. de octubre de 1788.

Mariano de la Rocque

4.15. St. Francis Barracks, 1771, elevation by Engineer Rocque, 1788. The English added wide verandas and exterior stairways, elements characteristic of contemporary styles in warm climates. (Photocopy by Ken Barrett, Jr., courtesy of SAHS)

Two tiers of colonnaded galleries with graduated columns stretched across the front and back and provided the soldiers plenty of shade, ventilation, and airy indoor-outdoor spaces for good health in the hot climate. All told, it was a handsome two-story building with a large circular lookout crowning its roof. It had its own harbor and wharf (fig. 4.16). Some materials had come from England; the hardware and shingles came from New York.[44] The Florida National Guard Headquarters owes its present day architecture to the British design.

When the Spanish returned to govern Florida, they too used the old monastery and its church for barracks. Their troop strength was much less, requiring no significant architectural changes. They surrounded it with a gated pine stake fence and converted kitchens into prisons."[45]

PILE OF BARRACKS

The largest building in colonial East Florida was called the "pile of barracks" by its draftsman, William Brazier, whose drawings are beautifully rendered. It was built to accommodate one battalion, and stood south of the St. Francis Barracks in 1772, about where the national cemetery is today. Some stones were recycled from one of the old Spanish southern redoubts to build the foundation. The first story was constructed with brick, and the two upper stories with wood. Verandas wrapped around the upper floors. This huge three-storied building with tall chimneys, cupola, and weathervane dominated the southern water-front (pl. 18).

In addition to the elevation, section, and floor plan, the materials estimate is conserved at the Public Record Office, England. The H plan had three central floors, each about 195 by 38 feet, and two three-storied wings about 85 by 38 feet, at the north and south ends, making a total of some 31,920 square feet. In addition, there were a fourth-floor garret, two stories of verandas, five detached kitchens in the back yard for the soldiers, and eighteen privies, called "necessary houses" or "boghouses" (pl. 19).[46]

In addition to its large size, there is another very compelling aspect of the history of this structure. The second and third stories had been prefabricated of wood in New York, which turned out to be a terrible blunder. The military never considered the climate and disdained the use of local materials, much to the chagrin of resident governors who had learned better. From their New York headquarters, the fulcrum of military decisions, the "experts" decided that northern wood was superior to the local stone and southern pine, but they were in for a rude awakening not long after completion of the prefabricated stories.

4.16. St. Francis Barracks, ca. 1835, detail from *View of Fort Marion and City of St. Augustine, Florida,* anonymous. The drawing captures the handsome English architecture of the soldiers' barracks completed in 1771, with its gabled pavilions and tall cupola, boat basin and wharf, and the King's bakery to the left. The officers' quarters in the former Spanish friary were behind the soldiers' barracks, out of sight of the artist. (Courtesy of SAHS)

Governor Grant forewarned the Lords of Trade in 1768 that the plans as approved by General Gage were wrong for the climate: "I am sorry that they propose to make them of wood as we have stone and lime in such plenty—which would be more durable and in the end would be less expensive to the Publick as a stone building would require fewer repairs."[47] The bricks, the two prefabricated upper stories, and all the shingles were shipped to St. Augustine from New York in five sailing vessels in 1770. With them came New York masons and carpenters employed to raise the building. It was left to Engineer Moncrief, however, to devise a method for the tide to flush the "necessary houses."[48]

Not long after the barracks were finished in 1772, it became obvious that the governors were right; the materials brought from New York were wrong for the Florida environment. Governor Tonyn, who replaced Grant, lamented to Lord Dartmouth and the Lords of Trade in May of 1776 that the upper story and the colonnades were built of wood that "is much inferior to the wood of this province" and was in need of major repairs. He indicated that even good bricks were made locally. Most of all, he complained that "It would have been much more beneficial if the construction had been of stone. All the houses in this town are built of very good stone, from a quarry in Anastasia Island, which forms this harbor. The Engineer assured me the barracks could have been built of this stone, at one third less expense, and would have lasted forever, with very trifling repairs."[49]

Lord George Germain replied for Lord Dartmouth, "It was certainly a great mistake in those who were intrusted with the construction of the Barracks to overlook the excellent materials for building which were upon the spot and to make use of such as cannot be of duration in the climate. The estimate of the repairs already necessary is proof of their error." John Hewitt, contractor, and Thomas Hannah and Ralph Laidler, masons, were hired to rebuild fifty-four wood pillars and ten staircases in stone, an expensive lesson costing £1,118.[50]

Estimates for the construction of the "pile of barracks" totaled £6,680, "New York Currency." Barracks built the same time in Quebec, also for one battalion and faced with stone, cost 6,893 in the same currency. The St. Augustine barracks estimate included 164 window sashes, 164 pairs of shutters, 800 panes of glass 9 by 10 inches, 88 four-paneled doors, 1,456 square yards of painting, 19½ barrels of paint, and 110 gallons of linseed oil. The kitchens had brick chimneys and walls on stone foundations and shingled roofs. The boghouses were wood frame built on stone foundations with shingled roofs. Only the officers' privies were lathed and plastered.[51]

Wrapping all the floors with seven-foot-wide verandas came about on the advice of Dr. John Lorimer, for fourteen years the military surgeon at Pensacola (fig. 6.5). He advised General Haldimand that "piazzas" enabled the men to walk about out of the sun. He believed that airy galleries and well-ventilated buildings prevented fevers and provided general good health. The barracks at Pensacola were similarly built with verandas. Originally, the prefabricated barracks shipped to St. Augustine had been destined for Pensacola.[52]

When the Spanish returned, they used only part of the "pile of barracks" for quarters, artillery and lumber storage, and military hospital, with temporary partitions. The building deteriorated, and on May 25, 1792, soot ignited in one of the chimneys and the shingle roof caught fire. The upper two wood stories were destroyed. A flat roof was laid over the brick first floor, and it was made into a prison. As late as 1821, the tall stacks of brick chimneys still pierced the skyline.[53]

Palacio Episcopal (The Bishop's House)

Early in the 1700s, a stone dwelling rose facing the plaza at the corner of St. George and King Streets, a stone's throw from the governor's house. The site is under the present Trinity Episcopal Church. By 1735, it was the residence (*palacio episcopal*) of Bishop Francisco de San Buenaventura y Tejada. San Buenaventura was the only bishop to reside in St. Augustine between 1702 and 1763. He had been a professor of theology and *guardián* at a Franciscan convent in Seville, Spain, before he was appointed auxiliary bishop of Cuba with residency in Florida. He resided in St. Augustine between 1735 and 1745, and applied great zeal to improving the moral life and amenities of St. Augustine. He renovated the parish church at Nuestra Señora de la Soledad (described below), and established a classical school for boys.[54]

The palacio episcopal, if it existed today, would look like many eighteenth-century houses in Spain and its American colonies. It was large, one-storied with a flat roof, L-shaped, and covered with white plaster and limewash. The windows did not have glass but were protected with wood shutters. Elíxio de la Puente's lot map of 1764 describes it as *Casa de Piedra de los Señores Obispos*. Like those in some regions of Spain, the flat roof (*sotea* according to Father Solana's description in 1759) might have had a parapet and projecting clay tile water spouts (*canales*) to carry off the rainwater. The principal entrance was centrally located and opened onto the plaza. At the rear, protected by its southern exposure, the long arcaded L shaped *corredor* had nine stone pier-arches, presumably facing a patio and garden. The arches had cornice-style capitals similar to those restored today at the Llambias, Seguí-Kirby Smith, and Espinosa Houses (figs. 5.11, 5.12, 5.14).[55] The *palacio episcopal* was a larger version of the Treasurer's House of 1741, which today forms the first floor of the Peña-Peck House (fig. 5.4).[56]

Under the flat roof and between the cool stone walls, the bishop had at least nine rooms: a principal formal parlor (*sala*), a chapel, and seven additional rooms. The house had approximately 3,548 square feet.[57] The cool, comfortable loggia must have given the Bishop great pleasure and a pleasant place to dine.

THE NEOCLASSIC BRITISH STATEHOUSE

After a very brief tenancy by the Church of England in 1764, the thirty-year-old Bishop's House became temporary barracks for British troops awaiting the completion of the St. Francis Barracks. Engineer Moncrief drew the conversion plans for the Bishop's House in 1765, including bed layout, labeling it "Soldiers Barracks as at Present." On his survey of St. Augustine of 1765 he entered it as "Bishop's House now a Barrack."[58] An added east wing increased the square footage to some 4,504 square feet and shows up on the property maps after 1764. Moncrief added two large fireplaces and chimneys and proposed a second story be built above the original Spanish house, to include a garret and pitched roof. The seven-hole outhouse drawn for the southeast corner of the lot was presumably built.

In 1773, the Bishop's House was renovated according to former governor James Grant's dream expressed to the Earl of Hillsborough and the Lords of Trade on December 14, 1770: "After the Troops get into the Barracks, I shall fit up the Spanish Bishop's House for Council and Assembly Rooms and for the other Offices of the Civil Government in such a manner as to have the whole under one Roof." He had saved a surplus of £3,283 19s. 2½d. for the statehouse and new roads out of the contingency funds voted by Parliament for the support of the "Infant Colony."[59]

The elevation drawings of the statehouse submitted to the Lords of Trade have not yet been found, a puzzle waiting to be solved in London. Many details, however, can be pieced together from correspondence, vouchers, and floor plans drawn in 1790 by Spanish Engineer Mariano de la Rocque. Governor Grant left the colony for London for personal reasons in May of 1771, and Lieutenant Governor John Moultrie, appointed acting governor, assumed responsibility for Grant's architectural projects with great enthusiasm (fig. 7.11). In 1773 he wrote, "In the erection of [the

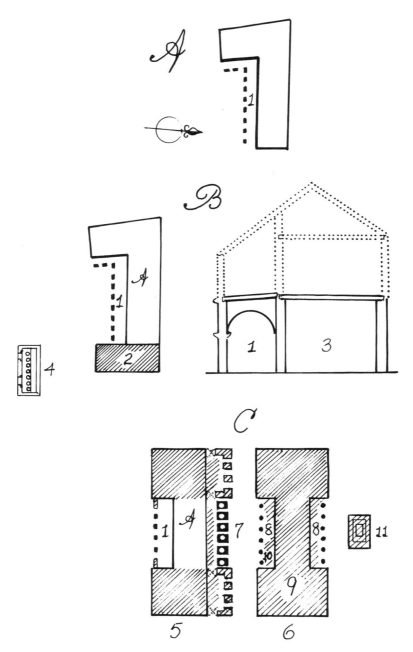

4.17. Spanish bishop's house (*palacio episcopal*) converted to British statehouse, St. Augustine. *A.* A Spanish-style house, with arcaded loggia (1) with nine pier arches. There were nine rooms. The site is under the present-day Trinity Episcopal Church. *B.* Former Bishop's House converted into temporary barracks for British troops in 1765, retaining arcaded loggia (1), adding new wing (2), and proposing second story (dotted lines) above original Spanish house (3). A seven-hole privy (4) was at farthest corner of the lot. *C.* British statehouse 1773: first floor (5) with new wings added to original Spanish house (*A*); second floor (6); grand arcaded entrance piazza (7); upper verandas (8). When the Spanish returned, they converted (ca. 1785) the first floor into their guardhouse and armory, and second floor into their church (9), sacristy (10). Former English cupola (11) became Spanish belfry with three bells. (Drawn by E. Gordon, *A.* after Elíxio de la Puente, 1764, SAHS; *B.* after Moncrief, 1765, PRO; *C.* after Rocque, 1790, SAHS)

church] as well as that of the State House I have earnestly endeavoured to throw as much Strength, convenience and ornament into them as could possibly be done for the money expended thereon. If your lordship should be of the opinion that I have tolerably succeeded in my intention I shall be happy. I flatter myself that those Edifices will be not only of real publick utility, but an Ornament to this Young Province."[60]

Both Grant and Moultrie were members of the landed aristocracy that prided itself on being gentlemen architects and owners of libraries that included architectural handbooks. They were tastemakers, and their tastes were classical, learned from books by Robert Morris, William Salmon, Colin Chambers, James Gibbs, Andrea Palladio, and others, and from their familiarity with London and neo-Palladian buildings by Burlington and Kent characterized by rusticated arcades and Roman orders.

Moultrie presided during the construction of the statehouse. His background would influence the results. He was from a prominent family of South Carolina, and had married into the very wealthy Austin families of South Carolina and Shropshire, England. His brother, William Moultrie, was governor of South Carolina. Moultrie forwarded statehouse plans along with the Georgian-Renaissance-style tower and steeple he had added to St. Peter's Church further south on St. George Street. His own plantation manor house at Bella Vista, south of St. Augustine, was Palladian inspired.[61] The statehouse that was to be the seat of British government in East Florida would not be anything less than his best attempt to bring forth a handsome building in the neoclassic style.

The statehouse was constructed during 1772–73. In April, 1771, Lord Hillsborough had asked Governor Grant to be more precise in his plan for "fitting up the Spanish Bishop's House for several public offices—An Assembly Room, Custom House, Land Surveyors Office, Secretary's Office, Register's Office, and Naval Office," and to submit the "necessary Plans and Estimates" for approval. Shortly after Grant left St. Augustine in 1771, he appeared before the Board of Trade in London to answer questions about the statehouse. He won the Board's approval and permission to appropriate from William Knox, Crown Agent, the surplus monies he had saved for this project. He then "directed Lt. Governor Moultrie to carry the works into immediate execution," and on March 1, 1772, he wrote Knox to pay Moultrie's bills "when they appear, which will probably be in June next."[62] The total amount expended on the statehouse is unknown, but £1,920.19 were spent on the masonry walls, some carpentry, and lead. (It has been previously published that £3,383 was spent on the statehouse, but an audit of 1786 shows that £1,763 of that sum was paid to contractors for road construction from Indian River to St. Mary's River.[63]) Additional monies were spent on the statehouse during 1777–78 after it had been completed, like the £15 10s. 9d. paid to Andrew Davitt for painting.[64]

John F. Millar, a historian researching the life of Peter Harrison, the gifted architect of Rhode Island, thinks Harrison had a hand in the design, but Harrison's work was destroyed in a fire, leaving no evidence. Millar's conjectural elevation is at the St. Augustine Historical Society. The East Florida statehouse is more likely to have been drawn by someone in St. Augustine, or perhaps Charleston, who adapted the design to the site and existing building. The case for Charleston rests on the design of the steeple for St. Peter's Church drawn about the same time as the statehouse and obviously linked to St. Michael's in Charleston, a fine example of church architecture influenced by James Gibbs and plates XXIX–XXX in his *Book of Architecture* (1728, London), a copy of which had been at the Charleston Library Society since 1770.[65] Moultrie, who forwarded the church drawing to London and supervised the statehouse, was well connected with architects in Charleston and at the Library Society.

There were several amateur gentlemen-architects as well as professional engineers in St. Augustine who were capable of designing the statehouse. In addition to Moultrie himself, there were Engineer Moncrief, William Drayton (the chief justice and designer of Charleston's courthouse), or even George Frederick Mulcaster, who was the "Engineer [and surveyor] in this province upon the same footing that Mr. Durnford [chief engineer] is in West Florida. Mr Mulcaster is God Son to the late Prince of Wales . . . under the immediate protection of the Royal Family and has the honor to be known to the King." (His eldest son, Sir Frederick William Mulcaster, was born in St. Augustine, and after graduation from Woolwich Academy, would distinguish himself as England's inspector general of fortifications.)[66]

During construction, Moultrie decided that "The old Spanish palace plagued me much. The walls were not square and many of them too thin and weak to build upon. I was therefore obliged to build the wings entirely new from the foundation and very strong to support the other parts. I intend to pave the lower story where the offices will be kept, and the front and back piazzas with red tile, as it will be cheaper, look very well, and be less liable to accidents from fire."[67]

Thus the statehouse rose around the old *palacio episcopal* and its arcaded gallery, which were incorporated into its central first floor (fig. 4.17). In 1790, engineer Mariano de la Rocque drew the layout of both

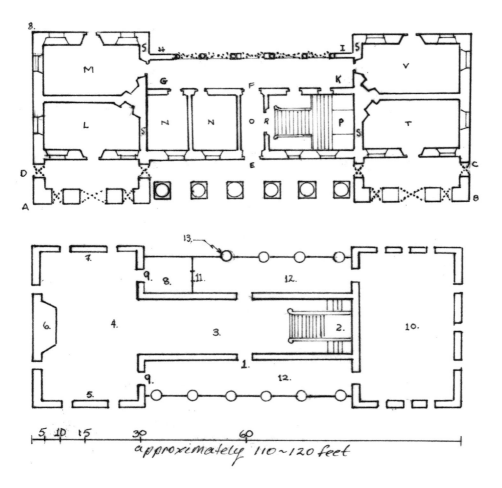

approximately 110~120 feet

4.18. British state-
house, 1773–85 floor
plan, St. Augustine.
Spanish engineer
Mariano de la
Rocque's plans of 1790
reveal the statehouse
had a grand entrance
facing the plaza. Veran-
das front and rear were
supported by columns.
After the British left,
Rocque converted the
assembly rooms into
the parish church with
altar and choir loft and
the cupola into a belfry.
(Redrawn by E. Gor-
don after Rocque, 1790,
from copy at SAHS.)

floors of the British statehouse, which he had converted into a church,
principal guardhouse, and artillery storage. Rocque's drawings, as well as
lot maps by surveyor Joseph Purcell (1777) and engineer Pedro Díaz
Berrio (1797) (map 4), reveal it was large and I-shaped, following examples set by government in London, with approximately 9,720 to
10,788 square feet, excluding the piazzas front and back.[68] Entering from
the plaza into the center hall, immediately to the right was an interior
divided staircase in an open well that led to the two large rooms upstairs
of the general assembly (fig. 4.18). The stairwell may have been lighted by
the rooftop cupola or belvedere (which the Spanish would later turn into
a belfry), the fourth to grace the British town skyline. In winter, the statehouse was heated by four fireplace hearths in two interior chimneys.

The entrance to the statehouse had an exceedingly grand effect; it was
a piazza composed of arcades and six large freestanding round columns
(fig. 4.19). The columns may have been constructed of specially molded
curved bricks or shellstone and covered with plaster to resemble the
stone of classical buildings. Their orders are unknown, but the drawing

of St. Peter's tower and steeple as well as English custom would suggest Roman Doric on the first floor, and Ionic on the second. Moultrie's own Bella Vista plantation house had this arrangement. Like St. Peter's Church, the statehouse might have had keystone arch surrounds and quoins to give the illusion of thick walls.

James Grant Forbes in 1821 recalled the "splendor" of the statehouse, describing it as a "handsome and spacious edifice, built in the modern style."[69] "Modern," according to William Salmon's eighteenth-century "Builder's Dictionary" meant architecture that borrowed Greek and Roman elements.[70]

On the evenings of March 3 and May 20, 1783, the citizens of St. Augustine attended the "theater in the State-House" to see a comedy and a tragedy. They had a choice of a 5–shilling seat in the "Pitt" or a 4–shilling seat in the "gallery," prices similar to the theater tickets bought by Thomas Jefferson in Williamsburg about the same time.[71]

4.19. British statehouse, 1773–85 conceptual view, St. Augustine. Acting Governor John Moultrie wrote the Lords of Trade in 1773 that the statehouse would be "an Ornament to this Young Province." The Spanish tore down the statehouse ca. 1804 after they constructed their new cathedral in 1797. Some of the statehouse stones went into the 1813 obelisk on the plaza dedicated to Spain's short-lived constitution. Some of the statehouse foundation stones remained in situ and are now thought to be part of Trinity Episcopal Church (1832). (Conceptual drawing by E. Gordon and Charles Tingley)

When the Spanish acquired the building in 1784, Engineer Rocque found it to be "in good condition." Its first floor became a weapons depository, guardhouse, and royal goods warehouse. He adapted the second floor for the parish church by knocking out a wall and chimney, adding an octagonal arch of pine to support the entrance to the sanctuary, and painting the interior white. He added a choir loft with turned and carved balusters, and a small staircase made of carved wood posts so close together they screened the entrance to the cupola that became the bell tower. The belfry had a door with shutters, and was large enough for three bells.[72]

In 1790, the roof or cupola-belfry was struck by lightning. It was temporarily covered, but not repaired. The statehouse was torn down in 1804 after the Cathedral was built. Stones from its walls were used in 1813 to build the obelisk on the plaza commemorating Spain's first but short-lived constitutional government, hence today's name, "Plaza de la Constitución." Some of the statehouse foundation stones may still be in place and part of Trinity Episcopal Church, which rose on the site in 1832.[73]

MENÉNDEZ MARQUÉZ HOUSE—SPANISH HOSPITAL —BRITISH COURTHOUSE

The house of the Spanish royal accountant, Don Francisco Menéndez Marquéz, with two stories and a courtyard, was built of stone in the 1730s on a large lot on present-day Aviles Street south of the plaza. After his death, the Spanish converted the house ca. 1743 into the Royal Hospital.[74]

Father Solana described the house-hospital in 1759 as having two large rooms, one above the other, two smaller back rooms, and a detached stone kitchen and staff apartment. The roof was shingled and a medicinal garden was planted.[75] Engineer Pablo Castelló made an inventory of the building in 1763 on the eve of the Spanish departure and English arrival. He confirmed its construction of stone, including stone pillars supporting the upper gallery, exterior stone stairs, stone floors, and a stone wall around the courtyard. The ceiling beams, gallery railings, doors, window shutters, shingles, and garden fence were wood. The stone pillars measured 7 varas tall (19 feet).[76]

Engineer Moncrief's floor plan and elevation of 1770 for its conversion into the British courthouse show a large house, with about 3,360 square feet excluding the detached stone kitchen and apartment (figs. 4.20, 4.21). It had a side yard entrance through the walled courtyard, which

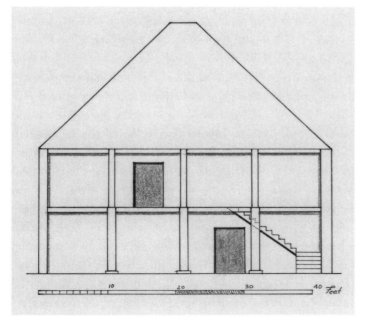

4.20. British courthouse, 1770, elevation by Engineer Moncrief, St. Augustine. The drawing is of the former Spanish hospital (1743–63). The stone house had two stories, shingled roof, loggia and *galería* with outside staircase. It was converted to the British courthouse in 1773. (Drawing by E. Gordon after Engineer James Moncrief's elevation of 1770, Public Record Office PRO: MPG 979)

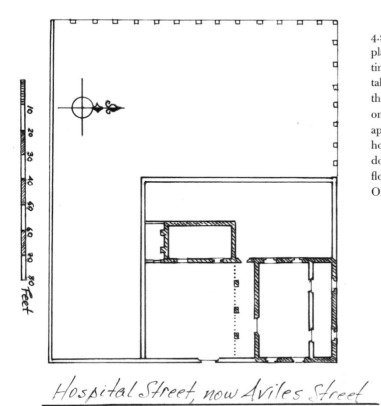

Hospital Street, now Aviles Street

4.21. British courthouse, 1770, floor plan by Engineer Moncrief, St. Augustine. When the former Spanish hospital was converted into the courthouse, the first floor held the court, the second became the provost marshal's apartment, and the detached kitchen house was a jail. (Drawing by E. Gordon after Engineer James Moncrief's floor plan of 1770, Public Record Office, PRO MPG 979)

measured 40 by 45 feet. The principal entrance was in the loggia under the gallery. It was a very good example of the St. Augustine-style dwelling described in chapter 5.[77]

Governor Grant wrote that the courthouse "will be one of the best in America." It was completed in 1773, and vouchers indicate glazed window sashes were added and the roof was raised. In the garret created under the new steeply pitched hip roof were stored the equipment, hoses, and buckets of the new town fire engine. The rest of the renovation was cosmetic: plastering and painting the large room for the Courts of Justice and the second floor apartment for the provost marshal, and planking the jail walls and erecting a new boarded fence enclosing the former medicinal garden. Benches and tables for the judges, juries, clerks, and lawyers were made. The apartments in the former kitchen became jail cells. Thomas Lawrence, blacksmith, added iron grates to the prison door and iron bars on the window and in the chimney vent. A jail yard was enclosed. Thomas Hannah, Godfrey Humber, and James Marlin were responsible for the carpentry and masonry. John Moultrie wrote he had to "expend a little more money of the furnishing of it than was first estimated owing to the old Spanish walls on which it was founded being in a worse condition than was expected." He added, "It is now a very proper and good building." Cost: £517.[78] In March of 1818, during the second Spanish period, the building burned.

COLONIAL CHURCHES

The Spanish built five stone churches in St. Augustine between 1718 and 1797. Some had facades with a "prodigious sight of carved stone";[79] four had *espadaña* belfries, and one a domed tower that became a city landmark. One of the Spanish churches was transformed by the British into an Anglican church with a neoclassical tower and steeple. In addition to the five freestanding church buildings, there was a chapel in the Castillo de San Marcos to which an impressive Doric entrance was added. The hands of professional engineers, *maestros de obras* and master masons, and stone carvers were evident in their design and construction. They fashioned classic orders, fluted columns, cornices, stepped and curved belfries, and at least one known handsome "broken" pediment.

Churches were important structures to the colonial community. Their thick stone walls shut out the world and provided safe havens. Catholic rituals demanded specific architecture. The ornate sanctuaries were made mysterious by the ethereal glow of candles; they lifted life to another level enriched with gilded altars, crosses, linens, silver chalices, silk damask, paintings, and statuary, much of it bought in Spain, Mexico, and Cuba. The summoning toll from the church bells, and the healing melodies from the pipe organs and choirs, were seminal to the church architecture. They were buildings to believe in.

Of the four churches profiled below (the Franciscan church has been described above), only one still stands; it is the parish church built between 1793 and 1797, now the Cathedral. In its walls and front facade are the stones and styles from three earlier churches.

Nuestra Señora de la Leche

North of St. Augustine and a cannon shot from the fort, a Franciscan mission church was erected in the Pueblo Nombre de Dios about 1587, when the first significant number of Franciscan missionaries arrived and Fray Alonso Escobedo was assigned to the mission. He was a scholar who wrote a metrical narrative about La Florida.[80] The first church might have been a small pole frame set in the ground and covered with thatch, built by Indians in their own idiom, until a larger church with a European floor plan could be erected. The larger church was also walled and roofed with palm thatch (figs. 2.1, 2.2).

Soon after the turn of the century, the church at Pueblo Nombre de Dios was described by Fray Pedro Bermejo as built with stone. By then it had become associated with a statue of the Blessed Virgin nursing the infant Jesus. This special devotion to Nuestra Señora de la Leche y Buen Parto (Our Lady of Milk and Good Birth) was reflected in the name of the mission church.[81] In 1678, Governor Hita Salazar boasted he had built the church "out of mortar and masonry, the only one like it in the provinces."[82] On November 14, 1702, the government scribe, Juan Solana, wrote, "in the Pueblo de Nombre de Dios . . . the enemy garrison has taken over the stone church."[83]

In 1728, an English and Indian force led by Colonel John Palmer burned the church and carried off the statue of the Virgin nursing the infant. Before midcentury, the church had been rebuilt of stone, but this time closer to town and inside the outer defense line, just north of the fort (fig. 4.22).[84] According to Father Solana in 1759, the front wall was the belfry and it faced east, a stone's throw from the edge of the river, with a view over the harbor and its tricky sandbar entrance. His description suggests the traditional *espadaña* belfry similar to the one at the Convento de San Francisco.[85] Lieutenant Todiman's drawing (he used a stock English map symbol) indicated there was a belfry by 1740 (fig. 4.2).

Solana described a nave of harmonic proportions. The width (9 varas)

4.22. Mission church, Nuestra Señora de la Leche, ca. 1740s, St. Augustine, sketched by Sam Roworth ca. 1769, when he was the English deputy surveyor general and the church was used by the English as a hospital. It is the only depiction known of one of Spanish Florida's most elaborate stone churches. It was dismantled by the Spanish ca. 1792 to save money on stones for the new cathedral. (Photocopy of a detail of Roworth's *A Plan of the Land Between Fort Mossy [Mose] and St. Augustine . . .* , courtesy of Florida State Archives)

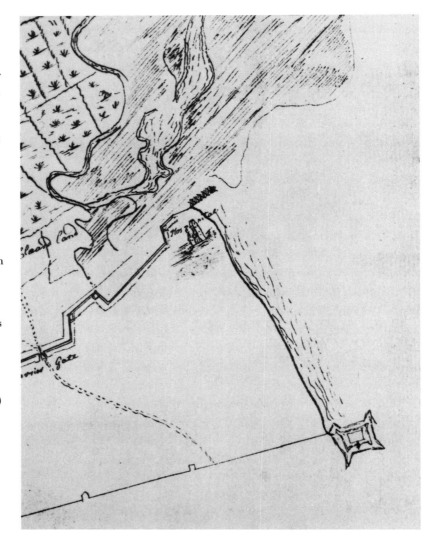

was half the length (18 varas) and the height (4½ varas) was half the width. Solana wrote there was a sacristy and an adjoining friary room to the north with a covered walk (*corredor*). Attached to the friary was another room (fig. 4.23), also to the north, reserved for pilgrimages to the statue of the Virgen de la Leche y Buen Parto ordered from Spain to replace the one taken by the English. A likeness of this sculpture was painted in 1760 and hangs today in Campeche, Mexico (pl. 11).[86]

John Bartram visited the church, which he called the "indian" or "milk church," in 1765. He found it to be "ye compleates piece of architecter" in the town, and he thought that the Spanish had bestowed on it "ten times more labor & charge on this indian church than any of

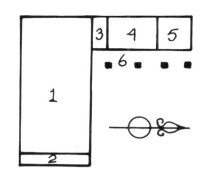

4.23. Mission church, Nuestra Señora de la Leche, ca. 1740s, St. Augustine. Conceptual elevation based on Roworth's sketch; floor plan based on descriptions by Father Juan Joseph Solana in 1759 and John Bartram in 1765: 1. nave; 2. *espadaña* belfry; 3. sacristy; 4. friary, sharing north wall of sacristy; 5. room to north for pilgrimages to the Virgin de la Leche; 6. *corredor*. (Drawing by E. Gordon)

their own in town." Bartram added that the gable-end was heavily decorated with fluted columns, Doric capitals, bases, and a frieze, above which was the "prodigious sight of carved stone according to their fancy."[87] The stonework was most likely the work of skilled Indian masons at the mission. La Leche resembled mission churches built at the same time in San Antonio, Texas, still standing today.

After the Spanish returned to Florida in 1784, they tore La Leche down, used its stones, and replicated its frontispiece in the construction of the new parish church, the Cathedral.[88]

Nuestra Señora de Guadalupe de Tolomato

A hermitage (*ermita*) associated with the Virgin of Guadalupe was located in the Tolomato mission village northwest of the city in what is now the Tolomato cemetery. The Tolomato Indians had originally resided on the coastal islands of Georgia. They were displaced to a Spanish mission village on the Guana Peninsula in the 1600s, then to St. Augustine. The cemetery and the Tolomato River bear their name.[89] The devotion to the Virgin of Guadalupe might have come from the miraculous statue in Estremadura, Spain, or the image that later was said to have appeared on the garment of a poor Indian in Mexico in 1531.

The smallest of St. Augustine's colonial stone churches, Guadalupe's nave was estimated by Father Solana to be 16 varas long, 7 varas wide, and 4 varas high, approximating harmonic proportions. James Moncrief, surveyed the entire church with tower at 24 yards long by 12 yards wide. The roof was palm thatched. The stone bell tower terminated in a dome and served as the main church entrance. Father Solana described the dome as a *semisirculo o media naranja* (semicircular or half orange).[90]

This tower may have resembled the tall sentry tower of the San Carlos bastion at the fort completed January 1740, under the direction of Engineer Pedro Ruiz de Olano, who had come from Venezuela in 1738 (pl. 8; figs. 9.5, 9.6). The *maestro de obras* was Blas de Ortega, from Havana, a likely candidate for the construction of the church tower.[91]

Before the arrival of the English in 1764, German immigrants used the church. The minutes of the British Council and Assembly in 1766 called it the "German Church" and ordered a road built around it.[92] William Stork wrote that there was a German settlement within the first fortified line of defense with a church of its own.[93] Four German families and Indians from the Tolomato mission were listed in the Spanish exodus in 1764, resettling in San Agustín de la Nueva Florida (or Ceiba Mocha), Matanzas province, Cuba.[94]

John Bartram called it the "dutch church" in 1765, a mispronunciation of *Deutsche,* meaning German. He described it as having interior "pillars and arches" that were broken by soldiers pulling down the wood roof beams of the thatch roof, which was in bad repair. The stone tower, however, remained. Bartram thought it was almost 20 feet square, with "A great Cupola of stone about four story high."[95] William Gerard de Brahm, surveyor general of the Southern District of North America, wrote that St. Augustine had "four churches, ornamentally built with stone in the Spanish taste . . . One is pulled down, viz, the German Church, but the steeple is preserved as an ornament to the town."[96] The tower was still standing twelve years later when Spanish engineer Mariano de la Rocque referred to the "tower of Tolomoto" in the cemetery north of the city.[97] The church and its tower, the "ornament to the town," was dismantled by the Spanish and its stone used to lessen the cost of the new parish church, the Cathedral.[98]

Nuestra Señora de la Soledad

Shortly after the Spanish colonists moved their settlement from Anastasia Island back to the mainland in 1572, they built both a parish church and a hermitage. They erected their parish church, Nuestra Señora de los Remedios, near the waterfront, close to the southeast corner of today's plaza. It was described as a plain planked building richly appointed in the interior (figs. 3.4, 3.5, 3.6). The hermitage was erected further west, on what is today a parking lot on St. George Street south of the plaza (maps 3, 4) , and was associated with the Virgin Mary of Solitude, an image that often refers to the life of Mary after the crucifixion. In 1597, Governor Méndez de Canzo built a hospital addition to the hermitage, the first hospital established in what is now the United States. In the late 1600s, Governor Quiroga y Losada enlarged the hermitage into a little wood church complete with a campanile.[99]

After 1702, the hermitage served as the parish church. It had been one of the few structures that survived the fires of the English raid.[100] When the energetic Bishop Francisco de San Buenaventura y Tejada lived in St. Augustine, 1735–45, he rebuilt the church and added the stone sacristy. He had seen that the parish priest was assisted by an elder sexton, organist, and two acolytes. The organist and altar boy were paid the "extremely high" salaries of 390 pesos and 5 reales. In 1759 Father Solana described the stone church as having a sacristy and two rooms on the second floor for the assistant priest and acolytes, a choir, and a stone belfry.[101] The hospital activities had been removed to the converted Menéndez Marquéz House described earlier.

The new stone front facade, according to Father Solana, had three arches of stone. Above the arches was "the stone wall in which the bells were rung," the traditional *espadaña* belfry that had also been built at the monastery church and La Leche. The belfry and entrance faced east. The altar was in the west, according to burials excavated by archaeologists in the nave floor. Heads were to the east, as if the deceased could rise up and face the altar in the west.[102]

The size of La Soledad was not "small," one of several deprecating adjectives used by Father Solana. He was upset that the Crown funds for the new parish church (construction was started on the south side of the plaza) had been diverted to other projects and left the new church unfinished. By his estimates, the nave was 20 varas long, the presbytery 5 varas, and the width almost 12 varas, roughly 2,200 square feet. Engineer Moncrief similarly surveyed the nave in 1765 at 23 yards long and 12 yards wide. In addition, Moncrief measured the stone sacristy to be 8 yards long by 12 yards wide and the stone entrance 8 yards long, totaling 4,320 square feet, excluding the choir loft and the two second-floor rooms (fig. 4.24).[103] La Soledad served as the parish church for sixty-two years, until 1764 and the departure of the Spanish from Florida. They took with them the furnishings. The inventory included 250 items, including tabernacles, altars, biers, images, and candlesticks.[104]

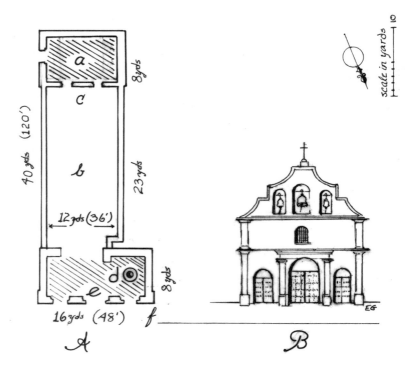

Above: 4.24. Parish church, Nuestra Señora de la Soledad, 1740–63 conceptual plan and elevation, St. Augustine. After 1702, La Soledad became the parish church. The church was rebuilt with stone ca. 1740. Conceptual view is based on 1759 descriptions of the parish priest, Father Solana, its form on various lot maps, and dimensions according to James Moncrief, engineer: stone sacristy (*a*) with two apartments above for assistant priest and acolytes; nave (*b*); altar (*c*) at western end; baptistry (*d*) and choir loft above; front (*e*) on today's St. George Street (*f*) had three stone arches, above which was the belfry wall. (Conceptual view by E. Gordon and Charles Tingley)

St. Peter's Church

Shortly after the British arrived in 1763, they set to work to remake Catholic La Soledad into Anglican St. Peter's. John Bartram wrote that it was still "repairing" in 1765.[105] Over the next twenty years they paid craftsmen more than £1,208, the total of the vouchers found to date in the British National Archives. This was a very large sum for the colonial period. For comparison, the historic brick Christ Church in Alexandria, Virginia, built at the same time, 1765–73, cost £820, excluding gallery and tower added after 1800.[106]

Work began in 1764, directed by the Anglican minister John Forbes. Forbes, a twenty-four-year-old Scotsman, was educated at the University of Aberdeen. He was related to Governor James Grant, and was appointed to Grant's ruling council in 1765. In 1768 he traveled "to Boston to be married to a young lady with some Fortune." She was Dorothy Murray (born 1738 in Boston, died 1815 in London), and her portrait was painted about 1760 by John Singleton Copley, America's leading portrait painter, well known in Boston and London as a master of realistic detail, from warts to beautiful gowns. Her portrait is in the collection of the Fogg Art Museum, Harvard University (fig. 5.16).[107] The Forbes family acquired considerable property in St. Augustine, three houses in town and two plantations.[108]

The church plan was influenced by Anglican architectural and liturgical practices of the day, as well as by the form of the preexisting Spanish building. The hand of Lieutenant Governor John Moultrie was also evident in the design. The widely respected physician and planter from St. James Parish and Charleston, South Carolina, was acting governor when in December of 1773 he forwarded a drawing of the new tower and steeple recently constructed at St. Peter's to the Board of Trade (fig 4.25).

The tower-steeple design was taken from plates XXIX–XXX in James Gibbs's *Book of Architecture* (London, 1728) (fig. 4.26). Gibbs wrote, "These two plates contain six of many more Draughts of Steeples made for St. Martins Church, with their plans."[109] His plates were widely used to design churches throughout the English colonies, many of which still stand in New England. The inspiration for using Gibbs in St. Augustine was undoubtably St. Michael's in Charleston, a church built in 1752–61 and said to be the south's most outstanding colonial adaptation of Gibbs's St. Martin-in-the-Fields (1724, London). Moultrie's father was a vestryman of St. Michael's as well as a member of the Charleston Library Society, which had a copy of the Gibbs book.[110]

St. Peter's tower and steeple cost £319, paid June 25, 1773, to the contractor John Hewitt, "being in full for building a spire to the Church of St. Peter in St. Augustine, agreeable to Plan and Elevation of the same delivered to me."[111] Practical instructions for constructing a wood steeple framework could be found in handbooks, for example, in plate 118 in William Salmon's *Palladio Londinensis, or, The London Art of Building*. Another £76 13s. 9d. were paid to Hewitt in connection with the installation of a sheet of lead that cost £17 13s. 10d. The church bells and the clock in the steeple, "the town clock," cost an additional £150. In 1778, James Watson cleaned, polished, and reinstalled the church clock. In 1772, Hewitt built a board fence with gates around the church yard for £40 and reglazed a window and installed two new locks and four bolts on the church door. He was also paid £62 in 1772 for building thirteen additional pews, two of which were more elaborate, each with a step and back.

4.25. St. Peter's Church tower and steeple, 1773, St. Augustine. St. Peter's (formerly La Soledad) was torn down by the Spanish to use the stones in the building of the cathedral. (Photograph courtesy of Public Record Office, PRO: CO 5/554, f. 3)

4.26. Church towers designed by James Gibbs: *left,* St. Martin-in-the-Fields, 1724, London; *right,* one of six drawings in plates XXIX–XXX in Gibbs's *Book of Architecture* (London, 1728). Gibbs was England's foremost church designer at the time. St. Peter's tower was adapted from Gibbs's plates and was in the prevailing style of eighteenth-century Georgian architecture influenced by Classical, Renaissance, and Baroque forms. (Sketches by E. Gordon)

He painted the pews with three coats of oil paint in imitation "stone" color and numbered them.[112]

The 70-to-80-foot tower and spire was an obvious point of pride in Moultrie's career. In July 1773, he wrote to the Lords of Trade that "I have entered into the expense of building a tower to the church of St. Augustine. I thought it necessary and almost of course as Government had most beautifully given a clock and bells to that church which had no place of reception for them; and I also thought that your Lordship would not be displeased that I expended a little on the Church, when not only real use was intended, but necessary in the appearance of the house of God for Publick Worship."[113] When he submitted the church drawing, he wrote the Lords of Trade that he had executed its construction with "as much strength, convenience, and ornament . . . as could possibly be done for the money expended thereon" in order that it "be not only of real publick utility but an ornament to this young province."[114]

The elevation drawing shows a graceful, tall, narrow spire and weathervane on a staged square and polygonal stone tower (fig. 4.25). The tower was embellished with classical quoins, keystone surrounds, Ionic columns, a clock, an oculus, and an Adamesque swag, all in the prevailing eighteenth-century Georgian style, influenced by Classical, Renaissance, and Baroque forms. The steeple was a handsome beacon and the tallest landmark on the skyline to bring sailor or horseman home.

A dramatic reversal occurred at the church with the British. Archaeology reveals that the heads of the Spanish burials in the nave were eastward, as if the deceased congregation could rise up and face the altar in the west. The British burials in the adjacent cemetery, however, were reversed; the heads were to the west. The Anglican altar was placed in accordance with Anglican practices in the 1760s in the eastern end of the church.[115]

A conjectural floor plan and elevation of La Soledad and St. Peter's is possible, based on the historical and archaeological data and the sequence of shapes on property maps by Jefferys (1763) and Moncrief (1765) before the tower was added, and those by Purcell (1777) and Rocque (1788) afterward (fig. 4.27). The conceptual plan uses the dimensions from Moncrief's large scaled lot map at the Public Record Office, England. (To test his reliability, his dimensions of the Franciscan convent on the same map match those of the Spanish carpenters and masons, and the dimensions of his Bishop's House more or less equal those drawn by Mariano de la Rocque after its conversion into the British Statehouse.)

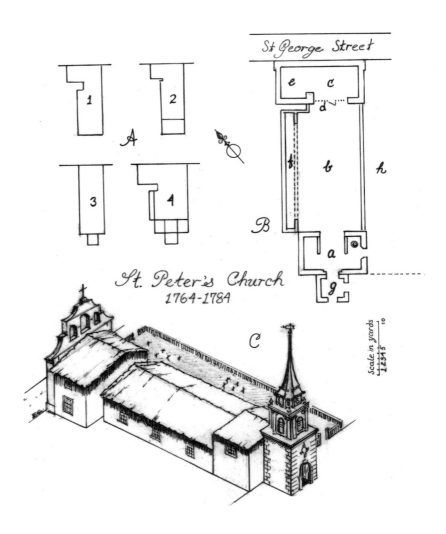

4.27. St. Peter's Church, 1764–84, conceptual plan, St. Augustine. *A.* Lot maps by: 1. Jefferys (based on Solis), 1763, and 2. Moncrief, 1765, before tower was added; 3. Pucell, 1777, and 4. Rocque, 1788, after tower was added. *B.* Conjectured floor plan: former Spanish sacristy (*a*) with attached tower (*g*); nave (*b*) with pews painted "stone" color and numbered; chancel (*c*) with chancel rail (*d*) and vestry (*e*); choir (*f*) "singing pew;" cemetery (*h*). *C.* Conjectured elevation after tower was added in 1773. (Conceptual view by E. Gordon and Charles Tingley)

When the Spanish returned to Florida in 1783, the British took leave with their pews and bells to the Bahamas. The Spanish tore down the church, tower, and spire, and used some of the stones to build the Cathedral. The site is now a parking lot owned by the Sisters of St. Joseph, beneath which are the old oyster shell footings of La Soledad/St. Peter's and many of the city's oldest burials.[116]

THE CATHEDRAL

The Cathedral is the only colonial church building still standing (pl. 22). The style of its belfry, its neoclassical portal with fluted columns, even the very stones within its walls, are relics from the earlier mission and parish churches. It was built during the second Spanish period, 1793–97. George Washington was president of the new nation to the north; Lewis and Clark had not yet seen the Pacific Ocean.

The story, however, begins much earlier, in 1572, when the parish church, Nuestra Señora de los Remedios, was built with wood planks and stood closer to the harbor. It was ransacked and burned by Sir Francis Drake in 1586, rebuilt and depicted by Hernando de Mestas about 1593 (figs. 3.4, 3.5, 3.6), and had embraced the baptism of an infant named Maria on June 25, 1594, recorded in the parish records that are now the oldest church records in the United States.[117]

The new church burned in a town fire in 1599, and a third church was erected at the site in 1602, the one that Governor Méndez de Canzo had boasted was "one of the neatest and best finished of its kind in the Indies." Governor Diego de Quiroga y Losada added a bell tower between 1687 and 1693, and in 1697 the parish church had a choir and a portico.[118]

This parish church smoldered with the rest of the town's buildings in 1702, torched by English invaders who were said to have been overwhelmed by the size of this church. After that dark day, no more churches would be built at the harbor site. The parish shifted their prayers and rituals to the church of the Virgin of Solitude (La Soledad) on St. George Street, described above. Meanwhile, a new parish church was begun near the governor's house on the southwest corner of the plaza but was never completed; its stone walls remained only a shell until Spain ceded Florida in 1763. When the Spanish returned in 1784, they converted the second floor of the British statehouse into the parish church. A decade later, the new stone Cathedral was begun.

The construction story begins on December 8, 1786, when the king of Spain ordered a new house of worship to be built in St. Augustine. Engineer Mariano de la Rocque drew plans that were rejected in 1788 as too expensive. During 1792 and 1793, Rocque reworked the construction drawings, received Crown approval, and solicited donations of tools, lime, and lumber, and recycled stones from the old churches of La Leche, Guadalupe, and La Soledad. He let out the construction contract to Miguel Isnardy, merchant-entrepreneur and former frigate captain. "Frigate captain" was a promotional route for engineers who were edu-

4.28. Cathedral, constructed 1793–97, St. Augustine. When designed by Spanish engineer Mariano de la Rocque, the front facade, of chaste design and exquisite proportions, was greatly admired. (Stereoscopic photograph before 1887 fire, courtesy of Florida State Archives)

cated in mathematics and experienced in measuring vertical angles, using triangulation and tools like the quadrant. In 1793 the cornerstone was laid.[119] Juan Nepomucena de Quesada, the new governor (1790–96), was responsible for the Cathedral; he watched its progress from his balcony. Rocque unfortunately did not live to see its completion.

Blocks of shellstone were layered up into walls 3 feet thick, 124 feet long by 42 feet wide (exterior dimensions) and 24 feet high, buttressed with pilasters and enclosing a nave calculated to hold 547 people, a presbytery, sacristy, and choir loft. The front facade rose above the gable roof and formed the belfry, stepped and curved gracefully in the *espadaña* style with five arches, four containing bells and the fifth a window. The belfry was a version of those that had graced the Franciscan church, the parish church, La Soledad, the mission church, La Leche, and, much earlier, many churches in Castilla y León and the church in Avilés, Spain, where Pedro Menéndez, founder of St. Augustine, is buried.

The main portal opened onto the plaza. This dominant motif was composed of a large wood door with wood panels and half-round wood head, set in a classical arch order flanked by paired fluted Doric columns. The columns support a full entablature with triglyphs alternating with metopes. Above was a "broken" pediment with receding planes, a design

Above: 4.29. Cathedral interior, 1797–1887, St. Augustine. The simplicity of the original nave and sanctuary matched the exterior facade. Details included a plain wood ceiling, Doric altar screen, three niches, chancel rail, box pews, movable Ionic side altars, and crystal chandeliers. (Photocopy of glass negative photo, ca. 1882, courtesy of Florida State Archives)

Left: 4.30. Parish church of Avilés, Asturias, Spain. The belfry facade of St. Augustine's cathedral is reminiscent of the parish church in the town that Pedro Menéndez de Avilés, founder of St. Augustine, came from and where he was buried in 1574. (Drawing by E. Gordon after a photograph by Homer N. Cato in Eugene Lyon's *The Enterprise of Florida*)

reminiscent of the lateral portal of the church of the Convento de San Francisco de Asís in Havana, from where Rocque had come, a beautiful example of eighteenth-century Cuban baroque.[120]

The exterior walls were plastered smooth with white plaster made from oyster shells. The flat chaste wall plane of the front facade descended from *herreriano desornamentado,* the style of Juan de Herrera at El Escorial (1563–84), the palace-monastery of King Felipe II, which became one of the most influential styles in Spain with Renaissance-inspired geometry and proportion but devoid of excessive ornamentation. The main facade of St. Augustine's *parrochial major* would be enlivened

4.31. Cathedral belfry, 1797, St. Augustine. A drawing by Harry Fenn published in William Cullen Bryant's *Picturesque America* (New York: D. Appleton, 1872) illustrates how the bells were tolled with mallets. (Photograph courtesy of SAHS)

only by the shadows cast from the neoclassical portal, corner pilasters, bell niches, and cornices that emphasized its main lines.

Behind the belfry, hidden from view, was a small shelter and a covered wood platform. Acolytes mounted steep stairs or ladders to the shelter and roof platform, and rang the bells with mallets or ropes attached to clappers. The oldest bell was cast in 1682.

Rocque, an architect of balance and harmony, designed two plain round windows in the front facade and one small round headed window in the belfry to light the choir and bell ringer's approach, repeating the arches of the bell niches and plaza portal. Two additional round headed windows were added to either side of the main doorway about 1862.

Disaster struck on the morning of April 12, 1887. The church roof caught fire and crashed into the nave. The porous nature and thickness of the coquina stone blocks saved the front facade and walls (fig. 4.32).

The sensitive restoration of the colonial church was masterminded by James Renwick (1818–1895) of New York, one of America's most accomplished architects, designer of St. Patrick's Cathedral in New York City. A brief story of the restoration follows.

4.32. Disaster struck! The cathedral roof caught fire and crashed into the nave, April 12, 1887. An anonymous photographer captured the firemen still hosing the flames. In the background is the unfinished tower of Henry Flagler's Ponce de Leon Hotel (far left), and the handsome newly built rectory with coquina cement walls and mansard roof. (Photocopy by Ken Barrett, Jr., courtesy of SAHS)

4.33. Cathedral, St. Augustine, restored after the fire of 1887 by James Renwick. His restoration was particularly sensitive to Mariano de la Rocque's colonial facade, making only one change: turning the choir window into a niche. Frances Benjamin Johnston photographed the cathedral front for the Library of Congress and Carnegie Survey of outstanding buildings in the South. In 1965, the facade was changed and the interior was even more drastically altered. (Photograph by Frances Benjamin Johnston, 1937; photocopy by Ken Barrett, Jr., courtesy of SAHS)

Epilogue

In the 1867 sketchbook of Henry J. Morton at the St. Augustine Historical Society are drawings of two structures that reveal more of colonial St. Augustine's neoclassicism, albeit as ghosts of their former elegance.[121] One is a drawing of a small building with keystone window and door surrounds (fig. 4.34). The site was on the outskirts of town, suggesting it may have been a military powder house or a hermitage. The other drawing shows a two-story wall along St. George Street with four graceful Ionic pilasters that resemble walls of eighteenth-century *palacios* in Havana (fig. 4.35). The dates and authorship of both buildings are a mystery, and both are now gone. These sketches, however, convey the cultural spirit that emboldened the little colonial town during its eighteenth-century rebirth in stone.

Some of the colonial buildings described earlier still exist in various ways. What happened to them in the postcolonial years?

Government House served as a courthouse and post office after Florida became a U.S. Territory in 1821. In 1827, Thomas Douglas, first U.S. attorney for the Eastern District, lived in the tower, which he described as five stories, 70 feet high, with excellent views of the city and comfortable during the heat of summer.[122] When Government House was renovated in 1833–34 by Robert Mills, the tower was removed, as well as the two-story wall and neoclassic portal along St. George Street, and the handsomely decorated balcony. Mills (1781–1855) was from Charleston, South Carolina, and was one of America's first native professional architects, having trained under Thomas Jefferson, Henry Benjamin Latrobe, and James Hoban, a designer of the U.S. Capitol and the White House. Mills was in Washington in 1833 as a draftsman with the land office and architectural adviser to the secretary of the treasury, who had jurisdiction over the Territory of Florida's public buildings. By 1836, Mills had been promoted to architect of public buildings. In the same year that he designed the renovation of Government House, he designed the Washington Monument.[123]

Mills did not visit St. Augustine; he drew his plan in Washington where he was influenced by new American trends. The building's Spanish facade was replaced by a facade based on one of Latrobe's Philadelphia bank designs of 1807, a project on which Mills had been superintendent of construction. Thus, Government House acquired a parapet and

4.34. Mysterious colonial building, St. Augustine. A building of unknown use, date, and site was sketched by Henry J. Morton in 1867. Constructed with coquina stone beyond the urban area, it might have been a hermitage or powder house. Whatever its attribution, the Tuscan door surround and keystone windows say much about the cultural aspirations of the eighteenth-century community. (Drawing courtesy of SAHS)

4.35. Mysterious colo-
nial wall, St. Augustine.
Long gone but fortu-
nately preserved in the
sketch book of Henry J.
Morton in 1867, it is
one more mystery in
the layers of St. Augus-
tine's colonial history.
(Courtesy of SAHS)

corner pavilions on its east facade, visible in Civil War and postwar photographs (fig. 4.36). The contractor was Elias Wallen of St. Augustine,
who ten years earlier had won the contract to renovate the old colonial
Spanish/English stone watchtower on Anastasia Island and turn it into
Florida's first Territorial Period lighthouse (fig. 4.6).[124]

In 1936, Government House was peeled back to its eighteenth-century
style by Florida architects Mellen Clark Greely and Clyde Harris (fig.
4.37). Today the building recalls the Spanish and English governors'
mansion of the colonial period but with adaptations for offices, a museum, and community events. Its formal colonial gardens, second patio,
stables and coach house, and other outbuildings were not reconstructed,
nor the tower and two-story wall with neoclassical entrance. Reduced in
its scope, Government House is nevertheless still a very important building and historical site, significant for its many government roles during
four hundred years of Florida history.

Of the two buildings that composed the British period St. Francis
Barracks, one was formerly the church and the other had been the monastery of the Spanish period Franciscans. The soldiers' quarters in what
had been the church burned in 1915. The coquina walls were left standing and were rebuilt (1922–24) in the same style as the original British
building, a central cube flanked by north and south pavilions, and
wrapped with verandas. The similarity can be seen by comparing Engineer Rocque's floor plan and elevation of 1788 and an anonymous sketch

of ca. 1835 (figs. 4,14, 4.15, 4.16), with Civil War depictions and a photograph of today's Florida National Guard Headquarters building (figs. 4.38, 4.39, 4.40).

The officers' quarters, formerly the monastery just north of the church, did not burn (fig. 4.41). Today one can walk inside the Florida National Guard Headquarters and see a few of the friars' cells and parts of the voussoirs of the arcaded cloister that have been preserved.

The site of the enormous Pile of Barracks is now the national military cemetery, containing the graves of soldiers killed December 28, 1835, in a battle of federal troops led by Major Francis L. Dade against Seminoles resisting forced relocation to western reservations. All the officers and all but two soldiers died. An African slave named Luis Pacheco also survived, but is rarely mentioned. Born and raised at New Switzerland, Francis Philip Fatio's colonial-period plantation, Pacheco could read and write and speak four languages and was an interpreter for Major Dade. He was accused of betrayal and made the scapegoat for the white-gloved career officer who ordered his command to march from Fort Brooke (Tampa) to Fort King (Ocala) despite delayed reinforcements and warnings of Seminoles in a war mood along the route.[125]

The church, Nuestra Señora de la Leche of the Pueblo Nombre de Dios, was dismantled by the Spanish and the stones were used in the construction of the new cathedral. Near where the former mission church had stood, a small chapel representing earlier churches built at the mission was constructed in stone in 1915 (fig. 4.42). It is not a reconstruction

4.36. Government House, 1870s, St. Augustine. Government House was converted in 1834 into a federal post office and courthouse by Robert Mills, who did not consider the cultural heritage of St. Augustine. His plans tore down the grand Doric entrance, the handsome balcony, and five-story tower, all built by the Spanish before 1763. (Photocopy of stereoscopic photograph by A. F. Styles, courtesy of Florida State Archives)

4.37. Government
House, 1937, St. August-
ine. Florida architects
Greely and Harris re-
stored Government
House's colonial plaza
facade in 1936 to its
original Spanish-style architecture. Many Span-
ish and English gover-
nors had entertained
lavishly in its parlors,
dining room, and gar-
dens, drinking wines and
Madeiras and eating deli-
cacies brought by sailing
ships. (Photographed by
Frances Benjamin
Johnston for the
Carnegie Survey of the
Architecture of the
South, commissioned by
the Library of Congress;
photocopy by Ken
Barrett, Jr., courtesy of
SAHS)

of La Leche based on archaeological data, nor is it large or ornate enough to fit the descriptions of Father Solana and John Bartram of the 1790s church that faced east, had a friary, *corredor,* fluted columns, frieze, carvings, and an additional room to the north reserved for pilgrimages to the statue of the Virgin nursing the baby Jesus. Its facade is closer in spirit to the simplified Doric facade that Engineer Rocque designed in 1792 for churches along the St. Johns and St. Mary's Rivers (fig. 4.43).[126]

The Cathedral stands today, but its colonial facade and interior are somewhat altered. After the 1887 fire, which spared the coquina walls, belfry, and entrance facade, the church was restored by James Renwick. Renwick was sixty-seven years old at the time and one of America's most accomplished architects. Working in more than one style throughout his career, he had designed churches in the Gothic and Romanesque styles in New York City. His design for the Corcoran Gallery (1859–61) in Washington (now the Smithsonian's Renwick Gallery) was one of

1. Calusa chief's house, ca. 1566, at capital town, coastal southwest Florida. According to Spanish documents, the structure, elevated on a platform mound, was large enough for two thousand people to stand inside without being very crowded. The structure may have been a community lodge rather than the domicile of the king himself. (Conceptual drawing by Merald Clark for the Hall of South Florida People and Environments, Powell Hall, copyright 2001 Florida Museum of Natural History, Gainesville)

2. Apalachee council house, ca. 1656, Mission San Luis, Tallahassee, reconstructed in 2000 by the state of Florida according to archaeological and historical data. The original Indian structure of ca. 1656 was said to hold between two thousand and three thousand people, the largest historic period Indian building in the Southeast. Built during the Spanish mission period, it was erected using traditional Indian construction practices, without European tools or hardware. (Photograph by Merald Clark, copyright 2001 Florida Museum of Natural History)

Above, 3. Apalachee council house interior, ca. 1656, Mission San Luis, Tallahassee, reconstructed 2000. During excavation and reconstruction, archaeologists discovered that benches and cabins had lined the circular wall of the original Indian council house in 1656. The council house was the seat of village government where delegations from other villages met. It also served as an overnight lodge and community center, where the Apalachee received Spanish officials, held feasts, and performed ceremonial dances. Underneath the cabins were corncob-burning smudge pits that produced light, heat for individual cooking, and enough smoke to drive away the mosquitoes. (Photograph by Merald Clark, copyright 2001 Florida Museum of Natural History)

Left, 4. Apalachee council house, interior framework, ca. 1656, Mission San Luis, Tallahassee, reconstructed 2000. The reconstruction of the circular timber frame required modern mechanical cranes and chain saws, and 56,000 palm fronds to cover. Three hundred and fifty years ago, however, the original structure was erected with hand labor and cordage. Dwarfed by the timbers, archaeologist Bonnie McEwan is standing next to the vertical post in the middle, demonstrating the tremendous height of the structure and the size of the roof opening that was both skylight and hearth ventilator. Indian construction technology was far more advanced than previously known. (Photograph by Merald Clark, copyright 2001 Florida Museum of Natural History)

5. Church, ca. 1690, Mission San Luis, reconstructed 1999, Tallahassee. Archaeological and historical data indicate the mission church was some 100 feet long by 50 feet wide and 50 feet high. In a triumph of faith, and with no pretense of monumentality, the Franciscan friars in the Florida wilderness probably laid out their churches using pegs and cords and a system of sacred numbers that had formulated the aesthetics of church building for centuries. Bishop Gabriel Díaz Vara Calderón visited the Florida missions in 1674 and wrote that the Indians were "great carpenters as is evidenced by the construction of their wooden churches which are large and painstakingly wrought." (Photograph courtesy of Florida Division of Historical Resources)

6. Church interior, ca. 1690, Mission San Luis, Tallahassee. The Franciscan mission church has been faithfully reconstructed with traditional long narrow nave and sanctuary. The architecture was European, but the large wooden church with palm thatch roof was constructed by Apalachee artisans. (Photograph courtesy of Florida Division of Historical Resources)

7. Castillo de San Marcos, begun 1672, St. Augustine. The plan of the fort was a square, equally strong on all sides, with a wide terreplein forming the gun deck and four bastions at each corner. The bastions were key architectural elements that allowed the cannons to crossfire in all directions. Each diamond-shaped bastion was four-sided and had its own name: San Agustín (southeast), San Carlos (northeast), San Pablo (northwest), and San Pedro (southwest). Around the fortress was a moat filled with seawater. Engineer Ignacio Daza laid out the initial plan, and many engineer-architects, *maestros de obras* (master contractors), and master masons arrived from Europe and Spanish America to complete the fort, which was designated a National Monument in 1924. (Photograph courtesy of Janet Goodrich)

8. Castillo de San Marcos, sentry tower and San Carlos bastion, 1740, St. Augustine. Construction of the massive fort began in 1672, with blocks of coquina stone quarried on Anastasia Island and rafted across Matanzas Bay. The sentry tower was completed just before General Oglethorpe and the English attacked in 1740. Construction of the tower was supervised by Engineer Pedro Ruiz de Olano, from Havana. It has a *media naranja* (half orange) dome similar to fortification towers in Nueva España (Mexico) and Cuba. Originally covered with white oyster-shell lime stucco and trimmed with red, the stone fort has weathered to gray over the course of some three hundred years. (Photograph by M. Gordon)

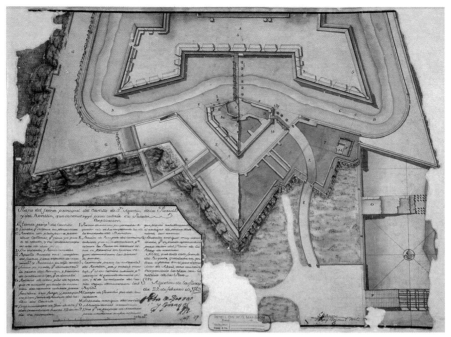

9. *Plano del frente principal del Castillo de San. Agustín de la Florida,* February 22, 1763, by Engineer Pedro de Brozas y Garay, who had come from Ceuta (Spanish Morocco) in 1752 to complete the enormous stone fort begun almost a hundred years earlier. Engineer Brozas y Garary drew plans for rebuilding the ravelin, the outer defense fortification that would protect the entrance gate and the curtain, the main wall between the bastions. (Courtesy of Public Record Office, PRO: WO 78/1017)

10. Castillo de San Marcos, chapel entrance, St. Augustine, 1785, restored 1915. Designed by the royal engineer, Mariano de la Rocque, the handsome portal with its Doric arch order was formed with the local stone and plaster. The fort chapel, storerooms, powder magazines, prisons, and quarters surrounding the courtyard were massively vaulted to withstand bombardment and support the ramparts and cannons above. (Photograph by M. Gordon)

Left, 11. Nuestra Señora de la Leche y Buen Parto, anonymous painting, 1760, of an icon in Saint Augustine dating from the late sixteenth century, when the mission church at Pueblo Nombre de Dios became associated with a statue of the Blessed Virgin nursing the infant Jesus. This painting of the statue "is the oldest known representation of the oldest known devotion to the Virgin Mary in North America," according to Dr. Miguel A. Bretos of the Smithsonian Institution. (Collection of the Regional Museum of Anthropology and History at Campeche, Mexico. Photograph by Renée Zapata, courtesy of Dr. Bretos)

Below, 12. Convento de San Francisco, founded 1588, St. Augustine, conceptual view about 1750. The monastery was the Spanish Franciscan mission headquarters; the site is now the Florida National Guard Headquarters. (Watercolor by Peg Richardson)

13. *View of the Governor's House at St. Augustine, in E. Florida, Nov. 1764*, anonymous. The Governor's House has been on the same site since 1598. Behind the wall and Doric portal was a very large *palacio* with many outbuildings, courtyards, a five-story tower and an exquisite Moorish-inspired balcony. (Courtesy of British Library, Maps K. Top. 122.86-2-a)

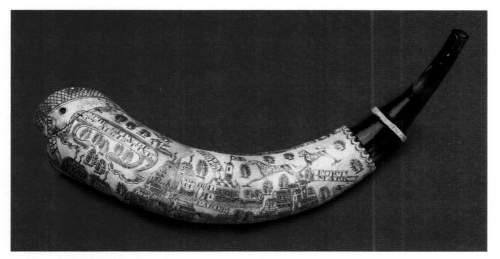

14. St. Augustine Powder Horn, 1765, carved by an anonymous seaman. In the center is the Spanish-built governor's mansion with its tower, balcony, Doric entrance, balustraded wall, and fruit trees brimming over the garden wall. (Collection of the Museum of Florida History, Tallahassee)

15. Spanish house, ca. 1656–1704, San Luis, Tallahassee, reconstructed on its original site, replicating the floor plan and materials found by archaeologists in 1999. (Photograph courtesy of Florida Division of Historical Resources)

The Old House
on St. Francis Street,
St. Augustine, Fla.

16. González-Peavett-Alvarez House ("Oldest House"), ca. 1720, 1775, St. Augustine, owned and restored by the SAHS. When the Spanish house of ca. 1720 was bought by a British couple in 1775, they turned it into a tavern. They added the wood second floor and many of the features that had worked well for others in the warm Florida climate. (Vintage postcard, collection of E. Gordon)

17. Llambias House, early eighteenth century and 1770s, St. Augustine. The Llambias House typifies the St. Augustine style, a combination of colonial Spanish, English, and Caribbean building practices that responded to the climate and available local materials. (Photograph by M. Gordon)

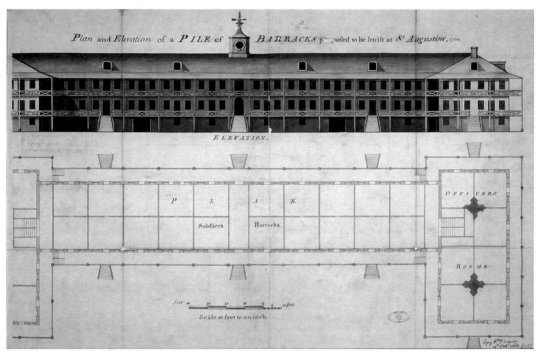

18. Pile of Barracks plan and elevation, St. Augustine, drawn by William Brasier, 1768. The largest building in English Florida was built in 1772 where the national cemetery is today on Marine Street. (Courtesy of Public Record Office, PRO: MPG 1/351 [1])

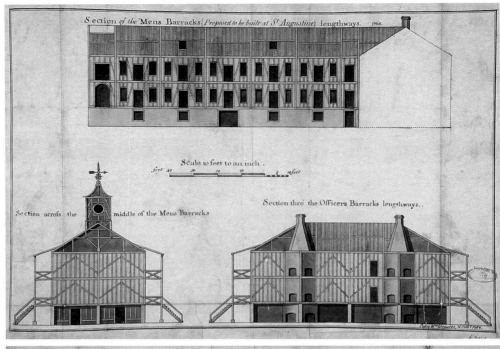

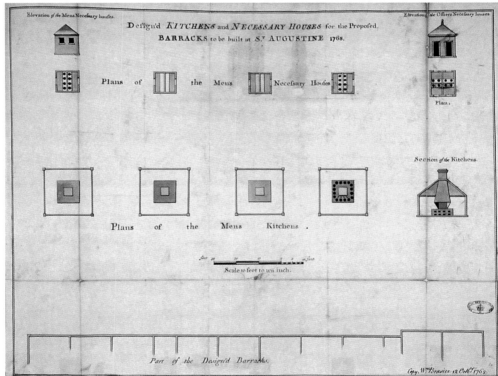

19. Pile of Barracks, sections, kitchens, and "necessary houses," drawn by William Brasier, 1768, St. Augustine. The estimated cost of construction was £6,680, including 164 pairs of shutters, 800 panes of glass 9 by 10 inches, 88 four-paneled doors, 19½ barrels of paint and 110 gallons of linseed oil. The wood stories burned during the second Spanish period. (Courtesy of Public Record Office, PRO: MPG 1/351)

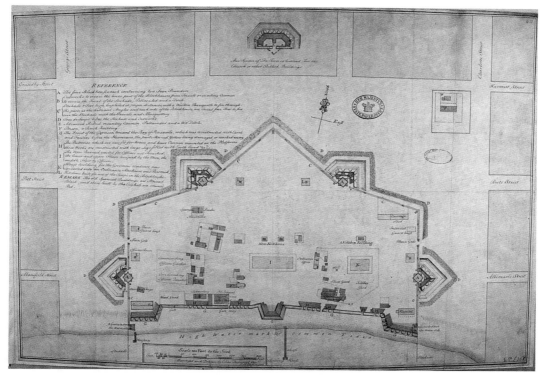

20. Pensacola, 1778. The plan drawn by Elias Durnford, captain of engineers, shows the English buildings in red and the former Spanish buildings in black. Governor Chester refused to live in the former Spanish governor's house (lower right) and had Durnford design a large new governor's mansion (*K*), half the size of the barracks (*I*). Begun in 1770 at an estimated cost of £2,500, construction came to a halt in 1778, the funds exhausted. (Courtesy of Public Record Office, PRO: MPG 358)

21. Greenfield Plantation, ca. 1767, conceptual elevation, British West Florida. Arthur and Eleanor Neil (he was keeper of British ordnance) owned 2,000 acres on which they built their raised house. (Conjectural drawing by F. Blair Reeves)

Left, 22. Cathedral, constructed 1793–97, in St. Augustine, during the second Spanish occupation of Florida. The facade, bathed in sunlight, faces the city's central plaza and reaches toward heaven with a stepped and curved belfry. (Photograph by E. Gordon)

Below, 23. Espinosa-Sanchez House, eighteenth century, St. Augustine. The beautiful arcaded loggia, composed of stone pier arches, was added soon after the Spanish returned in 1784 to a house built before 1763. This loggia is one of the best dating from the colonial era. (Photograph copyright 1995 Ken Barrett, Jr., from *The Houses of St. Augustine,* used by permission of Pineapple Press)

24. Murat House, ca. 1790, St. Augustine. Don Antonio Huertas, an Indian interpreter, built his small stone house on the site of an earlier stone house and incorporated some of its architectural details. The "Spanish" balcony, however, was a Victorian whimsy with novelty shingles and jigsawn balusters. The house was named for Prince Achille Murat, nephew of Napolean Bonaparte and friend of the Marquis de Lafayette, who briefly resided in the house before he married Catherine Daingerfield Willis Gray, grandniece of George Washington. The house is now part of Old St. Augustine Village, operated by the Museum of Arts and Sciences, Daytona Beach. (Photograph by M. Gordon)

25. Kingsley Plantation House, ca. 1798, Fort George Island. Situated on one of Florida's barrier islands, close to the rivers and inlets that were its main transportation routes, is Florida's only surviving colonial plantation house. The four-corner pavilions with pyramidal roofs are its most distinctive characteristic. (Photograph by M. Gordon)

26. Anna Jai House, ca. 1798 and 1817, Kingsley Plantation, Fort George Island. Originally the kitchen for the main house, part of the first floor was built with tabby bricks, an oyster shell concrete molded into bricks. There was a large clay brick cooking hearth. (Photograph by M. Gordon)

27. Tabby slave house ruins, ca. 1820, Kingsley Plantation, Fort George Island. In the ruins of the oyster shell tabby are the vestiges of the large fireplace hearth, lined with clay bricks, where the slave family cooked. (Photograph by M. Gordon)

28. Tabby slave house, ca. 1820, restored 1980s, Kingsley Plantation, Fort George Island. (Photograph by M. Gordon)

29. Lavalle-Bonifay House, ca. 1803–15, Pensacola, a duplex built for Carlos Lavalle and Marianna Bonifay. It is typical of the vernacular Gulf Coast or French Creole raised cottage style house that once dominated the region's architecture. The exterior red trim is a reproduction of the original color made from local red clay. (Photograph by E. Gordon)

30. Barkley House, early 1800s, Pensacola. Barkley House fronted the harbor of Pensacola and, like many French colonial plantation houses, was raised high off the ground and wrapped in a spacious veranda. (Photograph courtesy of Florida Division of Historical Resources)

31. New Smyrna sugar mill ruins, Volusia County. The pictured archways were part of the large sugar mill, once rumored to be a Spanish mission, built by Henry Cruger and William Depeyster of New York. (Photograph courtesy of Florida Division of Historical Resources)

32. Bulow Plantation ruins, Flagler County. More than sixty buildings were built ca. 1820–30 by John Joachim Bulow. The plantation was burned during the Second Seminole War in 1836, leaving only the chimney stacks and arches of the sugar works, the largest in East Florida. (Photograph by M. Gordon)

4.38. St. Francis Barracks, former Spanish church (1737) converted into British barracks in 1771, St. Augustine. When sketched in 1863, the 92-year-old British colonial barracks housed Union troops. (Sketch by Edward Clifford Brush, 1863; photocopy courtesy of Florida State Archives)

4.39. St. Francis Barracks, St. Augustine. The east facade was photographed ca. 1863–65, showing that the cupola had disappeared. The coquina facade is stuccoed and scored to look like stone, and upper window sashes have twelve lights. (Photograph by Samuel A. Cooley, courtesy of SAHS)

4.40. Florida National Guard Headquarters, formerly St. Francis Barracks, Marine Street, St. Augustine. The present building owes its architecture to the colonial English engineers who designed the barracks around the 1737 Franciscan church. (Photograph by M. Gordon)

4.41. St. Francis Barracks, St. Augustine. When the old friary was photographed ca. 1863–65, the south wall clearly revealed the random ashlar of the Spanish masons of the 1740s. The stonework can still be seen inside the building that is today the Florida National Guard Headquarters. (Photograph by Samuel A. Cooley; photocopy by Ken Barrett, Jr., courtesy of SAHS)

4.42. Our Lady of La Leche Shrine, St. Augustine. This small stone chapel faces north and is not an architectural reconstruction of the mission church Nuestra Señora de la Leche. (Photocopy courtesy of Florida State Archives)

America's first major Second Empire–style buildings. His career culminated with the Gothic design of St. Patrick's Cathedral in New York City (1858–89), conceived on a scale and style unmatched in America and considered the country's most prestigious church of the nineteenth century.[127]

Renwick sensitively restored the St. Augustine Cathedral's original front facade as designed by Engineer Rocque, removing only the clock and turning the arched window above the entrance into a niche held by a winged angel (fig. 4.33). He replicated the original wood paneled door and added fireproof tile to the roof. He added east and west transepts and twelve feet to the exterior length of the church. He designed the oak pulpit and main altar with its figures of Pope Pius V and St. Francis of Borgia sculpted by J. Massey Rhind of New York City in the finest Carrara marble. To enclose the church yard, Renwick added a cast concrete wall suggesting Gothic tracery, a section of which is preserved on St. George Street (fig. 4.44).[128]

Vista del Frente principal

San Agustín de la Florida 31 de Marzo de 1792

4.43. Principal facade of churches proposed for the St. Johns and St. Marys Rivers, by Spanish engineer Mariano de la Rocque, 1792. Rocque's respect for simplicity and harmonious proportions, is so apparent in this elegantly curved gable with a flat wall plane ornamented by the Tuscan portal. He applied these same characteristics to his design for the cathedral constructed during 1793–97. (Redrawn by E. Gordon after Rocque in East Florida Papers, Bundle 176g14)

The church fire had occurred just as Henry Flagler was completing his magnificent Hotel Ponce de Leon (fig. 4.32). He was promoting St. Augustine as the "Newport of the South" and Florida as the "American Riviera" to win tourists to his hotels.[129] The blackened skeleton of the church was only a block away on the plaza. He is thought to have provided financial assistance, if not his subcontractors, to hasten the church's restoration.

Renwick designed the new campanile west of the church. The 120-foot-tall bell tower reflected the spirit of the nearby architecture of Henry Flagler, and was cast in the same coquina shell concrete that was a hallmark of the Flagler hotels and churches (fig. 4.45). The steeple complemented the height, size, color, and texture of the nearby Hotel Ponce de Leon towers designed by John Mervin Carrère and Thomas Hastings, the young architects whose fame thereafter grew immensely. They were roofed by the same tile-roof contractor, J. K. Smith of Waterbury, Con-

4.44. Cathedral yard wall remnant, designed by James Renwick, 1888, St. Augustine. The wall was removed in 1966, but a section was saved and moved to St. George Street. (Photograph by M. Gordon)

4.45. Campanile, 1888, St. Augustine, designed by James Renwick. The bell tower (*far left*) stands west of the cathedral. During renovations in 1966, this distinguished link to the Flagler era was covered up with a modern white coating, and the separation in time between the Victorian era Flagler towers and the colonial cathedral slipped away. (Photograph by George Barker, ca. 1891; photocopy courtesy of Florida State Archives)

necticut. The working drawings were made by the supervising architect, William T. Cotter, of Sanford, Florida.[130]

In 1965–66, the church underwent extensive interior alterations. The ceiling was dramatically opened and the exposed beams painted; the Renwick altar was changed, hydraulic cement tiles were laid on the floor, and murals were painted on the walls. It is on the exterior, however, that an opportunity was missed to preserve the original colonial facade as designed by Rocque and restored by Renwick (figs. 4.28, 4.33). Commissioned by Archbishop Joseph P. Hurley, the Cleveland architect George Wesley Stickle removed the two 1797 roundels and the 1797-style paneled door, and squared the arched windows flanking the entrance, contrary to the original harmony of all the arches of the Spanish belfry, choir window niche, and main portal. Stickle also eliminated part of the original pediment. The simplicity of Rocque's chaste facade was supplanted by plaster swirls and coats of arms (pl. 22).[131]

A modern covering called Kenatex was applied to the exterior of both the two-hundred-year-old colonial coquina church and the hundred-year-old Flagler-era coquina concrete campanile.[132] This obliterated their unique connections to two different periods in St. Augustine's history. Such facade changes are today in marked contrast to restorations of historic churches like that of San Xavier del Bac, Tucson, Arizona, built in the same year (1797), and recently restored with such care that the original plaster coatings were replicated with the boiled juice of the cactus plant as binder. Changes of the nature described above may hopefully be past history. The Cathedral is now designated a National Historic Landmark (1972) and was proclaimed a Minor Basilica by Pope Paul VI, one of twenty-four so honored in the United States in recognition of historic significance.

5 | The St. Augustine Style

I believe that architecture has its own tasks and that its essence is the act of construction.[1]

Peter Zumthor, winner, 1998 International Carlsberg Architecture Prize

Out of colonial St. Augustine came a unique regional style of architecture—not a revival but a vernacular architecture of needs and place, history and culture.

The St. Augustine style was drafted at the site. Its form was somewhat controlled by the town plans of 1572 and 1598, cataclysmic events in history, the characteristics of the native shellstone that was its primary local material, the coastal climate, and traditions transplanted from other countries, particularly the "mother countries" of Spain and England. The Spanish gave St. Augustine's architecture initial direction and many of its most endearing elements, including the roofed balconies corbeled over public streets. The English grafted onto Spanish beginnings characteristics of their own Caribbean architecture. The amalgamation resulted from their mutual respect for the local coquina stone and architectural elements that were responsive to the climate (pl. 17).

The style endured. It was repeated over and over by arriving citizens without regard to nationality or any *one* country's tastes. Leitmotifs of the colonial St. Augustine style are thick and cool masonry walls, second stories of stone or wood, arcaded loggias and *galerías* overlooking rear gardens and patios, pitched roofs, glazed window sashes, roofed balconies suspended on double beams, and houses built up to the edges of narrow streets and entered through side gardens or courtyard walls and exterior staircases.

This chapter seeks an understanding of the cohesiveness and strengths of the vernacular St. Augustine style as a response to culture, history, and environment.

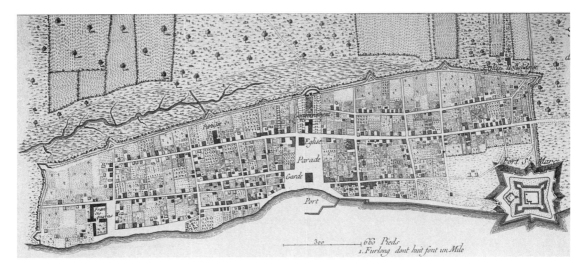

5. *St. Augustine, the Capital of East Florida.* Lot maps showing locations and ground floor plans of colonial streets and dwellings are gold mines for historians. The present map was engraved by Thomas Jefferys, London, from a survey of the Spanish town by Don Juan de Solis, ca. 1763, and was first published in London in 1763, republished in 1769 and 1777 by various publishers, including this edition by George Louis le Rouge, Paris, ca. 1777. (Courtesy of SAHS)

THE MAKING OF A FLORIDA STYLE

St. Augustine was established in 1565; for the next 137 years, colonists built their dwellings with perishable materials: wood and thatch. Fires, rot, hurricanes, pirates, and English raids repeatedly destroyed the sixteenth- and seventeenth-century buildings. The town was raked and torched by James Moore's marauders in 1702, but this time the flames were the catalyst that sent colonists scurrying to the shellstone quarries and oyster shell mounds to seek the fireproof material of their fort. The magnificent Castillo de San Marcos, constructed of coquina between 1672 and 1695, had survived while the town of wood burned.

Professional engineers, *maestros de obras,* stonecutters, and masons had been brought to St. Augustine to build the first phase of the fort at the end of the seventeenth century, and many more would come during the next century to enlarge and improve the defenses of the Spanish capital. The engineer-architects had been trained in Europe, and came to Florida from building experiences in Spain, Cuba, Mexico, north Africa, Venezuela, England, Scotland, and the West Indies. Their masters of construction were equally well trained after years of apprenticeships in Europe and the New World. They developed techniques for quarrying the submerged coquina shellstone on Anastasia Island and rafting it across the harbor, where they expertly layered it up into permanent walls enhanced with columns, pilasters, and arcades.[2]

During the eighteenth century, the talents of these Spanish and English engineer-architects and masters of construction were put to work enclosing and armoring the town against enemies and tidal surges and building barracks, churches, government buildings, hospitals, large residences, and the governor's house. The presence of these professionals and the availability of stone also held the promise for more permanent residences.

During the first two decades of the eighteenth century, the Spanish colonists made architecture in basic block forms, simple volumes with thick stone walls. Their dwellings consisted of one to three buildings with one to four rooms, flat roofs of wood and lime mortar, or gable roofs of palm thatch or wood shingles. Interior rooms were partitioned by walls of stone, wood planks, or oyster shell tabby cast in place in layers with wood uprights sometimes embedded for strength. Tabby floors with crushed coquina shellstone aggregate were similarly poured in place; when the floor wore out, a new tabby floor was poured on top. Window openings were protected by grilles and shutters (fig. 5.1).[3]

Like the wood houses they replaced, the stone *casas* lined the edges of narrow streets or footpaths to conserve as much of the lot as possible for detached kitchen houses, wells, storehouses, and kitchen gardens. Some house walls were constructed with large hewn stones; others were built with roughly trimmed small stones (*mampostería*). The porous stone was covered with smooth coats of white plaster and whitewashed inside and out to protect and seal. The new *casas* gleamed white under the Florida sunlight just like their guardian fort, the Castillo de San Marcos. The plaster was made from burned oyster shells to make quicklime, which was mixed in a pit in the backyard with sand and water. Whitewash was said to bind better with salt, a custom brought from Spain.[4] Later, the English in East Florida would add a sizing made from varnish or resins to their whitewash.

The built landscape in the early 1700s assumed a solidness that had been lacking in wood and thatch architecture. The houses and narrow streets were reminiscent of those in earlier Roman, Islamic, and Spanish towns. There was a new sense of permanency and cultural expectation, and an aesthetic link to eighteenth-century Spain, Cuba, and Mexico.

Construction of the González-Peavett-Alvarez House, known as the Oldest House, began about 1720 in the simple forms and materials described above (pl. 16; fig. 5.2). The Llambias House would soon follow, both on St. Francis Street, then called Convent Lane, south of today's

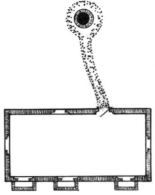

5.1. Llambias House, conceptual elevation and plan, early eighteenth century, St. Augustine. The Spanish-built stone house had one floor and a flat roof, with parapet and rain spouts. Walls were thick and cool, and the window openings were large, protected by grilles and wood shutters, traditions that came from warm Mediterranean and Caribbean climates. (Drawing by E. Gordon adapted from a drawing by Stuart Moffett Barnette, College of Architecture, Cornell University, restoration architect of Llambias House, courtesy of SAHS)

plaza (pl. 17; figs. 5.1, 5.3). Each had one story, a flat roof and parapet, and one or two rooms that today comprise their first floors. Their second stories, Spanish-style balconies and arcaded loggias would come during the British period.[5]

Variations of the simple rectangular floor plan were built at the Bishop's House (*palacio episcopal*) a decade or two later, and at the Treasurer's House about the same time. Their floor plans consisted of two rectangular blocks joined at right angles to form L-shaped houses. Both were one-storied and constructed in the Spanish idiom with flat roofs, parapets, and burnt clay or cypress waterspouts that carried off the rain water. Under their flat roofs were not only more and larger rooms but arcaded loggias opening onto patios and gardens.[6]

The Bishop's House, *la Casa de Piedra de los Señores Obispos,* had been built by 1735 when Bishop Francisco de San Buenaventura y Tejada, the first resident bishop, arrived from Seville, Spain. The house enclosed about 3,548 square feet in nine rooms, excluding the arcaded

5.2. Oldest House, ca. 1720, first floor interior, St. Augustine. Thick walls were laid up with blocks of coquina stone by some unknown Spanish owner, plastered and whitewashed to weatherproof the porous stone. The floor was coquina tabby. In the corner is a fireplace added by the English owners, who also added the second floor ca. 1775. (1954 photograph by Florida State News Bureau, courtesy of Florida State Archives)

5.3. *St. Francis Street* (Convent Lane), St. Augustine. Along St. Francis Street are some of the oldest St. Augustine style residences. The Oldest House (González-Peavett-Alvarez House), is on the right. Farther up the street, on the other side, is the Llambias House. (Wood engraving by Frederick William Quarterly after a watercolor painting by Henry Fenn, published in *Picturesque America,* edited by William Cullen Bryant, 1872, collection of E. Gordon)

loggia. During the British years, the Bishop's House would be greatly expanded, with two new wings and a second floor with pitched roof, when it became the statehouse (figs. 4.17, 4.18, 4.19).[7]

The Treasurer's House was a slightly smaller version of the *palacio episcopal*. It was L-shaped and flat-roofed in 1742 when Don Juan Estevan de Peña moved in and took up his duties as royal treasurer. It was still L-shaped in 1763 when Don Elíxio de la Puente platted it for the departing Spanish. After the British arrived, four chimneys and glazed sashes were added, and the house was enlarged with a third wing, extending the L into a U-shaped one-story house wrapped around a patio. Engineer Moncrief's 1765 scaled lot map shows the enlarged house had roughly 3,024 square feet. Several L-shaped houses had appeared on Elíxio de la Puente's property map drawn at the end of the Spanish period in 1763, and many more U-shaped houses would appear on the maps of the English and returning Spanish (map 5).[8] From 1772 to 1778, it was the residence of Lieutenant Governor John Moultrie. Later, during the Territorial Period, a wood second story was added by a doctor from Connecticut. The 1740s Treasurer's House still exists, now the first floor of the Peña-Peck House, on St. George Street north of the plaza.[9]

The flat roof at the Bishop's House was described in 1759 as *sotea* by the parish priest, Father Juan Joseph Solana.[10] Albert Manucy's definition of *sotea* (also *azotea*) in *The Houses of St. Augustine* is "flat roof, generally a tabby slab supported by solid board sheathing. Also a flat roof made of two or more layers of brick-like tile [with mortar between] supported upon spaced wooden slats."[11] However, the study of tabby by Janet Gritzner suggests that early flat roofs in La Florida during the sixteenth and seventeenth centuries were not tabby (a concrete made with an aggregate), but instead planks covered with a lime mortar similar to contemporary roofs in Andalucía, Spain (still a practice there today), and that the terminology for flat roofs in the eighteenth century does not make their material content all that clear.[12]

John Bartram described flat roofs in St. Augustine in 1765 as "flat roofed & terraced on top." He also described walks, seats, and staircases as "terraced."[13] William Salmon's popular builder's handbook, published in several editions between 1755 and 1773, has a "Builder's Dictionary" that defines "terras" as "an open walk or gallery, also a flat roof," without specifying any materials.[14] John Hewitt, master contractor during the British period in East Florida, submitted a voucher to the government for one gallon of linseed oil for the "terrass" on the new [wood] bridge on the road to the ferry.[15]

5.4. Peña-Peck House (Treasurer's House), 1740s, 1772, 1820s, St. Augustine. In 1742, the house was L-shaped, with the traditional Spanish flat roof and *canales* (waterspouts). A loggia opened onto the kitchen garden and orchard. In 1772, the English expanded the L into a U-shaped residence for British lieutenant governor John Moultrie. During the Territorial Period (1821–45), an American, Dr. Seth Peck from Old Lyme, Connecticut, chose to take up the St. Augustine style of building and added the wood second story and a balcony at the south end. (Photograph by Ken Barrett, Jr.)

Bartram distinguishes between walls of "hewn shel stone" and those of "ouster shells & morter" (tabby), going to great length to describe the latter as a concrete composed of an aggregate of oyster shells pounded into mortar. He does not, however, specifically associate oyster shell concrete (tabby) with his "terrace" roofs. Spanish flat roofs had, using John Bartram's words, "battlements" (crenelated parapets) made of stone, and "pipes" (waterspouts) projecting through the parapets, "A foot or more to carry of[f] ye [rain] water," made mostly of "burnt clay."[16] The presence of flat roofs in the wet tropical climate of Florida in the eighteenth century reveals that some Spanish colonists were still reluctant to abandon older traditions, even those that were not appropriate for the climate.[17]

The majority of the first Spanish stone dwellings were one-storied.[18] Two-story residences of stone were built on footings consisting of trenches filled with oyster shells and poured tabby, to which the first layer of the coquina blocks were mortared. Two examples of early two-storied stone houses were the Menéndez Marquéz House and the Elíxio de la

Puente House. The ample Menéndez Marquéz House was built as a residence for the royal accountant, Don Francisco Menéndez Marquéz. The house was converted into the royal hospital in 1743 and later into the British courthouse (figs. 4.20, 4.21). The house was a stone cube, its east facade flush with what is now Aviles Street. By the time it exemplified the St. Augustine style, incorporating Spanish and English characteristics, it had the requisite loggia (in this case, not arcaded, but stone post and wood lintel), second floor *galería,* exterior stone staircase, steeply pitched hip roof with cypress shingles, floors of both tabby and wood, and sash windows. The kitchen was a detached stone house. There were some four thousand square feet of roofed space. To enter the house, one passed through the side walled courtyard (40 by 45 feet) south of the house and thence into the loggia where the main door was located. The garden was to the west. The Menéndez Marquéz House is gone, destroyed by fire during the second Spanish period, but historical documents and the plans drawn to scale by engineer James Moncrief reveal its vernacular St. Augustine style.[19]

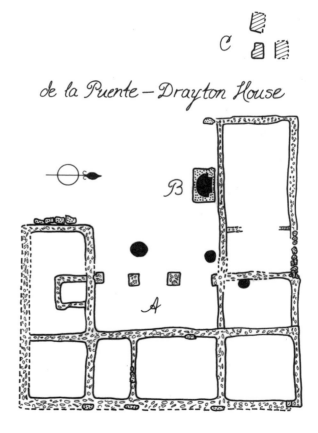

de la Puente — Drayton House

5.5. Elíxio de la Puente-Drayton House, eighteenth-century foundation, St. Augustine. The stone house faced the harbor on Marine Street and had a large quiet inner patio and loggia (*A*). The garden well (*B*) was formed with coquina stone in the shape of the scallop shell associated with the Apostle St. James, patron saint of Christian Spain and the Knights of Santiago. Discreetly hidden were the English privies (*C*). (Redrawn by E. Gordon from archaeological data, courtesy of SAHS)

The Elíxio de la Puente-Drayton House, on Marine Street south of the plaza, was also a very large stone house. The first owner of record before 1763 was the wealthy Don Juan Joseph Elíxio de la Puente, a Spanish treasury official, but its date of construction was several decades earlier. Between 1772 and 1784, it was owned by William Drayton, wealthy resident of Charleston, South Carolina, who came to East Florida to be chief justice. In 1784 he sold the house, office, outhouses, and waterfront lot to Frederick William Hecht, former deputy commissary general in New York, Boston, and Charleston, for £1,107. Excavations of its U-shaped foundations reveal an oyster shell bedding (fig. 5.5). It was a two-story block with pitched roof and a balcony facing the harbor, and wings in the rear enclosing a patio. Four piers or columns in the loggia supported a *galería* above. In the garden, an earlier Spanish resident (Elíxio de la Puente?) had added a very unusual stone well shaped like the scallop shell carried by pilgrims for drinking water en route to Santiago de Compostela and the shrine of St. James (*Yago,* or Santiago), patron saint of Christian Spain.[20] The house was still standing on the eve of the Civil War, but shorn of its balcony overlooking the harbor (fig. 5.6). The house was demolished in the 1880s.

Organizational patterns of town lots were the same during Spanish and English periods. Houses were built close to the streets. Kitchen houses were separate, as were storage houses and privies. Kitchen gardens, orchards, and wells took up the remainder of the lot. The British

5.6. Elíxio de la Puente-Drayton House, 1740s?–1880s, St. Augustine. It was about 140 years old when it was demolished in the 1880s, such was the enduring nature of the coquina stone. (Drawn and engraved on wood by John S. Horton, 1855; reprinted by St. Augustine National Bank, 1955)

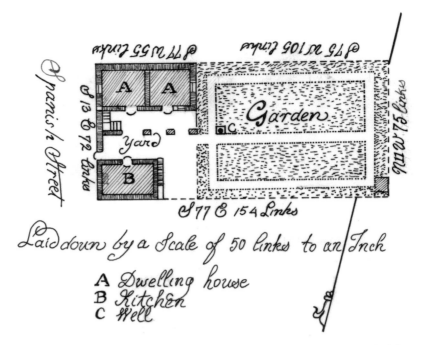

5.7. Samuel Hrabawski's town lot and house plan, 1771, St. Augustine. Typical St. Augustine style lot patterns developed early in the first Spanish period were similarly laid out through the English and second Spanish periods. Hrabawski's house was built up to the edge of the street and consisted of two buildings of stone: the two-story dwelling house (*A*) and the kitchen house (*B*). The kitchen garden with well (*C*) took up about two-thirds of the lot. (Drawing by E. Gordon after survey at Public Record Office, PRO: T 77/8, f. 206.)

loyalist claims reveal that kitchens and storage houses constructed with stone were the most valuable.

The lot layout of one Samuel Hrabawski, drawn by a surveyor for the owner's loyalist claim in 1784 when the English had to leave Florida, exemplifies the St. Augustine style dwelling. Hrabawski built his residence during the British period on a vacant lot granted to him in 1771, located on Spanish Street (described as "Number 2 in Box's Quarter, southwardly of the late James Box, east of George Rolfes"). The lot measured 105 feet by 50 feet (using 7.92 inches to the "link" in the surveyor's chain, the form of measurement used on his survey). Typical of the St. Augustine style, his residence was composed of two structures, the dwelling house and the kitchen house, both "built of stone and lime in excellent repair." The dwelling house was 36.6 feet by 16 feet, partitioned into two rooms on the ground floor (probably repeated on the second floor). There was a loggia opening onto a courtyard, protecting an outside stairway to a second-floor gallery (veranda, piazza) supported by three stone columns and the stairwell. Rooms were entered from the loggia and gallery. A gated wall along Spanish Street enclosed the "yard" (courtyard). The stone kitchen house, across the yard, opposite the main house, was a substantial kitchen (33 feet by 16.6 feet), and may also have served as a dining room and pantry. A ladder in the drawing hints that the kitchen was flat roofed, its terrace used for storage. A fenced garden with a well "of excellent good water" and "valuable" orange trees completed the description for Hrabawski's claim for £350. The "necessary house" was at the furthest corner of the lot.[21]

Eighteenth-century Spanish cooking differed from British practices. Spanish kitchens are somewhat revealed in the inventories of Spanish houses by Engineers Juan Joseph Cotilla and Pablo Castelló made in 1763 in preparation for the change of governments. There were ovens (*hornos*) and hearths of stone (*fogónes de cantería*) in detached kitchen houses (*cosinas*) erected with wood or stone, shingled and flat roofed. One kitchen is described with a masonry chimney (*chiminea*) and bell-shaped (*campana*) flue (*cañón*). The English detached kitchens had open fireplace hearths, built with coquina and clay brick vented by brick chimney stacks. Pots and kettles were hung over wood fires on cranes with trammels and hooks made from wrought iron. Remnants and replicas of detached colonial kitchens in St. Augustine can be seen at the González-Peavett-Alvarez House ("Oldest House") and the Ximénez-Fatio House, the latter rebuilt by a Spanish couple on the ruins of a British stone kitchen. Descriptions of many more exist in colonial narratives and estate inventories.[22]

5.8. Eighteenth-century Spanish cooking and baking ovens. Spanish and English alike had separate kitchen houses because of the threat of fire. The best were built of stone. (Drawing by E. Gordon)

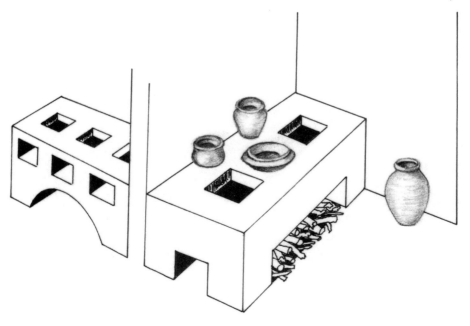

The St. Augustine style's most endearing characteristics are the suspended wood balconies, the arcaded stone loggias with wood gallery above (Spanish *corredor, galería*; English piazza, veranda). The covered wood balconies were a centuries-old Spanish tradition, descended from Islamic Spain, where they had relieved the flat, unadorned Christian Romanesque walls (fig. 5.9). In St. Augustine they were constructed as they were in Spain and in its American colonies, cantilevered over the public streets on hewn double beams that were first-floor ceiling joists rammed through the walls. This method of construction eliminated the need for vertical pillars that obstructed cart traffic in the narrow streets (figs. 3, 5.13).[23] Balconies were recorded in 1690 and 1713 at the governor's residence (Government House), and in 1702 on the residence of Joseph Rodríguez Meléndez, whose balcony faced the fort.[24] Throughout the Spanish-speaking world, such balconies were used to dry corn and clothing, and as places to sit with a fiery drink in the evening and discreet views of activities in the streets below.

The most handsome of all balconies in St. Augustine was that on the governor's house, suspended over St. George Street and looking toward the plaza and harbor (pl. 13; fig. 4.37). It was crafted similar to balconies in Andalucía and the Canary Islands, where balconies were inherently decorative in the *Mudéjar* style. The governor's balcony had columns, cornices, turned balusters, and panels painted a soft pastel blue. The house of Don Antonio Rodríguez and Don Juan de Salas on Charlotte

5.9. Suspended balconies, Aviles Street, St. Augustine. The balconies were a centuries-old practice brought from Spain and the Canary Islands, where they were highly decorative, influenced by the *Mudéjares* (or *Moriscos*), Muslim craftsmen who stayed in Spain under Christian rule after 1492. (Photograph by M. Gordon)

FLORIDA'S COLONIAL ARCHITECTURAL HERITAGE

Street also had a distinctive wood balcony, disclosed in an inventory of 1763 as "painted" and as having a shingled roof with a "painted" flat ceiling. Most unusual for the time, it was enclosed with glass windows.[25]

Loggias facing courtyards and gardens were indoor-outdoor spaces widely used as passageways into the house and cool, shady places in which to dine or relax in the quiet of the off-street garden side of the house. During the first Spanish period, there was an arcaded loggia with nine arches and cornice capitals at the Bishop's House and a pillar-and-beam loggia at the Menéndez Marquéz House (figs. 4.17, 4.20). The governor's eighteenth-century residence had a loggia and a roofed gallery above supported by sixteen stone columns with capitals.[26] The extent to which wood galleries were built above the loggias during the first Spanish period is unknown, but many are recorded during the British and second Spanish periods. The earliest mention of a gallery in Florida, however, dates from Laudonnière's house in 1564 at the French Fort Caroline: "On the other side toward the river was my house, around which there were covered galleries."[27]

Loggias and galleries were generally oriented away from cold northerly winds, but there were exceptions. The house of William Gerard de Brahm, surveyor general of the Southern District, for example, on lot Number 1, Governor's Quarter, was described in 1784 as a large stone house with eight rooms and "piazzas north and south." This was divulged in his loyalist claim, in which he valued his house, kitchen, other outbuildings, one-half acre lot, and large garden at £800.[28]

Perhaps the most elaborate and elegant loggia was built for the British statehouse entrance, with freestanding columns and flanking arcades (figs. 4.18, 4.19). Today, there are restored loggias from both English and second Spanish periods that can be seen at the Oldest House, Llambias House, Sequí-Kirby Smith House, Peña-Peck House, and the Espinosa House. Their stone pillars and arches were stylishly embellished with capitals, bases, and chamfered edges. Artists have been drawn to the romance of St. Augustine's evocative loggias. The Sequí House loggia, built ca. 1805–10, was sketched for the *Daily Graphic* (New York) in 1876 (fig. 5.10) and painted in an oil painting by Louis Comfort Tiffany in the early 1880s. When it was photographed in the late nineteenth century, its pier arches were captured with their original cornice capitals, bases, and chamfered edges (fig. 5.11). Frances Benjamin Johnston came to St. Augustine in 1937 to photograph the best of its architecture for the Library of Congress and the Carnegie Survey, and she too captured a second Spanish period loggia, one that had been added to the earlier Espinosa House (fig. 5.12). Ken Barrett, Jr., a professional photographer in St. Au-

Above: 5.10. Seguí-Kirby Smith House, ca. 1805, St. Augustine. Bernardo Seguí built his coquina house during the second Spanish period. Bernardo was a Minorcan from the failed New Smyrna colony of Dr. Andrew Turnbull. In St. Augustine he became a prosperous baker and member of a shipping network. His house illustrates the persistence of the St. Augustine Style, with loggia and gallery open to the garden. A balcony, later removed, was suspended on the street facade. The sketch shows Bernardo's preference for brick chimneys, glazed sashes, and English symmetry. (Drawing from the *New York Daily Graphic,* March 30, 1876; photocopy by Ken Barrett, Jr., courtesy of SAHS)

5.11. Seguí-Kirby Smith House, loggia, second Spanish period, St. Augustine. The late-nineteenth-century photograph poignantly captures the colonial loggia. Pier arches with bases, capitals, and chamfered corners were worked in coquina stone by an unnamed master mason. Long ago, through the arches could be seen the kitchen garden, fruit trees, and Bernardo Seguí's kitchen house, where he baked bread for the Spanish garrison. (Photograph by F. H. Meyer; photocopy by Ken Barrett, Jr., courtesy of SAHS)

5.12. Espinosa House (Perez-Sanchez House), loggia, second Spanish period, St. Augustine. When photographed by Frances Benjamin Johnston in 1937 for the Library of Congress Carnegie Survey, the original exquisite colonial masonry craftsmanship was still intact. Half-round arches, elaborate capital moldings, and chamfered corners might have been the work of master mason Juan del Pozo. (Photocopy by Ken Barrett, Jr., courtesy of SAHS)

gustine, is the latest to express the charm of the Espinosa colonial loggia (pl. 23).

Principal entrances and exterior stairways were built by the Spanish and English in loggias under galleries to shelter them from rain and sun, a practice noted by John Bartram in 1765.[29] When the English arrived in Florida in 1763, they, like the Spanish before them, were drawn to architectural elements that responded to the hot climate. Many had come from tropical and semitropical climates of the British West Indies and Charleston, but even in Virginia, English colonials had built courthouses with arcaded loggias as early as 1699–1705.[30] In eighteenth-century St. Augustine they also took up the Spanish tradition of building balconies suspended on joists rammed through walls.

The González-Peavett-Alvarez House (Oldest House) and the Llambias House mentioned earlier had both received their loggias and balconies during British ownership. The Oldest House had been one-storied and flat roofed from about 1720 to 1775, when it was bought by an

5.13. Llambias House, eighteenth century, St. Augustine. Houses built in the St. Augustine style had roofed balconies that were suspended over public streets (the sidewalk is modern) on first-floor ceiling joists and beams rammed through the walls. It was a very old tradition brought from Spain to the New World. Such construction eliminated the need for vertical pillars that blocked cart traffic in the very narrow roads. (Photograph by M. Gordon)

English couple, Joseph and Mary Peavett, who added many architectural elements that responded to the climate (pl. 16; figs. 5.2, 5.3). The Llambias House had similarly started with one story, flat roof, and Spanish-style windows (fig. 5.1) and was drastically altered by additions during the English period 1764–84 (figs. 5.13, 5.14). These additions were influenced by what the Spanish had constructed in St. Augustine, as well as other practices throughout the Caribbean world—English, French, and Spanish. At the Llambias House, the loggia and gallery were reconstructed by Stuart Moffett Barnette, College of Architecture, Cornell University, based on data and architectural remnants found in walls and footings during restoration (fig. 5.15).

The Reverend John Forbes, minister of St. Peter's Church, owned three houses in town and one on the outskirts, all with "piazzas" supported with stone columns. The Forbes house on the "parade" (plaza) was described by his widow, Dorothy Murray Forbes, in her loyalist claim of 1786 (fig. 5.16). She described the residence as "an Elegant Dwelling House Built of Stone containing six rooms two of which are 24 by 16 [feet] with a gallery and Piazza in front supported by six stone columns." Her choice of the words "in front" could mean either facade, facing the street or facing the side courtyard if that was where the main entrance was located, similar to the layout in the Hrabawski survey

5.14. Llambias House, south patio facade, ca. 1770s, St. Augustine, restored and reconstructed 1946–55. The strengths of the St. Augustine style were its responses to Florida's warm humid climate and use of the local wood and coquina stone. The one-storied Spanish house was expanded and dramatically changed by English owners during 1764–84, when they added architectural elements influenced by what they had seen in St Augustine, the Caribbean, and Charleston. An exterior staircase is hidden in the protection of the loggia. The hip roof's flaring eaves kept water off the plastered walls and foundation. (Photograph by Ken Barrett, Jr.)

5.15. Llambias House, loggia reconstruction, St. Augustine, 1950s. The coquina quarries on Anastasia Island were opened in 1672 for the construction of the Castillo de San Marcos. Indians were brought to the quarries to cut the slabs that were then barged across the river to the fort site where stonecutters shaped them with hand tools into construction blocks. In the 1950s, mechanical saws cut the stone to reconstruct the 1770s stone loggia. (Photograph courtesy of SAHS)

5.16. Dorothy Murray Forbes, portrait by John Singleton Copley, ca. 1760. John Forbes, from Scotland, the young Anglican minister of St. Peter's Church in St. Augustine, married Dorothy Murray of Boston in 1768. Forbes oversaw the conversion of the Catholic parish church into St. Peter's Anglican Church. The Forbes family owned four houses, in addition to a plantation on the Matanzas River. (Portrait photograph courtesy of the Fogg Art Museum, Harvard University Art Museums, gift of Mrs. David Simmons)

described above. The house also had "a store house built of stone and a kitchen and other out houses, and garden and arranged grove containing one-hundred trees bearing fruit," and was valued at £750.[31]

A second Forbes house (Number 2 Forbes Quarter, Charlotte Street), granted to Reverend Forbes, April 29, 1771, was described by his widow as also having piazzas. The house was "60 by 30 feet, the lower story built of stone containing six rooms, one of which is 30 by 18 feet, with a Piazza and gallery in front." From her words, one can deduce that the second story was wood, and that the gallery was stacked on top of the loggia, which she called the piazza. The kitchen was detached; another outbuilding was the stone store house, 30 by 14 feet. This residence was surrounded by a stone wall and was valued at £550. She and her deceased husband had also owned the adjoining house (Number 1 Forbes Quarter) described as stone with five rooms worth £350. Just outside the urban area, on two hundred acres on St. Sebastian River, Dorothy Murray Forbes testified that the dwelling they purchased was an "elegant commodious house, four rooms surrounded by Piazza," with separate kitchen and outbuildings, "planted with orchard of lemons, limes bearing fruit, formally arranged," and valued at £600.[32]

During the first Spanish period, window placement followed no rules of symmetry, but was dictated by interior requirements for light. "Spanish" windows generally did not have glass, a reflection of their evolution in southern European climates. They were large openings protected by interior wood shutters and *celosías* and *rejas,* carved lattice screens or spindled window grilles (fig. 5.17). Decorative *celosías* and *rejas* were Islamic in origin, characteristic of the work of the *Mudéjares* (or *Moriscos*), the Muslim craftsmen who stayed in Spain under Christian rule after 1492, when the Moors were ousted.

John Bartram described the Spanish windows in St. Augustine in 1765 as "large windows next ye street all banistered & projecting A foot or more from ye house wall[,] some had 3 & some 5 rows [of banisters] one above another each about two foot long . . . & many windows had a lattice with holes one inch square reaching half way or more up ye window."[33] In Cuba, such windows typically had a cloth or leather curtain (*guarda-polvo*) for privacy and blocking dust and insects. In Spain, transparent pigskin also did the job.[34] Interior wood shutters were closed to keep out

5.17. Spanish window with wood *rejas,* eighteenth century, Trinidad, Cuba. Spanish windows and their decorative *rejas* were a product of Spain's Mediterranean climate and the *Mudéjares.* They were protected with grilles (*rejas*) or lattice (*celosías*) and wood shutters, sometimes with a peephole (*postigo*). After 1763, English glazed sashes, symmetrically arranged, were the windows of choice. (Photograph, 1998, by E. Gordon)

cold and rain, and sometimes they had a little hinged peephole window (*postigo*) for peeking outside.[35]

Inventories of estates during the first Spanish period reveal that a number of windows had glass panes. The Rodríguez-Salas House, for example, had a balcony enclosed with glass windows in 1763, and ten window frames with glass in the bedroom and seven more in the living quarters.[36] This is not surprising. The history of window glass is very old, known in Rome before Christ was born and rediscovered in Europe in the twelfth century. In Spain, for example, twenty-six hundred windows had been glazed at the palace of Philip II, El Escorial, about the time that St. Augustine was founded. Glazed sashes were thought to have been brought across the Atlantic to the English colonies in 1620 and imported in larger quantities during the eighteenth century. In addition, glass panes were produced in domestic glasshouses. Glass could be obtained by St. Augustine residents who *wanted* glass and could afford it in external trade, legally if not illegally. Spain winked at trade restrictions, and Spanish policy toward the North American colonies was inconsistent, sometimes permitting the colonists of Cuba, Florida, and the British colonies to serve each other's commercial needs. For example, in 1683 a sloop from New York entered Matanzas Bay and the Spanish found a way to buy its cargo of gunpowder and flour. During the second Spanish period, it is even better documented that St. Augustine was a port engaging in virtual free trade, with Charleston its major trading partner.[37]

The English window, a product of that country's colder climate, enclosed a smaller opening than the Spanish window with sashes glazed with small "lights" (panes of glass), 10 by 12 and 8 by 10 inches. The panes were set in popular arrangements like nine panes over nine, or twelve over twelve, in a grid of wooden muntins and painted to protect them from the weather. The English governor's windows were painted with white lead in linseed oil; the shutters were painted the color of stone.[38] Double hung sashes with two movable sashes were counterbalanced, raised and lowered with pulleys and weights. In a less expensive arrangement, the upper sash was fixed in place (single hung) and the lower sash was held open with a peg in the jamb, or even a vertical stick. Window sashes meant residents no longer had to choose between darkness and rain, or darkness and cold. They were taken up by the second Spanish period house owners and became a characteristic of the St. Augustine style ever after.

The British period residents did not tear down Spanish houses in order to build typical English houses. They adapted the better-built stone dwellings for their own residences, retaining Spanish elements and adding what had worked best in the warm climates of the West Indies and Charleston, places they were familiar with. English houses in the cold climate of England generally focused inward, on interior halls and staircases and interior access to rooms; they followed rules of symmetry and modular geometry. In St. Augustine, the local architectural style focused on indoor-outdoor spaces, exterior stairs, single-width rooms, and cross-ventilation, characteristics also of Charleston "single houses" and Gulf Coast raised cottages.[39]

English residents constructed brick chimneys and open fireplaces for burning logs (a northern European practice).[40] A few chimneys had existed in St. Augustine before the British arrived. In the house of Don Antonio Rodríguez and Don Juan de Salas on Charlotte Street, there were two chimneys in the drawing room with a fireplace decorated with glazed tiles (*azulejos*). In their kitchen was a bell-shaped chimney (*chimenea campanario*), the more traditional Spanish chimney. It was similar to one inventoried at the principal guardhouse,[41] and was probably a fixture in a number of the kitchen houses of private residences. Like the sashes, the English-style brick chimney and fireplace became a fixture of the St. Augustine style after the British left and the Spanish returned.

The English replaced Spanish flat roofs with gable and hipped roofs with 45-degree slopes, covered with wood shingles. The roof of the Menéndez Marquéz House of ca. 1730s underwent a "raising of the peak" in 1772 by Engineer James Moncrief. The higher-pitched roof was cooler and provided garret space for the equipment of the town fire engine.[42] Hipped roofs withstood hurricanes better than gable roofs, a fact known to colonial builders in the Caribbean and recently learned by Florida residents after the destruction of Miami by hurricane Andrew in 1992.[43] At the Llambias House, the British replaced the flat roof with a hipped roof and flaring eaves, influenced by buildings in Charleston and the Caribbean where eaves sometimes had "outriggers" that kicked rainwater away from plastered walls and foundations. "Outriggers" also minimized hurricane damage: they were lighter and constructed separately from the main roof timbers and thus could be sheared off by wind turbulence under the eave without the entire roof lifting off (figs. 5.13, 5.14).[44]

The Seguí-Kirby Smith House and Ximénez-Fatio House, both standing today, are examples of second Spanish period houses that perpetuated the vernacular St. Augustine style. They were products of the best of the first Spanish period and English practices. The Seguí House, built by Bernardo and Agueda Villalonga Seguí, is a rags-to-riches story. Don Bernardo and Agueda, both from Minorca, walked penniless to St. Augustine in 1777 along with some six hundred "Minorcans" (the name for the cultural group from Greece, Italy, and Minorca from the failed plantation of Dr. Turnbull in New Smyrna). By the end of the British period, many of these Minorcans had amassed considerable capital supplying food and joining in shipping and trade ventures.[45] When Don Bernardo constructed his new house, he was a baker contracted to supply the Spanish troops with bread, and a member of the Cosifacio-Martinellis-Quevados merchant network that owned many sailing vessels trading directly with Cuba, Europe, New York, Philadelphia, and Charleston.

The Seguí family acquired the lot and pre-existing tabby and wood house in 1786. New construction began ca. 1805 with coquina stone and may have incorporated some of the old structure. Their two-storied stone house rose flush with the edges of Aviles Street and Artillery Lane. A balcony was suspended over Aviles Street, but was removed about a hundred years later. The cool loggia was masterfully built with stone arches, and a second-story wood gallery looked over the back yard and the kitchen-bakery, where Don Bernardo made his bread. The stairway to the second floor was in the loggia. Glazed windows, brick chimneys, and rigid English symmetry show in an 1876 sketch for the *Daily Graphic* of New York (fig. 5.10). Today the colonial Seguí House, with modifications from the 1880s and early 1990s, has been adapted for use by the St. Augustine Historical Society for its research library.[46]

Next door on Aviles Street, Andrés Ximénez, from Ronda, Spain, and Juana Pellicer, his Minorcan wife, built their coquina stone house during the second Spanish period with a similar architectural scheme in 1797 combining Spanish and English traditions. Two-storied, flush with the street, their design included a rear loggia, side entrance, and cantilevered street balcony (fig. 5.18). They reached the second floor by an exterior staircase, and cooked in a detached stone kitchen house. A pitched roof, glazed sashes, and fireplace and chimney were by then accepted necessities. Today it is owned by the Florida Colonial Dames, who have opened it to the public as a house museum and example of a successful historic boarding house.[47]

The Oldest House, Llambias House, and the Ximénez-Fatio House are excellent examples of colonial buildings to walk through and discover the spirit and strengths of St. Augustine's architecture. These houses convey at once why the local way of building persisted and was validated by repetition despite changes in nationalities of governments and owner-builders.

Today, the best characteristics of the St. Augustine style are being adapted to new construction and modern living in communities like the

5.18. Ximénez-Fatio House, ca. 1797, St. Augustine. Ximénez and Pellicer built a house in the St. Augustine style, with a balcony hanging over Aviles Street and a loggia and patio at the rear. Their detached stone kitchen was built on the foundation of an earlier English kitchen. In the 1850s, the colonial house was Miss Fatio's "private boarding house," with paying guests from the north who came to St. Augustine for their health. One such guest wrote, in praise of Fatio's comfortable lodging, "the hotels and boarding houses are all under the management of Southern individuals with 'Northern principles' of domestic economy." (Photograph courtesy of Ken Barrett, Jr.)

Village of Windsor in Vero Beach, and Rosemary Beach and Seaside in Walton County.

The pursuit of architecture on a frontier is difficult in any circumstance. Four changes in government nationality made architectural styles particularly vulnerable in St. Augustine. The stone and the climate, however, brought Spanish and English traditions together in pursuit of permanent and comfortable residences. Two English governors, Grant and Tonyn, had written the Lords of Trade that the local shellstone quarried by the Spanish was the superior and durable building material, needing the least amount of maintenance.[48] Newly arrived multinational residents after each change in hegemony, including Americans during the territorial period, saw no reason to alter the direction of St. Augustine's buildings. They erected dwellings and made additions with the same logic.

5.19. B. E. Carr house and store, St. Augustine. The Carr house and store on Bay Street (now Avenida Menendez) was owned by Burroughs E. Carr, the town's leading merchant in the 1830s. B. E. Carr's ownership reminds us of the colonial years, when merchants' houses and warehouse establishments were located by the waterfront, when the river and ocean were the main transportation routes. (Drawn and engraved on wood by John S. Horton, 1855; reprinted by St. Augustine National Bank, 1955)

5.20. B. E. Carr house reconstructed, 1888, St. Augustine. In 1887, the Carr House burned in the same fire that gutted the Cathedral. It was immediately rebuilt in its original St. Augustine style architecture, but instead of coquina stone blocks the house walls were cast with coquina concrete like that used in the Flagler hotels and churches. The replication of a colonial building was the first in the city's history. A private residence until 1976, it is now a restaurant. The side yard entrance coquina wall, with arch, is thought to be a vestige from the colonial period. (Photo, 1902, courtesy of Florida State Archives)

5.21. Side yard house, 1990–91, Village of Windsor, Vero Beach. Windsor is one of several new communities looking to the twenty-first century with architecture that respects the colonial St. Augustine style, emphasizing cool and quiet private spaces with elements like flaring eaves, roofed balconies, loggias, walled patios, and side yard entrances. These same elements had been repeated for centuries during the colonial period because they responded so well to the Florida climate. Architect: Scott Merrill. (Drawing by Thomas Spain, courtesy of the architect)

William Stork wrote in 1767, in his account of East Florida, that "the Spaniards consulted convenience more than taste in their buildings."[49] He was saying that ornamentation for ornamentation's sake was purposefully excluded. The English, the returning Spanish, and the Anglo-American residents who followed never lost sight of the architecture's regional strengths and its promises in the Florida environment. They stood in no need of architectural styles from the past or the fickleness of ornamental fashions to meet their real needs and comfort in St. Augustine.

6 | BRITISH PENSACOLA

Throughout this stream of human life, and thought, and
activity . . . men have ever felt the need to build; and from the
need arose the power to build . . . As they built, they made,
used, and left behind them records of their thinking . . .
Whatever the character of the thinking, just so was the
character of the building.

LOUIS SULLIVAN

The British period in Pensacola is like a mirage on a warm summer day. Wondrous architectural plans shimmered on the horizon with high hopes for a permanent future, but dissipated with the departure of the British and ensuing benign neglect of the second Spanish period and American territorial years. All that exist today of the British buildings are subterranean brick foundations and a well,[1] and beautifully drawn floor plans and elevations profuse with verandas and symmetry, conserved in the National Archives of Great Britain and the Library of Congress.

The British acquired Florida as a result of the Treaty of Paris in 1763 at the conclusion of the Seven Years War, but it was more land than could be efficiently administered from the former Spanish capital at St. Augustine. It was divided into two colonies, East Florida and West Florida. East Florida was east of the Apalachicola River to the Atlantic Ocean, with the northern border the St. Marys River, and the capital St. Augustine. West Florida, with Pensacola as its capital, encompassed the Panhandle and all the land westward to the Mississippi River, south to Lake Pontchartrain and the Gulf of Mexico, and north to latitude 32°28'. It included Mobile, Baton Rouge, and Natchez, but not New Orleans.

Architecturally, the Spanish had only six short years (1757–63) to build at the site they called San Miguel de Panzacola. Those six years had been interrupted by Indian tensions and a hurricane, but most of all there was

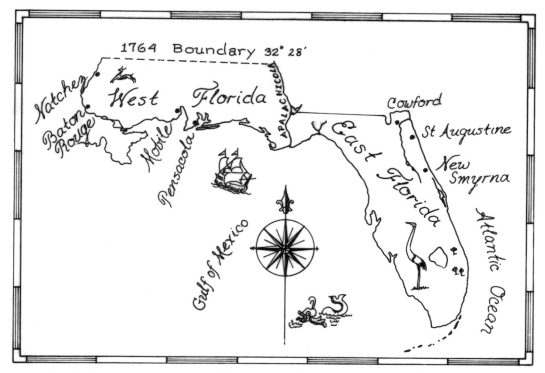

6. East Florida and West Florida, 1764. Great Britain acquired Florida in 1763 at the conclusion of the Seven Years War and the Treaty of Paris, but the territory stretching from the Atlantic Ocean to the Mississippi River was more than could be efficiently administered from the capital at St. Augustine. The solution was to divide Florida at the Apalachicola River into two colonies, East Florida and West Florida. (Drawn by E. Gordon)

a lack of architectural commitment. The construction labor was the garrison, mostly prisoners from Mexico (*Nueva España*) sentenced to hard labor. Making the most of this situation and the materials at hand, Royal Engineer Don Felipe Feringan Cortés had erected the requisite church, hospital, warehouses, barracks, and powder magazine, and a house within the stockade for the commandant-governor, Colonel Miguel Román de Castilla y Lugo. Houses for officers and their families, and townspeople, had been built outside the stockade and later dismantled to clear the environs in case of Indian attack.[2]

When the British arrived, they found houses with earthfast frames and walls that were either planks of cypress or slabs of "bark of trees" (the outside sappy planks sawn from the sides of timber), or "plaster," the *bousillage* typical of French colonial construction in Louisiana that was a mixture of clay, moss, and lime packed into lathwork, smoothed and lime plastered. The roofs were "palmetto leaves" or "bark." A small amount of brick had been used for the roofs of the gunpowder warehouses and the floor of the commandant-governor's house. Indian raids and a hurricane in 1760 had destroyed half the stockade and torn off the bark roofs.[3] Three years later, still in disrepair and generally conceded by historians to be a shabby village, Spanish Panzacola became British Pensacola.

Until archaeology proves differently, this story of Pensacola's British period architecture is told primarily through the meticulously drawn plans of the engineer-designers, the buildings they erected, and the many that were more dream than substance. But even dreams tell us much about a town, and the people who had come to stay and make it happen.

Dreams and Reality

British Pensacola looked to England, the West Indies, Mobile (formerly the French capital of Louisiana), and New Orleans for trade and some architectural direction. St. Augustine, the capital of British East Florida, was a world away. The trip took sixteen days or more, by boat to St. Marks and overland by horse, wagon, and ferry. British Pensacola was even further from Charleston and other English colonies along the Atlantic seaboard. It took four weeks by ship to New York. Veracruz, however, was only ten days away, Campeche eight, and Jamaica six. Mobile could be reached in a single day's sail.[4] Pensacola's architecture after 1763 would develop quite differently from that of older St. Augustine's.

The best Spanish architecture inherited by the British was the commandant-governor's house close to the waterfront, with its exterior stairway and two outbuildings, drawn the same on both Spanish and English plans. It is labeled "Casa del Gobernador" and "Governours House" on Spanish and British lot maps of 1763 and 1764, and "The House formerly the residence of the Governor" on Elias Durnford's 1778 plans of Pensacola.[5] A Spanish plan of the town had described it as thirty-six feet high, having a timber second story on a foundation and first floor of stone and bousillage. The first floor served as warehouse for groceries and had two rooms for the office of the paymaster; the second story was the commandant-governor's living quarters.[6] A detailed survey of this structure and its outbuildings was made by four British carpenters and the chief engineer, Elias Durnford, in 1770 when the newly arrived Governor Chester refused to live in this house, deeming it a "ruinous and uninhabitable" situation even though it had been repaired and lived in by his predecessors. Their report revealed much about earlier Spanish building practices, its French colonial influences and its earthfast framework and bousillage construction.[7] Lord Adam Gordon on a visit in 1764 had written in his journal that the house "has a balcony both ways up one pair of Stairs" (fig. 3.16).[8]

6.1. La Habana, Plaza Vieja, 1762, Havana, Cuba, painted by Elias Durnford (1739–
1794), chief engineer and town planner of Pensacola from 1764 to 1781. He laid out the
English fort and town lots on the site of the former Spanish presidio, and designed
barracks and the governor's residence. Some of his plans and elevations for Pensacola
were more dream than substance, but, nevertheless, they speak about the early town
and the people who wanted to make it happen. Durnford's painting of Havana, published in London, March 12, 1762, predicts the Caribbean influences that would appear in his architectural plans for Pensacola. (*A View of the Market Place in the City of
Havana,* published by T. Jeffries, London, reprinted in color in Havana, 1998, collection of E. Gordon)

George Johnstone (first English governor, 1763–67) decided to build
the capital of West Florida on the site of Spanish Panzacola. He directed
Engineer Durnford to prepare the plan and lay out the areas reserved for
public and military buildings, the streets, and the lots. The latter were
laid out at right angles in garden lots of 105 by 208 feet, and town lots of
80 by 170 feet. It is said that 113 good houses had been built by 1766 and
200 by 1768; Bernard Romans described the town as 180 houses built in
good taste. The colonial period town is about where Pensacola's Historic
District is today.[9]

Durnford was a capable engineer who became a member of the council as well as lieutenant governor, acting governor (1769–70), and owner of
Durnford's Dairy on the road to Mobile. At twenty-three, his first assign-
ment in the British arena in the Americas was to map the environs of
Havana during the British-Cuban campaign in 1762. While there, he
painted a view of Havana's Plaza Vieja titled *A View of the Market Place in
the City of Havana.* The painting, published in London on March 12,
1762, by Thomas Jefferys, reveals Durnford's drafting talent (fig. 6.1). His

West Indies experience and his training in London's neoclassic architecture are revealed in his architectural plans for Pensacola.[10]

George Gauld (1732–1782), surveyor and cartographer of West Florida, drew a view of Pensacola's waterfront about 1766–68 depicting a skyline of British Georgian hipped roofs. The former Spanish commandant-governor's house, "appropriated for the residence of the governor," George Johnstone, with its new brick chimney and shingled roof, may be seen just to the left of the masts of the ship at the right side of the drawing (fig. 6.2). The drawing was made before construction of the largest building in Pensacola, the three-storied "pile of barracks" (1776–78), left of the place where Gauld depicts the British flag.[11] Gauld, a seventeen-year resident of Pensacola, was educated at King's College, Aberdeen. He was a scholar, scientist, naturalist, a member of the prestigious American Philosophical Society, and a highly skilled naval cartographer whose drawings and maps have been much praised for their accuracy even into the nineteenth century.[12]

Somewhere among the roofs drawn by Gauld was the house and town lot bought by Daniel Boone in August, 1765. He had hoped to migrate to the new English colony, but his wife Rebecca put her foot down and told him to come back home in time for Christmas dinner.[13]

The British barrack plans received much attention and were designed and redesigned several times. Troop strength was never certain. The 1768 drawings called for two buildings that separated officers from the soldiers. The soldiers' barracks resembled colonial French Gulf Coast and English Caribbean architecture (figs. 6.3, 6.4). Exterior stairways,

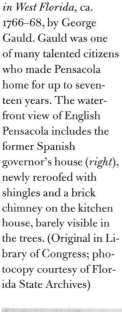

6.2. *A View of Pensacola in West Florida,* ca. 1766–68, by George Gauld. Gauld was one of many talented citizens who made Pensacola home for up to seventeen years. The waterfront view of English Pensacola includes the former Spanish governor's house (*right*), newly reroofed with shingles and a brick chimney on the kitchen house, barely visible in the trees. (Original in Library of Congress; photocopy courtesy of Florida State Archives)

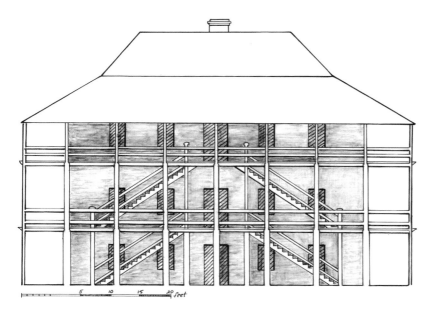

6.3. Proposed soldiers' barracks, elevation, 1768, Pensacola, British West Florida. Conscious of Pensacola's hot and humid climate and frequent "fevers," the designer looked to the architecture of the Caribbean and colonial French buildings of the Gulf Coast. He maximized ventilation with wraparound verandas under flaring eaves, exterior staircases, and many windows and doors placed across from each other. (Redrawn by E. Gordon, after Public Record Office, PRO: MPG 529)

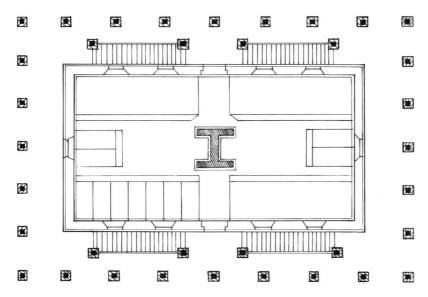

6.4. Proposed soldiers' barracks, floor plan, 1768, Pensacola, British West Florida. Rigid symmetry and wrapping verandas were characteristic of many British designs in colonial Florida. The barrack plan called for 81,400 bricks and 2,300 paving bricks to be made locally for its construction. (Redrawn by E. Gordon, after Public Record Office, PRO: MPG 529)

6.5. John Lorimer, M.D., for fourteen years the resident military surgeon in Pensacola, British West Florida. Dr. Lorimer was responsible for the many verandas included on every barracks plan. (Photograph courtesy of Library of Congress and William M. Straight, M.D.)

John Lorimer, M.D.
A.D. MDCCXCIV, Æt. 62.
Fellow of the Royal College of Physicians, at Edinburgh.

spacious wraparound verandas with graduating columns, hip roof, and flared eaves were right for the climate.

The officers' quarters, on the other hand, were to be more formal and Georgian, with interior stairs and no verandas. Both plans called for locally manufactured bricks, 81,400 bricks and 2,300 paving bricks for the soldiers' barracks, and 87,602 bricks and 2,740 paving bricks for the officers' building. The artificers and the 450 squares of glass, 47,000 shingles, barrels of lime, iron, and oil paints were to come from England or North America. Total cost was estimated by General Gage's military engineers in New York to be 2,419 "dollars, New York currency" for the soldiers' barracks and 2,363 dollars for that of the officers.[14]

The next barrack design (1771) combined living spaces for officers and soldiers. Drawn by William Brasier, it resembled the "Pile of Barracks" constructed in 1772 in St. Augustine, which, it turns out, was originally intended for Pensacola (pls. 18, 19). The Pensacola plan had an added flourish, a "palace" front with a classical pediment and coat of arms. The ground floor was to be constructed in brick for the storage of provisions, and the upper two stories to be constructed in wood, lathed and plastered, for living quarters. Once again, the plan was dominated by wrapping verandas.[15]

A notation on the 1771 plan specified that the barracks should be ranged along the north edge of the Bay of Pensacola, and that "each of these Barracks will on any particular occasion contain 300 men with their proper complement of Officers, but on account of the great heat in Summer fourteen men to each room, was judged the most proper for preserving their healths."[16] Dr. John Lorimer, seventeen years a military surgeon, including fourteen as the resident physician at Pensacola, was probably responsible for architectural ideas promoting good ventilation. He was scientifically curious, particularly about fevers, sanitation, and health, and like his good friend George Gauld was a member of the American Philosophical Society. He had recommended to General Haldimand that barracks should be at least two stories high with piazzas that sheltered the men from the sun.[17]

In the summer of 1772, a set of plans for a similar but slightly smaller barracks, minus the flourish and with double the chimneys, sent to London by General Gage, was probably closer to what was actually built. They were described as "now finishing" in 1776 and "occupied" in 1778 (fig. 6.6). In this plan, the soldiers were housed on the lower and upper floors and the officers on the middle floor.[18] These barracks were still

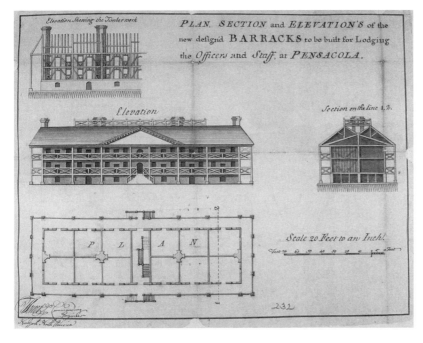

6.6. *Plan, Section and Elevations of the new designed Barracks to be built for Lodging the Officers and Staff, at Pensacola*, 1772, signed T. Sower, commanding engineer, New York. There was a central hall with entrance doors front and rear and a divided staircase. Rooms were entered from the wide encircling verandas. (Photograph courtesy of Public Record Office, PRO: MPD 1/194 [2])

standing in 1821, measured by American officers at 156 by 40 to 46 feet, the same measurements shown in the drawings. The Americans confirmed that the first floor was brick, and the second and third were wood with encircling verandas.[19]

British concern about architecture and climate showed up again on garrison plans for the "Red Cliffs" on the west side of the harbor entrance. Resembling raised cottage forms, the barracks consisted of four large single-width rooms on a second floor wrapped with verandas. Each room had six windows. The first floor was masonry, to prevent rot and provide cool food storage. Correspondence reveals that all English roofs were to be preserved against the weather by applying pitch and tar oil, that woodwork was to be kept painted, and that shades were to be built at blockhouses to protect the soldiers and cannon from sun and rain.[20]

The dapper Peter Chester arrived in 1770 to begin his term as governor. After only a month or two he vacated the former Spanish comman-

6.7. General Haldimand's house, 1770 lot plan, Pensacola, British West Florida. Haldimand's house, outside the stockade, was leased for Governor Chester in 1770 because Chester had refused to live in the old Spanish governor's house. The lot plan was drawn by Elias Durnford to send to the Lords of Trade in England. The rear (south) facade of the house had an eight-foot-wide veranda looking toward the garden and outbuildings, where all the domestic activities took place. (Redrawn by E. Gordon after Durnford, Public Record Office, PRO: MPG 611 [5])

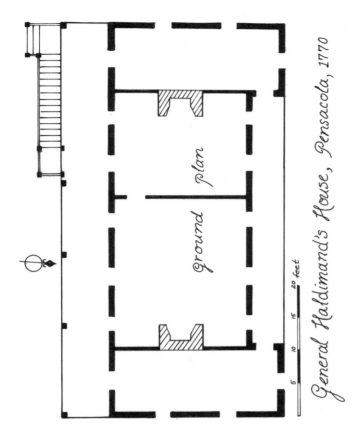

ground plan

General Haldimand's House, Pensacola, 1770

20 feet
15
10
5

6.8. General Haldimand's house, 1770 ground plan, Pensacola, British West Florida. The symmetrical house plan had many fine features for the climate. In addition to the veranda, there was a great room (repeated on second floor without partition) that was one room wide, with windows across from each other for good ventilation. There were twenty-four hundred square feet in the main house, and some fourteen hundred more in the outbuildings (excluding carriage house and stable) that nor-mally take up space inside houses today. (Redrawn by E. Gordon after Durnford, Public Record Office, PRO: MPG 611 [1–2])

dant-governor's house that had been requisitioned and renovated for his residence, and ordered a survey, which concluded it would be "impossible to repair properly without incurring more expense than rebuilding it."[21] Chester moved into a house in town that had been owned by General Frederick Haldimand since about 1767, when he was the newly designated commander of the Southern District of North America. When Haldimand left for St. Augustine in 1769, his house had been leased by Governor Montfort Browne for public offices and a courthouse, and in effect had become "Government House." When John Elliot became acting governor in 1769, he used it as a church.[22]

In a game of musical chairs, Chester moved into Haldimand's house, ordering the transfer of the church, courthouse, and public offices into the old Spanish commandant-governor's house he had just vacated. Money was no obstacle when it came to his own lodging. Chester directed Durnford to draw plans for upgrading the Haldimand building, and to design a new governor's residence for inside the stockade. Both sets of plans were forwarded to London on September 29, 1770.[23]

Four drawings of General Haldimand's house reveal much about the large residence that Chester moved into just outside and west of the stockade. The house was built at the north end of one of the long town lots (80 by 170 feet) laid out by Elias Durnsford when he planned the town in 1764. A large garden, wood yard, stables and coach house, and a number of outbuildings took up the remainder of the lot (fig. 6.7). The outbuildings ran down the west side of the lot, their entrances protected under a covered walkway that ended at the privy. The kitchen was ample (14 by 26 feet), and each of the servants and butler's quarters and storerooms were 13 by 14 feet. The house was some 60 feet long, 28 feet wide, with piazzas front and back and an outside staircase to the second floor (fig. 6.8). The doors had transoms and the rooms were single-width, encouraging as much cross ventilation as possible. The great room on the second floor was 40 by 20 feet. Symmetry was everywhere.[24]

While Chester was waiting for the new governor's mansion to be completed inside the stockade, he harbored fanciful dreams of ornamenting Haldimand's house. Durnford's drawings of the proposed upgrades are at the Public Record Office in England, labeled "plans, sections, and elevations of a house occupied by the Governor." The design shows an ambitious and symmetrical classical facade with pediment, balustraded roof piazza, and an elegant belvedere for harbor views, composed of eight columns arranged in an oval (figs. 6.9, 6.10).

6.9. General Haldimand's house, 1770 proposed changes to north facade, Pensacola, British West Florida. Elias Durnford drew up a set of four plans that were sent to the Lords of Trade. He proposed neoclassical ornamentation, a third floor, and a balustraded rooftop piazza with pavilion. The plans were never funded; Chester meanwhile built his own plantation, called Chester's Villa, and divided his time between the two places. (Redrawn by E. Gordon after Durnford, Public Record Office, PRO: MPG 611 [1–2])

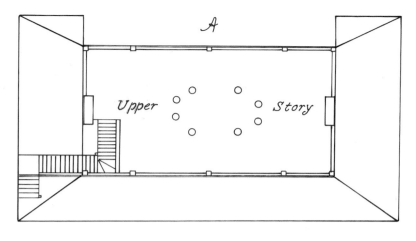

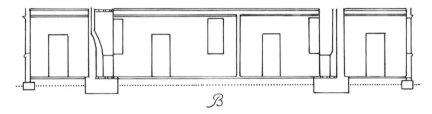

6.10. General Haldimand's house, 1770 foundation and proposed roof additions, Pensacola, British West Florida. (*A*) Third-story addition with an elegant belvedere of eight columns; (*B*) foundation plan showing footing and chimney bases. (Redrawn by E. Gordon after Durnford, courtesy of Public Record Office, PRO: MPG 611 [3])

Chester described Haldimand's house as "well built." The section reveals it was built above grade. The first and second floors had doors with glazed transoms and five windows front and rear opposite each other, pulling across the air cooled by the veranda.[25] Correspondence does not indicate that the proposed ornamentation and roof addition were funded or constructed. Chester lived in this house during his entire term as governor (1770–81), commuting frequently to his plantation, Chester's Villa, nearby but outside of town.

Haldimand's lawyers had offered to sell the house, with kitchen and outbuildings, for £1,500. Chester's letters, written during the negotiations, indicated that wood houses, even those "well built," had to be painted "in oyl" at least twice in five years, and that the roofs of houses and outbuildings had to be shingled or tarred, with tar oil, twice every year. Glass window sashes and fences constantly had to be kept in repair.[26]

Meanwhile, the new governor's house and office were under construction just north of the old Spanish governor's house (pl. 20).[27] It was impressive for its style, size, and estimated cost of £2,500. There were to be three inhabitable floors and a wide encircling veranda with divided stair-

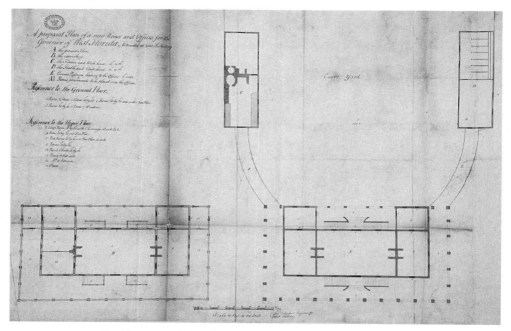

6.11. Governor Chester's dream house plan, 1770, by Elias Durnford, Pensacola, British West Florida. Peter Chester, governor of British West Florida (1770–81), intended to live well in a mansion with more than seventy-two hundred square feet. (Photograph courtesy of Public Record Office, PRO: MPG 611 [4])

cases front and back. The main floors each had about 3,600 square feet, or 7,200 square feet total, excluding verandas, rooms in the garret for servants, and the separate kitchen and other utility houses. The detached kitchen and wash house, and the stable and coach house were connected to the main house by a U-shaped covered passageway (fig. 6.11), a scheme similar to neo-Palladian plans in the London-published architectural handbooks by James Gibbs (*Book of Architecture*), Robert Morris (*Select Architecture*), and many others.

Governor Chester dreamed too big; the house was never finished. Work at the new governor's mansion in the stockade came to an end in 1778, its expectations unfilled; the £2,550 actually appropriated by Parliament (including a little extra for gardens) were exhausted. Chester blamed Durnford for erroneous estimates and plans too large; Durnford blamed Chester for demanding too fine a home and changing the plans. William Bartram visited Pensacola that year and wrote, "the governor's palace is a large stone building ornamented with a tower," which suggests a brick building with cupola, painted and scored to look like stone, a common practice of the time. (He thought the Spanish had built it.) The disappointed Chester did not move in, but assigned it to ordnance for more barrack and storage space.[28] In 1827, John Lee Williams wrote the three largest British Pensacola buildings were the two barracks and "the mansion house of Casa Blanca."[29] Its fate is unknown, but parts of its brick foundation have been excavated in Pensacola west of Old Christ Church.[30]

When Bartram visited in 1778, he noted "there are several hundred habitations in Pensacola. . . . The secretary [Philip Peter Livingston, 1740–1810, eight years as West Florida's provincial secretary] resides in a spacious, neat building: there are several merchants and gentlemen of other professions, who have respectable and convenient buildings in the town."[31] While his account does not disclose anything about style or building practices, there is a British drawing of about the same time that reveals a house design influenced by Gulf Coast practices. The drawing, *Plan of the Commanding Officer's Quarter at Pensacola*, was sent to London in 1779 by John Campbell, commanding officer of the British army in West Florida. The plan included "the present House built by General Taylor," and a floor plan and elevation of a proposed "Addition where the

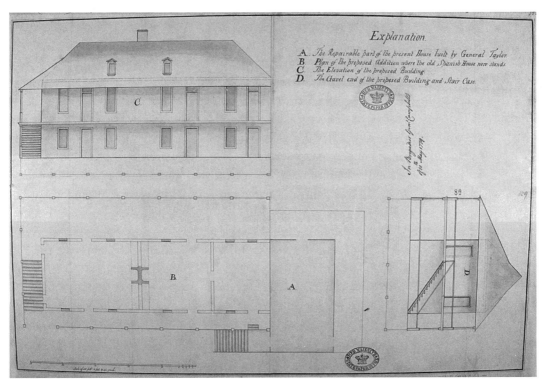

6.12. *Plan of the Commanding Officer's Quarter at Pensacola*, 1779, British West Florida. The drawing shows the house built by General Taylor (*A*), and a proposal for a new addition: floor plan (*B*), elevation (*C*), and section (*D*). The architecture was characteristic of the West Indies and Gulf Coast. (Courtesy of Public Record Office, PRO: MPG 1/980)

old Spanish House now stands," including the "Gavel [gable] end of the proposed Building and Stair Case." The new building was planned with a wide veranda, outside staircase, and flared eaves. In the original drawing now in England, the glass in the windows, dormers, and transoms is colored green, and the wood doors are colored a soft shade of coral.[32]

Pensacola was never a rich colonial town,[33] but the buildings were well planned for the climate and local materials: wood (cypress and pine) and clay for bousillage and fired bricks. The architecture of the town, from both Spanish and English periods, was barely in its twentieth year when the American rebellion was demanding the time and resources of the British military and officials in Florida. On October 9, 1778, the most violent hurricane in the colony's memory struck. Rose Island was breached and the surge at Pensacola destroyed the wharf, merchants' establishments, and a considerable number of houses. Ships were blown ashore, some as far as a mile into the woods. Cannon were found a half mile from the fort.[34]

The civilian urban buildings were mostly modest and made of wood. They belonged to the professionals, merchants, entrepreneurs, and trades people who were building Pensacola's future, and were influenced by the region's vernacular style of architecture, a composite of older practices from the West Indies and African slaves, the French in Louisiana, Natchez, and Mobile, and the earlier Spanish at the site. Respecting the region's moist ground, heat, and humidity, houses were raised off the ground to allow air to circulate under floorboards and had long, shady galleries covered by extended roof eaves and single-width rooms for cross ventilation. Some had dormers and central hall plans. The galleries were called "piazzas" by the British, "verandas" and "porches" by Americans, as the style became widespread across northern Florida in the nineteenth and twentieth centuries. George Washington Sully painted *The House We Lived in in Pensacola W. Florida, July 4, 1834,* portraying a raised cottage that was typical of the colonial period (fig. 6.13). The style did not originate with "crackers," a misunderstanding of recent vintage.[35]

The La Pointe-Krebs House in Pascagoula, Mississippi, may be the oldest standing example of one of the many raised cottage forms that stood in the Gulf Coast region that was once part of Florida (fig. 6.14). It was built by a French naval officer, Joseph Simon de la Pointe, who came to the Gulf Coast in 1699, and was passed on to his daughter, Marie Joseph, who married Hugo Krebs, and then to a British owner when what is now Mississippi was part of British West Florida. The house is sometimes labeled "Old Spanish Fort," but the Spanish were not a part of the

6.13. *The House We Lived in in Pensacola W. Florida, July 4, 1834,* painted by George Washington Sully, with watercolor, pen and ink, depicts a common house form of co-lonial Pensacola. It came out of an older tradition of framed cottages that were raised off the ground and cooled by wide front galleries that came to be called "porches" as the house form spread across Florida during the nineteenth and twentieth centuries. (Courtesy of Special Collections, University of West Florida Library, Pensacola)

early house history. The original structure of this house was composed of the two center rooms ca. 1718. The frame was raised off the ground on wood pilings or pieces of stone, and the walls were a combination of cy-press and cedar posts filled in with a bousillage of clay and moss, some-times called oyster shell cement when lime mortar from oyster shells was added. Its wall construction was similar to that of the Spanish governor's house built in Pensacola about 1760.[36]

Examples of raised cottages dating from Pensacola's colonial period are the Lavalle-Bonifay House and the Dorothy Walton House. They have been moved to the Historical District and restored, their original materials, building methods, and floor plans preserved. Both represent a house form influenced by Pensacola's large French Creole population.

The Lavalle-Bonifay House was built ca. 1803–15 as a duplex by Carlos Lavalle and Marianna Bonifay, a French widow who fled to West Florida from Santo Domingo during the slave revolt of the 1790s. Her name, "M. Bonifay," is imprinted on bricks found in old buildings around Pensacola. She and Carlos had purchased a brickyard in 1807 on the op-posite side of the bay where, with slave labor, they produced bricks and paving tiles. The house is framed in heavy timbers mortised and tenoned and raised off the ground. The front facade is shaded by a gallery (ve-randa or porch) the length of the house. The exterior red trim is a repro-duction of the original color made from local red clays (pl. 29).

6.14. LaPointe-Krebs House, ca. 1718, Pascagoula, Mississippi. The Gulf coast cottage house form came out of the West Indies, where it might have been influenced by African slaves, and was adapted to the wet and humid coastal and river sites in the American southeast by colonial French, Spanish, and English settlers. The LaPointe-Krebs House may be the oldest standing example. (Photograph, Thomas C. S. Wixon Collection, Jackson County Archives, courtesy of Jackson County Historical Society)

The raised cottage known as the Dorothy Walton House was built ca. 1810 by some unknown resident of Spanish Pensacola. It was named later, however, for Dorothy Walton (1760–1832), the widow of George Walton, governor of Georgia and signer of the Declaration of Independence. She came to Pensacola with her son, Colonel George Walton, Jr., secretary of West Florida under Andrew Jackson, and lived in the house rented by the government for the Waltons from 1821 until her death in 1832. It stood then at 137 West Romona Street, fronting on the "Public Washing Place." Among its many owners over the years was a "Yankee" who in 1910 added a dormer, four fat round Tuscan columns, and a Tiffany-style window. The house has been restored to its original appearance, with squared posts supporting the generous front and rear verandas. The wide central hall that runs from an equally wide front door to the back door creates a comfortable breezeway (fig. 6.15). There is a loft where the floor boards are secured with handmade wood pegs. The house is raised on brick piers imprinted with "M. Bonifay" that rest on oyster shell beds eighteen inches underground.[37]

The Barkley House is a French colonial form raised high off the ground. It fronts the harbor and might have been constructed before the end of the colonial period. It is Pensacola's oldest brick house. The difficulty in its dating is compounded by the possibility that it was constructed with recycled bricks that date from the British or second Spanish period. The brick walls, 16 inches thick, tapering to 12 inches, were stuccoed, scored, and painted to look like stone, a fashionable finish in colonial America that became popular again during the 1840s with the Picturesque and Italianate styles. The house today is 40 by 40 feet, but earlier it had two wings in the rear forming a U-shaped residence. Floor-length windows passed the summer breezes through the house, and eight fireplaces reduced the winter chill blowing off the bay water in the winter (pl. 30).

The first owner of record was George Barkley in 1835. He was born in London in 1793 and came to Pensacola in 1820, where he became a very successful merchant in coastal trade. By profession and by marriage, he had close links to French styles and to New Orleans, where his French wife, Clara Louise Garnier, was raised. Barkley died in 1854, followed by

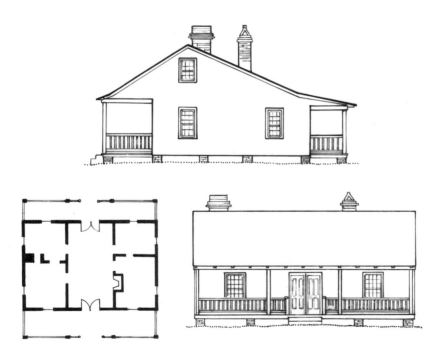

6.15. Dorothy Walton House, ca. 1810, Pensacola, Spanish West Florida. The raised cottage was of the vernacular style that had evolved along the Gulf Coast region in response to the environment. Moved and restored to the Historic Pensacola District. (Redrawn by E. Gordon after F. Blair Reeves before it was moved)

Clara in 1867 during a yellow fever epidemic. They brought up nine children in the house.[38] Like many French colonial plantation houses along the bayous and rivers in Mississippi and Louisiana, the Barkley House is raised 5 to 6 feet off the ground. This choice was a response to the climate and site, close to the water's edge of Pensacola harbor. In this respect, its high piers resembled those at the house built earlier by Arthur Neil, chief of British ordnance, at his plantation, Greenfield, twelve miles west of Pensacola. Greenfield was high enough off the ground to park his carriage underneath (pl. 21). Barkley House has generous verandas that might have been used like those inventoried at Greenfield for sleeping and for storage pantries, containing beds as well as the family's china, butter, sugar, and tea.[39]

The picture of colonial buildings in Pensacola, during English as well as Spanish hegemony, is incomplete. Until archaeology and history unearth more information, British Pensacola's aspirations, at least, can be presented in drawings and plans that are worth a thousand words of construction details.

7 | Haciendas and Plantations

The farmhouse was all dinginess. It sat snugly then as now
under tall old orange trees, and had a simple grace of line,
low, rambling and one-storied.

Marjorie Kinnan Rawlings

The farmhouse in the orange grove that moved Marjorie Kinnan Rawlings to write so eloquently of Cross Creek and Florida was built about sixty years after the end of Florida's colonial period. However, the house form, a wood-framed raised cottage with shady front veranda and shake roof, was not far removed from the houses constructed by the settlers of colonial Florida, which once stretched to the Mississippi River (fig. 7.1). Its form came out of the West Indies, perhaps owing in part to African slaves, and arrived in Florida with French, Spanish, and English colonists. Practical, expedient, conservative in design, and with an affinity for the land, the wet southern climate, and the job to be done, buildings on farms had little reason to change, generation after generation.

There were notable exceptions, however. Bella Vista, for example, was a splendid neo-Palladian stone plantation house of the British colonial period. It was constructed about four miles south of St. Augustine on Woodcutters Creek (now Moultrie Creek) during the 1770s, with formal gardens that included a bowling green. Kingsley Plantation, another exception, was developed by Americans during the second Spanish colonial period. The Kingsley buildings were constructed with stone, clay bricks, tabby, and wood on Fort George Island, to a design obsessed with classical symmetry and modular geometry. Both these plantation houses reflected the owners' personal histories and use of local materials.

This chapter, and the chapter about Kingsley Plantation that follows, search for the methods, materials, aesthetics, and environmental influences on colonial Florida's agrarian architecture.

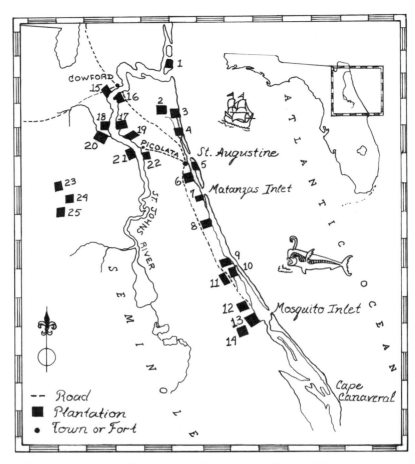

7. Colonial East Florida Haciendas and Plantations: 1. Kingsley Plantation (1797); 2. Hacienda San Diego (1703); 3. Mt. Pleasant (1780); 4. Grant's Villa (1768); 5. Vergell (1763); 6. Bella Vista (1765); 7. Forbes Plantation (ca. 1770); 8. Bulow Plantation (1820); 9. Rosetta (1765); 10. Mt Oswald (1764); 11. Swamp Settlement (1770); 12. Dunlawton (1804); 13. New Smyrna Plantation (1767); 14. Ambrose Hull, Cruger, and Depeyster Plantation (New Smyrna Sugar Mill Ruins), (1801); 15. San Juan Nepomuceno (1792); 16. Beauclerk's Bluff (ca. 1769); 17. New Switzerland (1771); 18. Hibernia (1785); 19. Mt. Hope (1776); 20. Tonyn's Plantation (1768); 21. Franco Ligarroa Hacienda (late 1600s); 22. Sanchez Risar Hacienda (late 1600s); 23. Hacienda La Chua (1620s); 24. Pilgrimage Plantation (1820); 25. Cuscowilla (1750s?). (Drawn by E. Gordon)

SPANISH HACIENDAS

In the late 1760s, John Bartram wrote, "its certain ye spaniards had formerly made plantations at great distance as well as all around Augustine before they quarreled with ye creek Indians."[1] A decade later, his son, William, made a unique journey exploring more of Florida's frontiers. Scattered among his wondrous descriptions of the land, rivers, and native plants, from the Atlantic coast to Mobile, then part of Florida, are many references to plantations. William saw remains of old orange groves and Spanish hacienda buildings: "There are to be seen plain marks or vestiges of the old Spanish plantations and dwellings; as fence posts and wooden pillars of their houses."[2] He was tight-lipped, however, about details. Nor did he describe the buildings of the English plantations he visited. He was, nevertheless, very effective in leaving the impression that Florida by then already had a long history of rural farm architecture.

Florida's cattle ranching began on Anastasia Island shortly after the Spanish built a town there in 1566.[3] Later, Spanish landowners would follow the missions westward, leasing cleared "old fields" from Indian chiefdoms whose native populations were dwindling in epidemics of European diseases. Some of these haciendas became large enough to create Florida's first landed aristocracy, but they left behind no sketches of their buildings.[4]

Hacienda La Chua was one of the most important ranches of the seventeenth century. It was established by Don Francisco Menéndez Marquéz, the royal treasurer, a descendant of Governor Pedro Menéndez Marquéz, nephew of Pedro Menéndez de Avilés, the founder of St. Augustine. The cattle ranch was established in the 1620s along the north

7.1. Raised cottage, ca. 1880s, Cross Creek. About sixty years after the colonial period ended, a raised cottage with shady front porch was built at Cross Creek. Later, a second and third raised cottage were added to the rear and side, and it became the home of Marjorie Kinnan Rawlings. The three houses were not far removed from houses built during the colonial period, when porches were called galleries, piazzas, or verandas. (Photograph by M. Gordon)

ridge of today's Paynes Prairie, south of Gainesville. *Chua* was a Timucuan word for the sinkhole; *la chua* became its Spanish name. In time,
Hacienda La Chua gave its name to the town and county of Alachua.
Cattle, horses, and pigs were raised and exported by 1672. Archaeology
has turned up hundreds of fragments of olive jars, Spanish majolica,
wrought iron hardware, spikes, and hinges. In addition to two African
slaves, the household included Gerónimo, a Mexican Indian servant.[5]
The principal Menéndez family homes, however, were in St. Augustine.

Spanish ranchers, following the missions to the valley of the St. Johns
River, established large haciendas near Forts Picolata and Pupo in the late
1600s and early 1700s. Don Franco Ligarroa's ranch was laid out on the
west bank and Don Juan Sanchez Risar's on the east bank, both worked
by Christian Indians from the missions.[6]

Twenty-two miles north of St. Augustine, Don Diego de Espinosa,
wealthy resident of St. Augustine, had built his hacienda, San Diego, by
1703, in savannas surrounded by woods and fresh water ponds. He supplied the presidio with fresh beef. Little is known about Espinosa's buildings except that he palisaded his ranch in the 1730s with cedar poles
fifteen feet high to "protect" his slaves from Indians. Thereafter called
Fort San Diego, the plantation was garrisoned by the Spanish and surrendered to General Oglethorpe's expedition against St. Augustine in 1740.
The British constructed an earthwork and moat around San Diego, and
departed after the siege without burning it. When Oglethorpe again
marched on St. Augustine in 1743, the fortified ranch had disappeared,
suggesting the Spanish themselves had demolished it as a defensive
move. "There are still some Ruins of it left, as a great Cross, Trench, and
Slaughter-House for Cattle. It must formerly have been a very fine estate," wrote a member of the expedition.[7] A map printed in 1742 showed
its location but not its architecture (map 9).

Moving west into the Apalachee region, Spanish colonists established
haciendas that grew wheat and corn and raised cattle and pigs. Hacienda
Asile was established by Governor Benito Ruíz de Salazar Vallecilla ca.
1645–46. He was an absentee owner; the spread was managed by Captain
Agustín Pérez de Villa Real and worked by soldiers, African slaves, and
Indians. The free-ranging animals of such western Spanish ranches,
however, destroyed Indian cornfields and ultimately were partly to blame
for the Indian revolt of 1704, and thus their own destruction. The ranch
buildings were constructed like those at San Luis, the region's administra-
trative center. There was a "tall dwelling with good timbers." Several others used combinations of "clay walls" (wattle-and-daub), and "palm
thatch."[8]

William Bartram described the western region as "frequently present-ing to view remains of ancient Spanish plantations" that were conve-niently situated near "one of the most beautiful navigable rivers in the world, and not more than thirty miles from St. Mark's on the great bay of Mexico."[9] St. Mark's was San Marcos de Apalachee, the Spanish fortified outpost at the confluence of the Apalachee (St. Marks) River and Wakulla River, from where the haciendas shipped products directly to and from Mexico, Cuba, and St. Augustine.

BRITISH PLANTATIONS

There is much more information about plantation architecture during 1764–84, when the British aggressively pursued a plantation economy. In England at the Public Record Office are loyalist claims that describe building materials and dimensions and surveys showing plantations me-ticulously laid out with contoured fields dedicated to rice, cotton, indigo, corn, and domestic gardens (fig. 7.6). Some surveys have sketches of houses for owners and overseers, and "Negro villages," as well as dams, mills, wharves, warehouses, barns, corn and poultry houses, and indigo works (figs. 7.3, 7.4). Small plantations had 300 to 1,000 acres; many large plantations had 5,000 to 20,000 acres belonging to absentee owners in London. More than a few St. Augustine residents had multiple planta-tions.

William Drayton developed Oak Forest, a three-hundred-acre planta-tion four miles from St. Augustine. He was educated at the Inns of Court in London, and had come from Charleston to be chief justice of East Florida in 1765. His principal residence (after Drayton Hall near Charles-ton, South Carolina) was in urban St. Augustine, where in 1772 he had bought one of the largest Spanish-built stone houses, the former home of Don Juan Joseph Elíxio de la Puente (fig. 5.5, fig. 5.6).[10] Drayton's villa at Oak Forest was described as "a neat dwelling house, kitchen, storehouse, stable, carriage house and other buildings," valued at £300. James Hume, Drayton's successor as chief justice, bought Oak Forest and hired up to twenty gardeners "constantly employed for several years" to lay out, raise, level, and turf "the pleasure ground, in erecting bridges, Chinese, Chevaux de frize, and other ornamental and useful fences," increasing the value to £1,000.[11]

Another town dweller, Mary Evans, like Drayton, had houses in town and a one-thousand-acre plantation twenty miles outside of town. She too was from South Carolina. Mary arrived in St. Augustine at age thirty-three in 1763, outlived three husbands, and was the city's best-known midwife. Her second husband, Joseph Peavett, was from England and was paymaster for the British troops. In time, he became a successful businessman and then member of the lower House of the General Assembly in 1781. Mary and Joseph bought the one-story stone house on St. Francis Street that is now called the "Oldest House" (figs. 5.2, 5.3). They added the wood second story, loggia, balcony, fireplace and chimney, and glazed sashes and turned it into an inn, tavern, and store for the garrison, and bought another town house, a two-storied tabby and wood house with two chimneys on Marine Street. As they acquired wealth, they also purchased 2,100 acres and fifty-seven slaves. Peavett died, and Mary married John Hudson, an Irish Catholic twenty-eight years her junior, who came from Havana. He was a notorious debtor, and plunged Mary into severe financial problems, but Mary held onto her plantation. It was named New Waterford after her Irish husband's birthplace in Ireland.[12]

Her plantation's main house was wood frame and weatherboarded, with a brick chimney and fireplace, a parlor, and two rooms. The outbuildings included a two-story house for storing corn, a detached wood planked kitchen, one stone or brick oven, seven slave houses for twenty slaves, including three families and five elderly men and women over age seventy, and four chicken coops. She died at her plantation house in 1792. Her estate inventory included numerous mahogany pieces, cupboards with glass doors, desks with drawers and mirrors, seventy-five books, and a silver tea service. Her clothing included kid and silk gloves, linens, silks, and capes of fine cloth.[13]

The Forbes family had a distant plantation in addition to three town houses and a country house just outside St. Augustine. John Forbes was minister of St. Peter's Church. His wife, Dorothy Murray, was from a wealthy Boston family (fig. 5.16). Their plantation of 300 acres was twenty miles south of St. Augustine on the Matanzas River. The dwelling house was described by Dorothy as consisting of five rooms and a "Piazza supported by stone pillars fit for the accommodation of a family." In addition there was an indigo house two stories high. Her loyalist claim for the plantation was £750.[14]

Owners of some of the largest Florida plantations preferred to live in the capitals, St. Augustine and Pensacola, or even further away in Charleston and London. Their plantations were run by resident overseers, and the architecture was modest, characterized by practical wood houses for the overseers and one built for the visiting owner. Rosetta, for example, was Lieutenant Governor John Moultrie's rice plantation on the Tomoka River, "being fit for indigo, rice, and provisions [domestic] with timber for building vessels, . . . also a good two story dwelling house, barn, and machine and other offices and [slave] houses." The house was described in 1787 with "piazzas before and behind." Another witness described it as "long and narrow."[15] Moultrie, meanwhile, lived in St. Augustine, in the former Spanish treasurer's house, and was building his very elegant neoclassical manor house at Bella Vista, his other plantation (figs. 5.4, 7.11, 7.12).[16]

Up and down Florida's east coast, from the Georgia border to the Mosquito Inlet (Ponce de Leon Inlet), along the rivers and inlets that were the main transportation routes, huge tracts of land—up to twenty thousand acres—were granted to capitalist-planters who speculated large investments in cash crops of indigo, rice, sugarcane, citrus, corn, naval stores, and Sea Island cotton (map 7). The majority of the grantees were from England, Scotland, or the British colonies in America and the West Indies, but some were French, German, and Swiss.[17] The details of their buildings and names of their builders and craftsmen have slipped into oblivion, lost with time and the dynamics of a frontier undergoing tremendous growth. A few are being excavated by Florida's archaeologists. Richard Oswald's plantation, for example, lies under Ormond Beach, and Andrew Turnbull's under New Smyrna Beach. Others are under twentieth-century highways and commercial developments.

Vergell (the owner's spelling of *el vergel*, Spanish for the garden or grove) was the plantation of Jesse Fish on Anastasia Island, once called Fish's Island or, even earlier, La Cantera and La Escolta Island. In 1763, Fish's house was the only dwelling on the island. William Brazier's 1760s copy of a survey shows the house surrounded by many cultivated fields. A year after Jesse's death on February 22, 1787, his son, Jesse, Jr., and the merchant John Leslie described the plantation as follows:

> Ten thousand acres, thirty acres of which known by the name Vergell, distant about one and a half miles from St. Augustine, and having a delightful prospect of the Town Harbour and shipping, also of the ten of it are highly improved and cultivated and bear between two and three Thousand of fruit trees come to maturity of which upwards of one thousand are China orange trees, the rest Seville oranges, peaches, lemons, limes, pomegranates, figs, etc. etc. etc. the fruit of which is annually worth about three hundred pounds sterling and annually increasing from a vast number of young trees transplanted and thriving, besides many thousands sweet oranges and other young trees fit to set out, all which with the buildings, fences, etc are valued at £2,500 . . . a stock of horses belonging to the tract consisting of upward of two hundred head, average at sixty shillings each is £600.

Total value of the plantation was £3,690.[18]

7.2. Vergell, ca. 1763, Anastasia Island, sketched by Henry J. Morton in 1867. Jesse Fish's thriving 10,000-acre citrus plantation, Vergell (from *el vergel,* the grove, garden), was across the river from St. Augustine. One hundred years after he constructed his coquina plantation house, it was still standing with arcaded loggia and roofed gallery. The house and Jesse's tomb were the solitary remainders of the island's long building history that had begun in 1566 when the first Spanish settlers moved to the island from Chief Seloy's Timucua village across Matanzas Bay. (Drawing courtesy of SAHS)

Fish's plantation house was built with coquina shellstone quarried on the island. Henry Morton sketched the solitary island house in 1867 (fig. 7.2). The hundred-year-old house was two storied and had an arcaded loggia across the ground floor facade, supporting a roofed veranda above—elements he was familiar with in St. Augustine and the West Indies. Fish was originally from New York but had lived in St. Augustine since boyhood, and he became an agent and master of trading sloops for the mercantile firm of Walton and Company. He married Sarah Warner of New York. Fish exported barrels of oranges and a mix of juice and spirits called "orange shrub." He was buried at his plantation, and his tomb was sketched in December 1874 for *Harper's New Monthly Magazine.* In 1870, the desolate house was still the only residence on Anastasia Island.[19] The island had seen much architectural history, including the germinal town of St. Augustine (1566–72), two early Spanish forts, a seventeenth-century lookout tower that was turned into Florida's earliest lighthouse, and Jesse Fish's manor house in an orange grove.

North of St. Augustine, James Grant, from Scotland, owned two plantations. Appointed governor of East Florida in 1763, he arrived August 29, 1764, and by 1768 had become a serious planter (fig. 4.9). His premier indigo plantation was known as Grant's Villa, on 1,450 acres that took up the tip of the peninsula between the Guana and Tolomato (sometimes

"Tolemato," or North) Rivers (fig. 7.4). The resident manager was Alexander Skinner, who came from South Carolina to serve the colony as Indian agent. His copious letters are now conserved at the Public Record Office in England and tell a poignant story of the development of this plantation.

Historian Daniel Schafer has extracted from Skinner's and Grant's letters a touching description of the sixteen years of hard work by enslaved men and women that made James Grant a wealthy man. The architectural details in these letters, however, are scant, but Dr. Schafer culled from them the following:[20] At first, forty working hands lived in "palmetto huts," but more substantial wood houses were built by the slaves during their free time. They used scantling, shingles, and clapboards, and the frames of their cottages were raised three feet off the ground. The "raised" houses were probably designed by the slaves themselves, who had experience in South Carolina's lowlands. These dwellings formed a "village" of twenty-two "Negro Houses" lining both sides of the main road that traversed the plantation, and led north eventually to Grant's other farm, Mount Pleasant Plantation (fig. 7.3).

Buildings at Grant's Villa were begun by a hired white carpenter, who was replaced by slave apprentice carpenters. These structures were sketched in 1783 by Benjamin Lord, then surveyor general of the colony, and described in Grant's loyalist claim. They included a framed overseer's house with kitchen addition, a large wood barn, stable, two fowl houses, large pigeon house, and a smith's shop on the river bank. A

7.3. Slave Villages, 1760s–84, details from Mount Pleasant Plantation (A) and Grant's Villa (B), British East Florida, based on Benjamin Lord's survey of 1783. Slave houses at Grant's Villa were described as a "village" of twenty-two "Negro Houses" lined along both sides of the main road. At Mount Pleasant, they were described as a "village" of thirty-seven "Negro Houses" lined up across from each other on both sides of an avenue planted with "Tallow Trees." (Redrawn by E. Gordon after Lord's survey at Public Record Office, PRO: T 77/7, ff. 375, 377)

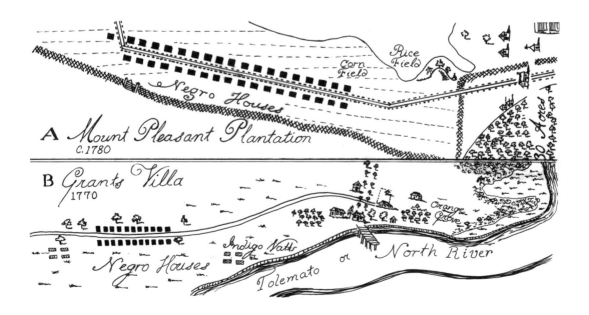

wide wharf built of the trunks of the cabbage palm jutted into the "Tolemato" River (fig. 7.4). The wharf led to Grant's "neat" dwelling house in the shade of a large pine tree, "with offices and outhouses," sketched showing an axial entrance, shingled roof, two gable chimneys, and perhaps a small entrance porch. Behind the house was an allée of formally planted trees leading eastward to a "good landing" on the Guana River.[21]

Mount Pleasant, Grant's plantation north of Grant's Villa, was developed in 1780, after Grant had left the colony and the soil at Grant's Villa was becoming exhausted. Located at the head of the Guana River, the plantation extended to the ocean coast, where Ponte Vedra Beach sprawls today. The cash crops were corn and rice. Alex Skinner had been

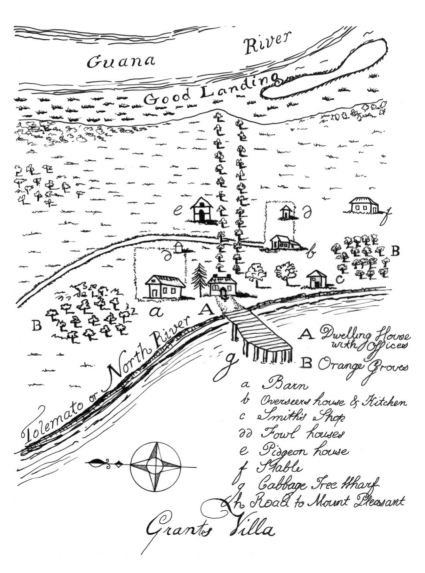

7.4. Grant's Villa, 1768, detail from *A Plan of 1450 Acres of Land in the Province of East Florida the Property of Lieuten.' Gen James Grant, called Grants Villa,* by Benjamin Lord, 1783. Grant's Villa was an indigo plantation north of St. Augustine, at the tip of the peninsula at the confluence of the Guana and Tolemato (or North) Rivers. (Redrawn by E. Gordon after Lord's survey at Public Record Office, PRO: T 77/7, f. 375)

A Dwelling House with Offices
B Orange Groves
a Barn
b Overseers house & Kitchen
c Smith's Shop
dd Fowl houses
e Pidgeon house
f Stable
g Cabbage Tree Wharf
h Road to Mount Pleasant

Grants Villa

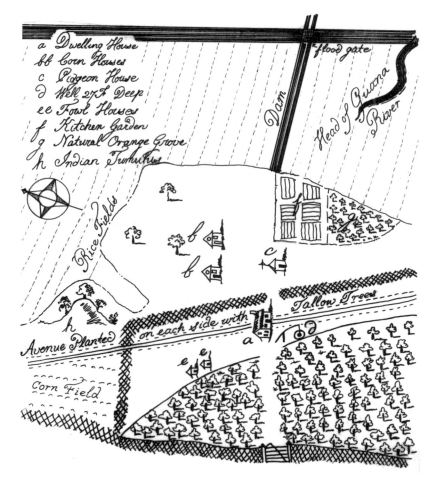

a Dwelling House
bb Corn Houses
c Pigeon House
d Well 27 ft Deep
ee Fowl Houses
f Kitchen Garden
g Natural Orange Grove
h Indian Tumulus

flood gate

Dam

Head of Guana River

Rice Fields

b
b

c

Tallow Trees

h

Avenue Planted on each side with

a

e e

Corn Field

7.5. Mount Pleasant Plantation, 1780, detail from *A Plan of Mount Pleasant Plantation belonging to Lieut' Gen' James Grant in East Florida,* by Benjamin Lord, 1783. The wooden overseer's dwelling, slave houses, corn houses, pigeon dovecote, and fencing, as well as earthen dams, reservoir pond, and flood gates were constructed by slave labor. (Redrawn by E. Gordon after Lord's survey at Public Record Office PRO: T 77/7, f. 377)

killed by Indians in Georgia; the supervision of the new plantation fell to David Yeats, physician, planter, secretary of East Florida, and business agent for Grant. Within five months, the principal African driver and fourteen male slaves had cleared the high ground and constructed their log cabins and the overseer's house. Benjamin Lord's sketch of Mount Pleasant shows a one-and-a-half story dwelling house with gable roof, axial entrance and brick chimney, two corn houses, a pigeon house with a weather vane, a well 27 feet deep, two fowl houses, kitchen garden and orange grove (fig. 7.5). There were extensive fences with gates, and a "village" of thirty-seven "Negro Houses" lined up across from each other on both sides of an avenue planted with "Tallow trees" (fig. 7.3). Thousands of Chinese tallow tree seedlings were raised, perhaps to extract wax from the seed capsules to manufacture soap and candles. To cultivate the rice, the slaves had constructed earthen dams, a large reservoir pond, and wooden flood gates.[22]

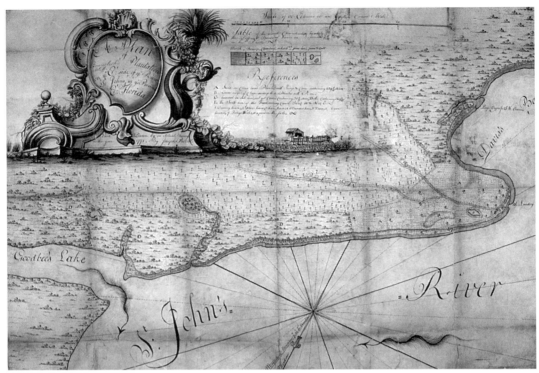

7.6. *A Plan of Beauclerk's Bluff Plantation on ye East side of ye River St. Johns in ye Province of East Florida, Laid Down by an Actual Survey in the year 1771, by Joseph Purcell.* The indigo plantation was on a point of land south of and opposite today's Naval Air Station. Indigo, rice, and corn fields are mapped; the slave houses and storehouse were erected near the bank of the river at the "landing;" the overseer's house and barn were on the road to Cowford (Jacksonville); the indigo works were along the river at a distance from the dwellings. (Photograph courtesy of Public Record Office, PRO: MPD 2)

Buildings necessary for the production of indigo were drawn by Joseph Purcell in 1771 at Beauclerk's Bluff plantation, on the St. Johns River, about opposite today's Jacksonville Naval Air Station. Purcell's drawing may be the only one known to illustrate indigo works in Florida (figs. 7.6, 7.7). Production took place near the river's edge, away from the overseer's house, because of the flies and obnoxious smell of putrification. His drawing depicts a water pump with platform and trough, three indigo vats of different sizes, the curing or dewing house, and the men bringing the indigo plants, pressing, and beating the liquid in the vats. After the sludge was pressed to squeeze out the remaining liquid, it was dried into a paste, worked by hand, put into boxes and cut into "bricks" that were air dried in the sun and in the dewing house to control the curing process. Purcell wrote on the drawing that it was made from an "Actual Survey."[23]

Patrick Tonyn, governor of East Florida after 1773, owned many tracts of land, the largest of which was a 20,000-acre indigo plantation called

Tonyn's Plantation twenty-four miles north from St. Augustine on Black Creek. Development began in April 1768, before Tonyn resided in Florida, and was productive until he left in 1785. The inventory of buildings made in 1788 for his loyalist claim included "a commodious dwelling house, wood framed, 14 by 16 feet, clapboarded, two storied, and lofted, with a brick chimney." There was a detached kitchen that was a "logg house," 24 by 15 feet, divided into two apartments and clapboarded (roofed with planks), with a brick chimney and oven. The outbuildings included three "logg houses," each 14 by 24 feet and a "complete cooper shop adapted for three coopers and their tools, 30 by 16 feet, with posts in the ground, weatherboarded and clapboarded.... A very large naval storage shed 30 by 16 feet was boarded and had a clapboard roof." There were nineteen "Negro Houses" and four complete sets of indigo baths, as well as fences and a "very costly [£300] machine for pulling up trees by the roots" shipped from England. Tonyn's claim for all his property losses came to the enormous sum of £18,347.[24]

The 2,500-acre Hope Plantation layout and building descriptions reveal the English obsession with symmetry (fig. 7.8). The plantation was on the east side of the St. Johns River across from Green Cove Springs, twelve miles from St. Augustine, bought by Robert Hope in 1776 to pro-

7.7. Indigo works, Beauclerk's Bluff Plantation, 1771. Detail from *A Plan of Beauclerk's Bluff Plantation on ye East side of ye River St. Johns in ye Province of East Florida, Laid Down by an Actual Survey in the year 1771*. Purcell depicted the following constructions: water pump platform with trough, three indigo vats of different sizes for different stages of the indigo production, and the curing or "dewing" house. He depicted slaves bringing the plants, pressing, and beating the liquid in the vats. (Photograph courtesy of Public Record Office, PRO: MPD 2)

duce rice, corn, and turpentine. There was a very good wharf on Six-Mile Creek and "a dam on Saw Mill Creek for the back water for the cleared rice ground on said creek." A survey and inventory for Hope's loyalist claim for £4,133 reveal all the buildings were wood frame, as follows: main dwelling house, two-storied, 40 by 20 feet, with a brick chimney; corn house, also 40 by 20 feet, with a lodging over it; cooperage, a larger 50-by-25-foot structure; two square pavilions, each 12 by 12 feet and of unknown use, built at the corners of the fenced kitchen garden and noted as having "boarded floors"; overseer's house, 24 by 16 feet, also with boarded floors; house of the slave driver, 20 by 14 feet; and the seventeen "Negro Houses," described with "boarded bedroom" or "boarded bedplace." The latter may have been a reference to a loft or wood sleeping shelf like those shown on plans for British barracks. The kitchen and

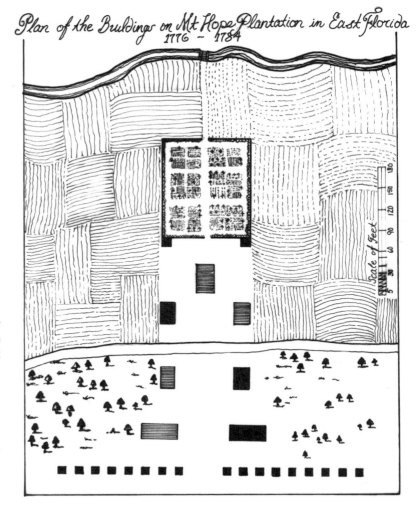

7.8. Mt. Hope Plantation, 1776, British East Florida. Robert Hope bought 2,500 acres on the east side of St. Johns River (opposite today's Green Cove Springs) and laid out his buildings in a rigidly symmetrical plan. The survey and list of buildings and their dimensions for his loyalist claim include buildings with "boarded floors," "boarded bedroom" and "boarded bedplace." There were seventeen slave houses and a very large cooperage. (Redrawn from survey at Public Record Office, PRO: T 77/8 folio 187)

oven were detached from the dwelling house, and the domestic garden of about an acre had a high boarded fence.[25] The wharf served as a convenient landing for travelers from west of the St. Johns River en route to St. Augustine, and as a loading and unloading dock for merchant ships.[26]

Boarded buildings required a great amount of wood: timbers, planks, and shingles. Trees were felled and split at the site, or lumber was purchased from one of the local water-driven sawmills. One of the earliest mills known was that of John Hewitt, British contractor whose name is associated with many works in St. Augustine. His mill on Pellicer Creek could turn out five hundred to fifteen hundred feet of lumber a day (fig. 7.9).

Many of these plantations were equivalent to small, self-sufficient company towns. The working farm buildings were site designed for domestic activities and cash crop production. In addition to the usual dwellings for owners, slaves, and overseers, and outbuildings for cooking, laundry, storage, making cheese, raising pigeons and chickens, and smoking meat, there were mills for processing cash crops, and barns, stables, carriage houses, lumber mills, carpentry shops, cooperages, blacksmith shops, dams, reservoirs, wharves, indigo houses, and churches. Such plantations produced, in addition to cash crops, the foodstuffs for domestic consumption and the materials for their buildings, canoes and flatboats, and carriages. Bricks, boards, timbers, shingles, lime, plaster, mortar, and turpentine were produced at the site to meet building needs. Making

7.9. John Hewitt's water-powered sawmill, 1770s, Pellicer Creek, south of St. Augustine. Mill production was an enormous improvement over hand-manufactured lumber, rived (hand-split) or pit-sawn. (Model made by William Jones; photocopy by Ken Barrett, Jr., courtesy of SAHS)

bricks was a long and tedious process requiring an experienced brick-maker, a process that will be described in chapter 8.

Among the largest plantation undertakings was Dr. Andrew Turn-bull's plantation at New Smyrna. Turnbull was a wealthy Scotsman who in 1768 brought fourteen hundred indentured settlers to Florida from Greece, Italy, and the Balearic Islands to develop a plantation on two 20,000-acre grants, which he named after Smyrna (now Izmir), a seaport in Ottoman Turkey, birthplace of his wealthy Greek wife, Gracia Maria Rubini. They had met in Paris, were married in 1753, and eventually had twelve children. Turnbull brought his family to St. Augustine in January of 1767, and from there set out to recruit his workers and develop the plantation. During the nine years of New Smyrna's existence, many buildings were erected, but few have been located and archaeologically described to date. The first homes of the indentured workers were hastily built palm thatch shelters that were superseded by wood frame houses constructed under the supervision of William Watson, an English car-penter hired by Turnbull. He resided on the plantation during its con-struction, and reported in 1777 that 145 houses were completed. His bill was £35 each for carpentry, totaling £5,075.[27]

The invoice signed by William Watson for "Carpenter Work on the Smyrna Settlement" also listed: "Dr. Turnbull's Dwelling House, £270; Two large stores for Provisions, £270; One small store for Provisions, £100; A Wind Mill, £3000; A Horse Mill, £30; One Indigo House, £100; 4 Bridges all of Cedar @ £30 each; and 22 Double Sett of Indigo vats @ £50 each, £1100."[28]

There were also shops for carpenters and blacksmiths, and the catho-lic San Pedro Church and rectory, which was described by a Cuban fish-erman as built of bricks. The design of Turnbull's own residence is some-what a mystery. It may have been on his 300-acre personal plantation adjoining the settlement to the north.[29] Watson's invoice for £270 would have been more than sufficient for a good two-story wood house with chimney and piazza, or it might have been for various dependencies, or a very large second story of wood on a stone foundation to accommodate his very large family and house servants. In the best of architecture, the detached kitchen and at least one storehouse would have been stone.

One of the settler's house sites has recently been excavated, revealing a two-room dwelling 13 by 27½ feet with tabby floor and central chimney. The chimney stack and two hearths were built of coquina stone covered with smooth mortar. The timber post-and-beam frame had horizontal hand-split wood laths nailed to squared vertical posts, plastered with mortar inside and out. The roof is believed to have been palm thatch.[30]

Turnbull's plantation was one of the largest in British East Florida, taking up most of today's New Smyrna Beach. The plantation was abandoned in 1777 after years of crop failures, deaths by disease and mistreatment, ethnic discontent, financial difficulties, and political feuding between Turnbull and Governor Tonyn. Some six hundred of the settlers, now generally called "Minorcans," walked to St. Augustine, where many established themselves with great success, adding much to the cultural heritage of the old city (figs. 5.10, 5.11).[31]

Another very large enterprise was that of Richard Oswald, a slaver originally from Scotland who invested in 20,000 acres in Florida on good navigable rivers in 1764. His plantation had five settlements. One called Mount Oswald was the heavily forested peninsula at the confluence of the Tomoka and Mosquito (Halifax) Rivers. In the seventeenth century, it had been the Timucua village of Nocoroco. Oswald sent slaves to Florida who were carpenters, sawyers, blacksmiths, coopers, and experienced indigo producers to develop his plantation. The first overseer, Samuel Huey, was a poor administrator and the slaves drowned him. He was replaced by an Indian named Johnson who proved to be an able overseer. The buildings constructed at Mount Oswald circa 1765 included a manor house (40 by 20 feet), a barn, stable, overseer's house, kitchen house, smithy, and slave houses. All that is left today is a network of drainage canals in the tidal marshes preserved in Tomoka State Park north of Ormond Beach.[32]

Five miles to the south, Oswald had another plantation named Swamp Settlement (Three Chimneys Site) that produced sugarcane and rum in 1772. A Jamaican planter who directed the making of the sugar and rum said, "the canes are as rich and produce as well as in most parts of the West Indies."[33] There was a very large overseer's house, described as "framed and shingled, floored and weatherboarded, one Storey high," and a large sugar works constructed of brick.[34]

Remains of Swamp Settlement's sugar works expose bricks laid in English bond, a course of stretchers alternating with a course of headers. While the architectural details are scarce, Oswald himself is documented in American history as the "wealthy statesman" who represented Britain in negotiations in Paris for American independence at the end of the Revolution. Brushed under the carpet, however, is Oswald's principal business in London. He supplied the slaves to the Austin & Laurens Company in Charleston, which sold thousands of enslaved people throughout the colonies and made Richard Oswald, George Austin, and Henry Laurens three of the richest men in North America. In 1748, Oswald had bought the slave franchise from the chiefs of the Temne tribe and leased Bunce Island, a walled prison on the west coast of Africa, for holding black captives.[35]

In British West Florida, the plantations were not as large. The land was not as consistently good for the indigo that brought such largesse to East Florida. Plantations near Pensacola, Mobile, Natchez, and Manchac were described as having several thousand acres with modest houses.[36] Unfortunately, no plans, elevations, or sketches of these West Florida plantations have been found. A few are described in letters and documents. For example, the plantation house belonging to one of the more wealthy entrepreneurs, James Bruce, council member, customs collector, and real estate speculator, was simple: one story, 16 by 16 feet, with a fireplace, planked floors, board walls, and shingled roof.[37]

The most substantial house description found to date in West Florida was of the plantation called Greenfield, built ca. 1767 by Arthur and Eleanor Neil. He was keeper of British ordnance and member of the council of West Florida in Pensacola. They owned 2,000 acres twelve miles west of Pensacola. The form of their manor house was influenced by colonial French practices in the lowlands of the Mississippi delta, raised high enough off the ground to park their horse carriage underneath. On the first floor were two rooms, a dining parlor and a bedroom flanking the central hall, and two substantial piazzas front and back (pl. 21).

The front veranda might have been screened with shutters, for it contained two feather beds, an oak bedstand, a pine writing table, two chairs, five stands of military guns, and a spinet, bow, and fiddle. The rear piazza had a pine table, tea chest, butter stand, two washbasins, and a closet full of sets of china and glassware, soup tureens, candlesticks, teapot stands, cases of silver-handled knives and forks, desert knives and forks, punch bowls, and various rolls of yellow wallpaper. Two feather beds on two bedsteads were in the bedroom, along with walnut chairs, night tables, bureau, and mirror. Six mahogany chairs and a dining table plus two arm chairs, two tea tables, one card table, a gilt mirror, bureau, and a pair of fire dogs in the fireplace graced the dining room. The second floor had a floor cloth, in addition to a mahogany table and a dozen new mahogany chairs upholstered with hair buttons, two mahogany chairs and card table, and four washstands.[38]

The rooms at Greenfield had to be spacious to accommodate all of the furniture inventoried. The wallpaper, floor cloth, extensive inventory of silver cutlery and china, and the gilt mirror indicate high expectations if not a gracious standard of living. Detached outbuildings included the usual kitchen, dairy, washroom, storage house, and slave house. The

Neils were in debt to merchants in Charleston and New Orleans, which resulted in this insightful inventory of the plantation. Just as thought-provoking are the titles of their ninety-two books and assorted pamphlets and magazines, which ranged from works by Homer and Virgil, *Caesars Commentaries, Antiquities of Rome,* and *Paradise Lost,* to several histories of England and revolution, a biography of Oliver Cromwell, debates in Parliament, seven volumes of Shakespeare's works, *Don Quixote,* and practical books of medicine, philosophy, religions, accounting, spelling, music, and *Stone's Geometrical Lectures, The Compleat Housewife, English Tradesmen,* and *Tradesman's Assistant.* The Neil's inventory of the architecture and furnishings of Greenfield is a treasure trove, revealing a frontier life lived in dignity and comfort in West Florida.[39]

Other descriptions of West Florida plantations are lean. Lieutenant Governor Montfort Browne, for example, had two plantations. The only description of his New Grove near Pensacola is of its wallpaper before the home was vandalized by Indians in 1771. His other plantation, which had no slaves, was located on Dauphin Island south of Mobile and known to have had cattle, horses, sheep, and turkeys that were numerous and unfenced. Daniel Hickey, overseer, could not stop the Creek and Alabama Indians from rowing their canoes out to the island to kill a few cattle for barbeque parties. The Indians unabashedly asked him for corn, flour, and tobacco to go with their beef. The cattle were so numerous and fertile on Browne's plantation that Hickey estimated the Indians slaughtered 114 cows plus bullocks and calves without diminishing stock.[40] Descriptions of the buildings were not included in the overseer's records.

After England retroceded Florida to Spain, and the English had left, a number of European planters stayed in Florida. Among them was Francis Philip Fatio, Sr., from Switzerland. He had arrived in Florida in 1771 during the British period. His 10,000-acre plantation, New Switzerland, on the east bank of the St. Johns River south of Mandarin, was a premier plantation of East Florida well into the second Spanish period. Fatio lived at the plantation where he surrounded himself with imported luxuries, including Chinese vases, a library, household silver, a piano, and a gold-headed cane. He was at the center of a large trading network, and received a special trading license in 1787 from Spanish officials that permitted him wide latitude in external trade, from Charleston to Havana. When his daughter, Sophia, married George Fleming, her dowry was said to be greater than the governor's annual salary.[41]

In 1812, during the mayhem of the so-called Patriot's War, Fatio's plantation was burned by Seminoles. Fatio and his family were saved by his two slaves, Dublin and Scipio, who led them through the garden and into a skiff that they rowed hard into the middle of the St. Johns River. Twelve years later, in 1824, the Fatio family returned and rebuilt New Switzerland only to suffer the same tragedy again in 1836 during the Second Seminole War.[42] No architectural details remain, but the plantation had been substantial and its owner, Fatio, had been an important player in colonial Florida.

George Fleming, Fatio's son-in-law, came from Ireland in 1785 and developed Hibernia, his plantation on the western shore of the St. Johns River, across the river from New Switzerland. The site is Fleming Island today, between Green Cove Springs and Orange Park. Hibernia also burned during the Patriot's War. Fleming's son Lewis and his wife, Margaret Seton Fleming, rebuilt the house in 1841. Their son Francis Philip Fleming would become Florida's fifteenth governor. The gracious second house, ringed by a two-story colonnade and verandas, was demolished in 1954. Under magnificent spreading oaks still stands the small board-and-batten church built by Margaret. It was one of a string of Episcopalian river mission chapels built along the St. Johns River in the 1870s and 1880s in the Carpenter Gothic style. The Fleming family is buried in the cemetery beside the chapel, a reminder that two large colonial plantations once stood nearby on the banks of the St. Johns River.

Since World War II, profound economic and cultural changes have radically altered Florida's agrarian landscape. With the exception of Kingsley Plantation, there are no colonial plantation buildings standing in situ to study or to compare their construction technology with historical descriptions. Until archaeology proves otherwise, some local building practices can be inferred from the loyalist claims and colonial correspondence. For example, cypress, cedar, and palm trunks were preferred woods for framing and for elements that came in contact with water, particularly verandas, roof shingles, and wharves. The application of tar oil to the roof shingles lengthened their durability. Resins were added to whitewash to make it more glutinous.

Separate buildings were constructed for domestic activities. The detached buildings, called outbuildings or dependencies, were distanced for practical and aesthetic reasons. Open cooking fires in the kitchen hearths burned day and night, causing mortar and bricks to crack and fires to break out in the flues. In tropical Florida, it was essential to remove the heat of cooking fires as well as the smells of unrefrigerated spoiled food and human waste. The choice material for storehouses and kitchens was masonry.

Archaeology has confirmed that chimneys and hearths were constructed in the centers of buildings as well as at gable ends. Chimneys

7.10. Eighteenth-century brick "kiln." Bricks were made at plantation sites by molding and firing in a "clamp," a temporary kiln made by stacking unfired "green" bricks under canvas stretched across poles. The clamp was plastered and sealed with an outer skin of clayey mud. At the bottom were "eyes" where wood fires burned day and night until the clamp slumped at about 2,550° F. After cooling for two weeks, the clamp was dismantled. Only half the bricks were hard enough for construction. Bricks on the outside, furthest from the fire ("samel" bricks), were too soft and were used as "nogging" to fill inside walls. (Drawing by F. Blair Reeves, F.A.I.A.).

were coquina stone or clay brick; the firebacks were brick. Fireplaces were large enough to burn logs, over which kettles and pots were hung on wrought iron cranes. On more modest farms, chimneys might have been built with poles, sticks, and mud, a version of wattle-and-daub methods that were used until the twentieth century in north Florida and coastal Alabama, once part of colonial Florida.[43] Bricks were imported during the British period, thousands being noted in cargo manifests at the Public Record Office. If clay was present on the plantation, bricks were molded and fired at the site in a "clamp," a kiln made of stacked bricks that required considerable expertise and produced uneven bricks (fig. 7.10).[44] One commercial kiln of record on the east coast was Don Juan McQueen's in the 1790s at his San Juan Nepomuceno plantation (today's Ortega) on the St. Johns River. West Florida was known to have excellent clay; a commercial brick kiln was noted in 1764 northeast of Pensacola by the cartographer George Gauld.[45]

Window glass was imported, but glazed sashes were expensive, and many plantations on the frontiers might have settled for wood shutters only.

Some British plantation buildings were no doubt planned and designed with the aid of tradesmen's handbooks. William Watson, for example, the carpenter at New Smyrna and later in St. Augustine, consulted "books of Architecture."[46] Handbooks for architectural design and tradesmen's instructions were published in England in many editions during the first half of the eighteenth century and widely used by colonists in America.[47] Practical books like William Pain's *Builders Companion* (with ninety-two copper plates) and William Salmon's *Palladio Londinensis, or, The London Art of Building* (with fifty-two copper plates) had many practical drawings and information on how best to design and construct buildings of various sizes. They were published with "clear and simple Instructions annexed to each subject of number, on the same plate, with estimates of materials and workmanship; being useful to all Masons, Bricklayers, Plasterers, Carpenters, Joiners, and others concerned in the several Branches of Building, etc. but also necessary for Gentlemen, who will be hereby enabled to know the exact Expenses of any Building, Alteration, or Repair."[48] Whichever books were locally available in private libraries would influence local designs.

Salmon's book had aids to finding the correct pitch and type of roof trusses, and how to figure the cost of paint in linseed oil in different colors. His painting instructions were accompanied by the admonition that wood sashes, sash frames, window shutters, doors, and door cases particularly should be painted three times with "oyl" to prevent decay.[49] There were illustrations and details for constructing and finishing stairs, fireplaces, frontispieces, porticoes, and windows, and for calculating proper proportions of rooms and corresponding sizes of scantling (timbers) for framing bearing posts, girders, joists, and roof rafters. The popular books by James Gibbs (*Book of Architecture*) and Robert Morris (*Select Architecture,* and *Rural Architecture*) were used many times in the English colonies to design the facades and floor plans of country residences. Plates in such books could be copied, or their classical elements extracted, combined, and reinterpreted to suit one's own taste, size, and purse.

Extant colonial farm buildings being absent in Florida, one might turn to Dudley Farm in Alachua County for some details of early wood frame farm architecture. Begun in 1850, thirty years after the colonial period, many of Dudley's original nineteenth-century outbuildings are still standing. The barn, four-hole outhouse, and cane and dairy houses carry on some of the traditions begun by English or Anglo-American planters late in the colonial period. They were built off the ground on limerock foundations, and had vertical board and batten siding and shingled roofs. The detached kitchen was the closest outbuilding to the farmhouse. Myrtle Dudley recently reminisced about living on Dudley Farm in the early 1900s, when as a little girl she ran down the porch steps, across a dirt yard, and into the kitchen that smelled deliciously of pumpkin and pecan pies.

BELLA VISTA

Bella Vista was exceptional, one of Florida's more grandiose colonial residences. The plantation house was built in the 1770s on 2,500 hundred acres on the west bank of the Matanzas River at Woodcutters (Moultrie) Creek, four miles south of St. Augustine. The design was the pursuit of a cultural ideal, a mansion of Georgian-Palladian proportions and details.

The personal history of its owner-builder, John Moultrie, Jr., is a large part of the architectural story (fig. 7.11). He was born in Charleston in 1729 and educated in Edinburgh, Scotland, studying medicine in the footsteps of his father, who had emigrated to South Carolina about 1733. The family home was called Scaffield Tower, on the coast of Fife, where its ruins are visible today. In Charleston, he led the life of a well-heeled physician and member of the extended and prominent Moultrie family.

7.11. Dr. John Moultrie, Jr. (1729–1798), of Charleston, South Carolina, St. Augustine, Florida, Aston Hall and London, England. He was acting governor of East Florida from May 1771 until March 1774, the peak period of British construction and renovations in St. Augustine. He resided on St. George Street in what is now the Peña-Peck House. John Moultrie owned several plantations, one of which was Bella Vista, four miles south of St. Augustine. (*Dr. John Moultrie, Jr.,* painted in England by Philip Reinagle [1749–1833], oil on canvas, courtesy of Gibbes Museum of Art, Carolina Art Association, Charleston, South Carolina, 1976.0150001)

One relative was the wealthy Sarah Middleton of St. James Parish, where Moultrie also acquired land and slaves. Fort Moultrie, and Moultrie, Georgia, are named for his brother, General William Moultrie, governor of South Carolina. Moultrie came to Florida at Governor Grant's request to assist in forming the government of East Florida in 1764. Grant considered Moultrie "our first and best planter." He was president of the council for seven years, and Grant insisted he be appointed acting governor while Grant was attending to personal affairs in England from May 1771 until the arrival of a new governor, Patrick Tonyn, in March 1774. During the years he was building Bella Vista, he lived in St. Augustine in the Spanish-built treasurer's house (fig. 5.4).[50]

Writing from Great Portland Street in London in 1787, Moultrie recounted that he

> became one of the first proprietors and planters, having moved with his family and a number of Negroes thither [to Florida] and in the year 1770, being honored with the appointment of Lieutenant Governor he broke up and dismantled his plantations in South Carolina and moved all his Negroes into Florida. This undertaking so prospered that for some years before the recession of the country to the Crown of Spain, he thought himself most happy and fortunate; settled with a numerous healthy family in a Country to them the most desirable on plantations upon which about 180 people were employed and maintained, the produce of which enabled him to live clear of debt, in plenty, ease and some elegance.

His memorial continues with the fact that he "lived 17 years in East Florida," and how with great expense and labor he established "his plantations for his children to leave them in ease and independence near each other." When England retroceded Florida to Spain in 1783, he suffered "in being obliged in hurry and confusion and at loss and destruction to get rid of much property consisting of household furniture, four wheeled and other carriages, boats, canoes, carts, and other plantation utensils, large stocks, consisting of about 140 head of working oxen, milk cows, and young cattle, horses, mares and colts, hogs, sheep, etc. of which he can make no just estimate but mentions them to show that he had settled in force in East Florida."[51]

Various testimonies for Moultrie's loyalist property claim (for some 14,000 acres totaling £9,432) described an elegant house with extensive formal landscaping and many outbuildings, valued at £2,974, a very large sum for a residence at the time. Moultrie had aspired to a countryseat as grand as those of his friends and family near Charleston. His wife, Eleanor Austin, was the granddaughter of Elias "Red Cap" Ball

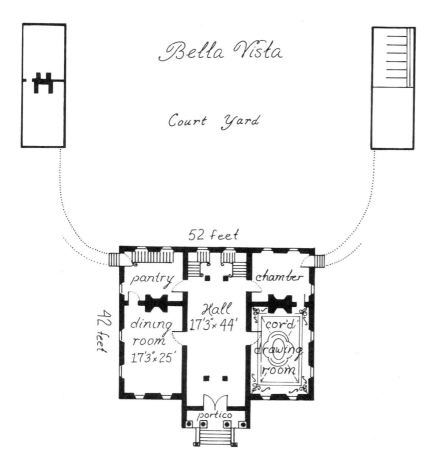

Bella Vista

Court Yard

52 feet

42 feet

pantry

chamber

Hall
17'3"× 44'

dining
room
17'3"×25'

cov'd
drawing
room

portico

7.12. Bella Vista, 1783, conceptual floor plan, British East Florida. Moultrie's plantation house was the pursuit of a cultural ideal. His mansion had Georgian-Palladian proportions and was probably inspired by builders' handbooks and the plantations he, his family, and friends owned in South Carolina. His loyalist claim revealed a large coquina stone house with ten rooms, six of which were bedchambers (4,368 square feet exclusive of the wings, detached kitchen, and other outbuildings). (Conceptual floor plan by E. Gordon and Charles Tingley)

and daughter of George Austin, one of the wealthiest men in the colonies, a partner in the slave-trading firm Austin and Laurens. She grew up in Charleston and on the Austin and Ball plantations, and inherited Aston Hall, the family estate in Shropshire, England.[52] She was "a woman of considerable property who would not have agreed to leave her favorite Carolina upon any other terms"[53] than Moultrie's appointment to the government of Florida and a home commensurate with her cultural upbringing.

The sworn witnesses attesting to Moultrie's claim of loss of property in 1784 described Bella Vista as follows, presented here in the original spelling and punctuation:

> a Stone mansion 52 by 42 feet lower Story rustic, upper Ionick, containing a rustick hall 44 feet long, Six arches supports the ceiling: a dining parlour: cov'd drawing room: six bed chambers: two unfinished porticos: Offices and other necessary buildings for a hundred people besides Kitchen garden, 10 acres fenced and laid out in pleasure gardens containing a bowling

green: laid walks planted with many trees Olives dates oranges lemons limes citrons figs chaddock vines white Mulberry pomegranate peach and plumb banana pines etc. A park in good order about the house of about 30 acres with many pea fowls, Poland geese Pidgeons, bees etc—100 acres hard marsh; fish ponds stock'd with fresh water fish 300 acres of land well clear'd cultivated and well fenced—planted this year 170 acres of corn pease potatoes rice . . . 25 thousand trees boxed for turpentine.[54]

In another testimony, the house was described as a large two-story stone house, built by his slaves, with shingled roof, three rooms on the ground floor, and five rooms on the second. The portico "and Wings" were said to be unfinished (fig. 7.12). There was "a good new Kitchen of stone pillars filled up with wood," and "a framed barn about 50 feet long." In addition to "a good many Negro houses," there was "an Overseer's wooden house framed one story high" in which Moultrie resided during visits to the construction site.[55]

The Bella Vista mansion comprised 4,368 square feet in the first and second floors, exclusive of spaces in the foundation, garret, wings, and the utilitarian outbuildings for the kitchen, laundry, storage, and toilet activities normally carried out inside houses today. The wellspring was Moultrie and his wife, who transplanted to Florida the styles and amenities they were accustomed to in Charleston. Architectural elements such as porticoes, wings, a central receiving hall running from front to back, coved ceiling, "rustick" first floor, and Ionic second floor were characteristic of the finest designs in the English colonies, copied from the same architectural books that spread Italian Renaissance neoclassicism up and down the eastern seaboard of America. Even the name, Bella Vista, was Italian inspired. Several plates in James Gibbs's *Book of Architecture* and Robert Morris's *Select Architecture* could have inspired the plan.

Eleven of the most popular architectural books in the American colonies used by gentlemen-architects of the landed gentry for designing their mansions were available at the Charleston Library Society, of which Moultrie's physician father was a member: Colin Campbell's *Vitruvius Britannicus* (London, 1715–25); Sir William Chambers's *Treatise on Civil Architecture* (London, 1759); Roland Fréart de Chambray's *Parallel of the Ancient Architecture with the Modern* (London 1733); James Gibbs's *A Book of Architecture, Containing Designs of Buildings and Ornaments* (London 1728) and *Rules for Drawing the several Parts of Architecture* (London 1732); William Kent's *The Designs of Inigo Jones* (London 1727, 1770); Giacomo Leoni's *The Architecture of A. Palladio, in Four Books* (London 1742); Robert Morris's *Lectures on Architecture, Consisting of*

Rules Founded upon Harmonick and Arithmetical Proportions in Building (London 1759); William Pain's *The Builder's Companion* (London 1758, 1762); William Salmon's *Palladio Loudinensis, or, The London Art of Building* (London 1755); and Isaac Ware's *The Four Books of Andrea Palladio's Architecture* (London 1737).[56] In addition, Robert Morris's *Select Architecture* was a favorite in many private colonial libraries including that of Thomas Jefferson, who advised a number of friends on their architecture. Morris overlaid his elevation drawings with circles to illustrate proper ratios, proportions, and harmony.[57]

Many kegs and casks of linseed oil, white lead, and pigments were listed in the cargo lists of the ships arriving in St. Augustine during the British period. One might assume Bella Vista was painted in the latest fashionable colors, perhaps the "stone" and "green" used at the governor's house (Government House) and St. Peter's Church.[58] Master painters mixed lead, oil, pigments, and turpentine to make quality paints. "Rustik" suggests that Bella Vista's first floor was Doric and was plastered, scored (rusticated), and painted to look like stone. Moultrie, like his friend Henry Laurens in Charleston, might have ordered items from Philadelphia such as marble fireplace frontispieces and chimney backs, hardware, glazed sashes, and wallpaper made in England.[59]

Moultrie had written in 1778 that he looked forward to living with ease and elegance at his "handsome stone house" that "will last forever, a good country house with ten rooms,"[60] implying that the wings, which added two rooms to the eight on the first and second floors, were substantially completed by that time. Bella Vista, however, did not last forever. The Moultrie family abandoned the plantation in 1784. There were no buyers for English plantations when Florida was retroceded to Spain. Eventually Bella Vista was burned by Indians disgruntled at the change of governments, and today its foundations might yet lie under the present housing development at Moultrie Creek.

Moultrie went to live at his wife's estate, Aston Hall, in England. He had four sons and two daughters. His youngest daughter, Cecelia, married Admiral William Bligh, of "Mutiny on the *Bounty*" fame. One son, George, became rector of Cleobury Mortimer, in Shropshire; George's son John grew up to be a well-known English poet. Another son, James, returned to Charleston, where his son married into the Ball family. Moultrie died in 1798, age 70, and is buried at Shifnal in Shropshire.[61]

Sugar Plantations

Along the coasts and rivers, once main arteries of transportation, weathered ruins of walls and chimney stacks of Florida's late colonial period sugar plantations testify to the tragedies of slavery and the Seminole Indian wars. The exact number of these plantations is still unknown, but all of them, and their pertinent architecture, were destroyed and depopulated in 1835–36 during the Second Seminole War. Beginning about 1770, in today's Volusia and Flagler Counties, sugarcane was planted and cut several times a year, crushed into juice by animal- and steam-powered cane crushers, and boiled in large iron kettles to produce crystallized brown sugar. Molasses was a byproduct from which rum was made. The operation required sizable sugar mills, many of which were erected with blocks of coquina stone and brick.[62]

Richard Oswald's Swamp Settlement (or Three Chimneys Site) sugar plantation, west of Ormond Beach, has been described earlier. Dunlawton (or Sugar Mill Gardens) near Port Orange, south of Daytona Beach, was the sugar plantation started by Patrick Dean and his uncle John Bunch about 1804 on land formerly part of the Turnbull grant. They had migrated to Florida from New Providence in the Bahamas. By 1819, their "house of two parts" with chimney had deteriorated. In 1832, the plantation was bought by Sarah Petty Anderson and her sons, John and James, also from the Bahamas as well as North Carolina. They hired John R. Marshall, a carpenter and master builder from Charleston, to build wood houses for themselves and their overseer, a kitchen house, landing and boat house, corn house, laundry, workshop, twenty-one slave cabins, and the very large sugar mill of coquina stone. An eight-horsepower steam engine was installed by Engineer John McMurchie. After its destruction, the mill was revived to produce sugar in the 1850s. The kettles at the site today were used by Confederates to make salt.[63]

The Cruger and Depeyster plantation, formerly part of the 1801 grant of twenty-six hundred acres belonging to Ambrose Hull, was one of the first to feel the flames of the Seminoles, on Christmas Day, 1835. The ruins, once thought to have been built by the Turnbull colonists or rumored to have been an old Spanish mission, are now identified with Henry Cruger and William Depeyster, who came from New York in 1830 to build the sugar mill, known today as the New Smyrna Sugar Mill Ruins (pl. 31). The mill had dimensions and a layout almost the same as the Bulow mill described below, the largest of the east coast sugar mills.[64]

The sugar mill ruins of Bulow plantation (Flagler County) tell another tragic story (pl. 32). In 1812, a 4,675-acre tract thirty miles south of St.

Augustine was sold by Don Juan José de Estrada, governor of East Florida, to John Russell, whose estate sold it to Charles Wilhelm Bulow of Charleston ca. 1820. Bulow added 2,000 acres and laid out his building plans on Bulow Creek, a tidal creek that flowed into the Halifax River and provided access to the Atlantic Ocean at Ponce de Leon Inlet. Bulow died unexpectedly and left his sixteen-year-old son, John Joachim, to take up his father's dream in Florida. John, who had been educated in Paris, was described as "wild." By 1835, the wealthy young Bulow (he also had a house on Marine Street in St. Augustine) had some sixty buildings at Bulow Ville and was living like a prince in the wilderness. His boat slips were said to be lined with the "spirit" bottles emptied by Bulow and guests.[65]

Bulow's buildings were built in the years immediately following the colonial period, but with the same materials, techniques, and related forms of earlier plantations. The main dwelling had two stories and measured 22 by 42 feet, or 42 by 62 feet with veranda. The walls were coquina stone blocks, eighteen inches thick. The house was heated by a large, central brick fireplace and cooled by cross ventilation. The second floor was the main dwelling area, and was wrapped with a wooden piazza ten feet wide with an exterior staircase front and back. The few archaeological findings to date suggest it was a plan similar to South Carolina's low country plantations, as well as to the French Creole and Spanish archi-

7.13. Colonel Charles Wilhelm Bulow (1779–1821). As the colonial period came to an end, the second son of Baron Joachim van Bulow of Charleston, acquired vast acreage in today's Flagler County on a creek that flowed to the Halifax River, formerly owned by Don Juan José de Estrada, governor of East Florida, 1811–12 and 1815–16. His sudden death left his sixteen-year-old son, John Joachim, to take up his dream, which he did in a very large way. (Photocopy courtesy of Florida State Archives)

tecture of the Gulf Coast region, which had developed in response to warm, moist climates, with raised foundations, single-width rooms, and wide verandas.

Behind the main house were the outbuildings. There were two detached kitchens, each measuring 20 by 20 feet, and forty-six framed slave houses, each about 12 by 16 feet, with tabby floors and shingle roofs. They were set in a crescent, an unusual arrangement that existed at only one other known Florida property, Kingsley Plantation.[66]

The ruins of Bulow's sugar mill structure reveal exemplary masonry craftsmanship (fig. 7.14). Once part of a huge enterprise, the steam engine house measured 18 by 31 feet, with a boiling room about 60 by 30 feet, and a sugar house about 90 by 118 feet.[67] Two massive stone chimneys testify to expert stonecutters and masons, who laid the squared stones with thin mortar joints. The four brick arches similarly reveal well-fired bricks and precision workmanship.

John James Audubon, famed naturalist and painter of birds, was a guest of young Bulow for almost a week in 1831. From Bulow's villa he visited St. Augustine, where he made studies for his engraving of the greenshank, engraved with Fort Marion as background. Another of Audubon's famous bird images, the greater yellowlegs, is thought to have Bulow buildings in the background.

Four years later, on Christmas Eve, 1835, Seminoles and allied former slaves began to ravage all the plantations around New Smyrna, prompting the militia, led by Benjamin A. Putnam under orders of General Joseph Hernández, to organize a defense and a refuge for neighboring planters at Bulow's plantation. They fortified Bulow's house with cotton bales and palm logs. Bulow, who had a close trading relationship with the Seminoles, is said to have resisted by aiming a four-pounder at the militia. Putnam placed him under arrest and locked him in an outhouse in order to dispossess him of his premises. Bulow predicted his plantation would be burned in retaliation. It was, violently, on February 7, 1836, except for the slave houses, which were left untouched. Before the year was out, Bulow had died and sugar mills were buildings of the past in East Florida.[68]

Pilgrimage Plantation

A plantation of a different kind was begun as the colonial period ended; the former colony entered the Territorial Period with promises of an enlightened Florida. Moses Elias Levy, one of only a few Jewish plantation owners in the entire south, bought 53,000 thousand acres in 1820 in Spanish Florida, part of the vast tract in Alachua granted in 1817 to Fernando de la Maza Arredondo. Levy established Pilgrimage Plantation two and one- half miles west of the present town of Micanopy. He had come to Florida from Cuba as the colonial period ended in 1821; previously he had lived in Morocco, Gibraltar, St. Thomas, and Puerto Rico, where he became an affluent planter-merchant with wide-ranging enterprises in timber, commercial sailing vessels, and a sugar plantation. He abandoned his profitable businesses, however, in order to establish the plantation in Florida as a refuge for Jews.

Moses Levy dreamed of an agricultural colony linked with a Hebrew school, intended for the education of Hebrew youth of both sexes. By 1824, he had spent a vast personal fortune creating a sugar plantation with twenty-five dwelling houses, a sawmill, and a road to the St. Johns River. Like so many others, Levy's Pilgrimage Plantation was burned by Indians during the Second Seminole War.

Levy's youngest son, David Levy Yulee, became Florida's first U.S. senator in 1845 and the first Jewish delegate to Congress. David had added to his name the honorary Moorish title "Yulee" that had been given to Moses Levy's father in Morocco. Moses, meanwhile, had become an ardent abolitionist and authored a pamphlet with a plan to abolish slavery, only recently discovered in the British Library by Chris Monaco. David, however, remained a pro-slavery "antebellum states-rights warrior." He spearheaded the drive for statehood, established the first cross-Florida railroad, and founded the town of Archer. Levy County and the town of Yulee today bear their family names.[69]

8 | KINGSLEY PLANTATION

*The House at the North end will be in the course of a month a
very comfortable habitation, & in any other country a
handsome situation.*

JOHN McQUEEN, JR., MARCH, 1798

On an island, near the Atlantic Ocean, there is an extraordinary plantation. The manor house was begun about 1795, during the ownership of
John McQueen, but it is named for its fascinating third owners,
Zephaniah Kingsley, Jr., and Anta Majigeen Ndiaye, his African-born
slave who became his wife and called herself Anna Jai Kingsley.[1]

Kingsley Plantation stands today in its unbelievably beautiful island
setting just as it did two hundred years ago, its surroundings unencum-
bered by developments and high-rise condominiums. Down a long sand
road that burrows through oaks, pines, cypress, and palms, the view
opens first to the slave houses, then the barn, the old kitchen house, and
finally the manor house on the bank of a river. The architecture is unique,
a product of its environment, the native materials at hand, slave skills,
contemporary building technologies, and the lives of its owners and their
respect for neoclassic symmetry. The plantation takes up the northern
end of Fort George Island, north of Jacksonville, where the St. Johns
River meets the Atlantic Ocean. The front of the house faces north, toward the marsh grass and oyster-rich mudflats of Fort George River and
Sisters Creek, the waterways that were its transportation routes north to
Savannah and Charleston, south to the St. Johns River settlements and
St. Augustine.

The story of the island plantation begins with the Timucua, for they
left the huge shell mound, forty feet tall, seven hundred feet long, that
yielded the lime that made the tabby that is a large part of the plantation
story (fig 1.3). The Franciscan friars were the first Europeans to build on

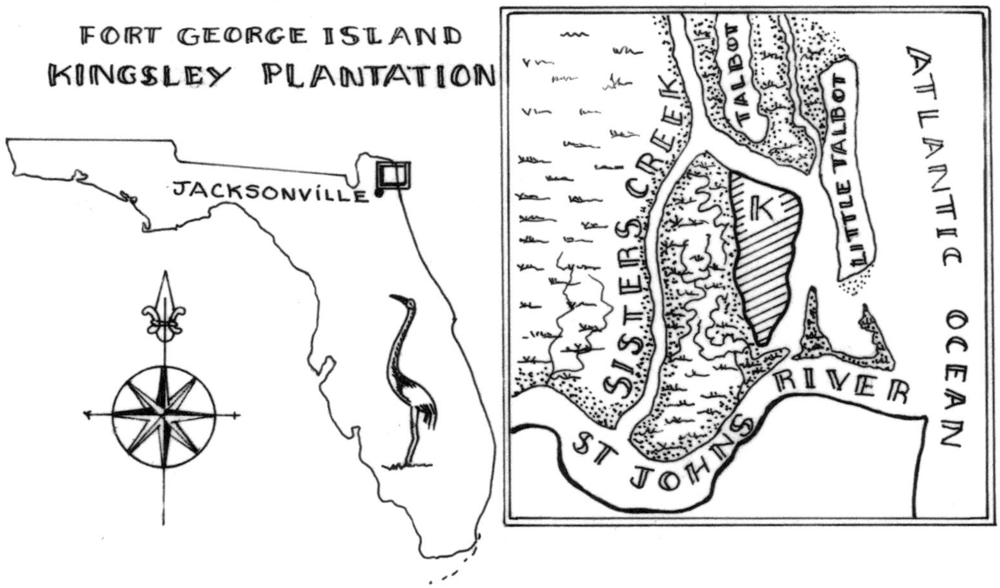

FORT GEORGE ISLAND
KINGSLEY PLANTATION

JACKSONVILLE

SISTERS CREEK
TALBOT
LITTLE TALBOT
ATLANTIC OCEAN
K
ST JOHNS RIVER

8. Kingsley Plantation, 1798, Fort George Island. (Drawn by E. Gordon)

the island and mine the oyster shell middens. Their mission of 1587 was named San Juan del Puerto (St. John of the Harbor), from which came the name of the St. Johns River. Next came General James Oglethorpe, who built Fort Saint George on the island in the 1730s. From the fort came the name of the island, Fort George Island.[2]

A planter, Richard Hazzard, was granted Fort George Island on June 5, 1765, and began the island's first agricultural enterprise. Very shortly thereafter, his plantation was visited by John Bartram and his son, William, but the time was too early in the plantation's history and they left no description of building activity.[3] The next three owners—John McQueen, John Houstoun McIntosh, and Zephaniah and Anna Kingsley—and how they shaped the architecture of their island plantation are the subject of this chapter.

THE OWNER-BUILDERS

The personal stories of McQueen, McIntosh, and the Kingsleys are integral to the plantation's development. The three men were of Scottish and English descent. They were educated beyond many of their contemporaries and moved in the circles of wealth and leadership in the English colonies to the north before they arrived, and in Florida after they came to the island. All three were alert to the neoclassicism of the Renaissance through their travels, friendships, and libraries, and were accustomed to living and entertaining graciously. Anna Kingsley's story, from slave to wife, is altogether unique, and shows such strength of character and independence that it suggests she had more than a passive voice in the development of the plantation, if not a few of its buildings.[4]

John McQueen (1751–1807) was granted the island by the king of Spain in 1792. He was born in Philadelphia, but reared in Charleston and educated in England. During the American Revolution, he was a courier for George Washington to the Marquis de Lafayette. Between 1785 and 1788 he was in Europe, where he renewed his friendship with Lafayette and met Thomas Jefferson, American minister to France from 1784 to 1789. Letters from Lafayette and Jefferson speak of McQueen's attending family suppers with the Jeffersons in France. He owned a small plantation in Savannah, Georgia, but that was not enough for a man who yearned for more expansive entrepreneurial opportunities. He went to Jamaica and brought back sugarcane to experiment with its cultivation in Georgia. Staying just ahead of debt collectors, he migrated to East Florida, where he helped the Spanish build defenses. In 1791, he was baptized into the Roman Catholic Church in St. Augustine, and took the name Don Juan Reyna. The Spanish governor, Juan Nepomucena Quesada, awarded him Fort George Island, surveyed to him in 1792.[5]

8.1. Road north to Kingsley Plantation, Fort George Island. The story of the plantation architecture is the story of the island setting, local materials, three owners, and the slaves who constructed the buildings. John McQueen authored the initial design, but the longest ownership was that of Zephaniah Kingsley, who married Anta Majigeen Mdiaye, his independent and courageous former slave who became a slave owner herself. She is thought to have set out the palm trees along the north-south island road that led to the slave houses. (Photograph by M. Gordon)

McQueen was granted another tract of 4,000 acres on the St. Johns River, which he named San Juan Nepomuceno in honor of Governor Quesada's patron saint, where he had a sawmill, made clay bricks, and manufactured cypress shingles. He built a house on the southern portion of Fort George Island in 1793 that burned in 1794. His wife, Anne, arrived from Savannah in 1795 to join him at a "camp" on the island. His son wrote early in 1798, "the house at the North end will be in the course of a month a very comfortable habitation, & in any other country a handsome situation."[6]

Houses were not built overnight, or even in a year or two in colonial times. It is possible that the foundation basement was dug in 1795 or 1796. At least, the sawyers were felling timbers and air-drying the lumber by then, and the coquina stone may have been brought from St. Augustine. The McQueens moved into the house, which was nearly finished, early in 1798. By 1799, the plantation was raising cotton, and in 1800 McQueen built a water-powered gin to clean his cotton. During the month of July, when the mosquitoes were particularly bad, the family annually sojourned in Savannah while McQueen stayed in St. Augustine with Father Michael O'Reilly. In 1801, he entertained General Nathaniel Greene, the soldier of the Revolution who had retired to Mulberry Hill on the Savannah River in Georgia. In 1802, McQueen wrote that there were "twenty-six at breakfast today at my table."[7]

McQueen's fortunes turned once again, and he was ruined by crop failure and financial difficulties. He sold his two plantations in 1804 for $28,000 to a wealthy Georgia planter, John Houstoun McIntosh. McIntosh (1773–1836) had inherited Refuge Plantation with hundreds of slaves in Camden County, and was married in 1792 to the wealthy Eliza Bayard, heiress to the fortunes of West Indian traders. After buying McQueen's plantations, McIntosh took the oath of allegiance to Spain and was recognized as a subject of Spanish Florida. McIntosh had a thriving timber industry on the St. Mary's River, shipping lumber to Liverpool, England, but had enough slaves to send around to his Florida properties: some 170–200 to the Ft. George Island plantation, and 40 to the Nepomuceno plantation, which he renamed Ortega. The McIntoshes traveled between Fort George Island and Refuge. However, it was not long before McIntosh (cousin of General John McIntosh) became a leader of the so-called Patriot's War of East Florida. As a result, he had to leave Florida with a price on his head in 1813.[8]

The third owner, Zephaniah Kingsley, Jr. (1765–1843), rented the island plantation from McIntosh from 1814 until 1817, when he purchased it for $7,000. He was born in England, his mother a British noblewoman and his father a Quaker merchant. From age eight he grew up in Charleston, South Carolina. His niece, Anna (daughter of his sister Martha), would become a renowned icon as the subject of a painting by her famous artist son, James McNeill Whistler (1834–1903), titled *Arrangement in Black and Gray: The Artist's Mother* (1871), now at the Louvre, Paris.

Kingsley was a wealthy entrepreneur, an enigmatic man with a dual nature. He owned slave ships, and bought and sold slaves, all the while championing their civil rights and expressing his view that the colored race was superior to the white race. His principal wife was formerly his slave, a young girl from Senegal who, in time, acquired her own slaves. On her behalf, he built a colony for free blacks in Haiti, using the earnings from his Florida plantations labored by slaves. He had more than one wife, but worked to uphold the laws of the new U.S. territory by serving in the territorial Legislative Council of 1823, and as a justice of the peace of Duval County. He also wrote the Duval County government bill, and chaired the site selection committee for Florida's permanent capital at Tallahassee.[9]

Kingsley's merchant ships sailed among Africa, the Caribbean, and North America, selling coffee, molasses, rum, and slaves. He came to Florida in 1803, where he purchased 2,600 acres on the west side of the St. Johns River and the plantation he called Laurel Grove (today's Orange Park).[10] Both plantations had two-story frame dwelling houses roughly 35 by 40 feet with brick chimneys, double piazzas, and many outbuildings. When he died in 1843 at age seventy-eight, he had owned five plantations in Florida, 32,044 acres of land, a fleet of schooners, and a town residence in Fernandina. One of his plantations, San Jose, was renamed Epping Forest by its later owner, Alfred I. du Pont, and today includes the site of Bolles School.[11]

Anna Jai Kingsley, his strong-minded wife, was a tall thirteen-year-old in 1806 in Havana, Cuba, when she was purchased by Kingsley, "black as jet but very handsome." Her African name, Anta Majigeen Ndiaye, reveals important lineages from the slave-owning class in Senegal. Kingsley claimed to have married her according to "her native African custom." They had four children, George, Martha, Mary, and John Maxwell, and for thirty-seven years, until his death, they lived as man and wife and she carried the Kingsley name.[12]

Anna managed their first plantation, Laurel Grove, and in 1811, when she was 18 years old, Kingsley formally emancipated her and her children. In 1812 she left Kingsley and moved across the St. Johns River to Mandarin where she had been granted five acres by the Spanish government. She had twelve slaves. They built a farm with slave cabins and a two-story house, masonry on the first floor and wood for the second. In the masonry first floor, she stored six hundred bushels of corn as well as other supplies and farming tools. She and her children lived on the second floor. In 1813, during the Patriot's War, Anna bravely torched her own house to prevent it being turned into a blockhouse by the marauding patriots. As a reward, she received a land grant of 305 acres from the Spanish government. Zephaniah's Laurel Grove plantation was also destroyed, and in 1814 he and Anna reunited to rent and eventually buy the Fort George Island plantation from John Houstoun McIntosh.[13]

MYSTERIOUS ARCHITECT

The plantation that can be visited today was built over the course of three decades, from the late 1790s until about 1830. The isolation of the site and the characteristics of the buildings themselves, suggest that John McQueen drafted the initial architecture on the spot using the popular literature of the day and the expertise of his slave master craftsmen.

The most striking characteristic of the main house is its modular symmetry. The plan seems to have been controlled by an extreme urge to balance and harmonize all of its parts. The original house (before late nineteenth-century additions) was a rectangular great room flanked by four identical square pavilions attached at the four corners (pl. 25). These five units were united in design by their pyramidal roofs, and were physically connected by two identical verandas north and south (front and back) and two passageways east and west (fig. 8.2). Fireplaces and chimneys were built alike at each end of the great room, and the great room was harmonically proportioned, its width (16 feet) half its length (32 feet).

This five-part countryseat design was current with the geometric classicism and Palladian symmetry that was the fashion in England, the American colonies, and English West Indies. The style was popularized by eighteenth-century handbooks brought to the colonies from England and used by gentlemen-architects and tradesmen. The books were inspired by sixteenth-century Italian architects like Andrea Palladio and Sebastiano Serlio who had published volumes of designs for country villas.

The Kingsley Plantation design might have come to the first owner, John McQueen, from one of these books or his travels and social connections in the northern colonies and West Indies. McQueen's island home was designed with the same aesthetics as Thomas Jefferson's geometrically balanced architecture and many other plantation villas of the southern landed gentry. For example, Mulberry Castle (1714), built near

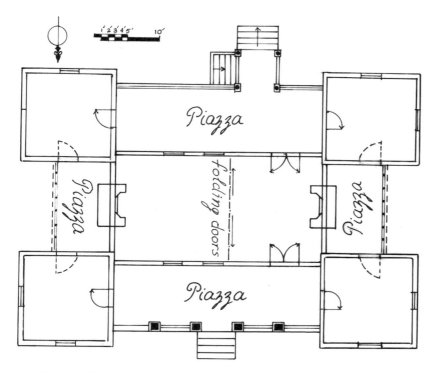

8.2. Kingsley Plantation main house, 1798, first-floor plan, Fort George Island. Geometrically balanced architecture was favored among landed gentry at the time John McQueen planned and built his plantation house in Florida. The square pavilions provoked an 1819 description of the house as being "fortified," prompted no doubt by its isolation, fear of Indians and slave revolt, and recent American patriot conspiracies. (Drawing adapted by E. Gordon from historical accounts and floor plans by Herschel E. Shepard and associates)

Charleston by Thomas Broughton, a colonist from the West Indies, and Stokes Hall (early 1700s) in Jamaica were both flanked with corner pavilions similar to McQueen's design. A plan in Serlio's *Five Books of Architecture* (1537–47, English edition 1611) described corner rooms as well lighted and cool (fig. 8.3).

One might even speculate that when McQueen dined with Thomas Jefferson in France, the seeds for the design were planted in discussions about the merits of architectural geometry, proportions, and symmetry, and about the most important authors on the subject. Jefferson was inordinately preoccupied with architectural design and had an extensive library of architectural books. His taste for Palladian architecture is well known; he is often quoted as having said, "Palladio is the Bible." In addition to Palladio's *Four Books of Architecture*, McQueen may have drawn upon Robert Morris, whose two books, *Select Architecture* and *Lectures on Architecture Consisting of Rules Founded Upon Harmonick and Arithmatical Proportions in Building*, were favorites of Thomas Jefferson. The

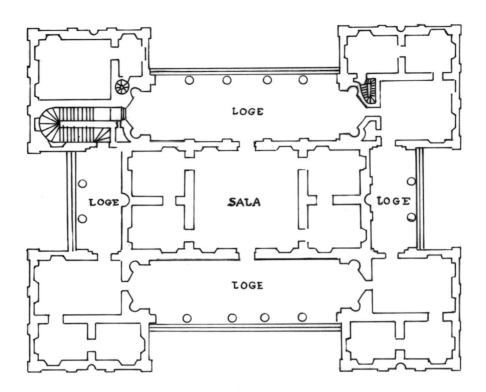

LOGE

LOGE   SALA   LOGE

LOGE

8.3. Plan from Sebastiano Serlio's *The Five Books of Architecture* (1537–47, English edition 1611). Books by Andrea Palladio and Robert Morris were among the favorites for planning geometrically balanced architecture in the English colonies. This particular plan shows an uncanny similarity to the Fort George Island plantation. (Redrawn by E. Gordon after Serlio's "Of Antiquitie")

frontispiece in the latter book says it was "Designed As an Agreeable Entertainment for Gentlemen: and to all who make Architecture, or the Public Arts, their study."[14]

The symmetry of the Kingsley Plantation house design is also notable for its response to the climate. The two verandas that flanked the great room served not only to shade the walls, doors, and open windows, but as shady indoor-outdoor spaces for dining and relaxing. All rooms were one room deep, similar to the "single houses" of Charleston, designed to reap the most benefit from cross ventilation. The first floor great room was spacious, with wide paneled double doors exiting to the verandas and large folding doors that could divide the room into two.[15] The second floor was accessed by an exterior stairway. There was an attic with an opening to the roof that led to a lookout, with views north to waterways, east to ocean, and south to the dependencies, farm activities, and the approach road. It is possible that the roof opening was used to vent warm air from the second floor.

Some changes to the original house plan were made by John Rollins, who owned the plantation from 1869 to 1923. He altered the symmetry and the flow of cross ventilation by adding rooms between the pavilions in 1877–78. He also partitioned the great central room, added an interior stairway, and an enclosed walkway to the former kitchen house in the 1880s.[16]

Stokes Hall, Jamaica, might have inspired the plan of the Kingsley Plantation house. Vintage drawings depict its square pavilions, with pyramidal roofs, built at each of the four corners of the rectangular wood house. The corner pavilions were solid masonry and had loopholes for firing. Stokes Hall was built in the same period (early 1700s) that two other fortified sugar plantations, Colbeck Castle and Stewart Castle, were similarly constructed with corner flankers, a period when English settlements in the West Indies were under constant threat of attack and houses were fortified.[17] In 1819, an account of a canoe trip in Florida by an Englishman describes "passing in our route the fortified private plantation of Mr. Kingsley, at Fort George."[18] Whether McQueen intended the house to be "fortified" or not is unknown. The isolation, Indian presence, fear of slave revolt, and American conspiracies were reasons enough for the McQueens, McIntoshes, and Kingsleys to sleep with a pistol under the pillow.

MATERIALS AND CONSTRUCTION METHODS

Kingsley Plantation buildings were constructed by slaves. McQueen had a large number of experienced slaves who produced lumber, hauled the sand and oyster shells, made tabby, molded and fired clay bricks, dug the foundation cellar, framed and weatherboarded the house. At the same time, these slaves raised the household food and the cash cotton crop, and erected their own expedient shelters. The construction of Kingsley Plantation is really their story.

The locally available natural materials, and how they were worked, are important to the story of the craftsmen. The abundance of wood on the island and Don Juan McQueen's own sawmill and brick-making enterprise on the St. John's River supplied the bulk of the house material. The main house was brace framed with hewn timbers of longleaf yellow (southern) pine (the same we call heart pine), joined by mortise and tenon. Slave sawyers were responsible for felling trees and squaring timbers. Others milled and rived boards, or split short cypress and cedar logs into shingles. Freshly cut green lumber was commonly air dried, sometimes up to three years to prevent warping in floors, windows, and doors.[19]

The McQueen home rose from its own cellar hole, a foundation-basement dug by slaves and lined with coquina stone, a material impervious to dampness.[20] The coquina stone, found only along the length of

Anastasia Island southward to the Halifax River, had to be shipped to Fort George Island. McQueen was frequently in St. Augustine, where he must have acquired local knowledge of the benefits of the stone that had long been the substance of the better buildings, including the new parish church, the Cathedral, under construction at the same time as his house.

Clay bricks were laid on top of the basement stone in a running bond, all stretchers and no headers. The bricks were gray-brown and oversized ($2\frac{3}{4}$ x $4\frac{1}{4}$ x $8\frac{1}{2}$ inches, similar to the standard British brick of $2\frac{1}{4}$ x $4\frac{1}{2}$ x $8\frac{3}{4}$ inches). They ranged from severely under-fired to well-fired, suggesting they were locally manufactured, if not at the plantation, then at McQueen's brick-making operation at San Juan Nepomuceno plantation (Ortega).[21] Lime mortar was made from sand, water, and quicklime produced by burning crushed oyster shells. Adding a crushed shell aggregate to the mixture, the slaves produced the tabby concrete floor. The full basement was unusual for colonial Florida, but it provided a cool, earth-insulated, storehouse.

The eighteenth-century method of making bricks was laborious and typically produced bricks of uneven firing. Ideally, the practice included the following: clayey mud and water were mixed in a shallow pit with hoes until a stiff lump could be rolled, folded into a loaf, and slammed into a wooden mold, a topless and bottomless box partitioned into four brick shapes and dusted with sand so the mud would not stick. The excess mud was struck off, and the mold was taken to an open-air drying area. The "green" bricks, at the mercy of rain and wandering animal feet, were released and turned daily. When they were dry enough to be stacked on edge, they were carried to the "kiln," which was not a fixed kiln but the stack of to-be-fired bricks called a "clamp" (fig. 7.10). Firing was an art, not a science, and an experienced brickmaster was the key. The green bricks had to be stacked just so, in intermeshed layers, with a finger-width space for the heat to circulate. For every three thousand bricks, there was an "eye," an arched fire tunnel, running through the center at ground level where fires could be built that would heat the entire stack. To protect the green bricks, a timber frame was erected and covered with canvas.[22]

The stack of the kiln and the quality of the fire were the secrets to good bricks. The clamp might reach eight or ten feet high before it was plastered with mud to keep the heat from escaping. The canvas was removed and the fires were started by striking a file against a flint rock, catching the sparks in a wad of dry cotton. For five days and nights, the fires were fed with hardwood, slowly at first to prevent bricks from exploding and moving the fires from eye to eye, until the kiln glowed red and the heat rose to

2,500° F. When the top of the kiln slumped in the middle, the bricks were hard and ready. The eyes of the kiln were then sealed and the bricks allowed to cool for two weeks before the kiln was taken apart. The bricks on the outside were too far from the fire to fully harden, and were called "samel" bricks. They were discarded or used for "nogging," filling inside walls. They would disintegrate into powder after many years. Only half of the bricks ("stock" bricks) were well fired and hardened. Those in the center, close to the fire eyes, burned so hot they took on a glaze. These glazed clinker bricks were used for decorative headers.[23]

Tabby was an even more important construction material in the history of Kingsley Plantation, where it was used in floors, bricks, and walls poured in place. Tabby was a concrete made of lime, sand, water, and oyster shell aggregate. It was used chiefly along the coasts of Georgia, South Carolina, and Florida during the colonial period, and was considered by many plantation owners in Georgia and South Carolina to be one of the best and cheapest materials for the erection of durable, fireproof, and handsome buildings. Tabby walls were plastered, rusticated (scored), and painted to look like stone. Thomas Spalding of Sapelo Island, McIntosh County, Georgia, frequently published articles in *Southern Agriculturist* early in the 1800s that advocated tabby construction of plantation outbuildings, kitchen houses, barns, mills, and slave quarters. He greatly influenced the construction of coastal plantations in Georgia, writing about his methods: "I generally made my people mix the materials one day and put it into [wooden] boxes the two following, very soft, as the better to amalgamate. 10 Bushels of lime, 10 Bushels of Sand, ten bushels of shells and ten bushels of water make 16 cubic feet of wall. I have made my walls 14 inches thick; below the lower floor 2 feet; for the second story 10 inches beyond that I would not erect Tabby."[24]

Tabby concrete had been known in Spanish St. Augustine since 1715.[25] In 1765 John Bartram described the tabby as follows: "ye common spanish houses was built of ouster shells & morter as well as garden & yard walls thay raised them by setting two boards on edge . . . then poured in limeshel morter mixt with sand in which thay pounded ye oister shels as close as posible & when that part was set thay raised ye planks & so on till thay had raised ye wall as high as wanted."[26] At Kingsley Plantation tabby was also formed into bricks (3 x 4 x 8½ inches) and used for "infill" in the basement of the main house, in the walls of the Anna Jai House, in the barn, and in the original chimneys of the slave houses.[27] Tabby was also poured and tamped, as described above by Bartram, into wood forms to layer up the walls of the thirty-two slave quarters and the south wing of the barn (fig. 8.4). It took a lot of oyster shells and much unpleas-

ant burning to make enough lime for all the tabby works at the Fort
George Island plantation.

The barn that was constructed of tabby is still standing, Florida's only
extant colonial barn. It was built in two stages, forming a T shape. The
north section was the earliest, with a poured tabby foundation on a clay
brick footer and walls constructed of tabby bricks. A protective layer of
lime plaster covered the rough tabby, smoothed and scored to simulate
stone in the size of the bricks underneath. The south wing of the barn was
constructed later, using the pouring and tamping method in wood forms
to layer up the walls. The roof was covered with cypress shingles. The
barn is spacious and high-ceilinged, and at various times probably served
to house livestock, cotton, citrus, other crops, and carriages. Kingsley
was well known for his stable of quality horses, "high-bred white charg-
ers."[28]

The Anna Jai House is the charming smaller house about sixty-five
feet behind the main house (pl. 26). Early in its history, it may have been
the detached kitchen house, connected to the main house by a tabby
walkway lined with orange trees. (The wood-covered walkway at the site
today was added during 1869 and 1877 by John Rollins.) The first floor of
the southern end was constructed of tabby bricks and had a large fireplace hearth lined with clay bricks for cooking. Kitchens were traditionally separated from houses during the colonial period due to the very real
threat of fire.

About the time the Kingsleys moved onto the plantation, the kitchen house assumed the form seen today. It was enlarged to the north with tabby and a second story of wood was added, with an outside staircase protected under extended eaves (fig. 8.5). Anna Kingsley had twelve slaves of her own, and might have been responsible for the design and construction of this renovation. She and her children lived on the second floor, just as she had in the stone and wood house she built in Mandarin. Tradition has long held that this was Anna's house. She lived separately from Zephaniah as was the custom among polygamous families in her native Africa. Zephaniah referred to it as "her house" when he deeded the plantation in 1831 to their son George.[29]

Anna lived at Kingsley Plantation twenty-three years. Her daughters married white men of Scottish descent and became two of Duval County's most wealthy citizens.[30]

8.5. Anna Jai house, ca. 1798, 1817, Kingsley Plantation, Fort George Island. After Anna Jai Kingsley was emancipated, she acquired twelve slaves of her own and built her own plantation in Mandarin. She reunited with Kingsley at Fort George Island, but lived separately from him in what had once been the kitchen house, built about 1798 with tabby. She added a second story of wood with an exterior staircase to the rooms in which she raised their four children. (Photograph by E. Gordon)

SLAVE HOUSES

While the architect of the manor house symmetry was probably John McQueen, the designer of the half-circle arrangement of slave cabins is more enigmatic. Early in the nineteenth century there were thirty-two tabby slave dwellings placed in the semicircle. The road, the main route from south to north, bisected the slave arc and led to the plantation wharf on the Fort George River, just east of the main house. There were sixteen cabins on each side of the road, built twelve feet apart. Four cabins, two immediately adjacent to the road and two at each end of the semicircle, were larger than the rest. They are thought to have been for overseers and their families.[31] A crescent arrangement of slave quarters has been found at only one other location in Florida, the Bulow plantation, north of Ormond Beach, built shortly after the Kingsley slave cabins.

8.6. Slave house site plan, ca. 1820, Kingsley Plantation, Fort George Island. The crescent arrangement of slave houses (5) behind the main plantation house (1), kitchen house that became the Anna Jai House (2), and barn (4), is very unusual. There were originally thirty-two houses placed in a semicircle, sixteen to each side of the north-south shell road (3) that led to the wharf on the Fort George River, the plantation's main transportation route. Like the plantation manor house itself, the slave arc was also preoccupied with symmetry and geometric harmony. (Drawn by E. Gordon, not to scale, after Daniel W. Stowell and Henry A. Baker)

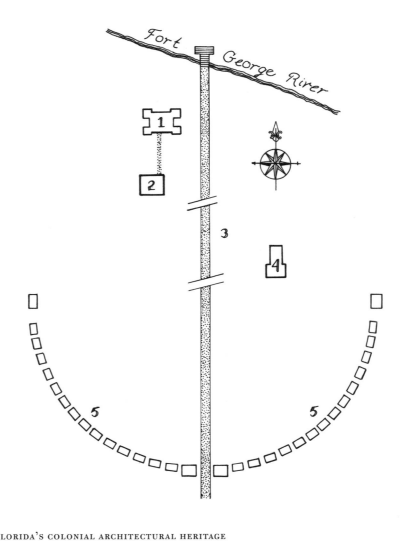

The symmetry of the plan and its relationship to the main house is very unusual. There might have been practical reasons for the arrangement; for instance, each cabin could be clearly seen from overseers' cabins and the main house. The author of the plan was most likely John McQueen, who was obviously enamored of architectural and geometrical balances and might have initiated the site plan with the first wood houses for his slaves. Like Thomas Jefferson, who continuously made drawings that coordinated Monticello to its site with roundabouts and an arc, McQueen might have played with similar ideas, taken from design books.[32] McIntosh, the second owner, possessed more wealth and more slaves at the Fort George plantation, but he was caught up in the Patriot's War and at present there is no evidence to connect him with the semicircular plan. Kingsley, the third owner, was described by Joseph White, Florida's delegate in Congress in 1825, as "a classical scholar."[33] One wonders if his scholarship extended to architectural books like Colin Campbell's three-volume work *Vitruvius Britannicus* (1715–25), James Gibbs's *Book of Architecture,* and Palladio's *Four Books of Architecture,* which were replete with semicircular designs for the grounds of neoclassic style farm houses.

Construction of the poured tabby slave quarters, probably dates from the tenure of Zephaniah and Anna Kingsley, particularly because of their more benevolent attitude toward their slaves. The slaves during McQueen's ownership were busy planting the first crops of cotton and corn, felling trees, making lumber and bricks, and constructing the manor house and a complicated water-gin to clean his cotton in 1800. It is unlikely that his slaves were assigned to make tabby cabins between 1798, when the main house was completed, and 1804, when he was bankrupt and sold the plantation.

The second owner, the wealthy John Houstoun McIntosh, had several hundred slaves, of whom seventy to eighty were workers, cultivating three to four hundred acres of Sea Island cotton.[34] (Figures given for the number of slaves are always misleading because of the unknown number that were too old, too young, or too sick to work, but were being housed and fed and counted.[35]) His slaves may have made tabby bricks for two crypts on the island thought to bear his daughter and sister-in-law, who died in 1808.[36] However, McIntosh was involved in various economic pursuits in Florida and Georgia, and eventually became preoccupied with the leadership (1811–13) of the Patriot's Rebellion, which kept East Florida in turmoil with American aggression and demanded the surrender of St. Augustine. In his absences, his plantation on Fort George Island was supervised by John G. Rushing. When the rebellion ended, he

8.7. Tabby slave houses, ca. 1820s, Kingsley Plantation, Fort George Island, stereoscopic photograph from the 1870s–80s. After the Civil War, freed slaves continued to live at Kingsley Plantation in some of the original slave houses built with tabby and roofed with hand-split cypress shingles. (Photocopy courtesy of Florida State Archives)

pressed his claim against the U.S. government for damage to his island plantation, declaring that all his buildings except his dwelling house were burned; this suggests that his slave cabins had been constructed with wood.[37]

Most likely, the thirty-two tabby slave houses were fabricated after the Kingsleys were in residence in 1814 (pl. 28). Zephaniah and Anna lived at the plantation the longest of the owners. In 1841, the cabin roofs had to be "recovered," and new shingles made.[38] The old cypress shingles might have lasted twenty years, suggesting they had been installed about 1820. Kingsley, furthermore, was known to be more concerned about slave welfare than either McQueen or McIntosh. He encouraged family units as well as the "task" system that was favored in South Carolina, setting aside time for the slave to grow his own goods or put up a supply of fish.[39] It also seems likely that Anna, once a slave herself, would have encouraged the building of the more permanent slave quarters. Lastly, the timing is commensurate with the proliferation of tabby plantation buildings, including slave quarters, in Georgia and South Carolina, on the advice and writings of Thomas Spalding.[40]

The tabby slave cabins had one or two rooms, central doorways, a loft of planks, and tabby chimneys with clay brick hearths (pl. 27). They had tabby floors, and wells in front. The window openings were shuttered and, like the Spanish residents of St. Augustine from 1565 to 1763, the slaves had to choose between darkness or cold on winter days, and darkness or rain in the summer (fig. 8.9). Perhaps a cloth kept out the mosquitoes. Slaves lived at Kingsley Plantation through the Civil War, and freed slaves lived in the cabins on the arc through the 1870s (fig. 8.7).[41]

Anna and her daughter, Mary, are thought to have set out the original rows of palm trees that lined the road to the plantation from the south, ending at the slave houses. In 1877, the road was described as "a magnificent avenue of palms" that "lift their round tops 50 or 60 feet in the air."[42] Only a woman of Anna's stature could have had the vision to beautify the utilitarian road to the slave community with what must have been thought of as frivolous elegance.

8.8. Tabby slave house ruin, twentieth century, Kingsley Plantation, Fort George Island. The first slave houses on the island, ca. 1795, might have been expedient pole-frame and palm-thatch shelters. After the cash crops and kitchen garden had been planted, the slaves might have turned to constructing wood frame houses in their free time. Their houses burned during the Patriot's Rebellion (1813), when John Houston McIntosh owned the island plantation. They were rebuilt with fireproof tabby during the ownership of Zephaniah Kingsley and his wife, Anna. When they were abandoned during the 1890s, their cypress shingle roofs rotted and the exterior plaster disintegrated, exposing tabby walls to weather and encroaching vines and trees. (Photocopy courtesy of Florida State Archives)

8.9. Tabby slave house restored, Kingsley Plantation, Fort George Island. The island slave house was restored in the 1980s to its 1820s architecture of tabby, brick, and cypress, with two rooms and a clay brick hearth. Walls were constructed by "pouring" layers of oyster shell lime, water, and sand in wood "lifts" and tamping in an aggregate of oyster shells to make a concrete known as tabby. Tabby was strong, but it was labor intensive, requiring much unpleasant burning of many oyster shells. Window openings had wood shutters. (Photograph by E. Gordon)

Kingsley Plantation, with twelve of its original acres, was bought by the state of Florida in 1955. The slave houses had greatly deteriorated (fig. 8.8). Today, one slave house, the barn, Anna's house, and the main house are restored and part of the Timucuan Ecological and Historic Preserve, protected and maintained by the National Park Service and open to the public.

9 | FORTS, REDOUBTS, PRICKLY CACTUS, AND A WOLF'S MOUTH

The cost of San Marcos Castle, as it was called, was estimated at $30,000,000, a sum that prompted the King of Spain to exclaim: "Its curtains and bastions must be made of solid silver."[1]

The Spanish colonists who settled Florida in the sixteenth to eighteenth centuries had to quickly face the reality of defending their new homes. Their New World not only belonged to Indians, but was coveted by England, France, and pirates.

They threw up palisades, redoubts, watchtowers, *casas fuertes,* and forts with bastions to protect early settlements, their harbors, and river crossings; to protect these defenses, they fashioned earthworks, palm log revetments, moats, and, for extra good measure, rows of prickly cactus or a trou-de-loup (wolf's mouth). The wood defense structures perpetually rotted. Some collapsed when hurricanes blew in and coastlines eroded. A stone fort somewhat assuaged the fears of St. Augustine after 1672. Requiring enormous expenditures and two and a half centuries of human labor, the contest for and defense of Florida were the most pressing issues of the day.

When the colonial era ended in 1821, Florida's fate fell to the Americans. The young nation had acquired a new territory with a vast coastline of harbors, inlets, and sea lanes that would be worth a fortune in maritime commerce, industries, and tariffs. The Americans, like the French, Spanish, and English before them, would spend the next century building harbor defenses to protect the coastline. Some of the American fortifications would be built on top of Spanish fortifications, which had been overlaid

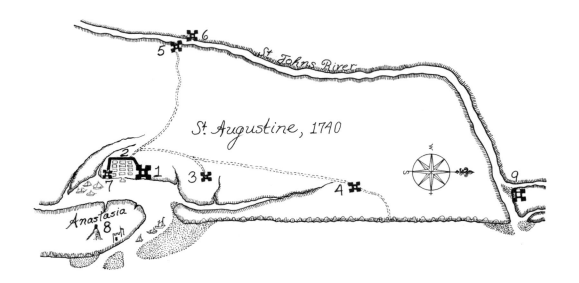

St. Johns River

St. Augustine, 1740

Anastasia

on French or superseded by English works, resulting in structures of complicated heritage that had, nevertheless, stood their course.

The inlets, rivers, and snug harbors of Florida are no longer scenes of strife, or even main arteries of transportation. The colonial moats, palm revetments, wood redoubts, lookouts, and most of the forts are not even a memory anymore, only obscure names in archives or on old maps.

Three colonial masonry forts are still intact, including the magnificent stone Castillo de San Marcos (1672) and *el fuerte pequeño,* the little fort now called Fort Matanzas (1740), both defending St. Augustine (pl. 7; fig. 9.12). The brick Batería de San Antonio (1796) exists today in Pensacola (fig. 9.17). Forts San Marcos de Apalachee in St. Marks and San Carlos de Barrancas in Pensacola are ruins. Fort Caroline (1564) in Jacksonville is reconstructed, and Fort San Luis (1656) in Tallahassee is an archaeological site soon to be reconstructed by the state of Florida. The history of building these and other isolated defensive structures reveals how difficult it was to settle the frontiers of Florida. To know how wood, earth, and stone were fashioned into defensive fortifications, and how they were garrisoned with great human effort by Indians, Africans, and Europeans charged with the lonely responsibility, is to know the real beginnings of Florida.

FORT CAROLINE (FORT SAN MATEO)

On a warm June morning in 1564, René de Goulaine de Laudonnière (1529–1582) and his French Huguenot colonists dropped anchor near the mouth of the St. Johns River. Men, women, and children disembarked at a chosen spot, armed themselves with shovels, axes, and billhooks, and began to build their fort and village. They had soon dug a moat, moved earth, cut stakes, erected a parapet and palisade, and enclosed a triangular area they named La Caroline, after their youthful king, Charles IX. The site was on the south side of the River May (now the St. Johns River) in present-day Jacksonville. The area had long been inhabited by the Timucua of the chiefdom of Saturiba.[2]

Construction proceeded according to Laudonnière as follows: On the west or land side of the triangular fort, they dug "a little ditch" and "built with turfs . . . a parapet nine feet high." They fortified the side toward the river with a "gabionade," a palisade of gabions, hollow cylinder-baskets without bottoms, made of stakes and wickerwork with iron straps, that were filled with earth or stones. The gabionade revetment made a shelter from enemy fire and a dike for the harbor. To the south, the colonists made a bastion of stakes and sand and parapets built up of turf, two to three feet high. In the south bastion, they erected a supply shed that was thatched with woven palm by the Timucua as directed by Saturiba. In the center of the fort, they marked off a square of eighteen paces, where they built a guardhouse facing south. A building north of it was two stories high, but the wind knocked it down. Laudonnière wrote that the "experience taught me that nothing should be built with upper floors in this land because of the high winds to which it is subject."[3]

His own house was constructed with wraparound covered galleries. The kitchen was built outside the fort "to avoid the risk of fire." Laudonnière noted that once the fire took hold of houses covered with palm leaves, they burned quickly. By November, the colonists were getting clay from an arm of the river and making bricks, and gathering oyster shells to make lime mortar with which to build the houses that would replace the initial palm thatch shelters.[4]

Jacques le Moyne, the artist-cartographer with the colony, sketched the fort-settlement. The drawing, however, would have to be started all over again in France from memory after he swam a river to escape the Spanish raid of September 20, 1565. This drawing has since been lost, but Theodor de Bry, of Liège, fortunately had etched its likeness in copper and published it in Frankfort in 1591 (fig. 9.1).

Meanwhile, the Spanish, led by Pedro Menéndez, had formally taken possession of Florida and established their campsite at St. Augustine on September 8, 1565, at Chief Seloy's village. While the colonists labored to fortify a large Timucua house and convert it into a fortified government house, Menéndez set out to attack Fort Caroline on September 18,

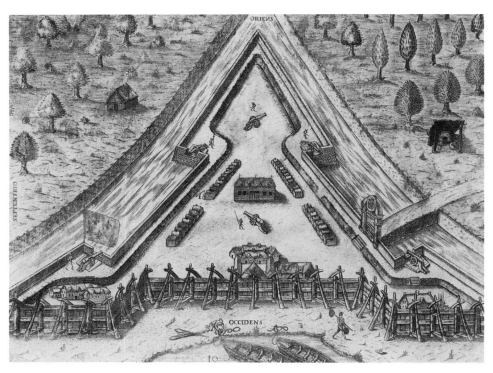

9.1. Fort Caroline, 1564, Jacksonville. Jacques le Moyne returned to France, where he recreated a sketch of the fort, which was engraved and published in 1591 by Theodore de Bry of Liège for his *Brevis narrato eorum quae in Florida Ameridae.* (Photocopy of de Bry's engraving number 10, *A Plan of Fort Caroline,* courtesy of Florida State Archives)

marching overland with some five hundred soldiers despite a storm that might have been a hurricane. They captured Fort Caroline while the larger part of the French force was sailing south, under the command of Jean Ribault, to destroy the Menéndez camp. In this cat-and-mouse maneuver, the French were the losers. Their ships were dispersed and sunk by the storm, Fort Caroline was captured, and many French were killed. Two groups of shipwrecked survivors, including Jean Ribault, surrendered to the Spanish at the inlet south of St. Augustine. They were systematically executed on orders from Menéndez.[5] The inlet and river today are called *Matanzas,* a Spanish word for slaughter.

The Spanish renamed the captured French fort San Mateo, for the saint on whose day it had been taken. They now had two forts in La Florida, Fort San Mateo and the fortified Timucua house at the campsite at San Agustín, improved with "a ditch and moat made around the house, with a rampart of earth and fagots."[6] The latter, however, did not last long, torched before the end of the colony's first year by Indians on April 19, 1566, prompting the Spanish to move to Anastasia Island, where they built the next two short-lived wood forts.[7]

In December 1566, the Spanish built Fort Santa Lucia (near today's Jupiter Inlet), but like those they erected near present-day Tampa and Miami, it lasted only months. It was destroyed by Indians who killed most of the garrison. The loss of frontier forts, however, had much to do with Spanish disrespect for natives, a persistence in harsh treatment of the Indians by soldiers as well as administrators who demanded their food and abused and killed them.[8]

Moats and palisades were not enough to quell the Indian hostility toward the Spanish, nor the appetites of France and England for colonial expansion. The Spanish built pine lookouts and blockhouses (*casas fuertes*), enclosed within stake palisades to defend strategic locations. Blockhouses were constructed at Matanzas Inlet, at Anastasia Island, and near Menéndez's first campsite (*San Agustín el viejo*) to guard the river routes and harbor entrance. Two blockhouses on the north and south banks of the mouth of the St. Johns River were erected to protect San Mateo.[9]

The French, however, had their revenge. Their Indian allies made a preliminary attack on San Mateo at dawn on March 30, 1568, followed by a combined force of Indians and French under Dominique de Gourgues, who attacked and burned the two wood blockhouses at the mouth of the river. On April 25, 1568, the French took Fort San Mateo. They left only a shell of a fort, and Spanish bodies hanging from trees (fig. 9.2). Defending the foothold on the St. Johns River with earth ramparts and palisades had failed both the French and Spanish, with a high cost in lives.[10]

9.2. Fort San Mateo, 1568 (formerly Fort Caroline), Jacksonville. The attack by the French on the triangular fort (with hangings depicted in the background) was engraved and published in 1706. (Photocopy from Pieter Vander Aa's *Verscheyde Scheeps-Togten Na Florida, Door Pontius, Ribald, Laudonnière, Gourgues en andere . . .*, courtesy of Florida State Archives)

9.3. Fort Caroline 1564, reconstructed 1964, Jacksonville, based on Theodore de Bry's engraving of 1591. Among the details omitted in the reconstruction were the guardhouse, René Laudonnière's quarters with its gallery, and dwellings of the colonials. In the south bastion there had been a supply shed that was thatched by the local Timucua Indians. Fort Caroline, nevertheless, symbolizes the beginning of European competition for Florida. (Photograph by M. Gordon)

Fort Caroline has been conceptually reconstructed based on the de Bry etching of le Moyne's sketch. The original site was washed away after the river channel was deepened and widened in the 1880s.[11]

CASTILLO DE SAN MARCOS (FORT ST. MARKS, FT. MARION)

The most impressive stone fort (*castillo*) in all of colonial North America was built to defend the harbor of St. Augustine, Florida (pls. 7, 8, 9, 10). The first workmen, who drew their pay on August 8, 1671, opened the coquina stone quarries on Anastasia Island, worked the stone blocks, built wheelbarrows, hauled and burned oyster shells to make lime mortar. Others forged tools or fashioned dugouts for rafting the stones to the mainland. Governor Manuel de Cendoya and Engineer Ignacio Daza, from Havana, staked out the outline of the fort, and on October 2, 1672, the first shovelful of dirt began the foundation trenches; on November 9, the first stone was laid. Twenty-three years later, the workmen put down their tools. The first phase of the massive stone fort, twenty feet high, surrounded by a forty-foot-wide moat, was finished.[12]

A series of wooden forts of indeterminate number had preceded the Castillo. The first fort was the Indian house fortified by the Spanish in 1565. The site is under investigation by Kathleen Deagan; its shape and method of construction might soon be known. The next two forts and a *casa fuerte* at St. Julián Creek were constructed on Anastasia Island between 1566 and 1570, when the population swelled to about eighteen hundred people. Dr. Eugene Lyon has found some descriptions in the Archives of the Indies at Seville, Spain. The forts were triangular, similar to Fort Caroline, with the usual support buildings inside, and are thought to have been at the northern end of the island.[13]

After 1570, a series of wood forts were constructed on the mainland north of the town, near the present-day Castillo. They began to rot in four to five years.[14] One was triangular, and several were squared blockhouses. Some were hastily built and rebuilt in similar form, but most followed current European fortification ideas, with palisades enclosing barracks, dungeon, powder house, treasury, chapel, and plaza, protected by moats, ditches, battered walls, and pointed bulwarks or bastions. A few of these forts are depicted in old manuscripts (fig. 9.4). One built about 1570–71, and its replacement in 1579, had two floors and similar layouts, according to a drawing made in 1580.[15] By 1586 there was a fort known as Castillo de San Juan de Pinos, "built all of timber, the walles being none other but whole mastes or bodies [trunks] of trees set uppe right and close together

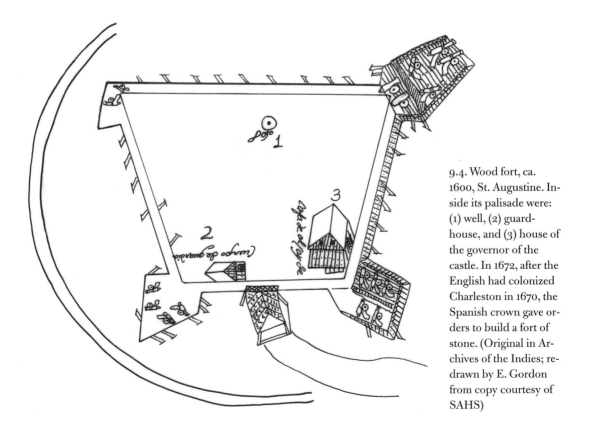

9.4. Wood fort, ca. 1600, St. Augustine. Inside its palisade were: (1) well, (2) guardhouse, and (3) house of the governor of the castle. In 1672, after the English had colonized Charleston in 1670, the Spanish crown gave orders to build a fort of stone. (Original in Archives of the Indies; redrawn by E. Gordon from copy courtesy of SAHS)

in manner of a pale [fence, palisade]."[16] Baptista Boazio depicted this fort before it was burned in the raid by Sir Francis Drake in 1586. Shortly thereafter, about 1593, Hernando de Mestas made a drawing of a successor triangular fort. Another wood fort, called Castillo de San Marcos, built early in the seventeenth century, was a square fort said to be in poor shape five years after it was built, "propped up by thirty-two supports . . . all of it is in danger of collapsing."[17] By 1668, after an untold total number of forts, the last fort to be constructed with wood was rotting away and feeling the crash of waves against its palisade.[18] In May, Robert Searles and his pirates sailed past this embarrassing fort in the night and attacked, setting in motion pressures to build a stone fort. By April, 1670, the English had become entrenched at Charleston. Spain had no choice but to build the next fort with masonry.

The wood forts had been imperfect solutions. The colonists' prayers for greater security were answered with the stone Castillo de San Marcos. It is a masterpiece of European textbook military architecture adapted to the river site by Spanish military engineers and their *maestros de obras,* master masons who were in charge of its construction. The plan of the fort was a square, equally strong on all sides, with a bastion at each corner (pl. 7). Each bastion was four-sided and had its own name: San Agustín (southeast), San Carlos (northeast), San Pablo (northwest), and San Pedro (southwest). The bastions were the key architectural elements, their shape permitting the cannon on its deck (terreplein) to fire from all angles in all directions. Around the entire fortress ran the wide moat, filled with seawater that flowed through an opening in the outer seawall.[19]

The engineer-architect of the brilliant initial design was Ignacio Daza. His design was influenced by current European practices and the forts he was familiar with in Havana: the Castillo de Real Fuerza in Havana (1562), designed by Bartolomé Sánchez and Francisco de Calona, and two forts designed by the well-known Italian fort designer Bautista Antonelli, the Castillo de San Salvador de la Punta (1589–1600) and the Castillo de los Tres Reyes del Morro (1589–1630). Antonelli also designed the forts of Veracruz, Cartagena, and Puerto Rico. His leitmotif was the rigidly symmetrical plan with an interior courtyard similar to that built in St. Augustine. Antonelli's influence can also be seen in similar designs by his son, Juan Bautista Antonelli, at the Castillo del Morro in Santiago de Cuba (1639) and the Fuerte de Cojímar (1645) in Havana.[20]

Daza's *maestros de obras* were Diego Díaz Mejia and Lorenzo Lajones. The fifty-six-year-old Lajones was a master mason with much experience who had worked on fortifications during thirty-six years in France, Italy, and Havana. Daza died a year after St. Augustine's fort was begun, and his engineering work was carried on by the new governor himself, Don Pablo de Hita Salazar, a veteran of many campaigns and most recently governor of Veracruz. Captain Enrique Primo de Rivera was his military construction overseer. The civilian master of construction, Lajones, died shortly thereafter and was replaced by new masters of construction Juan Márquez Molina, of Havana, and Simón Vázquez, civilian master stone-cutter and mason. A new military engineer arrived from Havana, Ensign Don Juan de Císcara, followed by Antonio de Arredondo, who designed the masonry vaults to replace rotted wood beams. In 1738, big changes to the fort were necessary due to English threats. From Venezuela came Engineer Pedro Ruiz de Olano to supervise more vaults and the tall watchtower on the San Carlos bastion (fig. 9.5; pl. 8). His *maestro de obras* was Cantillo, who sickened and was replaced by Blas de Ortega, of Havana. Finally came Engineer Pedro de Brozas y Garay from Ceuta, Africa, who completed the rest of the vaults during 1755–56 (fig. 9.7). In the last years of construction, Engineer Pablo Castelló, a mathematics professor at the Havana military college, arrived to help the aging Engineer Brozas y Garay enlarge the ravelin (pl. 9).[21] Brief are these biographies of some of the Spanish engineer-architects and their construction supervisors, but great was their contribution to Florida's architectural heritage.

The labor force represented many cultures. Hundreds of Indians were brought to St. Augustine to work in the quarries and as lime-burners and masons during 1673–75. Additionally there were African slaves, mulattoes and mestizos from Mexico and Cuba, and many creoles born in St. Augustine. Even Englishmen—prisoners from the Carolina colony— worked on the fort. John Collins (Juan Calens) rose in the Spanish crown's employment to be master of the kilns and quarry master.[22]

During the English siege of 1702, led by James Moore of Carolina, all of St. Augustine fled to the fort with their valuables and cattle. The spacious courtyard enclosed by stone walls proved a safe retreat. Three wells and some of the main rooms held enough provisions to wait out the siege until help came in four Spanish men-of-war. Meanwhile, the wood buildings in the city burned in the fires set by the raiders.

The attack in 1702 would be followed by more English attacks in 1728 and 1740. The Castillo was never breached, but it could not defend all of St. Augustine. From 1704 until the end of the colonial period, the defense of St. Augustine evolved into a complex plan that included various palisades, moats, earthworks, prickly cactus barriers, redoubts, and block-houses to protect approaches by land as well as by sea. The new defenses included the Cubo Line and the Rosario Line enclosing the city, and a hornwork and the Fort Mose Line creating land barriers to the north.[23]

9.5. Sentry tower, San Carlos bastion, 1740, Castillo de San Marcos, St. Augustine. The northeast bastion, San Carlos, had a tall sentry tower in time for the English attack led by General Oglethorpe in 1740. When the old fort and its tallest watch tower were no longer needed to defend Matanzas Bay from pirates and enemy sailing ships, it became a great favorite with tourists and artists alike. (1903 postcard, collection of E. Gordon)

Two older blockhouses, Forts Pupo and Picolata, were rebuilt where the Apalachee Trail crossed the St. Johns River, to guard against enemies approaching from the west. By 1755, Fort Picolata, on the east bank, had been rebuilt with a two-story coquina stone tower and a Spanish-style battlemented flat roof for cannons, and surrounded with a moat and stockade.[24] Twenty miles north of the city, Don Diego Espinosa, one of St. Augustine's wealthiest residents, had fortified his ranch, San Diego, in the 1730s. "Fort San Diego" had a palisade of cedar posts fifteen feet high, and two bastions armed with five small cannons.[25] Two miles north of the city, Fort Mose was built and garrisoned by former African slaves in 1738, and rebuilt in 1752 (map 9; fig. 9.10). South of the city, in 1740–42, the Spanish constructed *el fuerte pequeño,* the little stone Fort Matanzas, to defend the "backdoor" water route to the city (fig. 9.11). Both Fort Mose and Fort Matanzas are described later in this chapter.

The Castillo itself underwent changes. The walls were heightened to thirty-five feet and round-arched bombproof masonry vaults were constructed. A terreplein of six-inch-thick tabby concrete was poured above the vaults, forming a gundeck for cannon. By January 1740 the tall domed watchtower was built on the northeast San Carlos bastion, its *media naranja* dome a descendent of fortification towers built in Havana since the sixteenth century (fig. 9.6). The fort as such withstood General Oglethorpe's attack in 1740.[26]

G 15040 Old Watch Tower, Fort Marion, St Augustine, Fla.

9.6. Bastion tower, from early seven-teenth-century wall enclosing Havana, with *media naranja*-style dome similar to that built at the Castillo de San Marcos in St. Augustine. (Drawing by students of the Escuela Técnica Superior de Arquitectura de Barcelona/Universitat Politècnica de Catalunya)

A decade later, Engineer Brosas y Garay completed the vaults and added the row of two-story-tall Doric pilasters and cornices (fig. 9.7). The fort walls were covered with a smooth, gleaming white coat of lime plaster made from burned oyster shells to waterproof and protect the masonry. The sentry boxes were emblazoned with red paint. Today the fort looks like the artifact that it is; the plaster is gone, except for a small patch here and there to remind us that the colonists were serious about a *permanent* fort.[27]

The royal arms over the main gate indicate that the fort was completed in 1756. However, the covered way, the glacis, the stone parapet, and new ravelin were being worked on at the end of 1762 when the news came that Spain would cede Florida to Great Britain (pl. 9).[28] On July 21, 1763, the British took ownership of the fort and renamed it Fort St. Marks. The Spanish returned in 1784 and once again it was El Castillo. Engineer Mariano de la Rocque rebuilt the entrance to the chapel in the neoclassic style with an arch order, engaged pilasters and Doric entablature (pl. 10), and the beautiful baroque holy water stoup captured in a sketch in 1890.

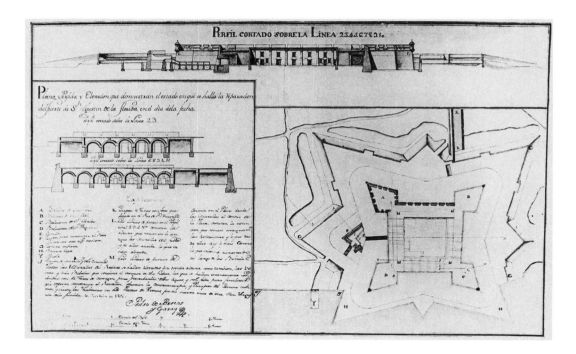

Above: 9.7. Castillo de San Marcos, 1756, St. Augustine, *Plano, Perfiles, y Elevacion que demuestran el estado . . .* by Pedro de Brozas y Garay. The stone fort was continuously worked on and improved by the Spanish. The vaulted rooms below the terreplein (cannon deck) were shellproof. (From *Cartografía de Ultramar*; photocopy by Ken Barrett, Jr., courtesy of SAHS)

Right: 9.8. Holy water stoup, ca. 1785, chapel, Castillo de San Marcos, St. Augustine. The baroque stoup in the chapel lent a touch of elegance to the massive military Castillo, and may have been the work of Engineer Mariano de la Rocque. (Drawing by Charles B. Reynolds, from *The Standard Guide, St. Augustine,* 1890; photocopy by Ken Barrett, Jr., courtesy of SAHS)

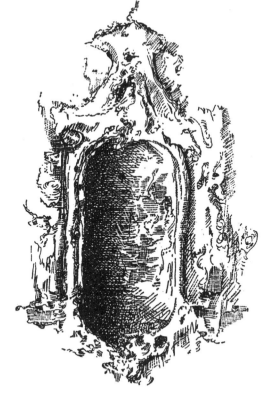

NICHE IN CHAPEL.

After Florida became a U.S. territory (1821), the venerable old fort was called Fort Marion, after Francis Marion, a hero of the Revolution and brilliant American guerrilla leader dubbed "the Swamp Fox" by the British. It was in Fort Marion that Osceola, leader of the Seminoles, was imprisoned after he was captured under a flag of truce in 1837. It was also in Fort Marion that the chiefs of Kiowas, Comanches, Cheyennes, Arapahos, and Apaches were locked up while white settlers moved into their homelands. An act of Congress restored the Spanish name to the fort in 1942, recognizing the success of the brilliant design and the unremitting suffering, labor, and sacrifices endured by its colonial builders. Today the Castillo de San Marcos is a National Monument and one of Florida's and America's greatest treasures.

The Walled City

The terrifying English raid of 1702 that resulted in the burning of most of St. Augustine's wood buildings spurred the construction of an enclosure around the city, to repel attacks by land from the north, west, and south. The northern bulwark was the Cubo Line, and the western and southern barrier was the Rosario Line. The Cubo Line extended from the Castillo west to the San Sebastian River. When completed in 1705, it was a long wood palisade with a ditch planted with prickly cactus, and six wood redoubts (small fortified platforms), each with two cannons enclosed inside a log palisade. By 1706, decay had already set in. The Cubo Line was replaced by a hornwork one-half mile to the north. It was an earthwork with a heavy log palisade and sizable wood bastions next to the Indian village Pueblo Nombre de Dios. The Indians planted corn between the old Cubo Line and the new hornwork.[29]

Between 1738 and 1743, the Cubo Line was rebuilt by Engineer Pedro Ruiz. The earthwork was planted with prickly cactus and had a moat and three redoubts where cannon could crossfire. The redoubts were named the Cubo, Medio Cubo, and Tolomato (later, Santo Domingo). By 1763, the defensive line was badly eroded. The British repaired it with pine logs, but in 1781 Engineer Elias Durnford, chief engineer of West Florida, erected a whole new Cubo Line (called the Intrenchment) with a string of wood redoubts. They too rotted. The Spanish returned in 1784 and reconstructed the Cubo Line in 1805–8 with palm logs. The Santo Domingo redoubt was 57 feet by 72 feet and had walls of vertical palm logs. Plans are underway for the reconstruction of the 1808 redoubt.[30]

The City Gate of today began about 1739–40 as a simple opening in the Cubo Line with a wood gate called "La Leche gate" at the head of St.

9.9. City Gate, St. Augustine. In 1821, the wood drawbridge from 1808 was removed and the road filled in. (Glass negative photograph, from north looking south, by Stanley J. Morrow, ca. 1882, courtesy of Florida State Archives)

George Street. In 1808, two strong pillars of stone were built by Engineer Manuel de Hita; these were hung with a wood gate, approached over a wood drawbridge, and protected by a wood guardhouse. Engineer Francisco de Cortazar completed the City Gate in 1818 with stone guardhouses and pomegranate decorations (fig. 9.9). Like the fort, the entrance was plastered white and had red trim. In 1821, the wood drawbridge was modernized, replaced with a stone causeway.[31]

The Rosario Line was built between 1718 and 1719. It was an earthwork planted with prickly pear cactus that began at the Santo Domingo redoubt of the Cubo Line and ran southward 3,575 feet, enclosing the west flank of the city, then turned east toward the shore of the Matanzas River for 478 feet, and north for 71 feet to its end. It was buttressed by five redoubts on the west, named San José, Santa Isabel, El Rosario, Santo Cristo, and Santa Barbara. Another redoubt, named Merino, stood where the line turned. Where the line met the river, they built the lunette-shaped San Francisco redoubt in stone (1720–25). The stones would later be recycled into the foundation of the British Pile of Barracks.[32] The prickly cactus plants and yucca, or Spanish bayonet, defied climbers, prompting William Stork to describe their pointed needle-sharp leaves in 1766 as "so many chevaux de frieze they make it entirely impenetrable." In this walled St. Augustine, the City Gate was "regularly shut at sunset."[33]

FORT MOSE

Two miles north of St. Augustine, on dry land surrounded by marsh, a small fort-settlement took shape in 1738. It was built by slaves who had fled from plantations in Georgia and South Carolina, and was named Gracia Real de Santa Teresa de Mose, or simply, Mosa, Moosa, Mossy, or Negro Fort. The Spanish had refused to return slaves escaping from English bondage and instead housed them, instructed them in Catholic doctrine, and baptized them. The males were made members of the Spanish slave militia. On March 15, 1738, Governor Manuel de Montiano granted the slaves in the militia their freedom and named as their captain an escaped slave named Francisco Menéndez. Anticipating attacks from the north by the English, the Spanish government moved the freedmen and their families, thirty-eight households of men, women, and children, to the northern site on which they were to build the fort-settlement. The African militia at Fort Mose would be the first line of warning and defense in an attack by land.[34]

The attack came in less than two years, with such strength that the African settlement was forced to take refuge in the Castillo along with the residents of St. Augustine. General Oglethorpe's troops, led by Colonel Palmer, occupied Fort Mose. On June 26, 1740, the African militia, Indians, and Spanish soldiers retook Fort Mose, but the fort and all the buildings were destroyed. It had been described by the British as four square with a flanker at each corner, banked with earth and prickly pear cactus, surrounded by a ditch. Within the enclosure were a well, a building, and a lookout.[35]

Fort Mose was rebuilt twelve years later in 1752, slightly north of the first destroyed fort. This second Fort Mose has been wrested from the ground as well as from the archives, with some architectural detail, by archaeologist Kathleen Deagan and historian Jane Landers. Much larger than the first fort, it was a rectangle enclosed on three sides by earthworks made of rammed earth faced with clay and sod, topped with needle-sharp cactus. The river protected the fourth side. Two bastions were formed at the northwest and southwest corners. There was also a six-foot-wide moat. Nine structures are depicted inside the earthworks on one map, likely to have included a powder magazine, kitchen, warehouse, quarters, and the church described by Father Solana in 1759 as 10 varas long by 6 varas wide (fig. 9.10). The small church had walls partially finished with wood planks; the sacristy was completed and housed the Franciscan friar Ginés Sánchez, who split his time with the mission church, Nuestra Señora de la Leche.[36]

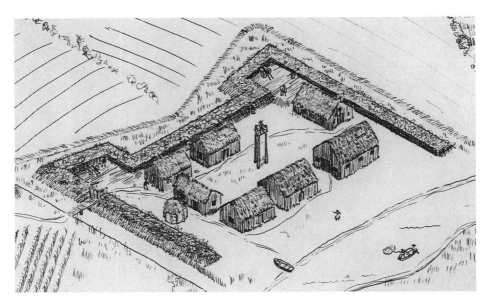

Nine black families of the free militia left Fort Mose and sailed with the Spanish to Havana in 1764, after Spain had ceded Florida in 1763. They were granted lots and given tools in a new settlement in the province of Matanzas, Cuba, called San Agustín de la Nueva Florida, or Ceiba Mocha. Ironically, they were also given "a slave newly imported from Africa to assist in the labor of homesteading."[37] Today Fort Mose is flooded by tidal creeks that wash over the site of what was the first legally free black town in the United States.

FORT MATANZAS

In colonial times, sailing vessels could navigate two inlets south of St. Augustine. Matanzas Inlet, the only one in existence today, is no longer navigable, changed by tidal currents, sand banks, and the diversion of the river to create the Intracoastal Waterway. The inlets allowed a backdoor surprise entrance to St. Augustine. Starting in 1569, they were guarded by wood watch towers with thatch huts, surrounded by palm log palisades, similar to the one described by Drake's men in 1586 on Anastasia Island as a "scaffold upon four long masts."[38]

Oglethorpe's attack on St. Augustine in 1740 prompted Engineer Pedro Ruiz de Olano to design a small stone fort to guard the inlets. Fort Matanzas was completed in 1742 on the east shore of Rattlesnake Island, facing Matanzas Inlet. The little fort was built on wood pilings sunk vertically in the sand and marshy subsoil to provide a stabile foundation. A sentry box and five cannons on the gun deck stood ready to stop any sailing vessel (fig. 9.12). A wood water trough channeled rainwater to a cistern for drinking and cooking. The tower was divided into a lower and upper story; the lower room housed six to ten soldiers, their cooking fireplace, and their munitions and provisions, and the upper story was for the commanding officer. The observation deck had a clear view of the inlet and river. At night, the wood ladder to the fort was drawn up for protection.[39]

9.11. Fort Matanzas, 1742, Rattlesnake Island, St. Johns County. Surprise attacks on St, Augustine could come up the Matanzas River from two inlets south of the city. Engineer Pedro Ruiz de Olano designed a small fort of coquina stone to guard the town's "backdoor." By 1872, when Henry Fenn made this drawing, the fort was tottering. Restoration finally began in 1916, almost too late. (Wood engraving by Frederick William Quarterly from a watercolor, *Ruins of a Spanish Fort at Matanzas Inlet,* by Henry Fenn, published in *Picturesque America,* 1872)

9.12. Fort Matanzas, 1742, restored 1916. In 1924, the fort was designated a National Monument, and today the National Park Service provides boat service to the fort. (Photograph copyright 2000 Ken Barrett, Jr.)

Fort Matanzas was turned over to the United States on June 4, 1821, a month before Florida formally became a U.S. territory. (The Adams-Onís Treaty of cession had been negotiated in 1819, but ratification and the exchange of flags did not occur until 1821, July 10 in St. Augustine, and July 17 in Pensacola.) By then the stalwart little fort was in very bad shape (fig. 9.11). Many good people fought to have the fort rescued, and repairs on the badly cracked fort finally began in 1916; in 1924 it was designated a National Monument, to preserve its unique construction and significant role in the contest for Florida between Spain and Great Britain.[40] Today the miniature fort, once very isolated, overlooks an anchorage for pleasure boats and a white sand beach, and is included in a popular boat excursion provided by the National Park Service. This is a fine example of what historic preservation has brought to Florida and the nation.

Fort San Luis and Fort San Marcos de Apalachee

Haciendas and cattle ranches followed the missions west in the 1600s. One of the most fertile regions was that of the Apalachee Indians, between the Ochlockonee and Aucilla Rivers. The haciendas grew food-stuffs and cattle that were shipped to St. Augustine, Cuba, and Mexico from a harbor at the confluence of the Apalachee (now St. Marks) and Wakulla Rivers. The harbor, the haciendas, and the missions had to be protected.

In 1656, the Apalachee chief promised to build a *casa fuerte* (block-house) for the Spanish in what is now Tallahassee. The site grew to become the Castillo San Luis in Pueblo San Luis, and headquarters for the western region of Spanish Florida. During the half century that San Luis evolved and developed before its destruction in 1704, a series of block-houses were built, before the "genuine fort" was erected in the 1690s. The fort had four features: the blockhouse, a surrounding palisade with three diamond bastions, a dry moat, and a covered way. The military engineer-builder (and deputy governor) was Captain Jacinto Roque Pérez. The fort was abandoned in 1704, and to prevent it from falling into enemy hands, it was set on fire. The next year, Admiral Antonio de Landeche documented the former fort with a map and drawing (fig. 9.13).[41]

Archaeology has turned up the following details: the blockhouse had massive wattle-and-daub walls, whitewashed with lime, strong enough to support the cannon on its roof. It was 40 by 70 feet, partitioned into a guardroom, quarters, and warehouses. The palisade measured 130 feet by 230 feet, and was about eleven feet high. The dry moat was three to five

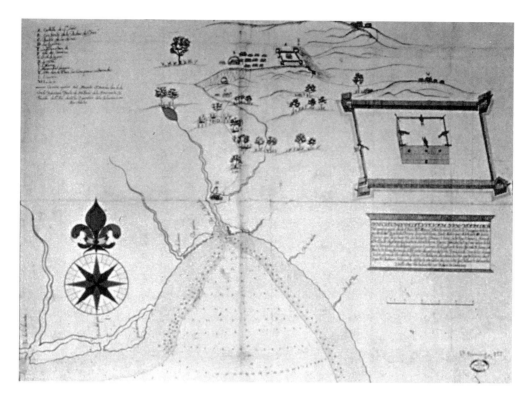

feet deep, planted with prickly pear cactus. The covered way led down into the ravine, where there was a water source. The remains of the fort were noted as a landmark in the 1760s when the British cartographer George Gauld noted that "Tallahassa" was on the road to "the old Spanish Fort."[42]

Fort San Marcos de Apalachee guarded the harbor that was south of San Luis, from where the produce of the Apalachee region was shipped and incoming supplies were received. The first of several small wood forts was begun by 1679. Logs were used, coated with lime whitewash to look like stone. The subterfuge did not deter French pirates, who burned the fort in 1682. In 1718, Captain José Primo de Ribera constructed a second wood fort. By 1739, the Spanish were rebuilding its parts with the limestone that was native to the mouth of the St. Marks River. The curtain, the bastion, a bomb-proof magazine, and the officers' and soldiers' barracks designed to hold two hundred men were built of stone by 1745. The fort-settlement became a popular trading post by the 1750s with a permanent settlement of Lower Creek Indians.[43]

In 1763, when British East Florida assumed jurisdiction, the fort, described by the surveyor George Gauld as a "small castle," was less than half finished. The British strengthened Fort St. Marks in the 1760s with a 12-foot-square tower, 45 feet high, on the bank of the Wakulla River oppo-

9.13. *Castillo de S^n Luis*, 1690s, Tallahassee, map of 1705. Built by the Apalachee, it was burned in 1704 to prevent it from falling into English hands. (Photocopy courtesy of Florida Division of Historical Resources)

site the fort. The tower walls, almost three feet thick, were pierced with loopholes to defend the workmen in the stone quarries a few yards away.[44] The fort was abandoned by the British in 1768 after severe storms and many repairs became a nagging problem. The strategic location prompted the Spanish to reoccupy the site in the 1780s, and General Andrew Jackson to move into the fort in 1818. The Americans abandoned the fort in 1825 and took some of the stone to construct St. Marks light-house in 1829.[45] In 1839 George W. Sully drew *A View of the Old Spanish Fort at the Town of St. Marks,* when the crenellated tower walls were still present, before they too were stripped of stones to build a marine hospital.

NEGRO FORT (FORT GADSDEN)

During the War of 1812 between England and America, a British expedi-tion was sent up the Apalachicola River (Spain did not object) to recruit Indians and escaped slaves. Fifteen miles up the river, on a strategic east bank called Prospect Bluff, Major Edward Nichols had built a strong wood fort by 1814. The fort had a wood palisade and was called British Point. It quickly became the headquarters for negotiations between the British and anti-American Indians. At the conclusion of the war in 1815, the British withdrew and turned the fort over to the Seminoles and former slaves. The fort became known as Negro Fort.

Negro Fort was a beacon of hope for slaves who fled Carolina and Georgia plantations. They rallied to the site, cultivated farms, and

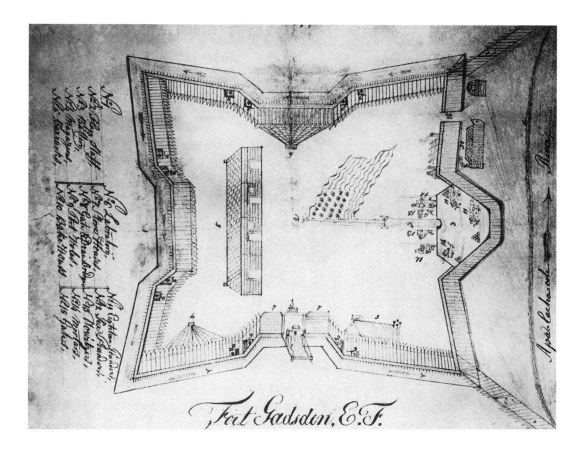

Fort Gadsden, E.F.

dreamed of freedom. But the fort became a scourge to the slave-owning planters, who looked upon it as a symbol for slave rebellion. Major General Jackson gave the order to "blow it up! Return the Negroes to their rightful owners!"

On July 27, 1816, Lieutenant Duncan Clinch, in command of a U.S. gunboat, fired a "hot" cannon shot into the fort, where 100 men and 234 women and children had gathered for safety. It blew the magazine and 270 runaway slaves were killed. Impressed by the strategic location of the fort, General Jackson directed Lieutenant James Gadsden in 1817 to build a new fortification at the site, ignoring the fact that it was within Spanish territory. The new Fort Gadsden had a wood palisade with many portholes, magazine, barracks, and a drawbridge flanked by storehouses. The bake oven was outside the palisade (fig. 9.15). The fort was garrisoned by Americans until the end of the colonial period, when Spain ceded Florida in 1821 to the United States.[46]

9.15. Negro Fort, 1815/ Fort Gadsden, 1818, Prospect Bluff, Apalachicola River. Built by the British during the War of 1812, Fort Gadsden, which was within Spanish territory, was garrisoned by Americans until Spain ceded Florida in 1821 to the United States. (Photograph courtesy of Florida State Archives)

Presidio Santa María de Galve and Fort San Carlos de Austria

Pensacola Bay was the primary focus of Spain's Gulf Coast empire. A Spanish settlement had been attempted by Tristán de Luna in 1559, but it was a tragic failure and was abandoned in a hurricane two years later. The de Luna site is unknown, long thought to have been in the Pensacola Bay area.

One hundred and thirty-nine years later, in 1698, Spain tried again to establish a presence at Pensacola Bay. This second attempt was successful. Spurred by fears that the French were planning to establish a colony, the Spanish sailed into the bay in November, beating the French to the site by only a month. While the Spanish were beginning to construct their fort-settlement, the French sailed on to occupy Mobile Bay. The Spanish chose a site high on the bluff on the west side of the entrance to the harbor, today's Pensacola Naval Air Station. They named the bay Bahia de Santa María de Galve, for the Virgin Mary and the viceroy of New Spain (Mexico), the Conde de Galve. They named their settlement after the bay. It was the beginning of a continuous Spanish presence.[47]

Santa María de Galve was founded by Governor Andrés de Arriola, from Veracruz. His engineer-architect was Captain Jaime Franck, an Austrian. He selected the site for the fort on the bluff, the Barranca de Santo Tomé, with a commanding view of the entrance to the harbor. He named the fort San Carlos de Austria, after the thirteen-year-old Charles of Austria, later Charles VI of the Holy Roman Empire. Unfortunately, the three hundred men who came with Arriola and Franck to build the colony were mostly military discipline problems or convicts from Mexico's prisons. It has been described as a penal colony, with "poles and palmetto thatch." The enclosure was roughly three hundred feet wide by six hundred feet long, and the fort was three hundred square feet, built of pine logs, with bastions at each corner. Outside the stockade was the town, with a church, a rectory, and houses.[48]

The fort and the town survived until 1719, but only with a large amount of contraband trade with French Mobile. In 1719, it changed hands in a series of surrenders that seesawed between the French and Spanish. Spain surrendered the settlement in May, the French surrendered it in August, the Spanish surrendered it in September, and the French occupied the site until the fort was destroyed in 1721. When it was given back to Spain in 1722 all that was left was a flimsy cabin, a bake oven, and a lidless cistern.[49]

Presidio Isla de Santa Rosa

The Spanish built a new presidio in 1723 at the western tip (Point Si-güenza) of Santa Rosa Island, the long, east-west barrier island defining the entrance to the harbor. The engineer-architect was Don José de Berbegal. He constructed the fort "upon a foundation of piles driven so far into the sand that wind and water could not too greatly weaken them." There were also the usual presidio buildings: a church, warehouse, pow-der magazine, officers quarters, and soldiers' barracks, houses for civilian workers, a hospital, bake oven, and a house for the governor, Lieutenant Colonel Alejandro Wauchope, a Scotsman who had served in Spain's Irish Brigade. It is said there was also a lookout tower sixty feet high. The new fort-settlement survived, like its predecessor, with assistance and il-legal trade with the French in Mobile and New Orleans. Santa Rosa, however, was also shortlived. Vulnerable to violent storms from the Gulf of Mexico, it was destroyed in a hurricane in 1752. This time only a store-house and the hospital were left.[50]

Fortunately, Dominic Serres had made a sketch of Santa Rosa in 1743, which was engraved in 1763 by T. Jefferys as *A North View of Pensacola, on the Island of Santa Rosa*. Despite refinements by the engraver, the view reveals something of what might have been achieved there architecturally. The legend on Jefferys' engraving identifies the fort, the church, the governor's house, and the commandant's house. Serres was French born, but he was serving on a Spanish merchant ship when he made the draw-ing, looking south from his ship to the north shore of the island. He de-picted the governor's house as two-storied, with *media naranja* domes topped with crosses. He drew the church with horizontal siding and po-lygonal plan, either an octagon or a decagon, with a central belfry (fig. 3.14). Such designs would seem suspect except for the fact that Serres (1722–1793) later became a founding member of the British Royal Acad-emy, and was well known for the accuracy of his marine paintings that today are considered to be more reliable than contemporary accounts often written with a bias to impress military superiors.[51] The engraving suggests that Don José erected something more than the ordinary under very limited conditions.

After the devastation of the 1752 storm, an expedient palisade of stakes and a warehouse and gunpowder magazine were hastily rebuilt. A new presidio, however, would have to be constructed on a more permanent site on the mainland across the harbor. In 1756, the Spanish moved to the site of an older blockhouse that had stood since 1740, northeast of the first settlement on the bluff at Fort San Carlos de Austria.[52] The Spanish, however, recognizing that the defense of the harbor rested on fortifications with cross-fire capability between Santa Rosa Island and the Red Cliffs, continued to maintain a blockhouse, battery, and signal tower on Santa Rosa Island and the bluff.

Santa Rosa would shine again in Florida's military history, when the massive brick walls of Fort Pickens rose out of the island's dunes in 1834 and stood ready for both the Civil War and the Spanish-American War of 1898.

Presidio San Miguel de Panzacola

The third Spanish presidio became today's Pensacola, and was built on the site of the present Historic District. Since 1740, the area was known by the name of its blockhouse, Fort San Miguel, but was commonly referred to as Panzacola, after the local Indians. In 1757, the new fort was officially named Presidio San Miguel de Panzacola. A new governor, Colonel Miguel Román de Castilla y Lugo, arrived from Veracruz.[53]

The engineer-architect, Felipe Feringan Cortés, ordered pointed stakes put in place quickly for a stockade on three sides, roughly enclosing a space 365 by 700 feet. The fourth side, on the banks of the harbor, was not palisaded, but had a pier sixty yards long, six yards wide. Within the stockade were the usual edifices: the royal chapel, grocery and gunpowder warehouses, soldiers' barracks and officers' quarters, bake ovens, jail, treasury, commandant-governor's house, and guardhouse (figs. 3.15, 3.16). They were built of wood boards or bousillage, clay packed on lath with a moss binder covered with lime plaster. The governor's house had a timber frame set directly into the ground, a first floor for offices, and the commandant-governor's dwelling on the second with a gallery and divided staircase. The style was influenced by French architectural practices in the Gulf Coast Region. The roofs, except that of the gunpowder magazine, were of cypress bark and palm fronds. Dwellings with similar materials were erected outside the stockade for the officers, married soldiers, and civilians.[54]

In June, 1760, in fear of Indian attack, the Spanish destroyed the buildings outside the stockade to clear the firing field. In August 1760, a hurricane destroyed half the stockade and blew the roofs off the houses. Cypress bark was in short supply and many houses were roofless during the winter of 1760–61. Indian attacks continued into 1762, and a new commandant-governor had been assigned to the presidio, Colonel Diego Ortiz Parrilla, an experienced Indian fighter. He found the buildings in terrible shape, but had only a year and a half to solve the Indian problem and make architectural repairs.[55] Time ran out. Spain ceded Florida to Great Britain in February 1763.

The British rebuilt the stockade and presidio buildings,[56] which they called "the garrison," and constructed Fort George north of the town on Gage Hill and two batteries above it. Their plans for military buildings show obvious concern for Florida's climate, with wraparound galleries, plenty of windows, and masonry foundations. General Gage wrote in 1768 that the troops were remarkably healthy, which he attributed to the removal of the stockade on the harbor side (as the Spanish had done before them), opening the garrison toward the sea breezes and to freer circulation of air around the fort.[57] Batteries were constructed with a "shade of three inch thick Plank laid above the Platforms, with a proper descent to carry off the water. . . . the shades will also cover the Guns, Carriages, and Platforms from the sun and rain in summer and winter." The blockhouses behind the batteries lodged the troops who worked the guns, and the engineer-designer made sure they were dry, their foundations "Piled, Plank'd, and reveted with bricks."[58]

Engineer Durnford's plans for Pensacola in 1778 showed the palisade reinforced with a *trou-de-loup,* or "wolf's mouth," a pit with pointed stakes that formed a formidable obstacle to the outworks (pl. 20). Fort George had a double stockade with the space between filled with sand. The plans, elevation, and section of one of the blockhouses "proposed for the Defense of the Town of Pensacola" (1765?) provided for a foundation reinforced by piles driven in marshy soft soil, battered and revetted walls, loop holes, bombproof barrel vaults, ground-floor powder magazine, bell-shaped flue, and cannon deck (fig. 9.16). The soldiers were to sleep in hammocks; the "officers apartment" was not described. To build the 40-by-40-foot blockhouse required piles 6 feet long preserved with pitch, 277,500 bricks, 1,000 barrels of lime, 1,116 feet of large timbers for the roof deck, 679 feet of twelve-foot boards 1½ to 2 inches thick, thousands of pieces of hardware, nails, spikes, bolts, and hammock hooks, and 434 hours of manual labor by bricklayers, carpenters, and laborers. The estimate of "4,935 Dollars" included transport of materials but did not specify whether the bricks, timbers, lumber, and lime were locally produced or imported.[59]

Like the Spanish, the British recognized the importance of the bluff at the harbor entrance (called Barranca de Santo Tomé by the Spanish and Red Cliffs by the English) as well as Santa Rosa Island in the defense of the harbor. Thus they built a masonry redoubt at the old site of the first Spanish fort, Fort San Carlos, on the entrance bluff. On Santa Rosa, they

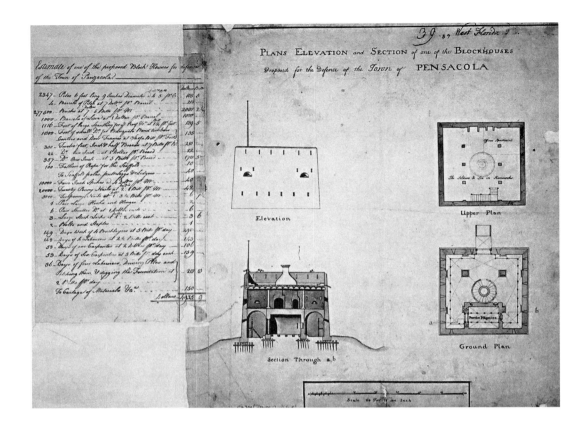

9.16. Plans, Elevation and Section of one of the Blockhouses Proposed for the Defense of the Town of Pensacola, 1765? Detailed English plans and estimates for materials to erect a blockhouse reveal how foundations were devised for soft soils as well as other construction practices. (Photograph courtesy of Public Record Office, PRO: CO 700 Florida 12)

erected a signal house and two new batteries with blockhouse in 1771, one of which was "stockaded to secure the Old Spanish Powder Magazine."[60]

Batería de San Antonio and Fort San Carlos de Barrancas

The masonry ruins on the west side of the entrance to Pensacola Bay descend from the decision of Jaime Franck in 1698 to build the first Spanish fort, Fort San Carlos de Austria, on the red bluffs. The ruins there today, however, called Fort San Carlos de Barrancas, are American. They are the remainder of the last layer of military architecture to be superimposed on the earlier Spanish and English forts.

When the Spanish returned to Florida in 1783, they fortified the bluff with a new Fort San Carlos. A plan of the fort drawn by Gilberto Guillemard in 1787 indicates building practices similar to those designed by French engineers Adrien de Pauger, at Mobile in 1724, and Bernard Deverges, at Fort Tombecbé in 1761.[61] During the second Spanish colonial period, the most important architects and builders in the region from Pensacola to Louisiana were French or American, and Guillemard was considered the most important of these. The French commonly used colombage or bousillage construction, and hipped roofs covered with split cypress shingles or with long slabs of bark laid on the roofs like clapboards. Colombage is a wood frame of timbers erected on timber sills and enclosed with horizontal boards. Sometimes the spaces between the timbers were filled with brick, known as brick-between-posts construction, or, in more remote areas, a mixture of mud and moss (bousillage) was used. If oyster shell lime was added to the mud mixture, it produced a more durable cement-like material.[62]

Batería de San Antonio is the brick *medialuna* battery that still exists at the water level, built in 1796 below the Spanish Fort San Carlos. It is a large horseshoe-shaped structure protected in the front by a dry moat and in the rear by a parapet (fig. 9.17). Iron tracks and granite pintle blocks for the cannon are still in place. The brickwork is exceptionally well crafted, composed of thin, long, locally handmade, Roman-style bricks.[63]

Fort San Carlos was destroyed by the British in 1813, during the War of 1812. In 1817, the Spanish reclaimed the ruins of Fort San Carlos and constructed wood barracks with bark roofs. Meanwhile, John Quincy Adams and Luis de Onís were negotiating the Adams-Onís Treaty of 1819, by which Spain agreed to transfer Florida to the United States. The Spanish flag came down in Pensacola on July 17, 1821, and the water battery and

9.17. Batería de San Antonio, 1796, Pensacola. Fort San Carlos was destroyed by the British in 1813, during the War of 1812, but the Batería de San Antonio stood fast and firm. (Photograph courtesy of Florida State Archives)

the fort on the bluff were transferred to the Americans. Fort San Carlos was in ruins, but only a few bricks were needed to repair the *medialuna* water battery.

The Americans built their fort during 1839–44 on the ruins of the 1790s Spanish Fort San Carlos. Today, the ruins of this American fort rise directly behind the colonial water battery and are connected to it by a long segmental arched brick tunnel.[64] Like the Spanish and English engineers before them, the Americans designed their Fort San Carlos de Barrancas to defend Pensacola harbor with a cross fire from Santa Rosa Island where Fort Pickens had been erected in the sand dunes a few years earlier. The strategy echoed the military tactics of the Spanish more than a century earlier.

It is difficult to make the tortuous route of complicated military architecture interesting to a generation long removed from the insecurity of the colonial period. Floridians no longer need to build stockades or dig moats or build earthwork barricades. One cannot even imagine the effort needed to dig them by hand or to burn and pound enough oyster shells to make lime to stucco the huge Castillo de San Marcos. The relics of Florida's colonial defenses are few, but the weight of their story is very heavy.

Appendix I: English Pound Sterling Equivalents

The British contribution to Florida's colonial architecture has been greatly undervalued or overlooked. To demonstrate England's financial commitment to architecture in the two Florida colonies, some English expenditures for maintaining Spanish buildings, including conversions and add-ons and new construction, are quoted in the present book, taken from English documents of 1763–84. The primary currency of the time in Florida as well as in English colonies to the north was the English "pound sterling." However, how much was an English pound sterling worth, or what would an English pound buy in the 1760s and 1770s in Florida? Below are listed some examples of costs, wages, and materials that will enable the reader to derive a sense of a building's worth comparable with costs of square footage today.

During Florida's colonial years, in addition to the English pound, many varying denominations and values of coins were circulating, struck in different countries. Dollars quoted for construction estimates in Pensacola, for example, might have been equivalent to the Spanish dollar, the silver peso that was widely used in English colonies and that became the prototype of the U.S. silver dollar, of the same value. The silver peso equaled eight *reales,* giving rise to the common American name "piece of eight." It was not until 1786, however, two years after the British left Florida, that the Continental Congress fixed the legal value of the dollars then circulating in the United States at 375.64 grains of pure silver per dollar.

Examples of construction costs, English colonial period 1763–84:

1. In New Smyrna, £158 would buy the following prepared lumber: 6,503 feet cypress planks, 870 feet 1½-inch-thick cypress planks, 5,760 feet pine boards, 516 feet cypress logs, 380 feet pine in logs, 7,720 cypress shingles.
2. The annual salaries of the governors of East Florida and West Florida were £1,200; the chief justices, £500; attorneys general, £150; church ministers, £100; schoolmasters, £25.

3. In Pensacola, £2,500 was the estimate to construct a very large house and office for the governor, with some 7,000 square feet (exclusive of verandas and garret) and outbuildings that included kitchen, stable, coach house, laundry, and covered walkways.

4. In St. Augustine, £95.2.6 (pounds, shillings, pence) bought a completed stable and coach house, heavy timber framed and weatherboarded. Materials came to £65.2.6, and included six windows, 929 feet of hanging timber, 649 feet of scantling, 850 feet of 1¼-inch boards, 1,500 feet of 1-inch boards, 800 feet lathing, and 8,000 shingles. Labor was £30.

5. In St. Augustine, two sentry boxes, constructed, painted, and sized, materials and labor, cost £8.15.

6. Construction of the King's Road from Ponce de Leon Inlet to Georgia border cost £1,763.

7. In St. Augustine, £319 covered the costs to build a church tower and steeple; £32 was paid for the construction of eleven pews, including labor and materials, and £7.8 to paint them three times in oil and number them.

8. In St. Augustine, the walls of one room in the governor's house were plastered and painted for £9.3.

9. In New Smyrna, £35 was the carpenter-contractor's bill submitted for each two-room, timber frame house, 13 × 27.5 feet, lathed and plastered, and roofed with thatch. It is not clear if the central chimney of stone and brick and tabby floor were included in the figure.

10. Loyalists filed claims after 1784 that their large, two-story stone houses in St. Augustine with five to six rooms, piazzas, stone kitchen houses and storehouses, were worth from £350 to £800, including lot and garden, with perhaps a little exaggeration to elevate their claims for reimbursement from the English crown. William Drayton, however, had sold his very large stone house (the former Elíxio de la Puente House) and lot on the waterfront to Frederick William Hecht for £1,107.

11. Respectable wood frame houses on Florida's plantations could be erected for £100 or less. For example, on governor Tonyn's plantation on Black Creek, a wood frame dwelling, 14 × 16 feet, with two stories and brick chimney, was valued at £60; a log kitchen with brick chimney at £20; a log barn 14 × 24 at £12; a cooper shop with earthfast pole frame 30 × 16 feet, weatherboarded and roof clapboarded, at £17.10.

12. A wood cypress bridge built by an experienced engineer over San Sebastian Creek and marshland, 195 feet long and 12 feet wide, including a road through the marsh cost £300.

13. In Pensacola, fees for grants of 1,000 acres of land were posted in dollars; in 1765, the governor's fee was 8 dollars and the secretary of state's fee was 4. The fees rose steadily: in 1772 they were 28 and 51 dollars, respectively, and in 1778 they were 80 and 106 dollars respectively.

14. Barracks for one battalion, brick and wood, with verandas, and New York labor, to be constructed in St. Augustine, were approved in 1769 at £6,680. As a comparison, barracks also for one battalion, approved on the same date, to be constructed in Quebec and stone faced, were approved at £6,893; in Pensacola, the barracks for five companies, brick, with separate buildings for officers and soldiers, were estimated at £4,782.

15. Theater tickets at St. Augustine's statehouse theater were 5 shillings for the pit, and 4 shillings for the gallery. In Williamsburg about the same time, the tickets to the playhouse were 5 to 7 shillings.

Appendix II: Colonial Builder's Glossary

Some Spanish and English colonial terms for materials, architectural elements, types of buildings, and construction techniques were extracted from old documents and used in the present text. The Spanish terms are in italics, and include some that are employed in the more frequently used documents as well as in the translations of Florida historians, particularly those of Eugene Lyon and Albert Manucy. Many of the English terms and their definitions came from William Salmon's very popular and practical architectural handbook, *Palladio Londinensis, or, The London Art of Building,* 5th edition, published in 1755 in London, to which he annexed his "Builder's Dictionary." His book was first published in 1734 and eight editions followed, used by gentlemen designers, carpenters, masons, brick layers, painters, plasterers, and joiners. Some of his words are no longer in English usage; several of his definitions have been expanded to be concurrent with their usage today.

Alarife: architect, builder.

Arch order: from Roman architecture, arches framed by engaged columns and entablatures.

Arcos de piedra: stone arches.

Ashlar: hewn or squared large stone blocks; random ashlar means stones of different sizes.

Atrio: church courtyard, sometimes surrounded by low wall.

Bark: outside sappy planks or boards sawn from the sides of timber.

Belvedere: rooftop pavilion, gazebo, lantern (lanthorn), or mirador; glazed or open roof superstructure larger than a cupola.

Boghouses: necessary houses, outhouses.

Bohío (bojío): house, a word used by the Arawaks of the Greater Antilles and adopted by the early Spanish settlers in Spanish America.

Bousillage (bouzillage): walling technique consisting of a mixture of clayey mud and moss packed between upright poles or hewn timbers (cypress preferred) on wood strips (lath), and usually plastered inside and out. Sometimes quicklime from burned oyster shells was added to the mixture. The walls were thick and over time hardened like cement. See also *Cuje y Embarrado* and Wattle-and-Daub.

Braced frame: heavy, braced wood frame, with timbers of full frame height, diagonally braced by lighter lumber in the angles.

Campana: bell; also bell-shaped; *campana de chiminea,* bell-shaped chimney hood.

Campanario: belfry.

Canales: water pipes, gutters.

Cantería: hewn stone.

Capital: top member of a column, consisting of an abacus (square slab at top of capital to bear the beam, or architrave) supported by decorative moldings (cornices).

Case of crown glass: contained 24 disks (the crown) handmade by glass blowers and called "tables," each table being circular or nearly so, about 3 feet 6 inches or 3 feet 8 inches in diameter.

Celosía: window lattice.

Clamp: stack of bricks forming a "kiln" built aboveground for the burning of the bricks.

Clapboarded: used to describe some eighteenth-century roofs; today it refers to wood siding on a frame building applied horizontally and overlapped (see Weatherboarded).

Clausura, claustro: cloister.

Clinkers: bricks that were glazed because they were closer to the fire.

Cloister: derived from Latin claustrum, claudere (to close), courtyard bordered by a covered walkway; it became the central organizing space around which the major buildings of monastic life were organized; an open colonnade.

Cocina: kitchen.

Comedor: dining room.

Convento: monastery, friary, the building or buildings containing friars' rooms, offices, library, chapel, and refectory; the religious community.

Corredor: covered walkway, gallery, see also Loggia and Cloister.

Cuje y embarrado: walling technique using horizontal sticks, cane withes, or split lath secured to upright posts and plastered with clayey mud (sometimes mixed with lime), and usually whitewashed or plastered. See Bousillage, Wattle-and-Daub.

Cupola: small room, circular, square or polygonal, on top of a building.

Curtain: Wall connecting two bastions of a fort; main wall.

Doric order: knowledge of the Greek Doric had not yet been regained and published at the time of the first Spanish period and first decade of English construction in Florida. The earliest published plates and handbooks revealing the antiquities of Greece occurred in the 1760s. Thus, what was built in colonial Florida before about 1770 was the taller, more slender Roman Doric with base and pedestal, or the shorter, Tuscan order.

Embarrador: plasterer.

Ermita: neighborhood church or hermitage to which a preacher came on the day of the mass; as the town and parish grew, traditionally the *ermita* became a more substantial church building.

Espadaña: portion of front facade raised above the gable ridge, often stepped and curved, sometimes highly decorated, and sometimes containing openings in which bells were hung (*espadaña* belfry).

Facines: bundles of sticks used to quickly build a defensive rampart parapet.

Fogón: hearth, cooking stove, kitchen range.

Foundation: raised basement; lowest floor.

Galería: veranda, piazza, porch, covered way; see also *Corredor.*

Gavel end: gable end.

Georgian-Palladian style: label not used in eighteenth-century Florida, but applied today to describe eighteenth-century neoclassic buildings characterized by rigid symmetry, geometrical proportions, hipped roofs, porticoes, axial entrances, sash windows, and various elements that were influenced by Palladio, or architectural handbooks published by English Palladianists; see also Palladian.

Guano: (Cuba) palm tree; guano thatch, palm fronds used for thatch roof; see also *Palapa.*

Headers: bricks laid endwise; stretchers are laid lengthwise.

Herreriano: and *estilo desornamentado:* major architectural style after Juan de Herrera, architect who introduced the style at El Escorial, the palace and monastery built 1563–84 near Madrid for King Felipe II of Spain and noted for its geometrical classicism, proportions, and simplicity, unadorned with embellishments.

Hipped roof: a roof that slopes back from each side of the building so that there are no gables.

Horno: oven; *horno de ladrillo,* brick-kiln.

Hornwork: defensive earthwork with two half bastions, resembling bull horns.

Intercolumnation: clear spaces between columns in a series.

Keystone: the central (often decorated) voussoir in an arch; when in place it forms the true arch.

Lead: for gutters, "flatts" [flat surfaces], pipes, cisterns, sinks, window glazing.

Link: measurement in a surveyor's chain equal to 7.92 inches.

Loggia: an arcade (covered walkway) forming part of a building.

Maestro de obras: professional master of construction, often a master mason.

Mampostería: rubble work; walls of roughly trimmed stones of many sizes that were not squared, but the uneven edges fitted against another as best as possible and the cracks filled in with smaller pieces and mortar.

Media naranja: type of dome in the shape of half an orange.

Metope, triglyph, mutule, and guttae: in the frieze of the Doric order, there are square spaces (metopes), often plain but sometimes decorated, between two triglyphs, vertical elements with two vertical channels and two half channels, related to the mutule above (projecting flat block on underside of Doric cornice) and guttae below (representing wooden pegs). The whole system is an interpretation in stone of earlier timber construction.

Modern: any architecture borrowing elements of Gothic and antique Greek and Roman (the 1750s definition).

Mudéjar: style of the Arab-Spanish craftsmen in Spain after the fifteenth century; the *Mudéjar* style is inherently decorative, as found in decorative clay tile, latticework, brickwork, window grilles, and balconies.

Muntin: a secondary framing member that holds the panes of glass in the window sash, also called a glazing bar or sash bar.

Nogging: soft bricks (samel) used as filling between members of a framed wall.

Paja: straw, thatch; *techado de paja, techar con paja,* thatch roof.

Palacio: splendid mansion.

Palacio episcopal: bishop's house.

Palapa: (Mexico) palm thatch roof.

Palisade: series of stout poles (or palm trunks) set in the earth close together as a fence or stockade.

Palladian (Palladianism): style of building based on Roman forms and the published designs of the Italian architect Andrea Palladio (1508–1580), particularly as it developed in England and its colonies in the

West Indies and America, derived from the influence of Inigo Jones
and Lord Burlington and popularized by many architectural handbooks thereafter.

Pallisication: piles driven in marshy soft soil (word no longer in English
use).

Parapet: little wall or rail enclosing a "tarrass" (flat roof).

Parlor: lower room for entertaining.

Parroquial mayor: cathedral, principal church.

Patio: courtyard.

Pediment: triangular space expressing the gable end of the roof, or an
ornamental triangle surmounting doors and windows, created by
horizontal and sloping cornices; sometimes with a rounded instead
of pointed top, or a "broken pediment" in which the sloping sides
are returned before reaching the top.

Piazza: British term for veranda, gallery, porch; broad open space or
square, whence it became applied to walks, porticoes of pillars,
verandas, and galleries.

Piedra: stone, block of stone.

Pilaster, *pilastra:* visible part of a square column against a wall.

Pillar: round column disengaged from wall.

Pisé: tapia, rammed earth construction.

Plaster: lime mortar, often with hair, daubed or smeared on lathing
(strips of split wood) or used as an exterior weatherproofing coat
over stone or mud-clay walls.

Postigo: peep-window, shutter.

Presbiterio: presbytery, chancel, part of the church before the sanctuary
where priests and bishops sit.

Presidio: fortified settlement.

Proportion: justness of members in each part of the building and
relation they bear to the whole.

Puncheon (punchin): short upright piece of timber (stud) in timber
frame placed under some weightier elements to support; a split log
or heavy slab with face smoothed to support flooring (puncheon
floor).

Quoins: reinforcement stones or bricks that form the external corners;
sometimes decorative in wood or rustication.

Rafa: buttress; *rafas y tapias,* architectural term for rammed earth-
with-buttress construction that was common for early churches in
Cuba.

Raja: chink, split; *paredes de raja:* walls of rived boards and chink.

Rejas: window grille.

Repartimiento: obligatory tribute of Indian labor.

Reredo: altarpiece or altar screen, backdrop for the celebration of the Mass, sometimes a simple painting on the wall, and sometimes a very elaborate frame with paintings and sculpture placed against the wall behind the altar.

Retablo: altarpiece, a painting on wood, part of the *reredo.*

Revet: to face with wood, stone, or concrete (a sloping wall or embankment, for example, to prevent erosion).

Rived: hand-split, as in planks and shingles.

Rustick (rustik): masonry (or imitation masonry) where joints between stones are emphasized, or where stones are rough or worked to give a contrasting textural effect, often associated with the first or Doric stories of Renaissance architects. English-Palladian architects, like James Gibbs and Robert Morris, published many designs with rusticated first stories. In the American colonies, exterior plaster and even wood siding was scored and painted to look like stone (rustication).

Sanctuary: the part of the chancel containing the main altar, separated from the nave and congregation by a low chancel rail.

Santos: saintly religious imagery, two- or three-dimensional.

Sash, window sash: framework of a window, fixed or movable, glazed with glass panes; a double-hung window has two vertically sliding sashes; a single-hung window has one fixed sash and one movable sash. Some movable sashes open and close using a system of counterweights suspended on sash cords that pass over sash pulleys. Some single sashes are propped open by a window stop or a stick.

Scantling: framing timbers cut to any desired size.

Shingles: for roofing, usually small wedges of wood, four to five inches wide, eight to twelve inches long, one inch thick at one end.

Size (sizing): glutinous material like varnish or resins added to whiting (lime and water) to make whitewash, which fills in porous holes of plaster, stone, and wood.

Sotea, azotea: flat roof of planks or timbers covered with a mortar mixture (cement) of sand and oyster shell lime and water.

Tabia or *tabbi* (Moorish North Africa) or *tapia real* (Spain): rammed earth (tapia) or mud wall stabilized with lime made from limestone and sometimes an aggregate of stone.

Tabby (American southeast coast): a concrete made of lime from burned oyster shells, water, and sand and an aggregate of oyster shells or, for floors, a finer aggregate of crushed coquina stone. (Not to be confused with cement, a cohesive and adhesive plastic mixture of lime and sand and water without aggregate, essentially a mortar.)

Tapia: rammed earth (also *pisé*); mud wall, as in adobe.

Tarras (tarrass): open walk or gallery, also flat roof; flat surfaces (Salmon's *Builder's Dictionary* did not imply a material).

Terreplein: gundeck.

Tie beam: in roof framing, the horizontal timber connecting the opposite ends of a rafter to prevent them from spreading.

Vara: Spanish unit of measurement of length equal to 32.9 inches.

Voussoir: wedge-shaped stones spanning the opening in an arch.

Walling: making of walls, of whatever kind.

Wattle-and-daub: walling technique using sticks of wood, twigs, branches, and withes (wattle), woven in basket-like manner and secured with cordage between and around upright framing poles set in the ground, and daubed (plastered) with clayey mud; see also *Cuje y embarrado* and Bousillage.

Weatherboarded: exterior wall covering with overlapping wood planks or boards, upper edge rabbeted to fit under an overlapping board above.

Wrought Iron: iron that is hammered or forged into shape when the metal is hot or cold.

Whitewash: quicklime and water (whiting), and a sizing like varnish or resin that is painted on walls and dries to a white protective coating.

NOTES

FOREWORD

1. William J. Murtagh, *Keeping Time: The History and Theory of Preservation in America,* rev. ed. (New York: John Wiley, 1997).

2. Boorstin, quoted in George Grant, *The Blood of the Moon, The Roots of the Middle East Crisis* (Brentwood, Tenn.: Wolgemuth and Hyatt, 1991), 9.

1. THE FIRST BUILDERS

1. Milanich and Hudson, *Hernando de Soto,* 82, 96.

2. Milanich, *Archaeology,* 216–18, 279–98, 312, 396–97; Milanich, "Late Nineteenth-Century Description," 75–79; Lewis, "The Calusa," 19–49; Madira Bickel State Archaeological Site brochure; Milanich and Fairbanks, *Florida Archaeology,* 242; Morgan, *Precolumbian Architecture,* 101–3, 225; Sears, *Fort Center.*

3. Bartram, *Travels,* 101–2.

4. Waselkov and Braund, *Bartram,* 178, fig. 28, 240 n. 31, 241 n. 32; Milanich, *Archaeology,* 3, 270; Morgan, *Precolumbian Architecture,* 212, 213.

5. Waselkov and Braund, *Bartram,* 49, 242 n. 37; Milanich, *Archaeology,* 257; Morgan, *Precolumbian Architecture,* 215.

6. Johnston, "Turnbull Plantation Site," 34; *Jacksonville Florida Times-Union,* September 6 and November 13, 1992; Arana, "Notes on Fort Matanzas," 64.

7. Hudson, *Southeastern Indians,* 206; Milanich and Milbrath, *First Encounters,* 26.

8. Cabeza de Vaca, *Journey,* trans. Bandelier, 10.

9. Shapiro and McEwan, "Archaeology at San Luis," 17; Hann and McEwan, *Apalachee Indians and Mission San Luis,* 75–79; Worth, *Timucuan Chiefdoms,* 1:93; Wenhold, "Seventeenth-Century Letter;" Dr. William Marquardt, correspondence with author, February 13, 2001.

10. Cabeza de Vaca, *Journey,* trans. Bandelier, 22–23, 25, 50; Clayton, Knight, and Moore, *De Soto Chronicles,* 1:190–91.

11. Bourne, *Narratives,* 23; Clayton, Knight, and Moore, *De Soto Chronicles,* 1:57, 187; Milanich, *de Soto Expedition,* 42–43.

12. Milanich and Hudson, *Hernando de Soto,* 63, 123; Milanich and Fairbanks, *Florida Archaeology,* 95, 107, 136, 187, 206.

13. Hulton, *America 1585,* 17, pl. 38, fig. 26.

14. Hudson, *Southeastern Indians,* 333.

15. Milanich, *Archaeology,* 272–74, 294–96.

16. Milanich, *de Soto Expedition,* 65, 66, 67, 375.

17. Bourne, *Narratives,* 38–39, 41, 47, 69, 72–73; Clayton, Knight, and Moore, *De Soto Chronicles,* 1:190–91, 2:197.

18. Bonnie McEwan, director of archaeology, San Luis Archaeology and History Site, Tallahassee, interview August 26, 1999; Ewen, "Anhaica," 110–18.

19. Lyon, *Enterprise,* 117–18.

20. Lawson, *Foothold,* 18, 19, 166, 200; Fort Caroline is described in chapter 9.

21. Lawson, *Foothold,* i, x.

22. Hulton, *America 1585,* 17–18; Milanich and Milbrath, *First Encounters,* 198–200; Lawson, *Foothold,* 150–60. The surviving painting is at the New York Public Library.

23. Kathleen Deagan, site archaeologist, interview, February 8, 2000.

24. Lyon, "First Three Wooden Forts," 131, 132; Lyon, *Enterprise,* 119.

25. Deagan, interview, February 8, 2000; Lyon, "The Three Wooden Forts," 134.

26. *New York Times,* July 27, 1993.

27. Lawson, *Foothold,* 75, 171.

28. Hudson, *Southeastern Indians,* 9–10.

29. Nebraska State Historical Society, Lincoln, Nebr., 1880s photograph of an Omaha Village.

30. Lawson, *Foothold,* 54.

31. Milanich and Hudson, *Hernando de Soto,* 205.

32. Lawson, *Foothold,* 75, 171.

33. Lawson, *Foothold,* 12.

34. Morgan, *Prehistoric Architecture, Precolumbian Architecture.*

35. Lawson, *Foothold,* 60.

36. De Landa, *Yucatan,* 32.

37. *Architectural Digest,* January 1999, 112–21; Colle Corcuera, *Mexico, Casas del Pacífico.*

38. Hulton, *America 1585,* fig. 23.

39. Hulton, *America 1585,* pl. 32, fig. 35.

40. Hulton, *America 1585,* 17, 20, 28, 35.

41. Hulton, *America 1585,* pl. 32, fig. 23.

42. Hulton, *America 1585,* 27–28, pl. 32, fig. 23, fig. 35; PRO: CO 5/577, f. 459; Rea, "Haldimand," 516; Mereness, *Travels,* 486; see chapters 6 and 9 and appendix II.

43. Faye, "British and Spanish Fortifications," 290; Wilson, "Gulf Coast Architecture," 123–24, 127–28.

44. Wilson, "Gulf Coast Architecture," 87–88, quoted from Le Page de Pratz, *Histoire de la Louisiana* (Paris, 1758), 2:172–75.

45. Ibid.

46. Ibid.

47. Lawson, *Foothold,* 13, 103, 176.

48. Bourne, *Narratives,* 47; Milanich and Sturtevant, 1613 *Confessionario,* 40–41, 48.

49. Bartram, *Travels,* 168, 170; Waselkov and Braund, *Bartram,* 159.

50. Hudson, *Southeastern Indians,* 299.

51. See chapter 8.

52. Lawson, *Foothold,* 79; Deagan and MacMahon, *Fort Mose,* 42; Bartram, *Diary,* 53; Hann and McEwan, *Apalachee Indians and Mission San Luis,* 78, 102.

53. Milanich, "Original Inhabitants," 4.

54. Milanich and Milbrath, *First Encounters,* 26; Johnson, "Mission Santa Fé," 141; Hann, "Missions of Spanish Florida," 94.

55. Bartram, *Travels,* 306–7; Mahon and Weisman, "Florida's Seminole," 183, 187, 188, 189; Hudson, *Southeastern Indians,* 5, 464–65.

56. Mahon and Weisman, "Florida's Seminole," 189.

57. Bartram, *Travels,* 163–69, 306–7, 314, 354, 359.

58. Patrick, *Florida Fiasco,* 179–80; Mahon and Weisman, "Florida's Seminole," 187; PRO: CO 5/548, ff. 62–77.

59. Bartram, *Travels,* 162–70.

60. Waselkov and Braund, *Bartram,* 156, 157, 172, 184; Bartram, *Travels,* 168, 200, 297, 357.

61. PRO: CO 700/54.

62. Mahon and Weisman, "Florida's Seminole," 190; Hudson, *Southeastern Indians,* 465.

63. Mahon and Weisman, "Florida's Seminole," 191–205; Coles and Waters, "Indian Fighter," 37.

2. The Spanish Missions

1. Bennett, *Twelve on the River,* 34; Parker, "Urban Indians," 3–4.

2. Hann, "Summary Guide," 46, 423, 417–513; Milanich, "Laboring in the Fields," 62, 65.

3. Lyon, *Enterprise,* 119, 162–63, 170, 178, 179, 197, 201, 202–3; Lyon, "First Three Wooden Forts," 142; Gannon, *Cross in the Sand,* 28–32; Milanich, "Laboring in the Fields," 60–62.

4. Worth, *Timucuan Chiefdoms,* 1:106, 109.

5. Deagan, "St. Augustine and Mission Frontier," 88.

6. Cather, *Death Comes for the Archbishop,* 276.

7. Worth, *Timucuan Chiefdoms,* 1:44, 103–5; Garcia-Weaver, "Private Archive," 101; Temple, *Carmel Mission,* 5, 6, 78.

8. Bennett, *Twelve on the River,* 30–46; Milanich and Sturtevant, *1613 Confessionario;* Gannon, *Cross in the Sand,* 38, 49–54, 57; the title page of the grammar is reproduced in Gannon, *New History,* 96.

9. Griffin, "Preliminary Report," 61–66; Dickinson and Wayne, "Archaeological Testing," 2–6.

10. Worth, *Timucuan Chiefdoms,* 1:111.

11. Hann and McEwan, *Apalachee Indians and Mission San Luis,* 142, 146, 149–53, 154, 162, 165–76; Gannon, *Cross in the Sand,* 73.

12. See McEwan, *Spanish Missions.*

13. See chapter 4.

14. Geiger, *Early Franciscans,* 2; Milanich and Sturtevant, *1613 Confessionario,* 14; Bennett, *Twelve on the River,* 42.

15. Hann and McEwan, *Apalachee Indians and Mission San Luis,* 32; Milanich, "Laboring in the Fields," 63–66.

16. Saunders, "Missions Santa María and Santa Catalina," 37; Marrinan, "Mission Patale," 276–79.

17. Bonnie G. McEwan, director of archaeology, San Luis Archaeological and Historic Site, Tallahassee, interview, August 1999.

18. Hann and McEwan, *Apalachee Indians and Mission San Luis,* 69.

19. Hudson, *Southeastern Indians,* 78, 113, 218–22; Thomas, "Mission Santa Catalina," 12; Saunders, "Missions Santa María and Santa Catalina," 40, 47–48; Weisman, "Archaeology of Fig Springs," 165, 179; Loucks, "Archaeology of Baptizing Spring," 202; Kubler, *Religious Architecture of New Mexico,* 74; Kubler, *Art and Architecture,* 69–70; McAndrew, *Open-Air Churches,* 216; Hann and McEwan, *Apalachee Indians and Mission San Luis,* 69–73; Milanich, *de Soto Expedition,* 63.

20. Hann and McEwan, *Apalachee Indians and Mission San Luis,* 89, 91; Bonnie McEwan, correspondence and interview with author, August–September, 1999; Herschel E. Shepard, F.A.I.A., correspondence with author, August 9, 1999; McEwan and Hann, "Reconstructing," 17.

21. See McEwan, *Spanish Missions.*

22. Arana, "Defenses," 34.

23. Wilson, *Gulf Coast Architecture,* 83.

24. Schuetz, "Professional Artisans," 18–19; Sunderland, "Symbolic Numbers," 94–103.

25. Saunders, "Spanish Mission Architecture," 533–34; Thomas, "Mission Santa Catalina," 9; Saunders, "Missions Santa María and Santa Catalina," 54; Johnson, "Mission Santa Fé," 146; Weisman, "Fig Springs Mission," 167, 173; Shapiro and Vernon, "Archaeology at San Luis," 202–19; Carley, *Cuba,* 69, 73–74; De Landa, *Yucatan,* 32.

26. Deagan, "St. Augustine and the Mission Frontier," 91–92; Bennett, *Twelve on the River,* 37; Milanich, "Laboring in the Fields," 66–65; Hoffman, "Material Culture," table 2; Worth, *Timucuan Chiefdoms,* 1:190.

27. Thomas, "Mission Santa Catalina," 9.

28. Lyon, "Richer Than We Thought," 20, 24, 37, 39, 46, 47, 48, 49, 50.

29. Weisman, *Excavations,* 34.

30. Wenhold, "Seventeenth-Century Letter," 12.

31. McAndrew, *Open-Air Churches,* 216, 133–134; Pierson, *American Buildings,* Vol 1, 171.

32. H. E. Shepard, correspondence with author, September 1, 1999; Hann and McEwan, *Apalachee Indians and Mission San Luis,* 87.

33. Von Simson, *Gothic Cathedral,* 8–14, 33–35, 56, 154–155, 208–210; Janson, *History of Art,* 231, 245; Sunderland, "Symbolic Numbers," 94–103.

34. Nuttgens, *Story of Architecture,* 178–82; Lawler, *Sacred Geometry,* 4, 6, 10, 53.

35. Dr. Bonnie McEwan, interview, August, 1999; H. E. Shepard, correspondence with author, September 1, 1999; Hann and McEwan, *Apalachee Indians and Mission San Luis,* 86.

36. Solana to Arriaga, 1759, 15; see chapter 4.

37. Hayes, *Four Churches of Pecos,* 4, quoting from Eleanor B. Adams and Angélico Chávez, *The Missions of New Mexico,* 1776, Albuquerque: University of New Mexico Press, 1956, 208–14.

38. Thomas, "Mission Santa Catalina," 12; Kubler, *Religious Architecture,* 30–31, 61; Hann and McEwan, *Apalachee Indians and Mission San Luis,* 87; see churches described in chapter 4.

39. Wenhold, "Seventeenth-Century Letter," 14.

40. Bushnell, "Situado," 88; see Convento de San Francisco, chapter 4. The music lesson method was suggested by Bonnie McEwan.

41. McEwan and Hann, "Reconstructing," 17.

42. Lyon, "Richer Than We Thought," 35; Milanich and Sturtevant, *1613 Confessionario,* 10; Thomas, "Mission Santa Catalina," 13; Marrinan, "Mission Patale," 280; Worth, *Timucuan Chiefdoms,* 1:57, 109; Hann, "Church Furnishings," 148, 149; Bartram, *Travels,* 198; Bartram, *Diary,* 53; PRO: CO 700/54.

43. Colle Corcuera, *Casas del Pacífico; Architectural Digest,* January 1999, 112–19, and August 1999, 112–18; personal observations in Mexico and Cuba.

44. Engraving of Boazio's battle plan showing St. Augustine at the time of Drake's raid; the Boazio drawing of St. Augustine was first published in 1588 in Latin by Bigges, an edition of which is in a bound portfolio at the British Library under the title *Expeditio Francisci Draki,* shelf mark "Draki G.345"; see chapter 3.

45. A copy of the Mestas drawing is in the SAHS collection.

46. Bushnell, "Situado," 88–89.

47. Lyon, "Richer Than We Thought," 11–12; 94–96; Hann, "Church Furnishings," 148–50.

48. Bretos, *Cuba and Florida,* 38; see chapter 4.

49. McEwan and Hann, "Reconstructing," 17.

50. Thomas, "Mission Santa Catalina," 9.

51. Milanich and Sturtevant, *1613 Confessionario,* 10; Bennett, *Twelve on the River,* 43; Johnson, "Mission Santa Fé," 142.

52. Lawson, *Foothold,* 7, 53, 169; Shapiro and Hann, "Documentary Image," 512; Hann and McEwan, *Apalachee Indians and Mission San Luis,* 114.

53. Lawson, *Foothold,* 7, 52.

54. Wenhold, "Seventeenth-Century Letter," 14.

55. Thomas, "Mission Santa Catalina," 13; Hoshower and Milanich, "Fig Springs Burial Area," 235; Milanich, "Laboring in the Fields," 65; Hann and McEwan, *Apalachee Indians and Mission San Luis,* 119–20; McEwan, interview, August 26, 1999.

56. H. E. Shepard, correspondence with author, August 9, 1999.

57. Shapiro and Vernon, "Archaeology at San Luis," 177–201, 220; Thomas, "Mission Santa Catalina," 16–19; Saunders, "Missions Santa María and Santa Catalina," 44–46; Johnson, "Mission Santa Fé," 156, 159; Weisman, "Fig Springs Mission," 177; Marrinan, "Mission Patale," 246, 277, 281; Hann, "Summary Guide," 485–86; Hann and McEwan, *Apalachee Indians and Mission San Luis,* 90–91.

58. Tour of site August 26, 1999.

59. Worth, *Timucuan Chiefdoms,* 1:168.

60. See chapter 4; Hoffman, "Convento de San Francisco," 63–65; Gannon, *Cross in the Sand,* 74, 76.

61. Wenhold, "Seventeenth-Century Letter," 13; Hann, *Apalachee*, 195; Gannon, *Cross in the Sand*, 65; Worth, *Timucuan Chiefdoms*, 1:93.

62. Interview with Bonnie McEwan at the site, November 29, 2000.

63. Shapiro and McEwan, "Archaeology at San Luis," 17–32; Shapiro and Hann, "Documentary Image," 511–21; Hann, *Apalachee*, 244–45; Hann and McEwan, *Apalachee Indians and Mission San Luis*, 75–78, 80; Thomas, "Mission Santa Catalina," 23; Weisman, "Fig Springs Mission," 179; Weisman, *Excavations*, 75–100.

3. THE DARK AGE OF WOOD

1. "A Map of the Road from Pensacola in West Florida to St. Augustine in East Florida from a survey made by order of the late Hon. Col. John Stuart, Esq., His Majesty's Superintendent of Indian Affairs, Southern District, in 1778 by Joseph Purcell," PRO: CO 700/54.

2. Lyon, "First Three Wooden Forts," 131–34; Deagan, *Creole Community*, 22–23; Deagan, "Excavations;" Deagan, interviews, *New York Times*, July 27, 1993, and *St. Augustine Record*, February 19, 1997.

3. Deagan, interview at site, February 8, 2000; Solís de Merás, *Menéndez*, 182.

4. Arana, "Defenses," 87.

5. Lyon, "First Three Wooden Forts," 134–36; Lyon, *Enterprise*, 92, 152; Solís de Merás, *Menéndez*, 184.

6. Lyon, "First Three Wooden Forts," 136–42; Lyon, conversation with author, March 3, 2000.

7. Lyon, "First Three Wooden Forts," 143–45; Lyon, "Settlement and Survival," 48, 51, 54–56, 58; Lyon, "Richer Than We Thought," 10.

8. Halbirt, "Redefining," 2–3; Deagan, *Urban Enclave*, 185–87; see note 44, chapter 2; Drake, *Exhibition*, 107, 108, 110.

9. Drake, *Exhibition*, 8–9, 108.

10. Deagan, *Urban Enclave*, 185–87; Elíxio de la Puente, 1764.

11. Deagan, *Urban Enclave*, 193; Lyon, *Enterprise*, 116; Johnson, "Spanish Community," 28–29.

12. Deagan, "Melting Pot," 27; H. E. Shepard, correspondence with author, August 9, 1999; Carley, *Cuba*, 74; De Landa, *Yucatan*, 32; Manucy, *Sixteenth-Century*, 77; Kathleen Deagan, interview, February 8, 2000.

13. Gritzner, "Tabby," 140–41; Laws, *Rural Spain*, 153.

14. Kelsey, *Drake*, 275–78; Deagan, "St. Augustine and the Mission Frontier," 91–92; Worth, *Timucuan Chiefdoms*, 1:190.

15. Parker, "Government House Overview," 2.

16. Carley, *Cuba*, 53, 59; Bond, "Tradition and Change," 133, 161; Hoffman, "1580 Research Project," 14–16.

17. Hoffman, "Material Culture," 99.

18. Hoffman, "Material Culture," 95; Bushnell, "Situado," 88; Arnade, *Siege*, 57–58; Hann and McEwan, *Apalachee Indians and Mission San Luis*, 32, 39, 146.

19. Bushnell, "Situado," 88.

20. See chapter 4; Arnade, *Siege*, 57–58; Bushnell, "Situado," 88.

21. Herschel E. Shepard, correspondence with author, August 9, 1999; Nuttgens, *Story of Architecture,* 21–22, 143.

22. Halbirt, "Of Earth, Tabby," 70, 75, 76.

23. Deagan, *Urban Enclave,* 185, 198–199.

24. Lyon, "Richer Than We Thought," 15–17; Cusick, "Across the Border," 278.

25. Lyon, *Enterprise,* 81–82, 93.

26. Lyon, "Settlement and Survival," 55–56, 64–67, 71; Lyon, "St. Augustine 1580," 24; P. Hoffman, "1580 Research Project," 17; Deagan, "Melting Pot," 29; K. Hoffman, "Material Culture" 96–98; *SAAA,* vol. 13(4), December 1998; Johnson, "Spanish Community," 31; Arana, "Defenses," 17; see also copies of parish records at the St. Augustine Historical Society.

27. Lyon, "Richer Than We Thought," 13; Hoffman, "Material Culture," 96, 105; Deagan, "St. Augustine and the Mission Frontier," 91, 92, 94; Cusick, "Across the Border," 279–82.

28. Deagan, *Creole Community,* 57; Manucy, *Houses,* 68.

29. Gritzner, "Tabby," 129–46.

30. Manucy, *Houses,* 157.

31. Arana, "Defenses," 62–63.

32. Lawson, *Foothold,* 62.

33. Lyon, "St. Augustine 1580," 25–26.

34. Manucy, *Houses,* 17–21.

35. See page 77 and chapter 6.

36. See chapter 6.

37. Manucy, *Sixteenth-Century,* 58; Bartram, *Diary,* 52.

38. Herschel E. Shepard, correspondence with author, August 9, 1999.

39. Manucy, *Houses,* 17, 20, 107.

40. Laws, *Rural Spain,* 28, 34, 115, 124; Manucy, *Sixteenth-Century,* 10.

41. See chapter 4.

42. Arnade, *Siege,* 42.

43. Bartram, *Diary,* 52; Carley, *Cuba,* 8, 13, 17; Laws, *Rural Spain,* 28.

44. Johnson, "Spanish Community," 28; Arana, "Defenses," 7.

45. Hann, "Leturiondo Memoir," 173.

46. Bonnie G. McEwan, director of archaeology, San Luis Archaeological and Historic Site, interview, August 1999; Hann and McEwan, *Apalachee Indians and Mission San Luis,* 50, 53, 54, 62, 96, 138–39.

47. Hann and McEwan, *Apalachee Indians and Mission San Luis,* 69.

48. McEwan, *Spanish Missions,* 299–301, 305, 311, 314; Hann and McEwan, *Apalachee Indians and Mission San Luis,* 75, 84, 93, 90, 96–97; site visit, December 2000.

49. Hann and McEwan, *Apalachee Indians and Mission San Luis,* 35, 48, 118; McEwan, *Spanish Missions,* 296, 314; Bushnell, "Situado," 112.

50. Hann and McEwan, *Apalachee Indians and Mission San Luis,* 93, 150, 153, 154, 162, 167; Jones, "James Moore and Destruction," 29–31.

51. Purcell, PRO: CO 700/54, 1778.

52. Gannon, *New History,* 34–36; *Florida History and the Arts,* Fall 2000, 16–19.

53. Judith Bense, interview, *St. Augustine Record,* August 13, 1995; Coker, "Pensacola" (1996), 117–120.

54. Manucy, "Founding of Pensacola," 239–40; Griffen, "Spanish Pensacola," 247–56; Coker, "Pensacola" (1996), 119–20, 122, 125; Coker, "Pensacola" (1999), 9, 13; *Gainesville Sun,* August 10, 1999.

55. Coker, "Pensacola" (1996), 126; Coker, "Pensacola" (1999), 15, 16.

56. Jefferys, 1769.

57. Greenwich Maritime Museum, England, gallery painting label; *Bryan's Dictionary of Painters and Engravers,* (London), Vol V, 69; Sotheby's Auction Catalog, November 23–24, 1998, 38–40, 228.

58. Coker, "Pensacola" (1996), 127–28; Coker, "Pensacola" (1999), 18; Griffen, "Spanish Pensacola," 259–62; see also chapter 9.

59. Joy, *Colonial Archaeological Trail,* 12; Temple, *Carmel Mission,* 13.

60. Coker, "Pensacola" (1996), 130; Hulbert, *Crown Collection,* 51, 52.

61. "Plano del Presidio de S^n Mig^l de Panzacola," reproduced and translated in Rush, *Battle of Pensacola,* 138; Durnford, 1778; Hulbert, *Crown Collection,* 51, 52; "A Plan of the Fort at Pensacola," British Library, Maps K. Top. 122.96; PRO: CO 5/577, ff. 454, 455, 459; Mereness, *Travels,* 382, 384; Ware and Rea, *George Gauld,* 25.

62. PRO: CO 5/577, ff. 459, 460.

63. Ibid.; see also Wilson, *Gulf Coast Architecture,* 124.

64. Joy, *Colonial Archaeological Trail,* 16.

4. THE POWER OF STONE

1. Arana and Manucy, *Castillo,* 25–37; see chapter 9.

2. "Records of Moore's Attack Reveal New Information of Buildings Here in 1702," MC63, 1702, Box 3, File 10, AGI 58-2-28; Bushnell, "Situado," 89; Waterbury, "Government House," 1–3.

3. Arnade, *Siege,* 5, 22, 26–27, 35, 39–40, 57, 58; Manucy, *Houses,* 8, 17.

4. Manucy, *Houses,* 17.

5. Bartram, *Diary,* 50, 52, 53.

6. For examples, Charlton Tebeau's *A History of Florida,* 91, and "Comprehensive Plan—Update: Historic Preservation," City of St. Augustine, September 1986, 8.

7. Arana and Manucy, *Castillo,* 12; Bushnell, "Situado," 88.

8. PRO: CO 5/551, pp. 53–65; CO 5/552, pp. 152–58; CO 5/555, pp. 204–15; Lyons, "Richer Than We Thought," 3–17, Cusick, "Across the Border," 277–99.

9. Arnade, *Architecture,* 173; see note 6 above.

10. Darlington, *Memorials of John Bartram,* 283; Manucy, *Houses,* 58.

11. Carter, *Gage Correspondence,* 1:87, 170–71, 201; CO5/540, p. 40.

12. PRO: MR 1816; CO 5/549, p. 59; CO 5/550, pp. 1, 22, 30, 63; CO 5/552, pp. 9, 64; CO 5/553, p. 59; CO 5/555, pp. 53, 103; Bartram, *Diary,* 34.

13. Bartram, *Diary,* 34; Taylor, *Lighthouses,* 15–18.

14. Carley, *Cuba,* 10, 12; discussion with preservation architects in Havana, Cuba, February 1998; see chapter 9. For a related discussion, see Delson, "Beginnings of Professionalization," 555–74.

15. Carley, *Cuba,* 12.

16. Arana and Manucy, *Castillo,* 19, 20, 28, 44; Arana, "Defenses," 27.

17. Arana and Manucy, *Castillo,* 17, 26–27, 30, 43, 51, 58; *Cartografía de Ultramar,* no. 68, 16 October 1756; PRO: WO 1017.

18. *Dictionary of National Biography* [England], 38:170–71; Siebert, *Loyalists,* 2:341–42; PRO: T 77/11, ff. 255, 292, 294, 296, 299, 315–40; CO 700 Florida no. 7 (MP 9922); CO 700 Florida no. 8; CO 700 Florida no. 9; CO 700 Florida no. 10; CO 700 Florida no. 11; CO 700 Florida no. 14; CO 700 Florida no. 15; CO 5/541, p. 97; MR 1816; CO 5/551, f. 108; MPG 979.

19. PRO: CO 5/540, pp. 178–209.

20. Jones, "British Period Sawmill," 84–105.

21. Rocque, 1788.

22. The title "Richer Than We Thought" is by Eugene Lyon, *El Escribano,* 1992.

23. Parker, "Government House Overview," 5; Waterbury, "Government House—1604 to date," 1.

24. Solana to Arriaga, 1759, 24; Rocque, 1788; Stork, *Account,* 32; Arnade, *Architecture,* 181–83; Government House file, SAHS, containing the following: An inventory by Pablo Castelló, December 28, 1763; De Braham's "History of the Three Provinces," photostat copy of manuscript at Harvard; Inventory by Capt. Bell to Secretary of War, August 14, 1821; John Rodman, Letter, 20 March 1823; Thomas Douglas, resident in tower, autobiography. The British ledgers are at the PRO as noted in the notes to follow. The original watercolor is in the British Library, shelf mark Maps K. Top. 122.86-2-a, one of five made by the same artist, beginning in October in Mobile and ending in December in Savannah. The powder horn is in the collection of the Museum of Florida History, Tallahassee.

25. Laws, *Rural Spain,* 102.

26. Piatek, "Urban Archaeology," 4.

27. PRO: CO 5/540, p. 178.

28. PRO: CO 5/540, pp. 222–23.

29. Wilson, "Window Glass," 150–64.

30. McLaughlin, *Jefferson,* 163–64.

31. Stork, *Account,* 32.

32. See note 34 below.

33. Arnade, *Architecture,* 183.

34. PRO: CO 5/541, pp. 77, 80, 81; CO 5/549, p. 59; CO 5/550, pp. 53, 63; CO 5/551, p. 47; CO 5/552, pp. 121–25, 128; CO 5/553, pp. 59, 63; CO 5/554, p. 54; CO 5/555, p. 103; CO 5/557, pp. 7, 287; CO 5/559, p. 33; Feldman, *Census,* 70.

35. Parker, "Government House Overview," 9, 10.

36. Anonymous, *Narrative of a Voyage,* 118.

37. Worth, *Timucuan Chiefdoms,* 1:57, 103, 104, 171, 172; Carley, *Cuba,* 63; Hoffman, "Material Culture," 93; Arana, "Defenses," 75.

38. British Library, Maps K. Top. 122.83a and 83b.

39. Governor Benavides, "Testimony of the situation concerning 40,000 pesos that were received with regards to 1702 seige," October 2, 1731, AGI 58-2-4/57, transcribed and translated, MC 63, 1731, Box 3, File 31, pp. 1, 47–51, SAHS;

Gannon, *Cross in the Sand*, 45–46, 82; Bushnell, "Situado," 88–89; Hoffman "Convento de San Francisco," 63, 65.

40. Bartram, *Diary*, 53; Moncrief, 1765.

41. Solana to Arriaga, 1759, 15; Bartram, *Diary*, 53.

42. Bartram, *Diary*, 53.

43. Hoffman, "Convento de San Francisco," 74.

44. PRO: CO 5/551, pp. 45, 89; Mariano de la Rocque, "Elevacion, vista, y Persil del Plano donde fue Convento de San Francisco . . . , and Plano inferior y superior por ser igual, del Quartel donde fue Convento de Sn Francisco," October, 1788, SAHS; "List of Bills Drawn upon His Excellency General Gage by Brig. General Haldimand," St. Augustine, 1769, MC 63, box 5, file 13, SAHS; Mowat, "St. Francis Barracks," 270, 271, 274; Fairbanks, *History and Antiquities*, 188; Waterbury, "Segui/Kirby Smith House," 18; Arana, "Defenses," 114–18.

45. Joyce, "St. Francis Barracks," 77, 78.

46. PRO: MPG 529; CO 5/87, ff. 48, 50, 121.

47. PRO: CO 5/550.

48. PRO: MPG 351; CO 5/87, ff. 95–106; CO 5/551 (35), p. 21, and (40), p. 83; CO 5/552 (43), p. 5; CO 5/556 (14), pp. 295, 297, 298; Mowat, "St. Francis Barracks," 274–78.

49. PRO: CO 5/556 (14), p. 295.

50. PRO: CO 5/556 (14), pp. 298, 347.

51. PRO: CO 5/87, ff. 48, 50, 121.

52. Straight, "Colonial Fevers," 154–66; Coker, "Pensacola" (1999), 29.

53. Joyce, "St. Francis Barracks," 79; Forbes, *Sketches*, 87.

54. Solana to Arriaga, 1759, 24; Gannon, *Cross in the Sand*, 78–79; Bushnell, Situado," 199, 200.

55. Puente, 1764; Solana to Arriaga, 1759, 24; Moncrief, "Plan of the Soldiers Barracks as at Present," SAHS; Laws, *Rural Spain*, 102.

56. See chapter 5; Waterbury, "Treasurer's House," 15–28.

57. Solana to Arriaga, 1759, 24; Moncrief, "Plan of the Soldiers Barracks as at Present," SAHS; PRO: CO 5/550, p. 40.

58. Moncrief, "Plans of the Soldiers Barracks as at Present," SAHS; Moncrief, 1765.

59. PRO: CO 5/552 (44), p. 9; CO 5/545, p. 77; AO 1, rolls 147 and 148, bundle 1261.

60. PRO: CO 5/554 (29), p. 1.

61. See chapter 7; Townsend, *John Moultrie*; PRO: CO 5/551, p. 92; Siebert, *Loyalists*, 2:237, 330–31.

62. PRO: CO 5/552 (38), p. 15; CO 5/545, pp. 59, 77.

63. PRO: AO 1, rolls 147 and 148, bundle 1261; Siebert, *Loyalists*, 2:331.

64. PRO: CO 5/559, p. 33.

65. Park, "List of Architectural Books," 124–129.

66. PRO: CO 5/551 (36), p. 25; *Dictionary of National Biography* [England], 39:274.

67. Schafer, ". . . not so gay a Town," 105.

68. Purcell, 1777; Berrio, 1797; Rocque, 1788 and report, 31 July 1789, 6; see Tavernor, *Palladio,* figures 130, 131.

69. Forbes, *Sketches,* 86.

70. See appendix II.

71. *East-Florida Gazette,* vol. 1, no. 5, February 2–March 1, 1783, and vol. 1, no. 16, May 10–17, 1783; McLaughlin, *Jefferson,* 91.

72. Rocque, Annual Reports, 1784, 1787, 1788, East Florida Papers, reel 73, SAHS.

73. Letter, Manuel de Hita to Governor Enrique White, 1804, SAHS; Waterbury, *Oldest House,* 17; *Episcopal Recorder,* November 12, 1831, 132.

74. Montiano to Crown, July 16, 1743, Menéndez Marquéz file, SAHS.

75. Solana to Arriaga, 1759, 23.

76. Arnade, *Architecture,* 184–85; Quesada, 1790 Inventory, SAHS.

77. Moncrief, PRO: MPG 979.

78. PRO: CO 5/548 ff. 202–3; CO 5/551 (37), pp. 45, 47, 48a, 51; CO 5/552 (16), pp. 121–25.

79. Bartram, *Diary,* 50, 53.

80. Gannon, *Cross in the Sand,* 38; Deagan, "St. Augustine and Mission Frontier," 92.

81. Gannon, *Cross in the Sand,* 43, 77; Bretos, *Cuba and Florida,* 36–38.

82. Bushnell, "Situado," 89.

83. AGI 58-2-8, 12931-12929, translation in MC 63 1702, box 3, file 10, SAHS.

84. Gannon, *Cross in the Sand,* 77; Roworth, 1770s.

85. Solana to Arriaga, 1759, 15.

86. Solana to Arriaga, 1759, 15–16; *Miami El Nuevo Herald,* January 22, 1991.

87. Bartram, *Diary,* 53.

88. Cathedral file, SAHS; Fairbanks, *History and Antiquities,* 115; Gannon, *Cross in the Sand,* 106, 108.

89. Parker, "Urban Indians," 4.

90. Solana to Arriaga, 1759, 15; Moncrief, 1765.

91. Arana and Manucy, *Castillo,* 44.

92. PRO: CO 5/570, p. 37.

93. Stork, *Account,* 34.

94. Johnson, *Ceiba Mocha,* n.p.

95. Bartram, *Diary,* 53.

96. Vorsey, "William Gerard de Brahm."

97. Rocque, "Public Buildings, Forts, and Defenses," 1789, SAHS.

98. Gannon, *Cross in the Sand,* 108; *Episcopal Recorder,* November 12, 1831, 132; Cathedral file, SAHS.

99. Lyon, "St. Augustine 1580," 22; Lyon, "Richer Than We Thought," 93; Gannon, *Cross in the Sand,* 46; Bushnell, "Situado," 88–89; Deagan, *Urban Enclave,* 190; Arnade, *Architecture,* 154.

100. Gannon, *Cross in the Sand,* 76; Arnade, *Siege,* 57, 58; Arnade, *Architecture,* 156.

101. Solana to Arriaga, 1759, 13; Cathedral file, SAHS, Deposition of Juan

Chrisostomo de Acosta, 1765; Bushnell, "Situado," 201; Arnade, *Architecture,* 154, 155; Gannon, *Cross in the Sand,* 79; Manucy, *Houses,* 18; Garcia-Weaver, "Private Archive," 108; Kapitzke, "Secular Clergy," 58.

102. Solana to Arriaga, 1759, 13; Deagan, *Creole Community,* 196–99.

103. Solana to Arriaga, 1759, 13; Moncrief, 1765.

104. Bushnell, "Situado," 89.

105. Bartram, *Diary,* 33.

106. Mullins, *Early Architecture of the South,* 132.

107. PRO: CO 5/550; Harvard University Art Museums Supplemental Publication Information, Reference Number 2814; Waterbury, "John Forbes, Man of Cloth," 9; Strock, *By Faith,* 1.

108. See chapter 5.

109. Gibbs, *Book of Architecture,* 29, 30.

110. Townsend, *John Moultrie;* Park, "List of Architectural Books," 125, 126.

111. PRO: CO 5/553, pp. 59, 74.

112. PRO: CO 5/552, pp. 121–25; CO 5/559, p. 270.

113. PRO: CO 5/553 (26), p. 33.

114. PRO: CO 5/554 (29), p. 1.

115. Deagan, *Creole Community,* 196–99; Addleshaw, *Anglican Worship,* 60, 61, 98–99, 148, 154–55, 190.

116. Gannon, *Cross in the Sand,* 106, 108; *Episcopal Recorder,* Nov. 12, 1831, 132; Strock, *By Faith,* 3; Siebert, *Loyalists,* 1:172; Lockey, *East Florida,* 694; Deagan, *Creole Community,* 196–99.

117. See chapter 3; Coomes, "Oldest Parish Records," 74–83. The records were taken to Havana in 1764 and returned to Florida in the early twentieth century. The originals today are in the archives of the St. Augustine Diocesan Center, Mandarin, Florida. Lyon, "Richer Than We Thought," 93–95.

118. Lyon, "St. Augustine 1580," 22; Bushnell, "Situado," 88, 89.

119. Gannon, *Cross in the Sand,* 106–8; Manucy, "Cathedral," 26–28; a copy of Rocque's 1789 plans are in the Cathedral file, SAHS; Florida Master Site file, 8SJ63, SAHS; Delson, "Beginnings of Professionalization," 568, 570.

120. Weiss, *Arquitectura Colonial Cubana,* 64–66, 247; HABS Survey No. 15-7, August 2, 1934.

121. Graham, "St. Augustine 1867," 4, 90. Original sketchbook is at SAHS.

122. Douglas, autobiography, 69–70, SAHS Government House file.

123. Contract, John Rodman and Elias Wallen, House Report Number 223, 25th Cong., 3rd sess., copy at SAHS; Pierson, *American Buildings,* 1:347, 373–94, 404.

124. Contract, Rodman and Wallen; Taylor, *Lighthouses,* 25.

125. The battle has been called the "Dade Massacre"; Matthews, *Edge of Wilderness,* 79–83.

126. Elevation drawing, bundle 176G14, East Florida Papers, revealed to the author by Susan Parker.

127. Renwick file, SAHS.

128. HABS Survey No. 15-7, August 2, 1934; Jean Waterbury pointed the author to the wall artifact.

129. Graham, *Hotel Ponce de León,* 13; Akin, *Flagler,* 116.

130. Cathedral and Renwick files, SAHS; HABS Survey No. 15-7, August 2, 1934.

131. Ibid.

132. Cathedral and Renwick files, SAHS.

5. The St. Augustine Style

1. Zumthor, *New York Times,* January 7, 1999, B12.

2. See chapters 4 and 9.

3. Deagan, *Creole Community,* 57, 60, 108, 109; Manucy, *Houses,* 68, 69, 118.

4. Bartram, *Diary,* 55; Laws, *Rural Spain,* 153–55.

5. Waterbury, *Oldest House,* 4; Waterbury, *East Florida Gazette,* vol. 19, no. 1, March 2001, 1; Waterbury, "Llambias House," 11.

6. See Bishop's House, chapter 4; Waterbury, "Treasurer's House, 15–28;" Bartram, *Diary,* 52; Manucy, *Houses,* 113.

7. See Bishop's House, chapter 4.

8. Elíxio de la Puente, 1764; Moncrief, 1765; Rocque, 1788.

9. Waterbury, "Treasurer's House," 17, 30–31; Moncrief, 1765.

10. Solana to Arriaga, 1759, 24.

11. Manucy, *Houses,* 153; see also 104–5.

12. Gritzner, "Tabby," 140, 141, 146, 147, 150; Laws, *Rural Spain,* 153.

13. Bartram, *Diary,* 52.

14. Salmon, *Palladio Londiensis.*

15. PRO: CO 5/553, p. 77.

16. Bartram, *Diary,* 34, 52.

17. See chapter 3; Arnade, *Architecture,* 181; Herschel E. Shepard, correspondence with author, August 9, 1999.

18. Arnade, *Architecture,* 156.

19. See Menéndez Marquéz House in chapter 4.

20. Puente-Drayton House file, SAHS; PRO: T 77/8, bundle 6, ff. 69, 79; *St. Augustine Record,* April 11 and May 31, 1986.

21. PRO: T 77/8, bundle 18, f. 206.

22. Arnade, *Architecture,* 176, 177, 178, 179; Waterbury, *Ximénez-Fatio House,* 6, 8; Bartram, *Diary,* 52, 55; Manucy, *Houses,* 29, 38, 59, 124; Parker, "Second Century," 16.

23. Bartram, *Diary,* 52; Manucy, *Houses,* 93, 94.

24. Waterbury, "Government House—1604 to Date"; Parker, "Government House Overview," n.p.; Arnade, *Siege,* 42.

25. Arnade, *Architecture,* 180; see Government House, chapter 4.

26. See Government House, chapter 4.

27. Lawson, *Foothold,* 61.

28. PRO: T 77/4, bundle 5, f. 28.

29. Bartram, *Diary,* 52.

30. Brownell et al., *Making of Virginia Architecture,* 10–13.

31. PRO: T 77/6, bundle 7, ff. 112, 117.

32. Ibid.

33. Bartram, *Diary,* 52.

34. Carley, *Cuba*, 8; Laws, *Rural Spain*, 28.

35. Bartram, *Diary*, 52.

36. Arnade, *Architecture*, 180; Parker, "Second Century," 17, 18.

37. Wilson, "Window Glass," 152; Lyon, "Richer Than We Thought," 15; Roorda, "Cuba, America, and the Sea," Cusick, "Across the Border," 279–87, 293; Arana, "Defenses," 61–62.

38. See Government House, chapter 4.

39. See Simons and Lapham, *Early Architecture of Charleston;* see chapter 6.

40. See also chapter 7.

41. Arnade, *Architecture*, 179, 182, 183.

42. PRO: CO 5/551, no. 37, p. 51; see Menéndez Marquéz House, chapter 4.

43. Beth Dunlop, "In Search of the Hurricane Proof House," *Miami Herald, Tropic*, October 18, 1992, 11–12.

44. Waterbury, "Llambias House," 25–26.

45. Griffin, *Mullet*, 105; Cusick, "Late Colonial Minorcan Household," 65, 66.

46. Cusick, "Late Colonial Minorcan Household," 67–96; Waterbury, "Seguí/ Kirby Smith House," 8.

47. Waterbury, *Ximénez-Fatio House.*

48. See chapter 4.

49. Stork, *Account*, 12.

6. British Pensacola

1. Joy, *Colonial Archaeological Trail*, 57–86.

2. See chapter 3.

3. Griffen, "Spanish Pensacola," 259–62; Rush, *Battle of Pensacola*, 138; Joy, *Colonial Archaeological Trail*, 12, 15, 16; PRO: CO5/577, p. 459; Mereness, *Travels*, 382, 384.

4. PRO: CO 5/541 (8), p. 162; Fabel, *Economy*, 127, Bartram, *Travels*, 331.

5. Rush, *Battle of Pensacola*, 138–39; PRO: MPG 349; MPG 528; Durnford, 1778.

6. "Plano del Presidio de Sⁿ Migˡ de Panzacola," in Rush, *Battle of Pensacola*, 138–39.

7. See chapter 3.

8. Mereness, *Travels*, 382.

9. PRO: CO 5/612, f. 163; Ware and Rea, *George Gauld*, 31, 33, 35, 194; Fabel, *Economy*, 14.

10. Gray, *Elias Durnford*, 1–5; Weiss, *Arquitectura*, 146.

11. PRO: CO 5/577, ff. 449–53, 455.

12. Ware and Rea, *George Gauld*, 34–35, 37, 115–16, 130, 190–91.

13. Lofaro, *Daniel Boone*, 20–21.

14. PRO: MPG 529; CO 5/585, ff. 37–43; CO 5/87, p. 29; see appendix I.

15. PRO: MPG 10.

16. PRO: MPG 10; MPD 194 (1).

17. PRO: CO 5/597, f. 54; Straight, "Colonial Fevers," 164; Ware and Rea, *George Gauld*, 116, 130; Coker, "Pensacola" (1999), 29.

18. PRO: MPD 194 (2); MPG 525; Durnford, 1778.

19. Joy, *Colonial Archaeological Trail,* 25.

20. PRO: CO 5/597, ff. 29–31; MPD 194/234.

21. See chapter 3; PRO: CO 5/577, ff. 459–60.

22. PRO: CO 5/577, ff. 212, 449–53; Johnson, *British West Florida,* 96, 274; Rea, "Brigadier Frederick Haldimand," 517, 521–22; Fabel, "British Rule," 144.

23. PRO: MPG 611, sheets 1–5.

24. PRO: MPG 611 (5), "Plan of Servants Rooms, Storerooms, Garden;" Number 20, "Casa de la Villa y Govierno Politico" on Spanish plans of 1781 reprinted in Rush, *Battle of Pensacola,* 131; Bense, *Archaeology,* Fig. 5.12.

25. PRO: MPG 611, sheets 1–3, 5.

26. PRO: CO 5/577, ff. 449–53, 463.

27. PRO: MPG 611 (4).

28. PRO: CO 5/577, f. 452; CO 5/592, f. 85, 205; CO 5/595, ff. 9–11, 196, 443, 445, 446; Bartram, *Travels,* 332.

29. Williams, *View of West Florida,* 74.

30. Joy, *Colonial Archaeological Trail,* figures 17, 18, 20.

31. Bartram, *Travels,* 332; Johnson, *British West Florida,* 96.

32. PRO: CO 5/597, f. 78; MPG 980.

33. Fabel, *Economy,* 198.

34. Col. Stiell to Lord Germain, October, 12, 1778, PRO: CO 5/595, ff. 12, 215.

35. Wilson, "Gulf Coast Architecture," 122, 127; see Haase, *Classic Cracker,* 46, 54.

36. Wilson, "Gulf Coast Architecture," 86, 124, 126; Crocker, *Historic Architecture,* 102; Betty Rodgers, records manager, Jackson County Archives, and board member, Jackson County Historical Society, correspondence with author, February 2001.

37. Sutton, *Walton House,* 1–4, 21–35; Newton, *Historic Architecture.*

38. Dorothy K. Wallace, executive director, Pensacola Heritage Foundation, supplied the information about the Barkley House and the Barkley family.

39. Greenfield is described in chapter 7.

7. Haciendas and Plantations

1. Bartram, *Diary,* 54.

2. Bartram, *Travels,* 198.

3. See chapter 3; Lyon, "First Three Wooden Forts," 143.

4. Worth, *Timucuan Chiefdoms,* 1:198–99; McEwan, *Spanish Missions,* 296; Hann and McEwan, *Apalachee Indians and Mission San Luis,* 56.

5. Bushnell, "Menéndez Marquéz," 412–18; Worth, *Timucuan Chiefdoms,* 1:199–203.

6. Sastre, "Picolata," 27.

7. Campbell, *Journal of a Late Expedition,* 22; Arana, "Defenses," 73–77.

8. Hann and McEwan, *Apalachee Indians and Mission San Luis,* 148–50; Worth, *Timucuan Chiefdoms,* 1:203; Bushnell, "Situado," 112.

9. Bartram, *Travels,* 198, 199.

10. See chapter 5.

11. Siebert, *Loyalists,* 2:37–41, 317; Mowat, "Enigma of William Drayton," 3–5;

SAHS file: Puente House Site BLK 24, 8 Marine Street; *St. Augustine Record*, April 11 and May 31, 1986.

12. Waterbury, *Oldest House*, 9–10; Griffin and Arana, "Mary Evans," 57–76.

13. Griffin and Arana, "Mary Evans," 57–76.

14. PRO: T 77/6, bundle 7.

15. Siebert, *Loyalists*, 2:245, 249.

16. Waterbury, "Treasurer's House," 31.

17. Fabel, *Economy*, 6–7, 8; Feldman, *Spanish Census.*

18. PRO: T 77/6, bundle 5, ff. 66–76; "Escolta" is in Arana, "Defenses," 69.

19. Graham, "St. Augustine 1867," 40, 41; Kingston, "Sarah Warner Fish," 63–84.

20. Schafer, "James Grant's Villa," 18.

21. PRO: T 77/7, bundle 18, ff. 254, 256, 262, 375; Schafer, "Early Plantation Development," 50.

22. PRO: T 77/7, bundle 18, f. 377; Schafer, "James Grant's Villa," 66–75.

23. "A Plan of Beauclerk's Bluff Plantation on ye East side of ye River St. Johns in ye Province of East Florida, Laid Down by an Actual Survey in the year 1771, by Joseph Purcell," PRO: MPD 2 (T 77/14); for indigo processing, see Schafer, "James Grant's Villa," 35–36.

24. PRO: T 77/17, bundle 10, ff. 204–5, 207–10, 226; see appendix I.

25. PRO: T 77/8, bundle 15, ff. 187, 189.

26. Schafer, "poor Billy Bartram," 4–5, 10.

27. Moore and Ste. Claire, "Dreams and Promises," 31–45; Griffin, *Mullet*, 3–10, 44–45; Cusick, "Late Colonial Minorcan," 66; Johnston, "Turnbull Plantation Site," 7, 13; Siebert, *Loyalists*, 2:155–60.

28. PRO: CO 5/548, f. 146; T 77/7, bundle 13 (Grenville).

29. Griffin, *Mullet*, 44; Moore and Ste. Claire, "Dreams and Promises," 38.

30. Grange, "Turnbull Colonist's House," 77–80.

31. Moore and Ste. Claire, "Dreams and Promises," 31–45; Griffin, *Mullet*, 93–94, 98–100.

32. MAAR Associates, "Archaeological Assessment," 11, 13–14.

33. PRO: CO 5/552, p. 9.

34. Siebert, *Loyalists*, 2:60, 61.

35. Tomoko State Park pamphlet; Ball, *Slaves*, 193, 238, 428, illustration between 90–91.

36. Fabel, *Economy*, 110, 112–15.

37. Fabel, *Economy*, 110; PRO: CO 5/612, f. 163; CO 324/42, f. 52.

38. PRO: CO 5/612, ff. 135–45; Fabel, *Economy*, 47, 110–11, 216.

39. PRO: CO 5/612, ff. 135–45.

40. Fabel, *Economy*, 111–12.

41. Parker, "Men Without God," 135–55; Cusick, "Across the Border," 295–96; Patrick, *Florida Fiasco*, 48, 187, 276.

42. Patrick, *Florida Fiasco*, 187, 276; Waterbury, *Ximénez- Fatio House*, 19–20.

43. Wilson, *Alabama Folk Houses*, 5, 54.

44. McLaughlin, *Jefferson*, 73; Mullins, *Early Architecture of the South*, 9; see chapter 8.

45. Wood, *Jacksonville's Architectural Heritage,* 348; see chapter 6.

46. Siebert, *Loyalists,* 2:155–60; PRO: CO 5/577, ff. 449–53.

47. Park, "List of Architectural Books," 115–30.

48. Pain, *Builders Companion,* frontispiece.

49. Salmon, *Palladio Londiensis,* 62–63.

50. PRO: CO 324/42, pp. 201, 237; *Dictionary of National Biography* [England], 39:202; Townsend, *John Moultrie;* Waterbury, "Treasurer's House," 30.

51. PRO: T 77/12, bundle 7, f. 143.

52. PRO: T 77/12, bundle 7, ff. 151–54; Townsend, *John Moultrie;* Ball, *Slaves,* 142, 145, 153, 177, 190, 191, 194, 428, 446–47.

53. PRO: CO 5/551, no. 42, p. 92.

54. PRO: T 77/12, bundle 7, ff. 151, 152, 153, 154; Siebert, *Loyalists,* 2:239.

55. Siebert, *Loyalists,* 2:244, 245, 249.

56. Park, "List of Architectural Books," 124–29.

57. McLaughlin, *Jefferson,* 38, 52, 56; Morris, *Lectures;* Morris, *Rural Designs.*

58. PRO: CO 5/552, p. 128.

59. Wallace, *Laurens,* 126, 424.

60. Schafer, ". . . not so gay a Town," 117.

61. *Dictionary of National Biography,* [England], 39:202; Townsend, *John Moultrie.*

62. Smith, Chance, and Ashley, "Cultural Resource Assessment," 13, 17, 20.

63. Wayne, Dickinson, and Shepard, "Dunlawton Sugar Mill," 16–23.

64. Smith, Chance, and Ashley, "Cultural Resource Assessment," 12, 20–27.

65. Baker, "Glimpses of Bulowville," 115, 120; Strickland, *Ormond-on-the-Halifax,* 14, 15, 20, 21.

66. Ibid.

67. Baker, "Glimpses of Bulowville," 115, 118–21; Strickland, *Ormond-on-the-Halifax,* 22.

68. Strickland, *Ormond-on-the-Halifax,* 14–15, 19–21; Knetsch, "Benjamin Alexander Putnam," 101–2.

69. Levy, *Plan for Abolition,* v–xxix; Huhner, "Moses Elias Levy," 323, 325, 330, 331; Fairbanks, *History and Antiquities,* xxvi–xxviii.

8. Kingsley Plantation

1. Schafer, *Anna Kingsley,* 8.

2. Wood, *Jacksonville's Architectural Heritage,* 309–14; the mission is described in chapter 2.

3. PRO: T 77/8, bundle 5, f. 66; Bartram, *Diary,* 48, 76; Stowell, "Historic Resource Study," 41.

4. Bennett, *Twelve on the River,* 61; Stowell, "Historic Resource Study," 40–42; Shepard, "Kingsley Plantation," 5; Schafer, *Anna Kingsley.*

5. Shepard, "Kingsley Plantation," 5–13; Stowell, "Historic Resource Study," 50–52; Kennedy, "Fortified Mansion," 8–13.

6. Stowell, "Historic Resource Study," 54, 105; Wood, *Jacksonville's Architectural Heritage,* 348.

7. Stowell, "Historic Resource Study," 40, 41–42, 50–52, 54, 56, 58, 105–6, 118; Shepard, "Kingsley Plantation," 8–10.

8. Bennett, *Twelve on the River,* 97, 99; Stowell, "Historic Resource Study," 58–61, 65; Patrick, *Florida Fiasco,* 48, 56, 268, 275, 301, 302, 311 n. 20; Shepard, "Kingsley Plantation," 13; Kennedy, "Fortified Mansion," 22.

9. Bennett, *Twelve on the River,* 89–113.

10. Schafer, *Anna Kingsley,* 8–14.

11. Stowell, "Historic Resource Study," 64, 65, 73; Fretwell, "Kingsley Beatty Gibbs," 82 n. 53; Kingsley file, SAHS.

12. Schafer, *Anna Kingsley,* 6–8, 13, 14, 29; Bennett, *Twelve on the River,* 90.

13. Schafer, *Anna Kingsley,* 14, 15, 16, 17, 18; Stowell, "Historic Resource Study," 61–65.

14. Brownell et al., *Making of Virginia Architecture,* 39, 47; McLaughlin, *Jefferson,* 38, 52, 54, 56–57, 61, 64; Serlio plan is in Sebastiano Serlio, *The Five Books of Architecture,* Dover Publications Unabridged Reprint of the English Edition of 1611 (1982), n.p.; Morris, *Select Architecture;* Morris, *Lectures.*

15. Gertrude Rollins Wilson, "Notes Concerning the Old Plantation," unpublished, at Kingsley Plantation.

16. Stowell, "Historic Resource Study," 104, 105 n. 140; Wilson, "Notes Concerning the Old Plantation."

17. Kennedy, "Fortified Mansion," 18; Buisseret, *Historic Architecture of the Caribbean,* 14; Higman, *Jamaica Surveyed,* 231–32.

18. Anonymous, *Narrative of a Voyage,* 52; see also Kennedy, "Fortified Mansion."

19. McLaughlin, *Jefferson,* 154.

20. Shepard, "Kingsley Plantation," 1–22; Shepard, "How old is old?" interview, *Jacksonville Florida Times-Union,* April 9, 1988.

21. Shepard, "Kingsley Plantation," 1–22.

22. Mullins, *Early Architecture of the South,* 9; McLaughlin, *Jefferson,* 72–74, 76, 77; F. Blair Reeves, F.A.I.A., per conversation with consultant at Williamsburg, February 12, 2001.

23. Ibid.; Buchanan, "Eighteenth-Century Frame Houses," 73, n. 11.

24. Sullivan, "Tabby," 4; Gritzner, "Tabby," 130–48.

25. Manucy, *Houses,* 164.

26. Bartram, *Diary,* 52.

27. Shepard, "Kingsley Plantation," 1–22.

28. Wood, *Jacksonville's Architectural Heritage,* 317; Schafer, *Anna Kingsley,* 29; Stowell, "Historic Resource Study," 107.

29. Stowell, "Historic Resource Study," 65, 106–7; Wood, *Jacksonville's Architectural Heritage,* 5; Bennett, *Twelve on the River,* 99; Schafer, *Anna Kingsley,* 15, 16, 20, 29.

30. Schafer, *Anna Kingsley,* 32, 37.

31. Stowell, "Historic Resource Study," 114, 115; Henry A. Baker, "Roads and Walkways at the Kingsley Plantation, an archaeological study," Bureau of Archaeological Research, Florida Department of State, 1985, copy at Kingsley Plantation.

32. Ackerman, *Villa,* 200–206; McLaughlin, *Jefferson,* 29–30, 140.

33. Snodgrass, Inventory-Nomination Form, National Register of Historic Places, 1970.

34. Stowell, "Historic Resource Study," 59.

35. Ball, *Slaves,* 47.

36. Wood, *Jacksonville's Architectural Heritage,* 312.

37. Patrick, *Florida Fiasco,* 56, 65, 103–4, 268; Stowell, "Historic Resource Study," 59, 65.

38. Fretwell, "Kingsley Beatty Gibbs," 73.

39. Stowell, "Historic Resource Study," 65, 66, 70, 112–14; Bennett, *Twelve on the River,* 92, 107–10; Patrick, *Florida Fiasco,* 268, 275; Schafer, *Anna Kingsley,* 10, 13, 19.

40. Sullivan, "Tabby," 1–25.

41. Stowell, "Historic Resource Study," 111–16; Shepard, "Kingsley Plantation," 1–22.

42. Julia Dodge, *Scribner's Magazine,* September 1877, quoted in Wood, *Jacksonville's Architectural Heritage,* 314.

9. Forts, Redoubts, Prickly Cactus, and a Wolf's Mouth

1. *The WPA Guide to Florida* (New York: Pantheon Books, 1939), 163.

2. Lawson, *Foothold,* iv, 60, 62.

3. Lawson, *Foothold,* 60–61; Lyon, *Enterprise,* 35, fn. 39.

4. Lawson, *Foothold,* 61, 79.

5. Lyon, *Enterprise,* 115, 119–24; Lyon, "First Three Wooden Forts," 144; Lawson, *Foothold,* 150–52; Kathleen Deagan, interview, February 8, 2000.

6. Lyon, *Enterprise,* 124; Lyon, "First Three Wooden Forts," 131; see chapters 1 and 3.

7. Lyon, "First Three Wooden Forts," 134, 136.

8. Lyon, *Enterprise,* 140, 150, 205; Hann and McEwan, *Apalachee Indians and Mission San Luis,* 59, 149, 171.

9. Lyon, *Enterprise,* 180, 200; Lyon, "First Three Wooden Forts," 139, 141, 145; Kathleen Deagan, interview, February 8, 2000.

10. Lyon, *Enterprise,* 140, 150, 180, 199–201, 205; Lawson, *Foothold,* 133, 141, 142, 145; Chatelain, *Defenses,* 36, 45.

11. Lyon, *Enterprise,* 35, fn. 39; Manucy, "How Did Fort Caroline Look?"

12. Arana and Manucy, *Castillo,* 16, 17, 25, 26, 27, 32, 36, 37; Arana, "Defenses," 34, 35.

13. Lyon, "First Three Wooden Forts," 130–47; Eugene Lyon, conversation with author, March 3, 2000.

14. Arana, "Cubo Line," 2; Manucy, *Sixteenth-Century,* 40.

15. Hoffman, "1580 Research Project," 8–9.

16. Manucy, *Sixteenth-Century,* 32; Arana and Manucy, *Castillo,* 10.

17. Chatelain, *Defenses,* Map 3, 534.

18. Arana and Manucy, *Castillo,* 12–13; Manucy, *Sixteenth-Century,* has a slightly different sequence and number of forts, 34–37.

19. Chatelain, *Defenses,* 66–67; Arana and Manucy, *Castillo,* 23; see chapter 4.

20. Arana and Manucy, *Castillo,* 17; Carley, *Cuba,* 60–62; discussions with architects in Havana and Santiago de Cuba, February 1998.

21. Chatelain, *Defenses,* 66; Arana and Manucy, *Castillo,* 17, 20, 26–27, 28–29, 30, 44, 51; Arana, "Defenses," 27, 54, 56, 119.

22. Hoffman, "Material Culture," 96; Arana and Manucy, *Castillo,* 18–20, 35; Arana, "Defenses," 17, 30, 50, 56.

23. Arana, "Cubo Line," 1–28.

24. Sastre, "Picolata," 25–64; Bartram, *Travels,* 87.

25. Arana, "Defenses," 73; see chapter 7.

26. Arana, "Defenses," 119; Arana and Manucy, *Castillo,* 43–53.

27. Arana and Manucy, *Castillo,* 53.

28. Arana and Manucy, *Castillo,* 53.

29. Arana, "Cubo Line," 5–6.

30. Arana, "Cubo Line," 10–15, 17–18; Halbirt, "Historic Redoubt Identified," St. Augustine Citizen's Report, April 1999, 3.

31. Arana, "Cubo Line," 10–12, 19–20, 28; Manucy, "City Gate."

32. Arana, "Cubo Line," 8, n. 24; Bartram, *Diary,* 78; see also *SAAA,* vol. 9(2), April 1994, and vol. 9(3), July 1994.

33. Stork, *Account,* 32; Bartram, *Diary,* 78; Anonymous, *Narrative of a Voyage,* 101.

34. Deagan and MacMahon, *Fort Mose,* 20, 30; *SAAA,* vol. 11(3), September 1996.

35. Deagan and MacMahon, *Fort Mose,* 22.

36. Deagan and MacMahon, *Fort Mose,* 24; Solana to Arriaga, 1759, 31; Arana, "Defenses," 82.

37. Johnson, *Ceiba Mocha,* n.p.

38. Arana, "Fort at Matanzas Inlet," 1–32; Taylor, *Lighthouses,* 15.

39. Arana, "Fort at Matanzas Inlet," 1–32.

40. Arana, "Notes on Fort Matanzas," 45–73.

41. Hann and McEwan, *Apalachee Indians and Mission San Luis,* 54, 56, 68, 93–95.

42. Hann and McEwan, *Apalachee Indians and Mission San Luis,* 93–95; Ware and Rea, *George Gauld,* 90.

43. Boyd, "Fortifications," 10–13; Arnade, "Raids, Sieges," 105; 108; Fabel, "British Rule," 137; Mahon and Weisman, "Florida's Seminole," 187; Fort San Marcos de Apalachee interpretative pamphlet, Florida Department of Environmental Protection, Division of Recreation and Parks.

44. Ware and Rea, *George Gauld,* 89.

45. Boyd, "Fortifications," 3–34; Garcia-Weaver, "Private Archive," 109; Taylor, *Lighthouses,* 171; Arnade, "Raids, Sieges," 105, 108, 114; Mahon and Weisman, "Florida's Seminole," 187; *The WPA Guide to Florida,* 486; PRO: CO 5/540, p. 46; Dailey, Morrell, and Cockrell, "St. Marks Military Cemetery," 2, 5, 7, 9.

46. Boyd, "Events at Prospect Bluff," 55–96; Dailey, Morrell, and Cockrell, "St. Marks Military Cemetery," 8, 9.

47. Arnade, "Raids, Sieges," 106; Coker, "Pensacola" (1996), 118–19; Coker, "Pensacola" (1999), 9.

48. Coker, "Pensacola" (1999), 9–10.

49. Manucy, "Founding of Pensacola," 239–41; Griffen, "Spanish Pensacola," 247–56; Arnade, "Raids, Sieges," 108, 118, 120, 121, 123, 125; Coker, "Pensacola" (1996), 118–25; Coker, "Pensacola" (1999), 12, 14.

50. Coker, "Pensacola" (1999) 15, 16; Coker, "Pensacola" (1996), 125–26; Griffen, "Spanish Pensacola," 257; Bense, *Archaeology*, 217.

51. British Library, Maps K. Top. 122.97; Greenwich Maritime Museum, England, gallery painting label; *Bryan's Dictionary of Painters and Engravers* (London), 5:69; Sotheby's Auction Catalog, November 23–24, 1998, 38–40; Coker, "Pensacola" (1996), 127.

52. Coker, "Pensacola" (1996), 127–28; Griffen, "Spanish Pensacola," 259–62.

53. Coker, "Pensacola" (1999), 128.

54. See chapters 3 and 6; Wilson, "Gulf Coast Architecture," 123, 124, 127–28; Rush, *Battle of Pensacola*, 138–39; Mereness, *Travels*, 382, 384.

55. See chapter 3; Coker, "Pensacola" (1996), 28–130; Coker, "Pensacola" (1999), 20.

56. See chapter 6.

57. PRO: CO 5/87, p. 25.

58. PRO: MPD 194 (3), enclosed in General Gag's letter, August 5, 1772, T 1/493, f. 233.

59. PRO: CO 700/12.

60. Faye, "British and Spanish Fortifications," 278–81, 286; McAlister, "Pensacola," 282; PRO: CO 700/32, Gauld, "A Survey of the Bay of Pensacola with part of Sta Rosa island etc.," 1766; CO 5/597, pp. 29–31; MPG 9 and MPD 194 (4), Brasier, "Plan of the Entrance of Pensacola Harbour shewing the situation of the New Batteries," 1771, enclosure to General Gage's letter, August 5, 1772, T 1/493, f. 230.

61. Wilson, "Gulf Coast Architecture," 115–16, fig. 25.

62. Wilson, "Gulf Coast Architecture," 90, 123, 124, 127–28; Proctor, *Eighteenth-Century*, fig. 13.

63. Anderson, "Pensacola Forts," 1–25, 32, 36–61; Bearss, *Fort Barrancas*, 4–21; Newton, *Historic Architecture;* Faye, "British and Spanish Fortifications," 277–92; McAlister, "Pensacola," 291.

64. Anderson, "Pensacola Forts," 72–131.

Bibliography

Unpublished Primary Materials

Unpublished primary materials include correspondence, reports, maps, floor plans and elevations, inventories, vouchers, memorials, testimonials, cargo lists, and loyalists claims. They are cited in the notes for each chapter, and can be found in the collections of the St. Augustine Historical Society Library, St. Augustine, Florida; the P. K. Yonge Library of Florida History of the University of Florida, Gainesville, Florida; the Florida Archives, Tallahassee, Florida; the Library of Congress, Washington, D.C., the British National Archives (Public Record Office), Kew, Richmond, Surrey, England; and the British Library, London, England.

   Maps and reports cited frequently are as follows:

Berrio, 1797: herein refers to: "Plano General de la Ciudad de Sn. Agustín en la Florida, 1797," by Engineer Pedro Días Berrio, copy at SAHS.

Durnford, 1778: herein refers to: "Plan of the fort [Pensacola] showing surrounding streets and an advanced redoubt, distinguishing old Spanish buildings and showing hurricane damage, surveyed and drawn by Elais Durnford, Capt. of Engineers," PRO: MPG 358, enclosure to Governor Chester's Letter of 25 November, 1775, CO 5595, f. 429.

Elíxio de la Puente, 1764: herein refers to: "San Agustín de Florida y Henero 22 de 1764," with key by Juan Joseph Elixío de la Puente, treasury official, copy made by Buckingham Smith July 21, 1858, of the original map in the Royal Deposit of Hydrography, SAHS.

Jefferys, 1769: herein refers to: "St. Augustine the Capital of East Florida, Thomas Jefferys sculp." (based on a survey of Don Juan de Solis) distributed by his partner, William Faden at No. 5 Charing Cross, London, and first published in 1763 in two publications: *Florida from the Latest Authorities,* by T. Jefferys, Geographer to His Majesty, and in William Roberts's *An Account of the First Discovery and Natural History of Florida.* It was published in William Stork's "Account of East-Florida," 1769, and in William Faden's *North American Atlas,* 1777. A copy of the Roberts book (1763) containing the map is in the Library of Congress; a copy of the map published by Stork (1769) map is at SAHS; the 1777 edition is at the British Library, Maps K. Top. 122.97.

Moncrief, 1765: herein refers to: "Plan of the Town of St. Augustine and its Environs," by Engineer James Moncrief, PRO: CO 700 Florida 8.

Purcell, 1777: herein refers to: "A Plan of St. Augustine Town and its Environs in East Florida from an actual survey made in 1777," by Joseph Purcell, copy at SAHS.

Rocque, 1788: herein refers to: "Plano Particular de la Ciudad de Sn. Agustín de la Florida . . . 25 de Abril de 1788" with key, by Engineer Mariano de la Rocque, copy at SAHS.

Rocque, 1790: herein refers to: "Plan de la Yglesia Parroquial de San Agustín de la Florida Oriental," June 2, 1790, with "explicacion," AGI 19 and AGI 184–85.

Roworth, 1769?: herein refers to: "A Plan of the Land Between Fort Mossy and St. Augustine in the Province of East Florida, Sam Roworth, Dept. Surv. Gen'l," (no date), copy at SAHS.

Solana to Arriaga, 1759: herein refers to: "Report of Conditions in St. Augustine," April 22, 1759, by Juan Joseph Solana, enclosure of April 9, 1760 to Ex. mo Sr. Bo. Fr. D. Julian de Arriaga, Secretario de Estado y del Despacho Universl de estas Yndias, AGI-86-7-21/41, transcribed copy at SAHS.

Published Books and Articles, and Unpublished Manuscripts

Ackerman, James S. *The Villa: Form and Ideology of Country Houses.* London: Thames and Hudson, 1995.

Addleshaw, G. W. O., and Frederick Etchells. *The Architectural Setting of Anglican Worship.* London: Faber and Faber Limited, 1968.

Akin, Edward N. *Flagler, Rockefeller Partner and Florida Baron.* Gainesville: University Press of Florida, 1992.

Anderson, Robert L. "A History and Study of the Pensacola Forts." Master's thesis, Auburn University, 1969.

Anonymous. *Narrative of a Voyage to the Spanish Main in the Ship "Two Friends;" the occupation of Amelia Island, by M'Gregor, etc—Sketches of the Province of East Florida, and Anecdotes. . .* London, 1819.

Arana, Luis Rafael. "Defenses and Defenders at St. Augustine, A Collection of Writings," edited by Jean Parker Waterbury. *El Escribano* 36 (1999).

———. "Notes on Fort Matanzas National Monument." *El Escribano* 18 (1981): 45–73.

———. "The Fort at Matanzas Inlet." *El Escribano* 17 (1980): 1–32.

———. "The Cubo Line, 1704–1909." Typed manuscript, Castillo de San Marcos National Monument, 1964.

Arana, Luis Rafael, and Albert Manucy. *The Building of Castillo de San Marcos.* Eastern National Park and Monument Association for Castillo de San Marcos National Monument, 1977.

Arnade, Charles W. "Raids, Sieges, and International Wars." In *The New History of Florida,* edited by Michael Gannon. Gainesville: University Press of Florida, 1996.

———. *The Architecture of Spanish St. Augustine.* Washington, D.C.: Academy of American Franciscan History. Reprinted from *The Americas* 18, no. 2 (October 1961): 149–85.

————. *The Siege of St. Augustine in 1702.* Gainesville: University of Florida Press, 1959.

Baker, Henry A. "Fifteen Years on Bulow Creek: Glimpses of Bulowville." *Florida Anthropologist* 52 (March–June 1999): 115–23.

Ball, Edward. *Slaves in the Family.* New York: Ferrar, Straus and Giroux, 1998.

Bartram, John. *Diary of a Journey Through the Carolinas, Georgia, and Florida.* Annotated by Francis Harper. Philadelphia: *Transactions of the American Philosophical Society* 33, 1942.

Bartram, William. *Travels of William Bartram.* Edited by Mark Van Doren. New York: Dover, 1955.

Bearss, Edwin C. *Fort Barrancas, Gulf Islands National Seashore, Florida, Historic Structure Report and Historic Resource Study, September* 1983. Denver: U.S. Department of the Interior, National Park Service, 1983.

Bennett, Charles E. *Twelve on the River St. Johns.* Jacksonville: University of North Florida Press, 1989.

Bense, Judith A. *Archaeology of Colonial Pensacola.* Gainesville: University Press of Florida, 1999.

Boazio, Baptista. "Opidum S. Augustini ligneis aedibus constructum . . . ," illustration in *Expeditio Francisci Draki,* London: Walter Bigges, 1588.

Bond, Stanley C., Jr. "Tradition and Change in First Spanish Period (1565–1763) St. Augustine Architecture: A Search For Colonial Identity." Ph.D. diss., State University of New York at Albany, 1995.

Bourne, Edward Gaylord. *Narratives of the Career of Hernando de Soto.* New York: A. S. Barnes, 1904.

Boyd, Mark F. "Mission Sites in Florida." *FHQ* 17, no. 4 (April 1939): 256–303.

————. "Events at Prospect Bluff on the Apalachicola River, 1808–1818." *FHQ* 16 (July 1937): 55–96.

————. "The Fortifications at San Marcos de Apalachee." *FHQ* 15, no. 1 (July 1936): 3–34.

Bretos, Miguel A. *Cuba and Florida: Exploration of an Historic Connection.* Miami: Historical Association of Southern Florida, 1991.

Brownell, Charles E., Calder Loth, William M. S. Rasmussen, and Richard Guy Wilson. *The Making of Virginia Architecture.* Richmond: Virginia Museum of Fine Arts, 1992.

Buchanan, Paul E. "The Eighteenth-Century Frame Houses of Tidewater Virginia." In *Building Early America: The Carpenters' Company of the City and County of Philadelphia,* edited by Charles E. Peterson. Radnor, Pa.: Chilton, 1976.

Buisseret, David. *Historic Architecture of the Caribbean.* London: Heinemann, 1980.

Bushnell, Amy Turner. "Situado and Sabana: Spain's Support System for the Presidio and Mission Provinces of Florida." *Anthropology Papers of the American Museum of Natural History* 74 (September 21, 1994).

————. "The Menéndez Marquéz Cattle Barony at la Chua and the Determinants of Economic Expansion in Seventeenth-Century Florida." *FHQ* 56, no. 4 (April 1978): 407–31.

Cabeza de Vaca, Alvar Nuñez. *The Journey of Alvar Nuñez Cabeza de Vaca and His Companions From Florida to the Pacific* 1528–1536. Translated by Fanny Bandelier. Barre, Mass.: Imprint Society, 1972.

Campbell, G. L. [Edward Kimber]. *A Relation or Journal of a late Expedition to the Gates of St. Augustine on Florida: Conducted by the Hon. General James Oglethorpe. . .* London: T. Astley, 1744.

Carley, Rachel. *Cuba, 400 Years of Architectural Heritage.* New York: Whitney Library of Design, 1997.

Carter, Clarence E. *The Correspondence of General Thomas Gage with the Secretaries of State and with the War Office and the Treasury, 1763–1775.* Vol 1. New York, Archon Books, 1969.

Cartografia de Ultramar. Madrid: Impr. de Servicio Geográfico del Ejército, 1953.

Cather, Willa. *Death Comes for the Archbishop.* New York, Random House, 1990.

Chatelain, Verne Elmo. *The Defenses of Spanish Florida* 1565–1763. Washington, D.C.: Carnegie Institution, Pub. 511, 1941.

Clayton, Lawrence A., Vernon James Knight, Jr., and Edward C. Moore, *The De Soto Chronicles,* 2 vols. Tuscaloosa: University of Alabama Press, 1993.

Coker, William S. "Pensacola, 1686–1763." In *Archaeology of Colonial Pensacola,* edited by Judith A. Bense. Gainesville: University Press of Florida, 1999.

———. "Pensacola, 1686–1763." In *The New History of Florida,* edited by Michael Gannon. Gainesville: University Press of Florida, 1996.

Coles, David J., and Zack C. Waters. "Indian Fighter, Confederate Soldier, Blockade Runner, and Scout: The Life and Letters of Jacob E. Mickler." *El Escribano* 34 (1997): 35–69.

Colle Corcuera, Marie Pierre. *Mexico, Casas del Pacífico.* La Jolla: ALTI Publishing, 1994.

Coomes, Charles S. "Our Country's Oldest Parish Records." *El Escribano* 18 (1981): 74–83.

Crocker, Mary Wallace. *Historic Architecture in Mississippi.* Jackson: University Press of Mississippi, 1973.

Cusick, James G. "A Late Colonial Minorcan Household: Archaeological Perspectives on the Seguí-Kirby Smith Site." *El Escribano* 30 (1993): 65–96.

———. "Across the Border: Commodity Flow and Merchants in Spanish St. Augustine." *FHQ* 69 (Jan. 1991): 277–99.

Dailey, Robert C., L. Ross Morrell, and W. A. Cockrell. "The St. Marks Military Cemetery (8WA 108)," Bureau of Historic Sites and Properties, Bulletin No. 2. Tallahassee: Division of Archives, History and Records Management, Florida Department of State, 1972: 1–24.

Darlington, William. *Memorials of John Bartram and Humphry Marshall.* Philadelphia: Lindsay and Blakiston, 1849.

Deagan, Kathleen A. "Excavations at the Menéndez Fort and Campsite, 1565–1572." *SAAA* 10, no. 2 (April 1995).

———. "St. Augustine and the Mission Frontier." In *The Spanish Missions of La Florida,* edited by Bonnie G. McEwan. Gainesville: University Press of Florida, 1993.

———. *Spanish St. Augustine: The Archaeology of a Colonial Creole Community.* New York: Academic Press, 1983.

———. *St. Augustine, First Urban Enclave in the United States.* New York: Baywood, 1982.

———. "Spanish St. Augustine: America's First 'Melting Pot.'" *Archaeology* (Sept.–Oct. 1980): 23–30.

Deagan, Kathleen, and Darcie MacMahon. *Fort Mose: Colonial America's Black Fortress of Freedom.* Gainesville: University Press of Florida, 1995.

De Landa, Diego. *Yucatan Before and After the Conquest.* Translated by William Gates. New York: Dover, 1978.

Delson, Roberta M. "The Beginnings of Professionalization in the Brazilian Military: The Eighteenth-Century Corps of Engineers." *The Americas* 51, no. 4 (April 1995): 555–74.

Dickinson, Martin F., and Lucy B. Wayne. "Archaeological Testing of the San Juan del Puerto Mission Site (8Du53), Fort George Island, Florida." Report prepared for Fairfield Communities, Jacksonville, Florida, Aug. 1985.

Drake, Sir Francis. *An Exhibition to Commemorate Francis Drake's Voyage Around the World,* 1577–1580. London: British Museum Publications, 1977.

Episcopal Recorder. Trinity Church, St. Augustine. November 12, 1831: 132.

Ewen, Charles R. "Anhaica: Discovery of Hernando de Soto's 1539–1540 Winter Camp." In *First Encounters,* edited by Jerald T. Milanich and Susan Milbrath. Gainesville: University Press of Florida, 1989.

Fabel, Robin F. A., "British Rule in the Floridas." In *The New History of Florida,* edited by Michael Gannon. Gainesville: University Press of Florida, 1996.

———. *The Economy of British West Florida, 1763–1783.* Tuscaloosa: University of Alabama Press, 1988.

Fairbanks, Charles H. *Seminoles of Florida.* Tallahassee: Peninsular, 1963.

Fairbanks, George R. *The History and Antiquities of the City of St. Augustine.* 1858. Facsimile reproduction, with an introduction by Michael V. Gannon, Gainesville: University Presses of Florida, 1975.

Faye, Stanley. "British and Spanish Fortifications of Pensacola, 1781–1821." *FHQ* 20, no. 2 (October 1941): 277–92.

Feldman, Lawrence H. *The Last Days of British St. Augustine, 1784–1785: A Spanish Census of the English Colony of East Florida.* Baltimore: Clearfield, 1998.

Forbes, James Grant. *Sketches, Historical and Topographical of the Floridas; More Particularly of East Florida.* Facsimile Reproduction of the 1821 Edition. Gainesville: University of Florida Press, 1964.

Fretwell, Jacqueline K. "Kingsley Beatty Gibbs and his Journal of 1840–1843," *El Escribano* 21 (1984): 53–88.

Gannon, Michael. *The Cross in the Sand.* Gainesville: University Presses of Florida, 1989 (1965).

———, ed. *The New History of Florida.* Gainesville: University Press of Florida, 1996.

Garcia-Weaver, Rosa Maria. "The Private Archive of the Count of Revillagigedo." *El Escribano,* 30 (1993): 97–112.

Geiger, Maynard J. *The Early Franciscans in Florida and Their Relation to Spain's Colonial Effort.* Patterson, N.J.: St. Anthony Guild Press, 1936.

Gibbs, James. *Book of Architecture, Containing Designs of Buildings and Ornaments.* London, 1928.

Graham, Thomas. "St. Augustine, 1867: Drawings by Henry J. Morton." *El Escribano* 33, 1996.

———. *Flagler's Magnificent Hotel Ponce de León.* Reprint, *FHQ* 56 (July, 1975).

Grange, Roger T. "The Turnbull Colonist's House at New Smyrna Beach: A Preliminary Report on 8V07051." *The Florida Anthropologist* 52 (March–June 1999): 73–84.

Gray, Robert Edward. *Elias Durnford, 1739–1794.* Graduate thesis, Auburn University, 1971.

Griffen, William B. "Spanish Pensacola, 1700–1763." *FHQ* 37, nos. 3–4 (January–April 1959): 242–62.

Griffin, John W. "Preliminary Report on the Site of the Mission of San Juan del Puerto, Fort George Island, Florida." *Papers of the Jacksonville Historical Society* 4 (1960): 61–66.

Griffin, Patricia C. *Mullet on the Beach.* Gainesville: University Press of Florida, 1993.

Griffin, Patricia C., and Eugenia B. Arana. "Mary Evans: Woman of Substance." *El Escribano* 14 (1977): 57–76.

Gritzner, Janet Bigbee. "Tabby in the Coastal Southeast: The Cultural History of an American Building Material." Ph.D. diss., Louisiana State University, 1978.

Haase, Ronald W. *Classic Cracker.* Sarasota, Fla.: Pineapple Press, 1992.

Halbirt, Carl D. "Of Earth, Tabby, Brick, and Asphalt: The Archaeology of St. Augustine's Historical St. George Street." *El Escribano* 34 (1997): 70–97.

———. "Redefining the Boundaries of 16th Century St. Augustine." *SAAA* 14, no. 1 (March 1999).

Hann, John H. "The Missions of Spanish Florida." In *The New History of Florida,* edited by Michael Gannon. Gainesville: University Press of Florida, 1996.

———. "Summary Guide to Spanish Florida Missions and Visitas: With Churches in the Sixteenth and Seventeenth Centuries." *The Americas* 16, no. 4 (April 1990): 417–513.

———. *Apalachee: The Land Between the Rivers.* Gainesville: University Presses of Florida, 1988.

———. "Church Furnishings, Sacred Vessels and Vestments Held by the Missions of Florida: Translation of Two Inventories." *Florida Archaeology* 2 (1986): 147–64.

———. "Translation of Alonso de Leturiondo's Memorial to the King of Spain." *Florida Archaeology* 2 (1986): 165–225.

Hann, John H., and Bonnie G. McEwan. *The Apalachee Indians and Mission San Luis.* Gainesville: University Press of Florida, 1998.

Hayes, Alden C. *The Four Churches of Pecos.* Albuquerque: University of New Mexico Press, 1974.

Higman, B. W. *Jamaica Surveyed: Plantation Maps and Plans of the Eighteenth and Nineteenth Centuries.* Kingston: Institute of Jamaica, 1988.

Hoffman, Kathleen. "The Material Culture of Seventeenth-Century St. Augustine." *El Escribano* 32 (1995): 91–112.

———. "The Archaeology of the Convento de San Francisco." In *The Spanish Missions of La Florida,* edited by Bonnie G. McEwan. Gainesville: University Press of Florida, 1993.

Hoffman, Paul E. "St. Augustine 1580, The Research Project." *El Escribano* 14 (1977): 59–19.

Howhower, Lisa M., and Jerald T. Milanich. "Excavations in the Fig Springs Mission Burial Area." In *The Spanish Missions of La Florida,* edited by Bonnie G. McEwan. Gainesville: University Press of Florida, 1993.

Hudson, Charles. *The Southeastern Indians.* Knoxville: University of Tennessee Press, 1976.

Huhner, Leon. "Moses Elias Levy: The Early Florida Pioneer and the Father of Florida's First Senator." *FHQ* 19, no. 4 (April 1941): 319–45.

Hulbert, Archer Butler, ed. *The Crown Collection of Photographs of American Maps.* Cleveland: Arthur H. Clark, 1915.

Hulton, Paul. *America 1585: The Complete Drawings of John White.* University of North Carolina Press, 1984.

———. *The Work of Jacques Le Moyne de Morgues: A French Huguenot Artist in France, Florida, and England.* London: British Museum Publications, 1977.

Janson, H. W. *History of Art.* Englewood Cliffs, N.J.: Prentice-Hall, 1968.

Johnson, Cecil. *British West Florida, 1763–1783.* 1942. Reprint, North Haven, Conn.: Archon Books, 1971.

Johnson, Kenneth W. "Mission Santa Fé de Toloca." In *The Spanish Missions of La Florida,* edited by Bonnie G. McEwan. Gainesville: University Press of Florida, 1993.

Johnson, Ralph B., ed. *Ceiba Mocha, Cuba, San Agustín de la Nueva Florida, Province of Matanzas, Cuba.* Gainesville: Research and Educational Center for Architectural Preservation, University of Florida, 1992.

Johnson, Sherry. "The Spanish St. Augustine Community, 1784–1795: A Reevaluation." *FHQ* 68 (July 1989): 27–54.

Johnston, Sydney. "The Turnbull Plantation Site: An Historical Evaluation." Unpublished research presented at Northeastern Florida Plantation Symposium, Volusia County, March 22, 1997.

Jones, B. Calvin. "Colonel James Moore and the Destruction of the Apalachee Missions in 1704." In *Bureau of Historic Sites and Properties, Bulletin No. 2.* Tallahassee: Division of Archives, History, and Records Management, Florida Department of State, 1972: 25–33.

Jones, William M. "A British Period Sawmill." *El Escribano* 18 (1981): 84–105.

Joy, Deborah. *The Colonial Archaeological Trail in Pensacola: Phase 1.* Tallahassee: Bureau of Historic Preservation, Division of Historical Resources, Florida Department of State, 1989.

Joyce, Edward R. "St. Francis Barracks: A Contradiction of Terms." *El Escibano* 24 (1989): 71–90.

Kapitzke, Robert L. "The Secular Clergy in St. Augustine During the First Spanish Period: 1565–1763." Master's thesis, University of Florida, 1991.

Kelsey, Harry. *Sir Francis Drake: The Queen's Pirate.* New Haven: Yale University Press, 1998.

Kennedy, Roger G. "A Fortified Mansion in Florida." Unpublished manuscript draft, SAHS, 1998.

Kingston, Clara Talley. "Sarah Warner Fish." *El Escribano* 24 (1987): 63–84.

Knetsch, Joe. "A Statesman on the Land: The Multifaceted Career of Benjamin Alexander Putnam." *El Escribano* 34 (1997): 98–129.

Kubler, George. *Art and Architecture in Spain and Portugal and Their American Dominions,* 1500–1800. Baltimore: Penguin Books, 1959.

———. *The Religious Architecture of New Mexico in the Colonial Period and Since the American Occupation.* Albuquerque: University of New Mexico Press, 1940.

Lawler, Robert. *Sacred Geometry.* London: Thames and Hudson, 1982.

Laws, Bill. *Traditional Houses of Rural Spain.* New York, Abbeville Press, 1995.

Lawson, Sarah. *A Foothold in Florida.* East Grinstead, England: Antique Atlas Publications, 1992.

Levy, Moses Elias. *A Plan for the Abolition of Slavery,* edited by Chris Monaco. Micanopy, Fla.: Wacahoota Press, 1999.

Lewis, Clifford M., "The Calusa." In *Tacachale,* edited by Jerald T. Milanich and Samuel Proctor. Gainesville: University of Florida Press, 1978.

Lockey, Joseph Byrne. *East Florida, A File of Documents Assembled, and Many of Them Translated.* Berkeley: University of California Press, 1949.

Lofaro, Michael A. *The Life and Adventures of Daniel Boone.* Lexington: University Press of Kentucky, 1978.

Loucks, L. Jill. "Spanish-Indian Interaction on the Florida Missions: The Archaeology of Baptizing Spring." In *The Spanish Missions of La Florida,* edited by Bonnie G. McEwan. Gainesville: University Press of Florida, 1993.

Lyon, Eugene. "The First Three Wooden Forts of St. Augustine, 1565–1571." *El Escribano* 34 (1997): 130–47.

———. "Settlement and Survival." In *The New History of Florida,* edited by Michael Gannon. Gainesville: University Press of Florida, 1996.

———. "Richer Than We Thought." *El Escribano* 29 (1992).

———. "St. Augustine 1580: The Living Community." *El Escribano* 14 (1977): 20–34.

———. *The Enterprise of Florida.* Gainesville: University Presses of Florida, 1976.

MAAR Associates. "Archaeological Assessment for the Three Chimneys Sites." City of Ormond Beach, 1995.

McAlister, L. N. "Pensacola During the Second Spanish Period." *FHQ* 37 (January–April 1959): 281–327.

McAndrew, John. *The Open-Air Churches of Sixteenth-Century Mexico.* Cambridge: Harvard University Press, 1965.

McEwan, Bonnie G., ed. *The Spanish Missions of La Florida.* Gainesville: University Press of Florida, 1993.

McEwan, Bonnie G., and John H. Hann. "Reconstructing a Spanish Mission: San Luis de Talimali." *Magazine of History* 14, no. 4 (Summer 2000).

McLaughlin, Jack. *Jefferson and Monticello.* New York: Henry Holt, 1988.

Mahon, John K., and Brent R. Weisman. "Florida's Seminole and Miccosukee

Peoples." In *The New History of Florida,* edited by Michael Gannon. Gainesville: University Press of Florida, 1996.

Manucy, Albert. *Sixteenth-Century St. Augustine.* Gainesville: University Press of Florida, 1997.

———. *The Houses of St. Augustine, 1565–1821.* St. Augustine Historical Society, 1978.

———. "The City Gate of St. Augustine." *El Escribano* 10 (1973): 1–13.

———. "How Did Fort Caroline Look? A Report on the Feasibility of Reconstructing Fort Caroline." National Park Service, 1960.

———. "The Founding of Pensacola: Reasons and Reality." *FHQ* 37 (January–April 1959): 223–42.

———. "The Cathedral of St. Augustine, Historic Site Report." Cathedral File, SAHS, 1946.

Marrinan, Rochelle A. "Archaeological Investigations at Mission Patale." In *The Spanish Missions of La Florida,* edited by Bonnie G. McEwan. Gainesville: University Press of Florida, 1993.

Matthews, Janet Snyder. *Edge of Wilderness.* Tulsa: Caprine Press, 1983.

Mereness, Newton D., ed. *Travels in the American Colonies.* New York: Antiquarian Press, 1961.

Milanich, Jerald T. "A Late Nineteenth-Century Description of Shell Mounds and Middens on the North Peninsula Gulf Coast of Florida." *Florida Anthropologist* 54 (June 2001): 75–79.

———. "Original Inhabitants." In *The New History of Florida,* edited by Michael Gannon. Gainesville: University Press of Florida, 1996.

———. "Laboring in the Fields of the Lord." *Archaeology* (January–February 1996): 60–67.

———. *Archaeology of Precolumbian Florida.* Gainesville: University Press of Florida, 1994.

———. *The Hernando de Soto Expedition.* New York: Garland, 1991.

Milanich, Jerald T., and Charles H. Fairbanks. *Florida Archaeology.* New York: Academic Press, 1980.

Milanich, Jerald T., and Charles Hudson. *Hernando de Soto and the Indians of Florida.* Gainesville: University Press of Florida, 1993.

Milanich, Jerald T., and Susan Milbrath, eds. *First Encounters.* Gainesville: University of Florida Press, 1989.

Milanich, Jerald T., and William C. Sturtevant. *Francisco Pareja's 1613 Confessionario.* Tallahassee: Division of Archives, History, and Records Management, Florida Department of State, 1972.

Mitchem, Jeffery M. "Artifacts of Exploration: Archaeological Evidence from Florida." In *First Encounters,* edited by Jerald T. Milanich and Susan Milbrath. Gainesville: University of Florida Press, 1989.

Moore, Dorothy L., and Dana Ste. Claire. "Dreams and Promises Unfulfilled: Andrew Turnbull and the New Smyrna Colony." *Florida Anthropologist* 52 (March–June 1999): 115–23.

Morgan, William N. *Precolumbian Architecture in Eastern North America.* Gainesville: University Press of Florida, 1999.

———. *Prehistoric Architecture in the Eastern United States.* Cambridge: MIT Press, 1980.

Morris, Robert. *Select Architecture Being Regular Designs of Plans and Elevations Well Suited to both Town and Country.* . . . 2nd ed. London: Robert Sayer, 1757.

———. *Rural Architecture: Consisting of Regular Designs of Plans and Elevations for Buildings in the Country.* London: Robert Morris, 1750.

———. *Lectures on Architecture Consisting of Rules Founded Upon Harmonick and Arithmetical Proportions in Building.* . . . London, 1734, 1759.

Mowat, Charles L. "St. Francis Barracks, St. Augustine, A Link With the British Regime." *FHQ* 31, no. 3 (January 1943): 266–81.

———. "Enigma of William Drayton." *FHQ* 32, no. 1 (July 1943).

Mullins, Lisa C., ed. *Early Architecture of the South.* Harrisburg, Penn.: National Historical Society, 1987.

Newton, Earle W. *Historic Architecture of Pensacola: Measured Drawings under the Supervision of Blair Reeves.* Pensacola: Historical Restoration and Preservation Commission, 1969.

Nuttgens, Patrick. *The Story of Architecture.* London: Phaidon, 1997.

Pain, William. *The Builder's Companion, and Workman's General Assistant: Demonstrating After the most easy and practical Method, all the Principal Rules of Architecture, from The Plan to the Ornamental Finish.* London: Wm. Pain and Robert Sayer, 1758.

Park, Helen. "A List of Architectural Books Available in America Before the Revolution." *Journal of the Society of Architectural Historians* 20, no. 3 (October 1961): 115–30.

Parker, Susan R. "The Second Century of Settlement in Spanish St. Augustine, 1670–1763." Unpublished manuscript draft, 1999.

———. "Spanish St. Augustine's Urban Indians," *El Escribano* 30 (1993): 1–15.

———. "Government House: Overview of Use and Residents." Unpublished manuscript draft, May 1994.

———. "Men Without God or King: Rural Settlers of East Florida, 1784–1790." *FHQ* (Oct. 1990): 135–55.

Patrick, Rembert W. *Florida Fiasco.* Athens: University of Georgia Press, 1954.

Piatek, Bruce John. "Urban Archaeology in St. Augustine: Volunteers Assist Research and Public Outreach." *SAAA* 9, no. 2 (April 1994): 4.

Pierson, William H., Jr. *American Buildings and Their Architects.* Vol. 1, *The Colonial and Neoclassical Styles.* New York: Oxford University Press, 1986.

Proctor, Samuel, ed. *Eighteenth-Century Florida and its Borderlands.* Gainesville: University Presses of Florida, 1975.

Rea, Robert R. "Brigadier Frederick Haldimand: The Florida Years." *FHQ* 54, no. 4 (April, 1976): 512–31.

Roorda, Eric. "Cuba, America, and the Sea." *Log of Mystic Seaport* 48, no. 4 (Spring 1997): 74–82.

Rush, N. Orwin. *The Battle of Pensacola.* Tallahassee: Florida State University Press, 1966.

Salmon, William. *Palladio Londinensis, or, The London Art of Building:* to which is annexed The Builders Dictionary 5th edition with Alterations and Improvement by E. Hoppus, surveyor. London: Birt, Hitch, 1755.

Sastre, Cécile-Marie. "Picolata on the St. Johns." *El Escribano* 32 (1995): 25–58.

Saunders, Rebecca. "Ideal and Innovation: Spanish Mission Architecture in the Southeast." In *Columbian Consequences,* vol. 2, edited by David Hurst Thomas, 527–42. Washington, D.C.: Smithsonian Institution Press, 1990.

———. "Architecture of the Missions Santa María and Santa Catalina de Amelia." In *The Spanish Missions of La Florida,* edited by Bonnie G. McEwan. Gainesville: University Press of Florida, 1993.

Schafer, Daniel L. "Governor James Grant's Villa: A British East Florida Indigo Plantation." *El Escribano* 37 (2000).

———. "'the forlorn state of poor Billy Bartram': Locating the St. Johns River Plantation of William Bartram." *El Escribano* 32 (1995): 1–11.

———. *Anna Kingsley.* St. Augustine: SAHS, 1994.

———. ". . . not so gay a Town in America as this. . ." In *The Oldest City,* edited by Jean Parker Waterbury. St. Augustine: SAHS, 1983.

———. "Early Plantation Development in British East Florida." *El Escribano* 19 (1982): 37–53.

Schuetz, Mardith. "Professional Artisans in the Hispanic Southwest: The Churches of San Antonio, Texas." *The Americas* 40, no. 1 (July 1983): 17–71.

Sears, William H. *Fort Center: An Archaeological Site in the Lake Okeechobee Basin.* Gainesville: University of Florida Press, 1982.

Shapiro, Gary N., and John H. Hann. "The Documentary Image of the Council Houses of Spanish Florida Tested by Excavations at the Mission of San Luis de Talimali." In *Columbian Consequences,* vol. 2, edited by David Hurst Thomas, 511–26. Washington, D.C.: Smithsonian Institution Press, 1990.

Shapiro, Gary, and Bonnie McEwan. "Archaeology at San Luis: The Apalachee Council House." *Florida Archaeology* Part 1, no. 6 (1992): 1–173.

Shapiro, Gary, and Richard Vernon. "Archaeology at San Luis: The Church Complex." *Florida Archaeology* Part 2, no. 6 (1992): 177–277.

Shepard, Herschel E., Jr. "Kingsley Plantation State Historical Site." Unpublished report at Kingsley Plantation, 1981.

Siebert, Wilbur Henry. *Loyalists in East Florida, 1774–1785; The Most Important Documents Pertaining Thereto.* 2 vols. 1929. Reprint, Boston: Gregg Press, 1972.

Simons, Albert, and Samuel Lapham, Jr. *The Early Architecture of Charleston.* Columbia: University of South Carolina Press, 1970.

Smith, Greg C., Marsha A. Chance, and Keith H. Ashley. "A Cultural Resource Assessment Survey of the New Smyrna Sugar Mill Ruins (8VO184-The Cruger and Depeyster Mill)." Volusia County, project no. P-4156-B, December 1994.

Solís de Merás, Gonzalo. *Pedro Menéndez de Avilés, Adelantado, Governor and Captain-General of Florida.* Translated by Jeannette Thurber Connor. Facsimile reproduction, Gainesville: University of Florida Press, 1964.

Stork, William. *An Account of East-Florida with a Journal kept by John Bartram of Philadelphia . . .* London: W. Nicoll and G. Woodfall, 1767.

Stowell, Daniel W. "Timucuan Ecological and Historic Preserve: Historic Resource Study." Unpublished manuscript at Kingsley Plantation, National Park Service, 1996.

Straight, William M. "Colonial Fevers and Fluxes." In *Born of the Sun,* edited by Joan E. Gill and Beth R. Read, 164–67. Hollywood: Florida Bicentennial Commemorative Journal, 1975.

Strickland, Alice. *Ormond-on-the-Halifax.* Holly Hill, Fla.: Southeast Printing and Publishing, 1980.

Strock, G. Michael. *By Faith With Thanksgiving: A History of Trinity Episcopal Parish,* 1821–1996. St. Augustine: Trinity Episcopal Parish, 1996.

Sullivan, Buddy. "Tabby." *Proceedings of the Conservation and Preservation of Tabby: A Symposium of Historic Building Material in the Coastal Southeast, February* 1998, *Jekyll Island.* Georgia: Department of Natural Resources, 1998.

Sunderland, Elizabeth Read. "Symbolic Numbers and Romanesque Church Plans." *Journal of the Society of Architectural Historians* 28 (1959): 94–103.

Sutton, Leora M. *The Walton House.* Pensacola: Pensacola Historical Society, 1968.

Tavernor, Robert. *Palladio and Palladianism.* London: Thames and Hudson, 1997.

Taylor, Thomas W. *Florida's Territorial Lighthouses,* 1821–1845. Allandale, Fla., 1995.

Tebeau, Charlton W. *A History of Florida.* Coral Gables: University of Miami Press, 1971.

Temple, Sydney. *The Carmel Mission.* Santa Cruz, Calif.: Western Tanager Press, 1980.

Thomas, David Hurst. "The Archaeology of Mission Santa Catalina de Guale: Our First 15 Years." In *The Spanish Missions of La Florida,* edited by Bonnie G. McEwan, 1–34. Gainesville: University Press of Florida, 1993.

———, ed. *Columbian Consequences.* Vol. 2, *Archaeological and Historical Perspectives on the Spanish Borderlands East.* Washington, D.C.: Smithsonian Institution Press, 1990.

Townsend, Eleanor Winthrop. *John Moultrie, Junior, M.D.* Paper presented at the Medical History Club, Charleston, S.C., Dec. 9, 1937, reprint at P. K. Yonge Library of Florida History, University of Florida, Gainesville.

Von Simson, Otto. *The Gothic Cathedral.* New York: Harper and Row, 1964.

Vorsey, Louis de, Jr. "A Colonial Resident of British St. Augustine: William Gerard De Brahm." Unpublished manuscript, St. Augustine Historical Society.

Wallace, David Duncan. *The Life of Henry Laurens.* New York: G. P. Putnam's Sons, 1915.

Ware, John D., and Robert R. Rea. *George Gauld, Surveyor and Cartographer of the Gulf Coast.* Gainesville: University Presses of Florida, 1982.

Waselkov, Gregory A., and Kathryn E. Holland Braund, editors. *William Bartram on the Southeastern Indians.* Lincoln: University of Nebraska Press, 1995.

Waterbury, Jean Parker. "The Many Lives of the Llambias House." *El Escribano* 34 (1997): 5–34.

———. "The Treasurer's House." *El Escribano* 31 (1994).

———. "Where Artillery Lane Crosses Aviles Street: The Seguí/Kirby Smith House." *El Escribano* 24 (1987): 1–38.

———. *The Ximénez-Fatio House.* St. Augustine: SAHS, 1985.

———. "Government House—1604 to Date." *East-Florida Gazette* 8, no. 3 (March 1985): 1–3.

———. *The Oldest House.* St. Augustine: SAHS, 1984.

———, ed. *The Oldest City: St. Augustine, Saga of Survival.* St. Augustine: SAHS, 1983.

———. "John Forbes: Man of Cloth, of his Times, and of St. Augustine." *El Escribano* 18 (1981): 1–32.

Wayne, Lucy B., Martin F. Dickinson, and Herschel E. Shepard. "Sugar Mill Botanical Gardens Archaeological and Architectural Study, Dunlawton Sugar Mill, 8VO189." Volusia County, 1991.

Weisman, Brent Richards. "Archaeology of Fig Springs Mission, Ichetucknee Springs State Park." In *The Spanish Missions of La Florida,* edited by Bonnie G. McEwan, 165–92. Gainesville: University Press of Florida, 1993.

———. *Excavations on the Franciscan Frontier: Archaeology at the Fig Springs Mission.* Gainesville: University Press of Florida.

Weiss, Joaquín E. *La Arquitectura Colonial Cubana, Siglo* 18. Havana: Editorial Pueblo y Educación, 1979.

Wenhold, Lucy L., trans. "A Seventeenth-Century Letter of Gabriel Díaz Vara Calderón, Bishop of Cuba, Describing the Indians and Indian Missions of Florida." *Smithsonian Miscellaneous Collections* 95, no. 16 (1936).

Williams, John Lee. *A View of West Florida.* 1827. Facsimile reproduction, Gainesville: University Presses of Florida, 1976.

Wilson, Eugene M. *Alabama Folk Houses.* Montgomery: Alabama Historical Commission, 1975.

Wilson, Kenneth M. "Window Glass in America." In *Building Early America, The Carpenters' Company of the City of Philadelphia,* edited by Charles E. Peterson. Radnor, Pa.: Chilton, 1976.

Wilson, Samuel, Jr. "Gulf Coast Architecture." In *Spain and Her Rivals on the Gulf Coast,* edited by Earle W. Newton and Ernest F. Dibble. 1971. Reprint, Pensacola: Historic Pensacola Preservation Board, 1977.

Wood, Wayne W. *Jacksonville's Architectural Heritage.* Jacksonville: University of North Florida Press, 1989.

Worth, John E. *The Timucuan Chiefdoms of Spanish Florida,* Vol. 1, *Assimilation.* Gainesville: University Press of Florida, 1998.

INDEX

Italics indicate a page with a figure and bold a page with a map.

Banqueting house (Seminole), 32

Bark (roof and wall material), 27, *32, 73,* 75, 77, 165, 256, 259

Barkley House, 181–82

Barmejo, Friar Pedro, 51, 113

Barnette, Stuart Moffett, 154

Barracks: Pensacola, 73, 75, 168–72, *169, 171, 177,* 255, 256; St. Augustine, 58, 263. *See also* Pile of barracks; Statehouse (British); St. Francis Barracks

Barranca de Santo Tomé ("Red Bluffs," "Red Cliffs,"), 73, 172, 254, 257, 258

Barrett, Ken, Jr., 151

Bartram, John: and Indian mounds 15–16; and Mission San Juan del Puerto, 38–39; and plantations, 184, 216; and St. Augustine, 69, 82, 83, 95–96, 114–15, 118, 144, 145, 153; and tabby, 145, 225

Bartram, William: and Cuscowilla, 29, 31–32; and Indian mounds, 15–16; and Pensacola, 176; and plantations, 184–85, 216; and West Florida, 187

Basements, 223–24

Bastions. *See* Forts

Batería San Antonio, 234, *259*

Bathing house, 85

Baton Rouge, 164

Beauclerk's Bluff, **184,** *194, 195*

Bella Vista, 109, 183, **184,** 189, 205–9, *207.* *See also* Moultrie, John, Jr.

Belfries (bell tower, campanile): at missions, 50, 51; at Pensacola, *75, 77,* 255; at St. Augustine, 46, *80, 81,* 85; styles of, 7, 46, *63, 98,* 116, 119, *120,* 121, *126. See also* Cathedral of St. Augustine; Convento de San Francisco; Nuestra Señora de Guadalupe de Tolomato; Nuestra Señora de la Leche; Nuestra Señora de la Soledad; Renwick campanile; Statehouse; St. Peter's Church

Benches, 27, 32

Benedit de Horruytiner, Major Pedro: house of, 68

Berbegal, Don José de, 73, 255

Bias (in architecture), 1, 6, 10–11, 83, 92, 117. *See also* Myths

Bigges, Walter, *Expeditio Francisci Draki,* 59

Biscayne Bay, 35, 36

Bishop's house (palacio episcopal), 6, 87, 103–4, *105,* 142–43. *See also* Statehouse

Blas de Ortega, 86, 116, 241

Blockhouses (casas fuertes). *See* Defensive structures

Boazio, Baptista, 44, 50, *59,* 60

Boghouses. *See* Necessary houses

Bonifay, Marianna, 179

Book of Architecture. See Gibbs, James

Boone, Daniel, 168

Boorstin, Daniel J., xx, 78

Bousillage construction, 6, 68, *76,* 77, 165, 166, 179, 256, 259. *See also* Earthfast construction; Wattle-and-daub

Braziers, 92

Brick-between-posts construction, 259

Bricks: clay, 10, 30, *76,* 77, 165, 199, 212, 224, 234; manufacture of, 10, 179, *203,* 218, 224–25; English bond, 199; nogging, 225; Roman-style, 259; running bond, 224; samel, 225; tabby, 225, 226, 229

British East Florida, 8, 87, 164, **165,** 251

British Library, 20

British Pensacola. *See* British West Florida

British Point. *See* Negro Fort: Fort Gadsden

British Royal Academy, 255

British West Florida, 6, 164–78, **165,** 200–201

Browne, Montfort (Governor), 173, 201

Brozas y Garay, Engineer Pedro de, 86, 241, 243

Bruce, James, 200

Builders Companion (Pain), 204

Building practices (colonial Florida). *See* Architecture; Balconies; Bishop's house; Bousillage construction; Church architecture; Coquina shellstone; Crenellated parapets; Earthfast construction; Elíxio de la Puente; Flat roofs; Forts; Friaries; Galleries; González-Peavett-Alvarez House; Government House; Hearths; Kingsley Plantation; Kitchens; Lime and limemaking; Llambias House; Lofts; Loggias; Lot plans; Missions; Outbuildings; Oyster shells; Palm thatch; Palm trunks; Plantations; Pile of barracks; Raised cottage style; San

Luis de Talimali; Spanish colonial architecture; Stairways; St. Augustine style; Symmetry; Tabby concrete; Treasurer's house; Wattle-and-daub; Windows; Wood

Bulow, Charles Wilhelm, *211*

Bulow, John Joachim, 211–13

Bulow Plantation (Bulowville), 11, **184,** 210–13, *212,* 228

Bunch, John, 210

Burial platform, *21*

Burials: in Anglican church, 121; Fleming cemetery, 202; in mounds, 15, 20; Spanish churches, 52–53, 73, 121

Cabeza de Vaca, Álvar Núñez, 13, 19

Cádiz (Spain), 66

Calos (Calusa capital), 15

Calusa Indians, 4, 15, 19, 35

Camino Real (Apalachee Trail), 39, 41, 242

Campbell, Colin, *Vitruvius Britannicus,* 229

Campbell, General John, 177

Canary Islands, 66, 70, 91

Canaveral National Seashore, 16

Cape Canaveral, 36

Capitals (of colonial Florida), xviii, 7. *See also* Pensacola; St. Augustine

Caribbean architectural influences, 6, 139, 154, *155,* 159, *167,* 168, *169, 177,* 178, 183, 220, 223

CARL (Conservation and Recreational Lands Trust), xx

Carnegie Survey of Architecture, 151

Carr, B. E., house, *162*

Carrère and Hastings, 136

Cartagena de Indias, 66

Casas fuertes. *See* Defensive structures

Castelló, Engineer Pablo, 86, 89, 110, 149, 241

Castilla y León (Spain), 66, 124

Castillo de San Marcos (Fort St. Marks, Fort Marion), xviii, 4; construction of, 9, 14, 68, 69, 80, 82, 86; depiction of, *10, 81,* **140, 234,** 238–45, *244,* 247, 260. *See also* Engineers

Cathedral of St. Augustine: belfry related to, 98, *115,* 116; construction of, 123–28, *124–26,* 224; 1960s alterations, 138; Renwick's restoration, *128,* 132, 135–37;

size of, 46; stones from other churches, 115, 116, 122. *See also* Nuestra Señora de la Soledad; Nuestra Señora de los Remedios

Cather, Willa: *Death Comes for the Archbishop,* 1, 36

Catholicism (dogma, faith, liturgy), 36, 37, 43, 46, 117, 217

Cendoya, Manuel de (Governor), 238

Central hall plan, *169,* 178, *181, 192, 200*

Challeux, Nicholas le, 24

Charles IX (King of France), 235

Charles, King of Spain (later Charles VI, Holy Roman Emperor), 73, 254

Charleston: architectural influences of, 107, 159, 222; connections with, 119, 153, 199, 205, 207, 208, 210, 215, 217, 219; establishment of, 9, 240; trade with, 201

Charleston Library Society, 107, 119, 208

Charnel houses, 15, 19–20, *21*

Chester, Peter (Governor), 166; house plans (Pensacola), *172–76*

Chester's Villa, 175

Chevaux de frieze, 167, 246

Chickees, *33, 34*

Chief's house: Apalachee, 40, *42, 43;* Calusa, 19; Timucua, 23–24, 56–57. *See also* Council houses

Chimneys, 92, 100, 103, 104, 108, 144, 159, 181, 198, 202–3, 219; bell-shaped flues, 149, 257. *See also* Hearths; Sugar plantations

Choir lofts, *48,* 49, 117, 123

Church architecture: at Fort Mose, 247; at missions, xix, xx, *39,* 41–50, *45, 48;* at Pensacola, 73–74, *75,* 77, 173, 255, *256;* at St. Augustine, 58, *61, 62, 63, 81, 83,* 110, 112–28. *See also* Belfries; Choir lofts; Church art; Convento de San Francisco; Missions; San Luis de Talimali

Church art, 51–52, 117

Císcara, Engineer Don Juan de, 86, 241

Cisterns, 73, 249

City Gate, St. Augustine, 85, 245–*46*

Clamp (brick kiln). *See* bricks

Classical orders, 7, 82, 106, 108, 151; Doric, 90, 91, *109,* 115, *124, 125, 128,* 132, 209, 243; Ionic, 109, 128, *130,* 207; Tuscan, *129, 136*

French: colonial architecture of, 6, 77, 164–82, *180,* 183, 200, 256, 258–59; colonization attempts (in Florida), xix, 2, 22–23, 73, 234–36, 254; trade with, 254, 255. *See also* Bousillage construction

Friaries (convento, monastery): architecture of, 37, 38, *39,* 42, 41, *45,* 53–54. *See also* Convento de San Francisco

Fruitland, 15

Furnishings, 93, 188, 200, 201

Gabionade (palisade), 235

Gadsden, Lieutenant James, 253

Gage, General, 83, 92, 102, 170, 171

Galleries (corredor, piazza, porch, veranda), examples of: barracks, *99, 100, 169,* 170, *171*; church, 75; Government House, 90; houses, 103–5; *111,* 139, 146–47, 148–49, 151, 153–54, 172–73, 178–81, 219; statehouse, 107, *109. See also* Loggias; Plantations

Galve, Conde de, 254

Gannon, Michael, 1, 61

Gardens: kitchen, 53, 66, *76,* 112, 141, *148,* 149, 156, *172,* 174, 187; pleasure, 7, 187, 207–8

Garnier, Clara Louise, 181

Gauld, George, 168, 171, 203, 251

Georgian-Palladian influence, 121, 205, 208. *See also* Handbooks

Germain, Lord, 102

German church and settlement, 116

Gibbs, James, 7, 106; *Book of Architecture,* 107, 119, *120,* 176, 204

Glass. *See* Windows

Golden Ratios, 47

González, Antonio (master carpenter), 95

González-Peavett-Alvarez House ("Oldest House"), 141, *143,* 149, 153–54

Gordon, Lord Adam, 166

Gourgues, Dominique de, 237

Government House (or Governor's House): Pensacola, *74, 76,* 77, 166, 173, 179, 255, 256, 262; St. Augustine, 1, 6, 23, 56, *62, 64,* **79,** *88,* 89–94, 129–30, *131, 132,* 150, 235

Governor's House. *See* Government House

Gracia Real de Santa Teresa de Mose. *See* Fort Mose

Granaries, 29, 38, *39,* 41, *54,* 196

Grant, Governor James, 83, 87, *91,* 92, 102, 104–6, 112, 161, 190, 206

Grant's Villa, **184,** 190, *191–92*

Greeley, Mellen Clark, 88, 130

Greene, General Nathaniel, 218

Greenfield, 182, 200–201

Gritzner, Janet Bigbee, 67

Guale Indians, 35

Guana River, 192

Guardhouse: Pensacola, 75; St. Augustine, *63,* 110

Guillemard, Gilberto, 258–59

Gulf Coast cottage. *See* Raised cottage style

Haciendas and ranches. *See* Plantations

Haldimand, General Frederick, 103, 171; house plan, 172–75, *172, 173, 175*

Halifax River (Mosquito River), 199, 211

Handbooks (builder's, architect's), 93, 106, 107, 109, 119, 203–4, 208–9, 220, 221–22, 229

Harris, Clyde, 88, 130

Harrison, Peter, 107

Havana, Cuba, 74, 86, *167,* 242

Hazzard, Richard, 216

Hearths: Apalachee, 55; European, 149, 159, 226, 230. *See also* Chimneys

Heating. *See* Braziers; Chimneys; . Hearths

Hecht, Frederick William, 147, 262

Herreriano desornamentado, 126

Hewitt, John, 85, 87, 93, 102, 119, 144, 197

Hibernia, **184,** 202

"Highways" (Indian), 15, *16*

Hita, Engineer Manuel de, 246

Hita Salazar, Governor Pablo de, 113, 241

Hornwork, 245. *See also* Defensive structures

Hospital: English, *114*; Spanish, 6, 73, 74, 75, 117, 146. *See also* Menéndez Marquéz House

House lots. *See* Lot plans

Hrabawski, Samuel: house and lot plan, *148*

Hull, Ambrose. *See* Cruger and Depeyster Plantation

Hume, James, Chief Justice, 7, 187

Hurley, Archbishop Joseph P., 138

Manucy, Albert, 24, 68, 144

Mariana, Queen of Spain, 29, 46

Marion, Francis, 245

Marquardt, William H., 4

Márquez Molina, Juan, 86, 241

Marshall, John R. (carpenter), 210

Masonry, 65; foundations, 100–103, 223, 257. *See also* Bricks; Coquina shell-stone; Tabby concrete

Masons. *See* Craftsmen and craftsmanship; Engineers

Matanzas Inlet and River, 188, 236, 237, 248

Materials (construction): costs of, British period, 261–63; descriptions of, 9–10, 25, 26, 28, 58, 77, 235, 257, 261–63; imported, 82; locally available, 6, 8, 9–10, 13, 30, 60, 73, 78, 83, 91, 178, 223. *See also* Bark; Bricks; Coquina shell-stone; Lime and limemaking; Oyster shells; Palm thatch; Palm trunks; Wood

May River (St. Johns River), 22, 235

McCluch, David (carpenter), 92

McEwan, Bonnie, 4, 72

McIntosh, John Houstoun, 216, 218, 220, 229

McMurchie, Engineer John, 210

McQueen, John (Don Juan Reyna), 203, 215, 216, 217–18, 220, 223, 229

Melchor Feliu, Governor, 83

Méndez de Canzo, Governor Gonzalo, 63, 89, 117, 123

Menéndez, Francisco (African slave/freedman), 247

Menéndez de Avilés, Pedro, 2, 4, 22, 50, 56, 63, 185, 235–36; campsite of, 23, 57, 237

Menéndez Marquéz, Don Francisco, 6, 185

Menéndez Marquéz, Governor Pedro, 185

Menéndez Marquéz House, 87, 110–12, *111,* 145–46, 151, 159

Merrill, Scott, *163*

Mesta, Hernando de, 24, 29, 37, *38,* 44, 61, 62, 123

Mexico (Nueva España), 3, 27, 29, 37, 44, 48, 49, 61, 68, 72, 74; prison labor, 73, 75, 165, 254

Militia, free black, 247–48

Millar, John, 107

Mills, Robert, 129

Minorcans, 159–60, 199

Mission Fig Springs, 46

Mission (Pueblo) Nombre de Dios, 37, *38, 39,* 40, 51, 80, *81,* 98, 113, 131. *See also* Missions; Nuestra Señora de la Leche

Missions (Spanish, Florida), xix, 4, 5, 30, 35, **36,** 250; architecture of, 38, 39, 41; baptism at, 49, *49;* compared with missions in Texas, 48, 49, 115; destruction of, 40, 116. *See also* Camino real; Convento de San Francisco; Mission (Pueblo) Nombre de Dios; Mission (Pueblo) San Juan del Puerto; San Luis de Talimali

Mission (Pueblo) San Juan del Puerto, 37, 38, 51, 216

Mission (Pueblo) San Luis de Talimali (de Apalachee). *See* San Luis de Talimali

Mission San Martín de Timucua, 52

Mission San Pedro y San Pablo de Patale, 40

Mission Santa Catalina de Amelia, 53

Mission Santa Catalina de Guale, 40

Mission Santa Fé de Toloca, 40, 51

Mississippi River, 6, 24, 183

Moats. *See* Forts

Mobile: British, 164, **165,** 166, 184; French, 254, 255, 258

Moe, Richard, xxi

Monastery. *See* Friaries

Moncrief, Engineer James, 86–87, 95–96, 99, 104, 115, 144, 146, 159

Montiano, Governor Manuel de, 247

Moore, James: raid of, 39, 54, 72, 80, 94, 110–11, 117, 241

Morales, Diego Marquéz (master carpenter), 95

Morgan, William N., 26

Morris, Robert, 204, 221. *See also* Handbooks

Mortars. *See* Lime and limemaking

Morton, Henry J., 128

Mortuary temples. *See* Charnel houses

Mosquito Inlet (Ponce de Leon Inlet), 83, 211, 262

Moss binder, 27, 165, 256, 259

Moultrie, John, Jr.: lieutenant governor, 7,

104–6, 119, 121, 144, 188–89, *205–7. See also* Bella Vista; Rosetta Plantation

Moultrie family (South Carolina), 205–6

Mound Key, 15

Mounds (Indian): as lookouts, 17; mined for construction lime, *17, 18,* 215–16. *See also* Indians; Lime and limemaking; Oyster shells

Mount Royal (Fruitland): Indian mound, *15–16*

Mt. Hope, **184,** 195–97

Mt. Oswald, **184,** 199

Mt. Pleasant, **184,** *191, 192*

Mudéjar style, 91, 150, 157

Mulberry Castle (South Carolina), 220–21

Mulcaster, George Frederick, 107

Mulcaster, Sir Frederick William, 107

Murtagh, William, *Keeping Time: The History and Theory of Preservation in America,* xx

Music (choir), 48–49. *See also* Choir lofts

Myths (about architecture), *3, 5,* 82

Narváez, Pánfilo de, expedition of, 4, 13, 19

Natchez, 164

National Guard Headquarters (Florida), 87, 96, 100, 130, *134*

National Historic Landmarks, xix–xx, 60, 138

National Historic Preservation Act of 1966, xx

National Monuments, 245, 250

National Park Service, xix, xxvi, 232, 250

National Register of Historic Places, xx, 17

National Trust for Historic Preservation, xxi

Native Americans, xviii, 2. *See also* Indians

Necessary houses, 101, 102, 104, 149, 204

Negro Fort: Fort Gadsden, 252–53. *See also* Fort Mose

Neil, Arthur and Eleanor, 182, 200–201

Neoclassical style elements, 99–100, 104–10, 112, *120,* 121, *174. See also* Classical orders

Nepomuceno, Plantation San Juan (Ortega), 203, 218

Nepomuceno de Quesada, Governor Juan, 124, 217

New Grove plantation, 201

New Smyrna Beach, 16, 17, 83, 189, 199, 213

New Smyrna Plantation, 160, **184,** 198, 199

New Smyrna Sugar Mill Ruins, xx. *See* Cruger and Depeyster Plantation

New Switzerland Plantation, **184,** 201–2

New Waterford Plantation, 188

Nichols, Major Edward, 252

Nocoroco (Timucua village), 199

Nombre de Dios. *See* Mission (Pueblo) Nombre de Dios

Nuestra Señora de Guadalupe de Tolomato, 40, 47, 83, 115–16, 123

Nuestra Señora de la Leche, 40, 47, 50, 113–15, *114, 115*; dismantled, 83, 123, 131; and special devotion to Virgen de la Leche, 113; twentieth century shrine to, *135. See also* Mission (Pueblo) Nombre de Dios

Nuestra Señora de los Remedios, 50, *61, 62, 63,* 116, 123. *See also* Nuestra Señora de la Soledad; Cathedral of St. Augustine

Nuestra Señora de la Soledad, 83, 103, 116–17, *118,* 123. *See also* St. Peter's Church

Ocaña, Friar Francisco de, 39

Ochlockonee River, 19, 250

Oglethorpe, General, 186, 216, 242, 247

Oldest House. *See* González-Peavett-Alvarez House

Onís, Luis de, 259

O'Reilly, Father Michael, 218

Ormond Beach, 189, 199. *See also* Mt. Oswald; Swamp Settlement

Ortega (Jacksonville), 30, 203

Ortiz Parrilla, Colonel Diego, 75, 256

Osceola, 245

Oswald, Richard, 189, 199–200. *See* Mt. Oswald; Swamp Settlement

Outbuildings (dependencies), 147–48, 166, *172,* 174, 176, 188, 195–96, 200, 202, 212. *See also* Kingsley Plantation

Outhouses. *See* Necessary houses

"Outriggers" (eaves), 159

Oyster shells (as construction material), 9, 17–18, 45, 61, 67–68, 122, 141, 145, 147, 215. *See also* Lime and lime-making; Tabby concrete

Pacheco, Luis (slave), 131
Paint: colors, 91, 92, 93, 121, 158, 177, 179, 243, 246; use of, 102, 121, 151, 158, 172, 175, 176, 204, 208, 243, 262
Palacio episcopal. *See* Bishop's house
Palisades. *See* Forts
Palladio, Andrea: *Four Books of Architecture*, 221; influence of, 87, 99, *174*, 205, 207, 220. *See also* Handbooks
Palmer, Colonel John, 113, 247
Palm thatch (construction material), 5, 22, 24, 25, 26–27, 30, *42*, 45, 50, 58, *61*, 62–63, *66*, 116, 186, 191, 235, 248
Palm trunks (construction material), *67*, 192, *192*, 245, 248
Panzacola. *See* Pensacola; Presidio San Miguel de Panzacola
Panzacola Indians, xviii, 73, 256
Pareja, Friar, 38, 41, 50, 51
Parish records, 123
Patio. *See* Courtyard
Patriot's War, 201, 202, 218, 220, 229
Pauger, Adrien de, 258
Peavett, Joseph, 188. *See also* González-Peavett-Alvarez House
Peavett, Mary Evans. *See* Evans, Mary
Peña-Peck House. *See* Treasurer's House
Pensacola: British Period, 6, 164–82; Naval Air Station, 72, 254; Spanish period, xviii–xix, 72–77, *74, 76*, 254–60. *See also* Fort San Carlos de Barrancas; Presidio San Miguel de Panzacola; Santa Rosa Island
Perez, Ensign Bartholome (master mason), 95
Peso, silver (eight reales), 261
Peterson, Representative J. Hardin, xxi
Piazzas. *See* Galleries; Loggias
Pile of barracks, 100–103, 131, 170
Piles (pilings), 38, 248, 255, 257
Pilgrimage Plantation, **184**, 213–14
Pitsaw, *69*
Plantations, 17, 175, 183–214, **184**, 250
Plaster, 141, 243, 246. *See also* Lime and limemaking
Plaza Ferdinand VII, xix, 75
Plazas (atrios, public squares, yards), xx, 31, 32, 41–42, 50, 64, 71, 117, 154
Point Siquenza, 255
Pomar, Doña María de, 89

Population, 30, 41, 58, 66
Pound sterling, equivalents, 261–63
Pratz, le Page du, 20, 28
Prefabricated building, 101–2
Presidios. *See* Forts
Presidio Isla de Santa Rosa. *See* Santa Rosa Island, Spanish presidio on
Presidio San Miguel de Panzacola, 6, 75, 256
Prickly cactus barriers, 233, 241, 246, 247
Primo de Ribera, Captain José, 251
Primo de Rivera, Captain Enrique, 241
Proportioned architecture, 7, 8, 47, 113, 115, 209, 220, *221*, 222
Public Record Office, England, 8, 101, 174, 187, 191, 203
Pueblo de yndios nombre de Dios, 24, 29, 37, *38*, *39*
Puerto Rico, 66
Purcell, Joseph, 33, 50, 72, 194

Quiroga y Losada, Governor Diego de, 117, 123

Raised cottage style, 172, *173*, 178–82, *179, 180, 181, 185*, 211
Rammed earth (tapia, pisé), 67, 247
Ranjel, Rodrigo, 19, 22
Rawlings, Marjorie Kinnan: farm house of, 183, *185*
Red Cliffs. *See* Barranca de Santo Tomé
Redoubts. *See* Defensive structures
Renwick, James, 127, 132–36; campanile design of, 136–38, *137*
Repartimiento, 41
Ribault, Jean, 236
Rocque, Engineer Mariano de la, 87–88, *99, 100, 104*, 107, 110, 123, 127, 132, *136*, 138, 243
Rodríguez Meléndez, Joseph: residence of, 70, 150
Rodríguez-Salas House, 150–51, 158
Román de Castilla y Lugo, Governor Don Miguel, 75, 165, 256
Roof construction, 27, 50, 110–12, *111*; roof shingles, 230, *231*, 259. *See also* Bark; Flat roofs; Palm thatch
Roque Pérez, Captain Jacinto, 250
Rosario Line. *See* Cubo and Rosario Lines
Rosemary Beach, 161

Elsbeth Gordon is a photographer/architectural historian living in Gainesville. She did graduate work on the architecture of Tulum in Mexico and was an artist/photographer for a *National Geographic* archaeological project in Veracruz, Mexico. For eleven years she owned a company that restored historic buildings in Florida.